FAITH, VALOR, AND DEVOTION

FAITH, VALOR, AND DEVOTION

The Civil War Letters of
William Porcher DuBose

Edited by
W. Eric Emerson and Karen Stokes

The University of South Carolina Press

E
605
.D85
2010

Published by the University of South Carolina Press
Columbia, South Carolina 29208

www.sc.edu/uscpress

Manufactured in the United States of America

19 18 17 16 15 14 13 12 11 10   10 9 8 7 6 5 4 3 2 1

Library of Congress Cataloging-in-Publication Data

Dubose, William Porcher, 1836–1918.
    Faith, valor, and devotion : the Civil War letters of William Porcher
DuBose / edited by W. Eric Emerson and Karen Stokes.
      p. cm.
    Includes bibliographical references and index.
    ISBN 978-1-57003-912-6 (cloth : alk. paper)
    1. DuBose, William Porcher, 1836–1918—Correspondence. 2. United ·
States—History—Civil War, 1861–1865—Personal narratives, Confederate.
3. Military chaplains—Confederate States of America—Correspondence.
4. United States—History—Civil War, 1861–1865—Chaplains. 5. United
States—History—Civil War, 1861–1865—Religious aspects. 6. Confederate
States of America. Army. Kershaw's Brigade. 7. Confederate States of America.
Army. Holcombe Legion. 8. Soldiers—South Carolina—Correspondence.
I. Emerson, W. Eric, 1966– II. Stokes, Karen. III. Title.
    E605.D85 2010
    973.7'82—dc22

                                                                2010006338

This book was printed on Glatfelter Natures, a recycled paper with 30 percent
postconsumer waste content.

CONTENTS

ILLUSTRATIONS

ACKNOWLEDGMENTS

T he Civil War letters of William Porcher DuBose published in this volume have been a noteworthy part of the South Carolina Historical
Society's (SCHS) collections since 2005. Early that year Dr. Nicholas Butler,
director of the Charleston Archive at the Charleston County Public Library
(CCPL), contacted the South Carolina Historical Society regarding the letters. Mrs. Clelia Peronneau McGowan, an early supporter of the library, had
donated the DuBose correspondence. Library personnel made photocopies
of the letters, arranged them chronologically, and stored them in acid-free
folders and boxes. Afterward the collection received little attention from
researchers.

Butler, formerly an archivist at SCHS, became familiar with the letters
during a survey of the CCPL collections. He contacted Dr. W. Eric Emerson,
who was at the time executive director of SCHS, and together they agreed
to an exchange. SCHS would get the DuBose correspondence, and CCPL
would in turn receive four boxes of mid-nineteenth-century field notebooks
kept by Charles Parker, city engineer for Charleston. The exchange took
place on July 7, 2005, and in 2007 the editors of this volume began work to
transcribe, annotate, and publish the DuBose letters for the South Carolina
Historical Society.

The letters contained herein are probably not the only surviving war-
time correspondence from DuBose to family members or vice versa. DuBose
destroyed some of his wife's letters before battle to ensure that they did not
fall into enemy hands. Much DuBose correspondence is located at the Jessie
Ball duPont Library in Sewanee, Tennessee. Little of that correspondence
deals with the war. Other letters likely exist in private hands.

This project would not have been possible without the assistance of
many people. First, the editors would like to thank Dr. Faye Jensen, SCHS
executive director, and the SCHS board of managers for allowing the anno-
tation and publication of these letters. We also would like to thank the staff
of the South Carolina Historical Society for their assistance with this project,

ACKNOWLEDGMENTS

especially Mike Coker. Thanks are no doubt due to Dr. Nicolas Butler for bringing these letters to light and having the foresight to see their value to researchers. Dr. Allen Stokes of the South Caroliniana Library, the University of South Carolina, Columbia; the staff of the Southern Historical Collection at the University of North Carolina, Chapel Hill; and the staff of the Rare Book, Manuscript, and Special Collections Library at Duke University were all helpful during this project. Special thanks to John Tilford of the University Archives and Special Collections at Sewanee for his assistance, to R. Hugh Simmons of the Fort Delaware Society, and to Robert B. Cuthbert. Finally, we would like to thank our families for their patience as we pursued the completion of this project.

EDITORIAL METHOD

The editors transcribed the letters in this volume as they were written. No changes were made to spelling or abbreviations. With some exceptions, DuBose used British orthography, so that "honor," for instance, is spelled "honour" and "recognize" is spelled "recognise." Obvious mistakes are indicated by *sic* in brackets. Some abbreviations are also indicated by *sic* and are sometimes explained by the full word in brackets ("Bp" meaning "Bishop," for example). In some cases words or passages were obliterated by tears or holes in the paper or rendered illegible by fading or water damage; any consequent omissions are indicated by ellipses. Words or brief passages that were uncertain are bracketed and represent the transcriber's best interpretations.

INTRODUCTION

D uring the summer of 1863 Thomas F. Davis, Episcopal bishop of the Diocese of South Carolina, and Joseph B. Kershaw, a brigadier general of the Confederate States Army, conspired to remove an able-bodied young lieutenant from the front lines of the American Civil War. The officer was the scion of one of South Carolina's oldest and wealthiest families. Davis's and Kershaw's efforts were, to some extent, based on personal motives. Both men knew the officer well and were fond of him, and Kershaw and the man were cousins. This intervention by the bishop and the general, however, did not come at the request of a timid young man interested in self-preservation.

By the end of the war's second year, William Porcher DuBose (1836–1918) had commanded a regiment during some of the conflict's fiercest combat. He was wounded before and during the battle of Second Manassas, and he was captured during a solitary nighttime reconnaissance of Union lines after the battle of South Mountain. He was imprisoned at Fort Delaware for a short time and then exchanged. Upon returning to duty, he was wounded again, this time more seriously, during the battle of Kinston in North Carolina. In combat DuBose had proved himself to be a brave and selfless leader. His experiences had left him with the mental scars of battle and the physical scars of three wounds, all received within a six-month period. If survival in combat is a game of chance, then DuBose's luck was running out.

Davis and Kershaw saw great promise in the young man. He was intelligent and well educated, but more important in their estimation, he was a man of profound faith and devotion to God. DuBose had left behind a promising career when he abandoned his seminary studies to serve his state. Davis and Kershaw believed that he was destined to serve a higher calling as a clergyman. To fulfill that calling, however, he had to survive the war, so the young lieutenant was slated for duty as a chaplain in the Confederate army.

Their efforts on behalf of this aspiring clergyman paid great dividends. DuBose survived the war and was ordained an Episcopal minister. His greatest contributions, however, came when he joined the faculty of the

University of the South at Sewanee, Tennessee. There he helped to establish a seminary and became, in the eyes of some, the greatest of America's Episcopal theologians. He gained worldwide acclaim, and his writings continue to shape Episcopal thought nearly one hundred years after his death. His contributions are due in large part to the confidence and faith of two men, one by profession a man of God and the other a man of war.

The Civil War letters of William Porcher DuBose, which comprise this volume, cover the period October 1861–April 1865. They provide fascinating insight into the values, thoughts, and deeds of a young man who would live a remarkable postwar life as an Episcopal minister, teacher, and theologian. During our nation's deadliest conflict, he served in the forces of South Carolina and the Confederacy. He was adjutant of the Holcombe Legion, which was attached to Brig. Gen. Nathan G. Evans's "Tramp" Brigade, so called for its service throughout much of the Confederacy. Through a sense of modesty, DuBose turned down opportunities for advancement, though his combat command experience and accolades almost guaranteed him higher rank. In 1863 he left the Holcombe Legion to become a chaplain in Kershaw's Brigade, and for the remainder of the war he served in that capacity.

DuBose wrote the majority of his surviving war-time correspondence to his fiancée, and later wife, Anne Barnwell Peronneau, or "Nannie." The letters are filled with news of the war and its pivotal impact on family and friends, and they provide eye-witness accounts of some of the conflict's most brutal and important campaigns. As a witness to war, DuBose could boast of a nearly unbroken war-time service record as a commander, staff officer, and chaplain, and he participated in campaigns that took him from South Carolina to Virginia, Maryland, Delaware, North Carolina, Mississippi, Alabama, Georgia, and Tennessee. His letters provide insight into a man of considerable intellectual depth who could claim the widest breadth of war-time experiences.

DuBose's religious thought and intellect were by-products of a fortunate upbringing. He was a descendant of Norman French Huguenots who thrived in the plantation culture of many of South Carolina's prominent families. He was the son of Theodore Samuel Marion DuBose and his first cousin Jane Sinkler Porcher, who had moved to the South Carolina midlands to escape the heat and disease of their families' lowcountry plantations. The couple initially rented a home in Winnsboro, South Carolina, thirty miles north of Columbia, prior to purchasing a plantation nearby. William Porcher DuBose was born in that rented house on April 11, 1836.[1]

William Porcher DuBose was first honor graduate and ranking cadet in his class at the Citadel in 1855. Today the Citadel presents an award in his name to the first honor graduate of each graduating class. Courtesy of the Jessie Ball duPont Library, Sewanee, the University of the South

By mid-nineteenth-century standards the DuBose family was among the wealthiest in the state. Theodore DuBose, who had been educated at Partridge Academy and Yale University, purchased Farmington Plantation, a three-thousand-acre holding along Wateree Creek and nine miles north of Winnsboro. He became a captain in the local militia, a commissioner of free schools, a member of the Board of Visitors of Mt. Zion Schools, and a member of the South Carolina Historical Society. In 1860 he owned 204 slaves in Fairfield District, real estate valued at $40,000, and a personal estate worth $27,716.[2]

When William was eight, the DuBose family moved to nearby Roseland Plantation, another of his father's holdings, which was much closer to Winnsboro, where he and his siblings began their education. In 1852, at the age of fifteen, he enrolled at the South Carolina Military College, which comprised the Arsenal Military Academy in Columbia and the Citadel in Charleston. DuBose excelled at the Citadel, finishing first in his class in two of the three years he was there.[3]

DuBose always had been religious, but the rigorous military life of the Citadel dampened his zeal. For a brief time he began to lose interest in his studies, and he went through what he described later as "my farthest religious aberration. At this period I even neglected my prayers."[4] A conversion experience in 1854 gave him new focus and started him on a path to religious study. While staying at an inn on a return trip to Charleston, he felt a presence enter his room. As he later described the experience, it was "as if a new world had opened to me, a new presence had come into my life and it was so absolute and positive, there was no mistaking it." He was confirmed at St. Michael's Church in Charleston on November 19, 1854, during the final year of his enrollment at the Citadel.[5]

DuBose finished his education at the Citadel as captain of cadets and an assistant professor of English, but he believed that his education was incomplete. He enrolled at the University of Virginia, where he received degrees in Latin, French, Greek, moral sciences, mathematics, and physics.[6] Then in October 1859 he began his formal religious studies in Camden at the Theological Seminary for the Protestant Episcopal Church of South Carolina.[7] His health deteriorated while he was in Camden, and he developed a lingering cough. He left the seminary in the summer of 1860 for an extended camping trip through the mountains of North Carolina. At Dunn's Rock, forty miles southwest of Asheville, he met and became acquainted with Anne Barnwell "Nannie" Peronneau, who was vacationing with her mother and sister. Nannie's father, Henry William Peronneau, had been a prominent Charleston attorney before his death the previous year. DuBose was so impressed by Nannie that he remained at Dunn's Rock for a week before returning to Camden to continue his studies.[8]

DuBose was in Charleston for Christmas break, and he witnessed the signing of the Ordinance of Secession on December 20, 1860. His real purpose for visiting the city, however, was to see Nannie. He later noted, "I have to confess that in the intense interest that prevailed my immediate concern was not so much in the momentous event taking place, as in the rather smaller question of whether a certain person was present in the audience." Nannie was present for the ceremony, and DuBose and the Reverend Christopher Gadsden escorted her and her sisters to their home on Tradd Street, where DuBose made the first of several visits. He later wrote that he made his intentions "tolerably evident."[9] He returned to the seminary after the holidays, but he was in Charleston once again to visit Nannie during the next pivotal event that would lead to war. On the evening of April 11, 1861, DuBose's birthday, he, Nannie, and her sisters promenaded along the Battery with large crowds; all were anxious to witness the impending Confederate bombardment of Fort Sumter. Later that evening DuBose escorted the ladies to their home and returned to his hotel. Like many other potential spectators, they were all asleep when the bombardment began in the early hours of April 12.

DuBose visited Charleston once again during the summer of 1861 to call on Nannie and her family. The visit ended with the couple engaged to be married.[10] On October 4, 1861, DuBose returned to the Episcopal seminary in Camden. He and Nannie had made tentative plans to marry after DuBose completed his seminary education. However, the intensifying war would greatly affect the timing of their nuptials. DuBose wrestled with whether or not duty to state and country trumped duty to God. His initial answer was no: "I go so far as to believe that one who has devoted his life to God can no longer call it his own, & therefore has no right to give it away, or even to endanger it in any other cause whatever, even though it be so sacred a one as that of Country. Of course the emergency may become such as to break down all such scruples." In that last statement DuBose was correct. Soon thereafter he received a letter from his father, Theodore S. DuBose, who had always served as a compass for DuBose's sense of duty. The letter, which DuBose later characterized as "a turning point to me . . . which lives in my memory," convinced him that it was his duty to serve his state and his new nation.[11]

During this period of transition from seminarian to soldier, DuBose was buoyed by his feelings for his fiancée and his deepened gratitude for God's blessings. He wrote to Nannie and expressed his thanks for the joy that both she and God had bestowed upon him: "I see only the <u>beauty</u> of God's creation & think only of his <u>love</u>. . . . And among them all, you come & sit by my side & in your presence, I can think of nothing but truth, & beauty & goodness & love. A Father that loves & blesses us both in His dear Son—a spirit of holiness that draws us nearer to each other in drawing us nearer to our Savior, a providence watching over us, infinite power & wisdom pledged to make 'all things work together for our good.'"[12]

On November 21, 1861, DuBose became adjutant of South Carolina's newly formed Holcombe Legion, which was named in honor of Gov. Francis Pickens's beautiful young wife Lucy Holcombe Pickens. The Holcombe Legion was a composite organization with a regiment of infantry, a battalion of cavalry, and a battalion of artillery. It was commanded and staffed by a number of former Citadel cadets and faculty, including Col. Peter Fayssoux Stevens, Maj. F. Gendron Palmer, and its new adjutant, William Porcher DuBose.[13]

Soon after its organization the Holcombe Legion was stationed in St. Andrew's Parish, which was across the Ashley River from Charleston. The unit was there on December 11, 1861, when flames from a massive fire, which would eventually burn over 135 acres of the city, lit the lowcountry sky. Realizing the danger to his fiancée and her family, DuBose left camp and traveled across the Ashley River to the Peronneau residence on Tradd Street. To both his and the family's relief, the fire stopped just short of their home.[14]

On December 26, 1861, the Holcombe Legion was transferred twenty miles southwest of Charleston to the village of Adam's Run. Located between the Edisto and Wadmalaw rivers, the village was a logical posting for Confederate troops. From there the Holcombe Legion could defend local rivers and the strategically vital Charleston and Savannah Railroad.[15] DuBose and his unit remained at their camp at Adam's Run for several months, during which time they were involved in operations against nearby enemy units, including raids on Edisto Island. When not on duty, DuBose spent much time visiting Nannie at nearby Dungannon Plantation, which was the home of her uncle.[16]

DuBose realized that his military service would necessitate postponing his religious education, but he continued to place more value on the ultimate victory of salvation than on the triumph of the Confederacy. In late February 1862, long before Confederate military reversals generated doubts regarding the conflict's eventual outcome, DuBose speculated about his country's defeat, asking his fiancée to "imagine our great cause finally unsuccessful & our beloved country conquered & ruined." He wondered if God's purpose in allowing defeat might be to teach his people a lesson, "that here 'we have no continuing city,' but that 'we seek a better, even a heavenly' [city]." The city to which he and the scriptures refer is the New Jerusalem foretold in the Book of Revelation. DuBose's thoughts echo those of Saint Augustine, who, in response to the destruction of Rome by the Visigoths in 410, wrote *The City of God*. In it Augustine consoled Christians with the assurance that though earthly governments may fail, their ultimate citizenship was in the Kingdom of God. Along similar lines DuBose wrote, "we ought to remember that we belong to a kingdom that is above the kingdom of this world" and that the Christian life "consists in the gradual withdrawal of our affections from things temporal & fixing them upon the eternal."[17] DuBose also noted that God often used "wicked nations to accomplish his judgments upon those that were less so." He continued, "He maketh the [wrath] of man to praise Him & the remainder of wrath He restraineth."[18]

DuBose and his unit remained near Adam's Run until the spring of 1862, when the Holcombe Legion was transferred to Virginia following the Peninsula and Seven Days campaigns of April–July 1862. Upon the unit's arrival near Richmond, DuBose and his friend Richard Y. "Dick" Dwight experienced their first close contact with the enemy. The two men, armed only with a small pistol, captured a heavily armed Union cavalryman after the soldier mistakenly asked them for directions.[19]

The Holcombe Legion's arrival in Virginia signaled the beginning of intense combat operations for the unit. It moved to Gordonsville to join Gen. Robert E. Lee's Army of Northern Virginia, which opposed Union major general John Pope's Army of Virginia. On August 23, during the battle of Rappahannock Station, DuBose received the first of his wounds when a piece of shrapnel hit him in the knee and temporarily hobbled him.[20] Soon thereafter, on August 30, at the battle of Second Manassas, DuBose's unit experienced its first desperate combat when, as part of Evans's Brigade, they participated in the attack of Lt. Gen. James Longstreet's corps on Pope's left flank. DuBose was fortunate to survive. During the assault he stopped to pick up a fallen Confederate banner. In doing so, he left himself exposed to Union fire, while his unit moved into a wooded area. DuBose and his flag thus became a conspicuous target for Union troops. He later commented, "The few men that were with me were a little to the left and were shielded somewhat from sight by some stray pine saplings. It so happened that I was the only one visible to them at that moment, standing with the flag in my hands. I had the pleasure of seeing rifles deliberately aimed at me. At the charge I fell purposely and the flag was hit and not me. I then rose and turned to run to the left. At that moment a minie [sic] ball hit me, tearing my clothes and the flesh off my back and just scraping my back bone. The enemy resumed their retreat and I was left standing there—paralyzed."[21] Amazingly, his wound was not debilitating, and DuBose moved to the rear to seek medical care. The Holcombe Legion, including its officers, was devastated during the attack. DuBose was ordered to reorganize the one hundred or so survivors into three companies under his command.[22]

Lee's army was victorious at Second Manassas, and the Holcombe Legion advanced with it across the Potomac River, as part of Lee's efforts to move the war into Maryland.[23] DuBose's unit passed through Frederick City on its way to Hagerstown, where the men hoped to rest. Soon after arriving, they were rushed with Evans's Brigade to Turner's Gap at South Mountain. There the brigade participated in the battle of South Mountain, where it attempted to slow Maj. Gen. George B. McClellan's Army of the Potomac as it pursued Lee's scattered Confederate forces. After resisting Union assaults for much of the day, Lee's men, including the Holcombe Legion, retreated from the mountain passes.[24]

Afterward DuBose received orders to extend his unit's picket line to the left side of the mountain's base. He was exhausted from the forced march and the battle, so after moving his skirmishers forward under the cover of darkness, DuBose lay down to rest. He was asleep for only a short time before a subordinate woke him to tell him that Lee wanted a reconnaissance of Turner's Gap, where DuBose and his men had fought earlier that day. DuBose led his pickets uphill toward the battlefield, but their movement was so noisy that DuBose continued the ascent alone. When he reached the moonlit plateau, he was able to recognize the site by the fallen soldiers of both sides. He conducted a quiet reconnaissance of the battlefield, until he was challenged by a sentry. Glimpsing a figure in the dark, and uncertain whether or not he had stumbled into his own pickets, DuBose moved forward until the man stood a few paces away. The sentry was a Union soldier, who raised his rifle to fire. DuBose grabbed the weapon and discharged his pistol at him. The sentry yelled, dropped his rifle, and tackled DuBose, who struggled to escape. DuBose soon discovered that he had been moving within a large Union encampment. The surrounding troops quickly subdued him.[25]

The following day DuBose began traveling to a prisoner-of-war camp. He and other Confederate prisoners were marched to Baltimore, where they boarded a ship that transported them up the Chesapeake Bay to Fort Delaware. While imprisoned, DuBose met a number of acquaintances, including some from the University of Virginia. Many of the prisoners received supplies from Baltimore, which lessened the severity of confinement.[26]

Within one month DuBose and some of the other officers were exchanged for Union prisoners. The Confederate prisoners were taken by ship to Aiken's Landing, near Richmond on the James River. Little food was available for them on the return trip or when they arrived, but upon disembarking, DuBose met a close friend from Virginia, who invited him to dine with him and rest at his nearby camp before walking the eight miles to Richmond.[27]

In Richmond, DuBose was surprised to learn that he had been reported killed during the reconnaissance mission. His men had heard the gunshot and the Union soldier shout, and they had waited for DuBose for a long time before retreating to Confederate lines. Colonel Stevens, who was temporarily in command of Evans's Brigade, gave official notification to the government and the family. DuBose even read his own obituary in a piece written by Richard Yeadon of Charleston. DuBose quickly sent letters to family and friends, especially to Nannie, whose family had moved to Anderson, South Carolina. Although DuBose was supposed to remain in Richmond until exchanged, Dr. Edwin Gaillard, the chief surgeon of the Confederacy, examined him and granted him a sick furlough. DuBose returned to his home in Winnsboro, where he spent time with his family and, more important, with Nannie, who was staying with his family as their guest.[28]

DuBose was officially exchanged on November 10, 1862, and he rejoined his unit near Wilmington, North Carolina. Though stalwart in his religious convictions throughout the war, DuBose suffered a brief period of spiritual malaise following his return to service. On November 16, 1862, he wrote, "I find that the same difficulty has grown upon me in my intercourse with God. I find it hard to be still, & rest in His presence, to rejoice in dwelling quietly in the light of His countenance, as I used to do in my more favored hours. Restlessness & impatience have taken possession of me & have robbed my devotional hours of much of their joy & peace." Seven days later he had rallied: "I read a beautiful & admirable sermon of Robertson's this morning on the text, 'Eye hath not seen, nor ear heard &c.' As often happens with me, that was sent to me which I most needed at the time. There was much in it calculated to comfort and encourage me in the state of mind in which it found me." DuBose enthusiastically elaborated that man should seek "the same intimate filial communion" with God as that of Jesus. "God sees us in His Son, in proportion as we see ourselves in Him, & the only relief for us in our hours of bitter self-condemnation & self-abhorrence is to look away from ourselves infinitely unrighteous in ourselves to ourselves perfectly righteous in Him."[29]

On November 6 Evans's Brigade was ordered to Weldon, North Carolina, and by December 1862 the brigade moved south to defend Goldsboro, which was a vital point on the East Coast Railway. On December 11 Union major general John G. Foster launched a raid from New Bern with the objective of destroying the Whilden-Wilmington Railroad bridge over the Neuse River at Goldsboro.[30] Evans moved his brigade east from Goldsboro to Kinston to confront Foster's force. On December 13 he arrayed his forces in a wooded area with the Neuse River and its bridge to their rear. Evans placed his South Carolinians, including the Holcombe Legion, on the left side of his line. The following day Foster's forces attacked the Confederates, and Union troops quickly turned the left flank of the South Carolinians.[31] Du-Bose was once again in command of the Holcombe Legion, and he ordered his men to retreat to a more defensible position on a hill to their rear. The retreat, however, quickly became a rout. DuBose skillfully managed to halt his fleeing men on the hill, where they turned to face the advancing Union forces. DuBose moved up and down the line steadying his troops, until he was shot in the hip by a minié ball that ricocheted off the ground, penetrated several layers of clothing, and entered his side. Fortunately for DuBose, the round hit no arteries or organs.[32] General Evans stopped the stretcher bearers as they rushed DuBose to the rear. Showing great concern for his young subordinate, Evans gave DuBose whiskey to dull the pain. He later mentioned DuBose in the official report of the battle and recommended him for promotion.[33] Once again DuBose was spared from the worst possibilities of a wound. Surgeons successfully removed the ball from the hip while he was still on the battlefield, and an ambulance carried him to Goldsboro and then to a hospital in Raleigh. Soon thereafter a surgeon ordered him to be removed to his own home in South Carolina. DuBose returned to Winnsboro to convalesce once again, having received his third wound in less than six months.[34]

During his convalescence Nannie served as a foil for DuBose's theological thought. She wrote to him and asked for "some scriptural proofs of the divinity & personality of the Holy Ghost." DuBose's response was thoughtful and detailed. There were only two ways that one could be led to belief in the Trinity: "The first is to receive it on the authority of the Church until we come to a practical knowledge of it for ourselves. The second is so to study the Gospel and accept its teachings as to be taught of God all that it contains." DuBose then confirmed the divinity of the Holy Ghost while delivering a disquisition upon "His personality."[35]

DuBose returned to his unit in North Carolina, but as spring approached he was feeling his mortality. He asked Nannie if her mother would agree to the couple being married before the end of the war. "But to say that we are to wait until this war is over, or until I am ordained . . . is in fact to postpone it indefinitely." He urged haste regarding the wedding: "After the summer campaign opens, everything is dark & uncertain." She agreed, and DuBose received a furlough and married Nannie on April 30, 1863. The Reverend John H. Elliott conducted the wedding in a small ceremony in Anderson, South Carolina. DuBose and Nannie honeymooned in nearby Greenville, where they visited their friend Paul Trapier.[36]

After this respite, DuBose traveled to Mississippi, where he joined his unit as it lay encamped along the Pearl River outside of Jackson. Evans's Brigade was part of the forces of Gen. Joseph E. Johnston, which were attempting to relieve a besieged Confederate army at Vicksburg. During the first two days of July, Johnston moved his forces westward toward Vicksburg and arrived at the Big Black River. Johnston's army bivouacked along the river's banks believing that they would cross it the following day, attack the army of Union major general Ulysses S. Grant, and lift the siege of Vicksburg. DuBose and his comrades, however, were saddened deeply when they retreated away from Grant and moved eastward toward Jackson. Vicksburg had surrendered, and Grant quickly turned his forces to pursue Johnston's army. Johnston's forces stopped their retreat and constructed earthworks in Jackson. Union and Confederate troops traded desultory fire in front of the city for a few days before Johnston once again retreated eastward out of Mississippi.[37]

Evans's Brigade moved first to Mobile, Alabama, and then to Savannah, Georgia, where they occupied a nearby sea island. DuBose attempted to coordinate with Nannie so that she could join him in Savannah. Unfortunately, as she traveled south to meet him, DuBose and the Holcombe Legion were transferred north to Charleston. Upon their arrival they were stationed in Mt. Pleasant and on Sullivan's Island to guard against Union attacks.[38]

In the fall of 1863 DuBose's circumstances changed dramatically. He received a commission from the Confederate government to serve as a chaplain in Brig. Gen. Joseph B. Kershaw's brigade. Of the commission, DuBose later commented, "It had been secured by General Kershaw and Bishop Davis, without my knowledge or consent. I had been very near ordination at the beginning of the war and I suppose my friends thought that I had had my share of hard service." DuBose resigned his commission as adjutant on November 1, 1863, and in December he traveled to Camden, where he was ordained as a deacon. His ordination launched him on a different military path, transforming him from a combatant to a counselor for those who waged war.[39]

As a newly commissioned chaplain, DuBose traveled with Lt. Col. Franklin Gaillard to join Kershaw's Brigade, which was stationed in eastern Tennessee. The route there took the men from South Carolina to North Carolina and then on to Tennessee. One of DuBose's most vivid letters records a winter trek through the gloomy, majestic, snow-covered mountains of North Carolina. During the journey DuBose was once again spared, when a "chance" encounter with a lone woman in the wilderness saved him and his party from riding directly into an encampment of bushwhackers and certain death. In Greeneville, Tennessee, DuBose began his ministry to Kershaw's Brigade.[40]

His quiet time with the brigade in Tennessee allowed him to align his ministerial functions with the needs of the unit. It also served as a training period prior to the brigade's transfer to Gordonsville, Virginia, during spring 1864 to participate with the rest of the Army of Northern Virginia in the nearly continuous combat operations of the Overland campaign.[41]

From May 5 to May 7, 1864, Kershaw's Brigade played an important and costly role in the battle of the Wilderness. As a chaplain, DuBose was behind the firing line for the first time during the war. Lieutenant Colonel Gaillard, who had had a premonition of his death, presented DuBose with a package, which DuBose was to give to Gaillard's family after he died. Shortly thereafter Gaillard was shot and killed. DuBose oversaw Gaillard's battlefield burial the following day. He also officiated at the burials of Brig. Gen. Micah Jenkins and the colonel of the Third South Carolina, both of whom were friends from the Citadel.[42] DuBose spent much of his time ministering to the wounded. While doing so, his haversack, with Lieutenant Colonel Gaillard's package, was stolen.[43]

Kershaw's Brigade participated in other battles during the campaign, including Spotsylvania and Cold Harbor. By July the brigade had retreated to Petersburg. DuBose's letters during this period include a litany of references to friends and family members who had been consumed by the war's deadliest campaign. DuBose wrote, "There continues to be a good deal of religious interest manifested in the Brigade. There is no doubt that battles & the prospect of battles do much to startle men into seriousness."[44] The strain of nearly continuous combat deeply affected DuBose and the soldiers to whom he ministered. One day he openly wrote to Nannie regarding the macabre actions of a nearby soldier who was grinding his coffee in the skull of a soldier and using one of his bones as a pestle: "It is wonderful how matter of fact they become. Though I do not think I could quite do that, I find much 'sentiment' on such matters wearing off. The mind becomes easily accustomed to almost anything."[45] The ongoing campaign left DuBose little time for correspondence or contemplation: "I have not been writing on regular days lately & the consequence is I can never remember when I wrote last."[46]

As the opposing forces reached an uneasy stalemate around Petersburg, both Confederate and Union commanders sought advantage elsewhere. Kershaw's Brigade, which was part of Anderson's division, was transferred to the Shenandoah Valley to serve under Gen. Jubal Early. After brief service there, the division was ordered back to Petersburg, but halfway there it was ordered back to the Shenandoah Valley to help stem the advance of Union forces under Maj. Gen. Philip Sheridan. On October 19, 1864, Kershaw's Brigade participated in the pivotal battle of Cedar Creek. Of the engagement DuBose later wrote, "Kershaw's Brigade, which had never slept behind a field of battle, but always on it or before it, slept that night fifteen miles behind one. To others besides myself I think that night's experience was the turning point of the war. . . . To me—that night!—I felt as if everything was gone!"[47] In another memoir he added, "I could not sleep; the end of the world was upon me as completely as upon the Romans when the barbarians had overrun them."[48] Eleven days after the engagement he wrote to Nannie, "The fact is that since that unfortunate reverse of the 19th I have been laboring harder to make my life & ministry what they ought to be."[49]

The end of the Valley campaign began a period of almost constant movement for Kershaw's Brigade, as it returned to Petersburg and then moved to Charleston to contest Union major general William Tecumseh Sherman's forces as they invaded South Carolina. The greatest break in the DuBose correspondence occurs during this period from October 31, 1864, to February 5, 1865.

Despite Confederate efforts to slow his advance, Sherman captured Columbia on February 17, 1865, and moved toward Camden and Cheraw. To avoid encirclement, Confederate forces abandoned Charleston on the same night that Columbia was captured and burned. Kershaw's Brigade and garrison troops from Charleston moved north to unite with other forces coalescing under Johnston's command. During the march DuBose stopped at Back River to visit his aunt, Mrs. Anna Maria Stoney. En route to Cheraw his brigade also marched through St. Stephens, where DuBose's grandfather was buried at the old Huguenot Church. At Cheraw, Confederate forces futilely attempted to slow Sherman's advance. Kershaw's Brigade retreated with other Confederate units into North Carolina, where it participated in the battles of Averasboro and Bentonville.[50]

DuBose later wrote that during the war's final days, he had "one of the most painful little duties to perform that I think was ever imposed upon me." Desertion from South Carolina regiments increased as Sherman's forces moved through the state. Six deserters from Orangeburg, who "were deserting mainly just to see how things were at home," were "caught, court-martialed, and sentenced to be shot." DuBose was ordered to prepare the men for execution. "It was the most awful thing I was ever asked to do, the worst I ever experienced. Fortunately, the surrender came and the sentence was not executed."[51]

The war's final days were a period of great anxiety for DuBose. There is a break in his correspondence between February 8 and March 2, when mail service in South Carolina dissolved as Sherman's forces moved through the state.[52] In one of the last letters in the collection, DuBose, like Confederate soldiers from South Carolina (and previously Georgia), sought news of loved ones and property after Sherman's men had passed. On March 2, 1865, DuBose wrote to Nannie because he had heard that his house had been burned. The news was so distressing that he was tempted to leave his unit in Cheraw and return home: "You may imagine my anxiety to get home & I have been sorely tempted to make an effort . . . it w'd cut me off indefinitely from my command." Fifteen days later he received news from Nannie that she and the house had been spared the worst depredations of Sherman's men.[53]

To all but the most optimistic Southern observers, the fate of the Confederacy had been sealed. Years later DuBose wrote that on the night when "it came over me like a shock of death that the Confederacy was beginning to break," he went out by himself, and "under the stars, alone upon the planet, without home or country or any earthly interest or object before me, my very world at an end, I redevoted myself wholly and only to God, and to the work and life of His Kingdom."[54]

DuBose's war-time correspondence concludes without providing the reader with insight into the struggles that he, Nannie, and their family faced once peace arrived. The final complete letter, dated April 3, 1865, finds DuBose enjoying a beautiful spring day near Smithfield, North Carolina. In it there is no anticipation of the forthcoming demise of the Confederacy. The letter provides no portent of Lee's surrender at Appomattox on April 9, 1865, or of Johnston's surrender to Sherman at Bennett Place on April 26. The reader is left with the impression that DuBose is enjoying a peaceful afternoon, both grateful and relieved that his family and home have been spared destruction. The letter is, like previous correspondence, full of news and best wishes. Little is written of the war, which he would ultimately survive and which would shape the postwar fate of DuBose, his family, and his church.

Notes

1. DuBose, "Reminiscences," 3, South Caroliniana Library (hereafter SCL).
2. Ibid.; Davidson, *Last Foray,* 193; National Archives, United States Bureau of the Census, 1860, *Eighth Census of the United States (South Carolina),* Fairfield District, 282.
3. DuBose, "Reminiscences," 28–31, SCL.

INTRODUCTION

4. DuBose, *Turning Points in My Life,* 20.

5. DuBose, "Reminiscences," 30–31, 34, SCL.

6. Ibid., 34–40, 46.

7. Ibid., 58.

8. Ibid., 63–66.

9. Ibid., 67–68.

10. Ibid., 68–69.

11. DuBose, "Reminiscences," 69–70, SCL.

12. W. P. DuBose to A. B. Peronneau, October 23, 1861, South Carolina Historical Society (hereafter SCHS).

13. Lewis, *Queen of the Confederacy,* 143–44; National Archives, War Department Collection of Confederate Records, RG 109, Compiled Service Records of Confederate Soldiers Who Served in Organizations from the State of South Carolina [hereafter Compiled Service Records], Microcopy 267, Holcombe Legion, roll 372; Scarborough, *Masters of the Big House,* 117.

14. DuBose, "Reminiscences," 73, SCL.

15. In early November 1861 a Union fleet captured Port Royal Sound and the adjacent sea islands in South Carolina. Using Port Royal as an operational base, Union gunboats made forays into the rivers bisecting the coast, testing Confederate defenses and enforcing the blockade. See Compiled Service Records, Holcombe Legion, M267, roll 372; Stone, *Vital Rails,* 68–70.

16. Compiled Service Records, Holcombe Legion, M267, roll 372; *War of the Rebellion: The Official Records of the Union and Confederate Armies* (hereafter *Official Records Army* and series 1 unless otherwise indicated), 6:77–82, 113–20; DuBose, "Reminiscences," 69–70, SCL.

17. W. P. DuBose to A. B. Peronneau, February 28, 1862, SCHS; Hebrews 11:16 and 13:14; Augustine of Hippo and Bettenson, *City of God.*

18. Ibid.

19. Compiled Service Records, Holcombe Legion, M267, roll 372; DuBose, "Reminiscences," 82, SCL.

20. *Official Records Army,* 12(2):630; DuBose, "Reminiscences," 84, SCL.

21. DuBose, "Reminiscences," 85–88, SCL.

22. Ibid., 88; *Official Records Army,* 12(2):629–32. Lt. Col. F. G. Palmer and Major Crawley of the Holcombe Legion were both wounded at Second Manassas, leaving DuBose as the unit's senior officer.

23. Confederate general Robert E. Lee (1807–70) believed that a campaign in Maryland could be advantageous for a variety of reasons. It could draw potential recruits from the border state; the farms of Maryland could feed his starving army and free Virginia of Union troops during the important harvest season; Lee could cut the rail links that connected Washington, D.C., from the west; and perhaps the Confederacy could win recognition by foreign powers. See McPherson, *Battle Cry of Freedom,* 534–35; Sears, *Landscape Turned Red,* 65–69.

24. DuBose, "Reminiscences," 89–93, SCL; *Official Records Army,* 19(1):147, 939–42; Sears, *Landscape Turned Red,* 134–43. Union troops had found a copy of Lee's

orders, which outlined the fragmented disposition of Lee's army. Union major George B. McClellan (1826–85) swiftly moved his Army of the Potomac to shatter the fragments of Lee's army before it could consolidate. Lee tasked part of his army, including Evans's Brigade, with holding the gaps at South Mountain to buy time for him to gather the rest of his men near Sharpsburg, Maryland. After stiff resistance, Union troops forced the Confederates from the mountain passes. See Sears, *Landscape Turned Red,* 112–19.

25. DuBose, "Reminiscences," 93–96, SCL.

26. Ibid., 104–5.

27. Ibid., 109–11.

28. Ibid., 112–14, 116; *Official Records Army,* 19:147, 939–42. In his official report of DuBose's "death," Stevens wrote, "Whether that single shot proved fatal or whether he is a prisoner, I know not, but in him I have lost my right arm, and the service of as noble, as pure minded, as fearless an officer as ever battled for his country."

29. W. P. DuBose to A. B. Peronneau, November 16, 1862, SCHS; W. P. DuBose to A. B. Peronneau, November 23, 1862, SCHS.

30. Barrett, *Civil War in North Carolina,* 139.

31. *Official Records Army,* 18:112–14; Barrett, *Civil War in North Carolina,* 140–43.

32. DuBose, "Reminiscences," 119, SCL.

33. Ibid.; *Official Records Army,* 18:112–14. In his official report of the battle of Kinston, Evans noted that DuBose was "conspicuous in the battles of Saturday and Sunday" and that he was "wounded while leading his regiment."

34. DuBose, "Reminiscences," 119–20, SCL.

35. W. P. DuBose to A. B. P. DuBose, January 10, 1863, SCHS.

36. Ibid., March 25, 1863; DuBose, "Reminiscences," 120–21, SCL.

37. DuBose, "Reminiscences," 121–23, SCL; McPherson, *Battle Cry of Freedom,* 634–35.

38. DuBose, "Reminiscences," 124–25, SCL.

39. Compiled Service Records, William P. DuBose, Brig. Gen. Joseph B. Kershaw to Gen. S. Cooper, August 4, 1863, roll 374. Thirteen days prior to Kershaw sending his request to Confederate adjutant general Samuel S. Cooper, Brig. Gen. Nathan G. Evans had sent the Confederate adjutant general a letter requesting that DuBose receive an appointment as inspector general for Evans's Brigade. The request was denied because "it is not customary to allow an Inspt. Genl. to a brigade." DuBose, "Reminiscences," 124–25, SCL.

40. W. P. DuBose to A. P. B. DuBose, February 8, 1863(4), SCHS.

41. McPherson, *Battle Cry of Freedom,* 725; DuBose, "Reminiscences," 130–31, SCL.

42. In his "Reminiscences," DuBose remembered the colonel of the Third South Carolina as "Col. Means," but Col. James D. Nance was commander of the Third South Carolina when he was killed at the battle of the Wilderness. Nance was a Citadel graduate and probably the person to whom DuBose refers. See DuBose, "Reminiscences," 131, SCL.

43. DuBose, "Reminiscences," 131, SCL.

44. W. P. DuBose to A. B. P. DuBose, May 30, 1864, SCHS.

45. Ibid., June 14, 1864, SCHS.

46. Ibid., June 24, 1864, SCHS.

47. DuBose, "Reminiscences," 133–34, SCL.

48. DuBose, *Turning Points in My Life,* 49.

49. W. P. DuBose to A. B. P. DuBose, October 31, 1864, SCHS.

50. DuBose, "Reminiscences," 134–35, SCL.

51. Ibid., 135.

52. Once Sherman's forces had swept through South Carolina, DuBose sent letters to Nannie through friends and acquaintances, who served as couriers. See W. P. DuBose to A. B. P. DuBose, April 3, 1865, SCHS.

53. W. P. DuBose to A. B. P. DuBose, March 2, 1865, SCHS; ibid., March 17, 1865, SCHS.

54. DuBose, *Turning Points in My Life,* 49.

FAITH, VALOR,
AND DEVOTION

1

DIVERGENT LOYALTIES

October–December 1861

"It is not only the cause of our country that I regard, but the cause of religion & the Church."

November 11, 1861

During the final months of 1861, William Porcher DuBose witnessed a dramatic change in his plans for the future. Recently engaged to Nannie Peronneau, DuBose hoped to finish his seminary studies, get married, and begin a career in the clergy. Instead, his father convinced him to leave the seminary to serve in the army of the Confederacy. By December the Holcombe Legion, with DuBose as its adjutant, was stationed near Charleston.

Fort Beauregard[1]
Oct 4th 1861

Dear Nannie,

I am glad you wrote to tell me of your engagement—it was kind and cousinly. I won't say I am sorry or rejoiced; I am content, for I am sure your choice must be worthy, if not of you, of respect & love. I have for several years cultivated self control & have restrained many strong impulses & feelings so that I am sure few know how strong my love can be. But dear Cousin you must believe me when I say that I can scarcely recognize any difference in my love for yourself & Sue[2] than from that I feel for my own sisters & that I earnestly pray for you as I would for one of them that God may grant you happiness in this world; for the other you have already I believe every assurance. The grave stern antics of manhood are now my chief delight; but deep down in my heart is a wellspring of affection, & whenever dear Cousin you need a friend either for your sympathy or advice I hope you will find me ready unasked to give you both or either. Mr. DuBose I do not know but will be most happy to do so. Pray say so for me to him. Goodbye dear Nannie. I will try to write a line to my second mother Aunt Mary[3] tonight. Kiss Sue & tell Mr. D.B. that no never mind. Kiss Aunt Mary for me too.

Your aff Cousin Ned[4]

1. "From Cousin Ned Parker" is penciled on the back of the letter.

2. This is Nannie's sister Susan Hayne Peronneau (d. 1910). See Patey, *Whaley Family*, 198.

3. Aunt Mary is Nannie's mother, Mary Sarah Coffin Peronneau. See Patey, *Whaley Family*, 197, 212.

4. This possibly is Edward Frost Parker (1830–88). He married Serina Waring Parker in 1866. See Parker, *Genealogy of the Parker Family*, 40.

Camden, S.C.
Oct. 8th 1861

I have delayed writing to you a whole long day—no easy matter, I assure you—until I could have leisure & quiet to turn my whole mind & heart toward you, My own dear Miss Nannie. We have just closed our first weekly prayer-meeting, during which our hearts have been drawn, I trust, close to our Savior & close to each other. And now I feel like communing with you, nearer & dearer to me than anything else, except Him who in His great mercy gave you to me.

I am once more established in my dear little room, surrounded by many old familiar things—engravings, books & c. A year ago as I sat thus, I used often to say to myself "What could God do for me than He has done? He has given me health, friends, pure and moderate tastes & the means of satisfying them, the highest & holiest of callings & an ardent love for it." But His infinite love has discovered another blessing to bestow upon me. Oh, may it humble me to reflect upon His goodness & my own great unworthiness!

I feel that God blesses me in my love for you, that He graciously uses it as a means of drawing me nearer to Himself. During the past week the light of His countenance has not been withdrawn from me for a moment, and whenever I begin to "fore-date the day of woe"[1] & look forward to the conflicts & clouds which have always seemed inseparable from the Christian life—the words which we read last Sunday in the Psalter come back to reproach me for my want of faith—"Be strong and <u>He</u> shall establish your heart, all you that trust in the Lord." So I enjoy the peace which He gives me now & leave the future to Him.

Thank you for that little note & the tablets; they have helped me to bear the separation better than I could have done without them. I am longing for the daguerreotype—please send it soon. I was tempted tonight to ask Miss Sarah, if she had one, to lend it to me until mine comes. My trip up had no incident worth recalling, it was not an unpleasant one, though the day was rather warm. I took charge of Miss Susan[2] as far as Orangeburg, but as she could not talk while the cars were in motion I had plenty of time to think of you. On my arrival here I received of course a hearty welcome from my friends. That night Johnson[3] & I sat & talked until a late hour when we parted with prayer. He showed me more of himself than he had done before, & we both, I am sure, felt that our friendship was, to say the least of it, unimpaired by my recent acquisition. The fact is, I believe, that my love for you has expanded & deepened my whole nature, that my capacity for loving others has been increased too. I shall be disappointed in myself if I am not hereafter a better son, brother & friend than I have ever been before. That which I believed God was going to effect by chastening, He chose to accomplish by blessing, viz: give me a deeper & more real & practical sympathy with human nature, its joys & its sorrows. I never doubt that He has given us to each other for our good & for His glory. I paid a delightful visit to the Trapiers[4] yesterday afternoon. Miss Sarah was very good to me, but I would insist upon calling her Miss Sue. I made the mistake several times. She has told you I suppose how the news first reached her. I have seen no one else yet; I was so busy yesterday that I had no time to go out.

We have all the seminary back except the professors. Mr. Hanckel has not come yet, & Mr. Trapier goes to Col. today.

I found several very affectionate letters from home awaiting me here. I suppose you have heard from my sister. She wrote me a note too, but she cannot write very comfortably to herself yet [sic].

I have not opened a book yet—as soon as I get regularly into traces I will tell you all about my duties & studies.

There is a mockingbird singing most enthusiastically just out of my window. It carries me back to Tradd St.[5] & into your presence.

"Oh for the touch of an absent hand!"

You must excuse this letter—it is not written under as favorable circumstances as I hope to write hereafter. I commenced it late last night (later than you would have approved) & am finishing it hurriedly for the mail this morning (9th). Much love to Mamma & Sue & Miss Carrie Winthrop.[6] I hope to hear from you before the close of the week. God guard & guide you!

Yrs most truly & affectionately W. P. DuBose

1. These lines are attributed to Thomas Ken (1637–1711), an English prelate and hymn writer: "When by God the heart is riven, / Strength is promised, strength is given; / But fore-date the day of woe, / And alone thou bear'st the blow." See Carey, *Esther,* 29.

2. This is probably Susan Eliza Lovell (1818–92) of Charleston and Orangeburg, South Carolina, daughter of Josiah Sturgis Lovell (1779–1821). See Dominick, "Poinsett Genealogy," 72.

3. John Johnson (1829–1907), an Episcopal priest and Confederate engineer, was a friend of William Porcher DuBose and also attended the Camden seminary of Bishop Davis. Johnson married in 1865. He was the author of *The Defense of Charleston Harbor.* See *Cyclopedia of Eminent Men of the Carolinas,* 512; *Works Progress Administration Cemetery Index* (hereafter *WPA Cemetery Index*).

4. Reference here is to the family of the Reverend Paul Trapier (1806–72), a professor at the theological seminary in Camden and formerly rector of St. Michael's Episcopal Church in Charleston. His wife was Sarah Dehon Trapier (1815–89), the mother of twelve children, some of whom included daughters Sarah, Mary, and Alice and sons Paul, Theodore, Pierre, and Richard. See Trapier, *Incidents in My Life;* Thomas, *Protestant Episcopal Church,* 687ff.; Jervey, *Inscriptions in St. Michael's,* 270, 315.

5. Nannie lived at 97 Tradd Street in Charleston. See Charleston (S.C.) City Council, *Census for 1861,* 205.

6. Caroline Winthrop (1836–1918) was the daughter of Joseph Augustus Winthrop (1791–1864), a prominent Charleston merchant who was married to Maria Evelina, daughter of Thomas Parker. Early in the war Winthrop purchased a house and lot in Anderson, South Carolina, and moved his family there. See Mayo, *Winthrop Family,* 280.

Piedmont Oct. 10th 1861[1]

Well, my beloved Nannie, what shall I say to the news contained in your letter of the seventh? I reply this, that I don't think that I was ever so surprised in the whole course of my life before! And I could not for the life of me, tell at first, whether the surprise was pleasant or painful. But before telling you how unprepared I was to hear of your engagement, I must say how rejoiced I am at your happiness, and assure you that I am not skeptical—at least in your case—& though it seems very strange to me, sometimes, that you should be engaged to a man I have never seen. I am astonished at the amiability of my feelings toward him, and am really quite willing to like him whenever I have an opportunity. I receive your descriptions as if they were written by an impartial hand, & believe them implicitly. Indeed I have too much confidence in you to think for one moment that you could have chosen unworthily—but O Nannie I do feel very lonely & forsaken. I am not foolish enough to think that you will love me less now than formerly, but I fear that I will see less of you and I am not yet accustomed to this great change in your circumstances. You must forgive my selfishness and believe me when I say that I really do rejoice with you, and think your lot a most happy one. I could not wish you a better destiny than the wife of an intelligent & earnest minister—it is what I would like best for myself; and am delighted that it is selected for you. I must thank you dear Nannie, for letting me hear this news first from you & not from strangers, for as you will perceive from this letter, not a breath of it had reached Flat Rock until your letter came yesterday.

Now I want you to write me some particulars, as to how long Mr. DuBose has been in Charleston, whether he was in Camden when you were there, & everything about you or himself which you are willing to tell. I will be only too glad to hear. I am not at all alarmed for his stature, for, as you have probably found out, my opinion on this & on many other subjects has undergone many changes. I am afraid that I have written very incoherently, & that you will find my letter very unsatisfactory, for I have not yet recovered from the shock of yesterday sufficiently to collect my [focus]. I find it hard to leave this engrossing subject for any less interesting, and I am delighted to think that I will see you before long, and can then say all that I now leave unsaid. We sometimes talk of staying up here this winter but I believe it is only talk.

[Maury] will enclose a note to [you]. Grandmamma, Aunt Carey[2] & Mary [S.] send you much love & many fond wishes. With much love to your Mother & Sue I am dearest Nannie,

Yours always C. P.[3]

What is the matter with [Mrs.] Gilchrist?[4]

1. Piedmont (located in Flat Rock, North Carolina) was the summer home of the Reverend Charles Cotesworth Pinckney (1812–98), a South Carolina Episcopal clergyman. See Reuther, *Flat Rock,* 17.

2. Caroline Pinckney, the writer of the letter, was the niece of Caroline Pinckney Seabrook (1816–92), the wife of Archibald Hamilton Seabrook (1816–94). See *South Carolina Genealogies,* 3:306, 4:217.

3. Caroline Pinckney was the daughter of the Reverend Charles C. Pinckney. She married Julian A. Mitchell (1836–1907). See *South Carolina Genealogies,* 2:81, 3:306.

4. The Gilchrist family of Charleston was apparently related to the Peronneaus through the Gibbes family. See Patey, *Whaley Family,* 140.

Charleston Oct 11th 1861

At last a quiet moment has arrived in which I can reply to your most welcome letter, My Dearest Friend. All day has been employed in business which would not leave me calm enough to write until it was duly accomplished, and now I fear I am too late for tomorrow's mail. My morning was spent in answering some of the kind loving letters I have received from your home. Your father's I answered first, taking a long time to do it, for I wanted very much to please him, and did my very best. Mrs. Bratton's[1] sweet note was next answered and when it was nearly done, a very charming epistle from your elder sister was put into my hands. That is reserved for another day, it is one of the style of letters which awakens a strong desire to reply to it, so you need not fear that I am troubling myself in doing so.

Your letter only reached me last night and as I had been longing for it ever since you left, you may be sure it was most thankfully received and enjoyed. These quiet peaceful hours at the end of the day are so well suited for writing that I fear both of us will be ensnared into staying up later than is good for us. We must try to be conscientious however. I am glad you wrote to me after the prayer meeting for your thoughts were still hallowed by their recent communion with heavenly things, and they have breathed some of their own spirit into my heart. In so very active a life as mine there is great need for an influence which will draw one away from earthly to higher thoughts, and which will lead me to carry all my joys as well as trials to my Savior to sanctify and bless them to me. You will I hope always be that blessed influence to me. You see I am depending on you already for a great deal.

We have all missed you very much indeed. Sue sends her love and says that she at least has missed you horribly. I have your likeness open before me now, looking straight into my eyes, but with a much sterner expression than I'm accustomed to see in them. I have not quite forgotten yet how you look with your lips apart.

Yesterday we spent delightfully, in the country. My dear cousin Nannie,[2] had written me so very nice a letter in answer to a short, stiff note of mine, that an uncontrollable desire to talk to her, seized me, and I persuaded Sue and Mamma to go with me and spend the day at Uncle Edward's. Every circumstance favored us. The weather cool and very bright, and our friends

Thomas Frederick Davis (1804–1871) was the bishop of South Carolina from 1853 to 1871. Along with Gen. Joseph B. Kershaw, he was instrumental in William Porcher DuBose's transfer from active military service into the chaplaincy. Courtesy of the Episcopal Diocese of South Carolina; photograph by David Harley, 2009

affectionate and amiable as possible. Nannie listened to all I had to say, pronounced the ambrotype excellent, and wound up by sending her love to you. Just see how many new friends you are forced to make. Carrie Winthrop too sends her love, tho' I think she considers such a proceeding improper. Sue talked so much yesterday that she was very much exhausted. Our day ended as happily as it began, for when I got home, there was your precious letter ready for me—quite a climax it was to the past pleasures. The only small drop of alloy (an eight paged letter from Miss Susan) was so completely swallowed up in happiness that it never disturbed me. Think of Miss Susan's sending me eight pages of congratulations and commissions! and still more strange, a formal request for my consent to your going to Orangeburg, before she writes to the Bp [Bishop]! Imagine Leila Davis's[3] enjoyment at reading a letter from

Miss Susan, telling her father that you and I consent to his giving you the Church at Orangeburgh! As the request is not to be made for you, until my consent is given, I think Miss Susan shall have a little time to calm off before I write.

Sue and I spent a delightful evening at the Miss Johnson's.[4] They were so affectionate and enjoyed so much the little teasing they allowed themselves to give me. Miss Catherine ensnared me into taking your cup at tea, and then was so much afraid I wouldn't like to be made conspicuous, that she could not enjoy the joke at all! Miss Charlotte presented me with a beautiful bunch of flowers, because she said it had sweet williams in it. A good many of the sisters charged me to find a wife for their brother John. It will be a difficult thing I'm afraid, tho' after Fort Sumter we ought never to despair. Mrs. Porcher[5] had to write me that message herself about Messrs Johnson & Hutcheson. She ought not to have expected you to cast reproaches on your friend, ought she? The three letters which have come to me from Winnsboro have been far more kind and affectionate than I had the least right to expect. They trust me at once for everything I ought to be. I will send the daguerreotype early in the week if nothing prevents. Brother and all his party arrived last night in excellent health and spirits. His company has diminished rather than increased in numbers, but he is very hopeful.

I am very glad Mr. Johnson is not estranged or rather, saddened by this affair. Sarah thinks he looks sad. My love to the Trapiers and kind regards to Thomas and the Miss Davises if you like. I hope that mockingbird sings often for you. Are you quite well? Believe me

Yrs most affctly
Nannie

In spite of your robbery, I have now on my table two French Broad apples, a handful of chinquapins, and a piece of hemlock from Hoxad (?) falls![6] Will you not think of me more especially on Sunday, and pray for me. I am particularly fond of that prayer contained in the concluding verses of Eph. 3rd. I find it constantly rising to my lips for both of us.

Yrs. N.

1. William Porcher DuBose's sister Elizabeth Porcher DuBose (1838–75), or "Betsey," married Dr. John Bratton (1831–98), a Winnsboro planter (Wynn Dee Plantation) and physician. Bratton rose through the ranks of the Confederate army to become a brigadier general in May 1864. After the war he continued farming and served in the South Carolina Senate and the U.S. House of Representatives. See Bailey, *Biographical Directory of the South Carolina Senate,* 1:180–81; MacDowell, *DuBose Genealogy,* 232.

2. Anna Coffin Peronneau (b. 1836) was the daughter of Nannie's uncle Edward Charles Peronneau. See Patey, *Whaley Family*, 198.

3. Leila Davis was the daughter of Bishop Thomas Frederick Davis (1804–71), founder of the theological seminary in Camden attended by William Porcher DuBose. See Thomas, *Protestant Episcopal Church*, 706–8.

4. These were members of the Reverend John Johnson's (1829–1907) family.

5. This probably refers to William Porcher DuBose's sister Eliza Marion DuBose (1829–95), who was the widow of Augustus Henry Porcher (1824–52). See Mac-Dowell, *DuBose Genealogy*, 12.

6. Nannie could possibly mean the falls on Hogshead Creek (N.C.), the source of Maidenhair Falls (near Brevard). She questions the spelling. See Tinsley, *Land of Waterfalls*, 124.

[*Enclosed note:*]

Oct. 12th

I am truly disappointed that my letter has not gone Dear Mr. DuBose, but the post-office was shut this morning and I could get no stamp. However I shall immediately get a supply to guard against future misfortunes of the kind.

I had no room to tell you that I started to pay Miss Malvina[1] her promised visit when I heard she was out, so I postponed the visit, sending her only a message. Remember me to Mr. Johnson if you think it best and, Believe one,

Yrs ever, N.

1. Malvina Murden (d. 1890) kept a well-known school in Charleston with her mother and sisters Victoria, Rosaline, and Octavia, the latter of whom married Jacob K. Sass. See Tison and Stoney, "Recollections of John Safford Stoney," 209.

Camden, S.C.[1]
Oct. 14th 1861

Your letter reached me this morning, my dearest Miss Nannie, and would have been answered on the spot, if I had yielded to the temptation of the moment. But I had two others to write, to accelerate which I determined to put yours last—the consequence was that they were soon dispatched & here I am ready for you.

I don't know which gratified me most, that the people of home should have written to you so promptly, cordially, & affectionately, or that you should have taken so much pleasure in answering them all for yourself. I know that you will have no difficulty in learning to love them very much—and they certainly will not find it hard to love you, if they are anything like me. Sister and some of the others have been for some time distressed by the fear that I was incurably infected with old bachelor tastes & predilections (hateful heresy) & I have no doubt are truly grateful to you for rescuing me from the saddest of fates. I must confess that my views on that subject have undergone some change lately.

Our professors are still away and I find it harder than I expected to come down to systematic work. I can sympathize with Pegasus in his restiveness under harness; however I hope to be more successfully broken in than he was.

My plan just now is as follows—get up at 6 ½ exactly; prayers at 7; break-fast 7 ½; walk from 8 to 9; study from 10 to 2; dinner 2 to 3; read until 4; drill from 4 to 5; prayers at 5; anything until supper at 6 ½; then study or write until 10, and to bed by 11 o.c. It is hard to adhere to this routine, & I haven't succeeded remarkably well so far, but you know one of our mottoes is: "forget past errors & past failures & press forward." I have been twice into "my parish" in the lower part of the town & have seen enough wretched-ness & vice to sadden & sicken my heart. Poor things! I think that I can say with truth that there is not an individual in my district proper who has not spent the summer under the influence of chill & fever. I was quite touched by the evident joy with which many of them, even the lowest, welcome me back. May He who came to save sinners make use of me for their good & His glory!

I have nearly got through my first round of visits, after which I will rest for a while. Miss Mary Boone desired to know whether her promise to you was still binding. I told her I would absolve her, but she made very little use of the privilege to which she was thus restored—& no one else seemed much inclined to do so. My cousins the Kershaws[2] who are my most devoted & affectionate friends rec'd me very cordially. I had the pleasure of telling them of my engagement, of which they had not heard a suspicion.

On Sunday evening as I came up from my mission I joined Miss Sarah at church & walked home with her. It was the first time I had seen her by herself & we had a delightful talk & all about you. All your friends shall be my friends, if any exertions on my part can make them so.

I am getting a sermon on the stocks & hope to finish it in a week or so; you see I can only devote a small part of each day to it. I want to overcome my procrastination. We are reading on Church History & studying an analysis of the books of the O.T., nothing else until the professors come. I have quite a hopeful squad of seminary recruits preparing for coast service in case we are required.

My health is excellent. I take regular exercise & am careful of it otherwise. It is a blessing which I try to appreciate & be grateful for, & in which, more than any other, I realize the agency of that good Providence which numbers the hairs of my head & without which "not a sparrow falleth to the ground." May He make us both strong, both in soul & body, for His precious service!

There now, that will do for news-details, a thing I never succeeded well in. As I have broken my rules already, I will bid you good night. May He who is nearer to you than I can ever be, dearest, & who never slumbers nor sleeps, bless and keep you this night & for evermore.

15th 10 A.M. I will give you an hour of my studying time this morning. I feel particularly fresh & buoyant & the morning is bright & bracing, irresistibly suggestive of a brisk walk up to Dunn's Rock, not by myself though, but with one who is fast becoming a part of myself. My mockingbird has been singing fitfully & irregularly this morning, poor fellow, he is cold—never mind I don't require any aids in my present mood; I am with you without the assistance of his wings. He must have been peeping over my shoulder, for he has just begun again quite vigorously this time.

I have just been reading Colossians II, the whole epistle is beautiful. It is sweet to me, dearest, to believe that you love me, to hear you say that my presence or my letters make you happy. But it is sweeter to me to think of you looking beyond me, up to Christ your master & mine, and rejoicing in Him. "I choose her who first has first chosen Christ" says Bp . . . Beverly I believe. I think I can say so; I pray God to make us both His, really & entirely, lent to each other here "for this world's work" & for our mutual comfort, but not resting in each other; rather resting together in Him. I will remember you particularly on Sundays, & use that prayer with you from Ephesians. I love to think that there is no limit to the "closeness" to our Savior which we may attain, if we only make proper use of God's grace. The holiest saint that ever lived was not so holy but that he might have been a hundred times more so. Let us have a high standard, even Christ himself, & when we are nearest to Him, let us always remember to pray to Him to bring us a thousand times nearer.

You see I write very freely & unreservedly to you. Excuse me when I am too much so, but I feel that in writing to you, I am but communing with my own heart. I will enclose you a scrap which you must keep & read occasionally.

Give much love to Miss Sue & tell her I am very much gratified that she should have missed me so much. Beg her for my sake not to be too lavish of her colloquial energy, otherwise when I go down rested & fresh, all the talking will devolve on me. Tell her I am looking out for my letter. My other sisters never wait for me to write first, and she must not be behind them. Tell your Mother I do not feel disposed yet to give you back, & what is more I don't see any prospect of ever becoming so. So she had better give up all hope at once & learn to look upon me as a son for life. Tell her I wore a pair of yellow kid gloves on the cars coming up, but forgot again to wear any in church on Sunday—however I do not give up all hope of one day becoming respectable. And lastly, & more respectfully, give her my warmest love & tell her I hope you will find it as easy & natural to love a second mother as I will.

I am sorry Miss Susan Lovell annoyed you, as it was natural that her letter should have done—& more sorry because I am partly to blame for it. I am afraid Miss Susan drew me a little beyond the line of prudence, if out of propriety. However we forget little annoyances too & press forward, more careful next time. Couldn't you settle her by giving your consent to the Orangeburg scheme on the condition—pleasantly but firmly—that no allusion is made to you in the letter of application to the Bp. which I hope she will never write. She has a good heart & is really interested in you, which makes me feel amiably toward her.

Give my love to Miss Nannie [C.].[3] I am not afraid of you giving me too many friends if they are all like those I know. Tell Miss Lowndes that [look] on the stair-case was a very unsatisfactory one. I am anxious for a better one. I commission you to give any other messages you please, or to withhold any that I have given, if you prefer it. One person I will always remember, and that is Miss Winthrop.

The likeness will be heartily welcomed & appreciated when it comes. I hope it will be good—mind you are to keep the old one for me too.

That little sketch of the visit to the Johnsons' was particularly pleasant to me. They are our good friends.

My mockingbird is silent. Cold looking clouds are covering the bright skies. I must turn from you now to other thoughts & duties. But if my eye cannot always be turned towards you, there is one that can & will be. He will keep & bless us.

Goodbye.

Yrs truly & affectionately,

W. P. DuBose

1. The envelope is addressed to Miss Nannie B. Peronneau, care of Capt. Ed. Parker, Charleston, South Carolina. This is Edward Lightwood Parker (1828–92), the son of William McKenzie Parker and Anna (or Anne) Smith Coffin. He was a captain in the Marion Light Artillery. After William M. Parker's death, Anna S. Coffin married Edward Charles Peronneau, Nannie's uncle. The maiden name of Nannie's mother is also Coffin (Mary Sarah Coffin). See Parker, *Genealogy of the Parker Family,* 49.

2. William Porcher DuBose was related to Gen. Joseph Brevard Kershaw (1822–94) of Camden, whose mother was Harriet DuBose (1791–1845), daughter of Isaac DuBose (1754–1816). See MacDowell, *DuBose Genealogy,* 323.

3. Nannie was the daughter of Henry William Peronneau (d. 1859) and Mary S. Coffin (d. 1864). The other children of Henry W. and Mary Peronneau were Mary Coffin Peronneau (1821–95), who married Dr. Henry William DeSaussure (1815–87); William Henry Peronneau (d. 1874), who married Martha Washington (d. 1876); and Susan Hayne Peronneau (d. 1910). See Patey, *Whaley Family,* 197–98, 212.

Camden, S.C.

Oct. 23rd 1861

I wish it were always possible, my dearest Miss Nannie, to devote only my freshest & most elevated moments to communing with you; on the contrary I am compelled to give you my flattest & dullest. For example, if it were possible, for it to be anything but a pleasure to write to you, it would be so tonight. I am tired, without the satisfaction (sweet & rare) of being "able to look back upon a day every moment of which has been profitably spent." However it is only a natural & healthy weariness, & it is quite refreshing to forget myself in thinking of you. Oh, that I were by your side—in an easy chair! I feel like saying nothing tonight, except repeating in all possible forms how much I long to see you. When the mind lacks most the power to think, the heart is often freest [*sic*] to feel, and that is just my condition now.

Mr. Hanckel[1] arrived Friday, or Thursday night I believe, & could not even wait for Monday, but made us recite on Saturday. We are regularly under

way with him now, studying "Wager on the Atonement." All the Hanckels
are looking remarkably well. Tell your sister Martha I rec'd very submissive-
ly the scold she sent me. Mrs. Trapier was quite sick some days ago, so much
so that Mr. T. came over from Columbia on Saturday but returned on
Monday. Edith has also had some fever again. I would have enjoyed several
days in Ca. very much, but thought it best not to go.

I am very anxious to hear further particulars of the Virginia project. How
I would enjoy going with you, if you go. Not only the delight of being with
you, but the pleasure of being engaged with you in such a work! The
University of Va. is classic ground to me, if I ever have an opportunity of
writing to you there, I will describe localities endeared to me by the pleasantest associations—from the "Blue Cottage"[2] (which was neither blue, nor
a cottage), my home for three years—to a rock on the side of Lewis Mt (you
are a good walker) where I went on the 11th April 1857 to reflect on the
responsibilities of "manhood." It is a place I never came to visit again, except
to see some friends whom I have there still. Things change so at an institution like that, & I could not bear to be a stranger where I was once so much
at home. I am not sure that the Univ. is in operation this session.

We have only heard tonight of our victory under Evans near Leesburg[3]—
it might be the precursor of operations on a larger scale, which we have been
expecting for some time.

My brother Robert arrived at home some time ago, looking much better than they expected, & much improved in many respects by his campaign,
but really far from well. I hope home treatment will restore him. You may
imagine how anxious my two sisters must feel at the prospect of an early battle on the Potomac.

But I find even you cannot prevent my feeling stupid & sleepy, so good
night.

24th This is the first regular Fall day we have had, quite a relief after the
gloominess of the past few days. I hope you are feeling as well & are enjoying it as much as I am. I think one way of worshipping God is to feel and
enjoy Him in Nature. We ought to cultivate in ourselves a delicate susceptibility to all the sources of pleasure which He has bountifully spread around
us, just as we seek to cultivate in our souls a tender sensitiveness to all sweet
& holy spiritual influences. There is nothing that so awakens in me the "religious faculty" as music, next to that scenery, particularly among the mts, with
waterfalls for music. There is danger in indulging too much in this poetical

sort of religion—it is apt to make piety more reflective than practical, more dreamy than real; but I don't think it should be altogether discarded because it may be abused. The deep solemn notes of an organ, being alone during a thunder storm, or on a mountain without a sign of life around me, & nothing but vastness on every side—these things used to, more than they do now, fill me with the most indescribable emotions. It was very delightful to me, but it made me reserved. Since I have been actually engaged in preparing myself for the ministry, I have endeavored by God's grace to become more practical, to deal more with the awful <u>realities</u> with which we have to do— sin & suffering, salvation, & c. But still sometimes, particularly on a bright, bracing autumn day like this, the old feelings creep over me. I forget for a time what a poor wretched world this is that my imagination is dressing up in such beautiful colours. I see only the <u>beauty</u> of God's creation & think only of his <u>love</u>. And then His numerous blessings rise up before me. My whole frame thrills with a sensation of health, while through every sense come pouring in the rich "treasures of delight"[4] which He bestows through these channels upon my thankless heart.

And among them all, <u>you</u> come & sit by my side & in your presence, I can think of nothing but truth, & beauty & goodness & love. A Father that loves & blesses us both in His dear Son—a spirit of holiness that draws us nearer to each other in drawing us nearer to our Savior, a providence watching over us, infinite power & wisdom pledged to make "all things work together for our good"—"a new Heaven & a new Earth wherein dwelleth righteousness."[5] Is it wrong to indulge in such reveries—to forget for a while that there is such a thing as sin & sorrow, & imagine this world a Paradise & ourselves sinless & happy? Does not God Himself in viewing His redeemed children, regard them as sinless? Is it not a legitimate source of enjoyment sometimes to look away from ourselves as we are in ourselves & to think of ourselves as we are in Christ Jesus? "<u>Rejoice</u> evermore."[6] I do not think we rejoice as much as we are directed by St. Paul to do.

Do not think that I ever write with a view to <u>instruction</u>. I believe that your <u>experience of guilt & grace</u> (the truest "gauge" of the Christian life) is deeper than any <u>I</u> have ever undergone, although of course you will not agree with me. I write because it is in my heart to write, & because I believe that what comes from that source will interest you.

My mockingbird (I have given it out publicly among the students that he is exclusively mine, without telling them <u>why</u>, of course; they can't understand the words of his song as I do) <u>my</u> mockingbird, then—if he were to

15

look over my shoulder again—might be slighted at not seeing himself mentioned. So as he will soon probably be silenced by the cold weather, & as you seem to take some interest in him, I will gratify him by one more notice. I have discovered that he is a preacher in his way—a missionary to the blacks, he seems to be. Last Sunday morning he collected together on a large dead tree just in a line from my window, where he usually sits, a large congregation of blackbirds. Then seating himself on one of the highest branches, he perfectly electrified them with his eloquence. He knows how to manage them too. In the midst of one of his loftiest strains, he suddenly paused, pounced down upon a fellow who must have been misbehaving, expelled him from the church, & then very quietly resumed his pulpit & took up his discourse where he had left off.

Much love to your Mother & Miss Sue & all others to whom I should send it.

I do not write half as often to you, you may depend upon it, as I would like to do, but time I find makes no more allowances for my letters to you than for any others. I will not attempt to express the pleasure your letters give me. So write as often as you can conveniently or without interfering with any other duty.

Johnson is hurrying me to go & pay a visit, quite reversing matters you see.

Good bye—

Yrs very affectionately

W. P. DuBose

1. The Reverend James Stuart Hanckel (1817–92) was a professor at the seminary. See Thomas, *Protestant Episcopal Church,* 688; Barnwell, *Story of an American Family,* 135.

2. This house was located on Carr's Hill, the present-day site of the University of Virginia's president's house. See Bruce, *History of the University of Virginia,* 3:271, 315.

3. The battle of Leesburg, or Ball's Bluff, in Virginia, was fought on October 21, 1861. It was a victory for the Confederates under the command of Col. Nathan G. "Shanks" Evans, who afterward was promoted to brigadier general. See Long, *Civil War Almanac,* 129–30.

4. This is possibly a phrase from *The Christian Year* (1827) by John Keble (1792–1866), an English churchman and poet.

5. 2 Peter 3:13.

6. 1 Thessalonians 5:16.

∞

Camden S.C.
Nov. 4th 1861

Your letter, my dearest Miss Nannie, besides coming in that part of the week when I believe, on the whole, they are most acceptable, gave me still more pleasure from the fact of its having come earlier than I had expected. You need never be afraid of writing too often or too much for me, nor of my growing "tired" either of you or of your letters. I w'd [sic] not even use the word without quotation marks. I succeeded in finishing my week's work (rather more to my satisfaction than I had expected) in full time to have devoted a large portion of Saturday to you, as I was anxious to do. But I was prevented from doing so by a summons to military duty & an invitation to dinner. A few days ago the Capt of the Camden Beat (in the absence of a better name) called upon me & requested me to act as his orderly sergeant & assist him in drilling his company; I accepted the honour & "turned out" in that capacity on Saturday.

The invitation was to dine at Mr. Jno. DeSaussure's with Mr. & Mrs. Henry Des.[1] who have been on a visit to Camden on their way home from N.C., & also Miss Fanny, who seized a good opportunity at table to give me a private congratulation & assure me that she considered me a very fortunate man, a sentiment in which I expressed a hearty concurrence. Mr. Trapier insists on calling me nothing but the "Lucky Man." So you see I am constantly being fortified in an opinion at which I had arrived myself, without the aid of external assurances.

Of course we are all anxiously expecting to hear something of the fleet; which in all probability we will do by the time this reaches you. Still I surprise myself by my coolness on the subject, so much so that I sometimes reproach myself for feeling too little interest & excitement. It has not interfered at all with my interest in my studies. I was very anxious to spend this session quietly, & to be able to approach in a proper frame of mind the important subjects that belong to it. With this strong desire I have smothered & resisted my natural ardour & anxiety to mingle in the exciting scenes that are going on around us. I have strong views on the subject of a minister's, or even one in my situation, entering military service, stronger than I would like to express to one who might misunderstand my position. Besides the necessity which it involves of neglecting the service of God for one which however important & urgent, cannot possibly be more so than the work of the ministry, I go so far as to believe that one who has devoted his life to God can no longer call it his own, & therefore has no right to give it away, or even to endanger it in any other cause whatever, even though it be so sacred a one

17

as that of Country. Of course the emergency may become such as to break down all such scruples, & render it necessary, and therefore right, for even these to take up arms; & in that case I do not think I w'd be behind others in offering myself—but I trust that it will be a <u>real necessity</u> only that tempts me from my steadfast pursuit of God's service in the ministry to which He has called me.

This view of my duty renders me more settled & satisfied than I was at the beginning of our troubles, & enables me to make as good use as I can of my advantages here. Do you think that my views are right?

I am glad you heard some good sermons of the [C] from the members of the Convention. You do not seem to have been as much struck with Mr. Peterkin[2] as with the others & yet he stands very high in Va. He is spoken of as likely to be the next asst. Bp. of that state, & is a man of lovely character. Neither of the three that you heard belong to the very first class of our preachers.

Bp Davis gives us <u>two</u>, not three, lectures a week, & I do enjoy them wonderfully. I am not studying too hard, & am particular about my regular exercise. Oh, that we could have peace, & could go quietly and uninterruptedly about our regular occupations & duties! I feel ashamed to be so comfortably & happily situated when others are enduring & suffering so much.

I read my sermon this morning before the seminary. Mr. Hanckel seemed to like it better than I was afraid it deserved. I think I shall have to leave you in ignorance of "what sort of sermon I write" until you hear me from the pulpit. Mr. Hanckel does not often write his criticisms upon the sermons, but he has done so with some of mine. I will give you one extract from the remarks on one of them, which I value as much as any other, because I believe that in the main it is his opinion of my sermons generally; "—thoroughly scriptural (or to use a cant phrase, Gospel) sermon." Are you willing to wait that long for any further satisfaction on the subject? If I can write one sermon every month it will be enough. I see you are disposed to spur my procrastination occasionally, so I will rely on you to keep me up to this mark. Two more before I see you again; I think that probably will be the best point of view to regard it from. It will hasten me if anything can.

Mother is pretty much as usual, a little better I hope, if anything. Sister Betsey is improving though not well yet. Robert is much better. I do wish some of them could go to St. Johns[3] this winter & pass through Chstn while I am there, but I am sure they cannot. Did Miss Malvina have an opportunity to talk with you?

We have another student engaged. Robt. Wilson[4] to Miss Nanna Shand. I have just rec'd a sweet letter from Miss Catherine. She says she has tried to procure a flag for our squad, but failed.

I have been visiting a good deal among the poor, and do meet with some encouragement but not a great deal. I am glad to hear your school is progressing. Give my love to your household, including your sister Mattie, in spite of her message. I feel confident that I shall write to Miss Sue before the end of this week to shame her for having neglected me so long. I don't like encourage disobedience to parents, but I hope you will not regard your Mother's sentiments on the subject of writing. Give her my love & tell her she must not treat me so badly. Remember me to your Aunt Eliza[5] & all who remember me. I thought of you yesterday during the Communion service.

Yrs affectionately
W. P. DuBose

1. Dr. Henry William DeSaussure (1815–87) married Nannie's older sister Mary Coffin Peronneau (1821–95) in 1840. Dr. DeSaussure had a brother named John Boone DeSaussure. See Patey, *Whaley Family*, 197.

2. This is probably the Reverend Joshua Peterkin of Virginia. See *Appleton's Cyclopaedia*, 4:740.

3. St. John's Berkeley Parish is in the South Carolina lowcountry.

4. This is the Reverend Robert Wilson (1838–1924), who served as a surgeon in the Confederate army. His wife Nanna (Ann Jane) was the daughter of the Reverend Peter J. Shand. See Snowden, *History of South Carolina,* 5:75; Quinn, *Descendants of Robert Gibbes,* 1:127.

5. Elizabeth Peronneau Coffin Ravenel (1807–69) was the wife of Henry Ravenel (1795–1859). See *South Carolina Genealogies,* 2:73.

Charleston Nov 10th 1861

Tho' it is Sunday evening My Dearest Friend, I must write you a few lines to meet you tomorrow in case you are still in Camden. I know you will need sympathy and encouragement of all your fellow students have left you behind [*sic*].

As to your natural inclination to come and fight for the safety of Carolina I cannot imagine that any one who knows you will doubt. It is the first impulse of every one and I do indeed wish I were a man to do my part. But you have dedicated yourself soul and body to the service of God in another way, and no one has the smallest right to interfere with your private judgment of which is the right moment to yield to the pressure from without. I for my part feel the most undoubting confidence in your patriotism courage and unselfishness, and your friends are not likely to think less of you than I do. Prospects are very dark [still]. Beaufort is believed to be in ashes tho' it is uncertain who set fire. Ripley had ordered it burned, but some say the fleet sent hot shell into it before our men had time to obey Ripley.[1]

We have been relieved by hearing that not a man in Bay Point Fort was hurt.[2] It was there that our friends were. Oh how we must pray for God's help now. We must think of Sumter when faith fails and of the innumerable ways in which God's hand has been visible to us heretofore.

Personally I am not frightened, but I dread the idea of being sent off from Charleston (tho at present we know of no such plan) and then your passing thro without our being able to see each other. Some persons are talking of moving, but we shall not go unless the necessity is very apparent. My two nephews Harry & Alexander[3] are away on service at Simon's Bluff I believe. The cadets are joyous. And now Good bye dearest.

May our Father open a way for us thro' the dangers that threaten to overwhelm us. Sue sends love and

I remain

Yrs most affectionately

N. B. P.

1. Union forces captured Port Royal Sound, the surrounding sea islands, and Beaufort following the battle of Port Royal Sound on November 7, 1861. Their victory provided the Union with army and naval bases to conduct operations against the southern Atlantic coast of the Confederacy. Beaufort did not burn during or after the battle. Brig. Gen. Roswell Sabine Ripley (1823–87) was in command of the Department of South Carolina and its coastal defenses at the time of the battle. Ripley was a native of Ohio but married into the Middleton family of Charleston. See Rowland, Moore, and Rogers, Jr., *The History of Beaufort County, South Carolina,* 257.

2. The official name of the fort located at Bay Point was Fort Beauregard, which was named after Confederate general Pierre Gustave Toutant Beauregard (1818–93). It was one of two fortifications (the other being Fort Walker) guarding the mouth of Port Royal Sound. Confederate forces evacuated both forts following Union bombardment during the battle of Port Royal Sound. See Rowland et al., *History of Beaufort County,* 444–45, 452–54.

3. Henry William (1842–97) and Alexander Baron DeSaussure (1845–1905) were sons of Dr. Henry W. DeSaussure and Mary C. Peronneau. Both Harry and Alexander were cadets at the Citadel in 1861 and evidently were "joyous" to be in

active military service with the Confederacy. See DeSaussure, *Lowcountry Carolina Genealogies,* 28; Gary R. Baker, *Cadets in Gray: The Story of the Cadets of the South Carolina Military Academy and the Cadet Rangers in the Civil War* (Columbia, S.C.: Palmetto Bookworks, 1989), 204–5.

Camden S.C.
Nov. 11th 1861

As Johnson is going down to Chstn tomorrow my dearest Miss Nannie, I will send a note by him, to give you some further notice of my plans for the future as far as I can see.

I hear of a good many families that are going to leave the city, and am anxious to hear whether you think it secure enough to remain. I am so imperfectly apprised of the condition of things there & on the coast by the newspapers, that of course I do not feel competent to advise.

Johnson is only going down to see his sisters & look around. We are in such ignorance here that it is impossible to decide upon any thing from this stand point.

Gadsden[1] also goes down tomorrow, & several others will leave, at least temporarily. If I were as most of the other students here, I w'd remain quietly in the Seminary on the grounds that many more men will be sure to offer their service than can possibly be armed, & therefore of any use. But the case is different with me. If any new regiments or companies are organized, drill masters will be needed, particularly now that the cadets are in active service. In that case I shall feel called upon to offer my services. If I can find employment of that kind here, I w'd prefer remaining. Next to that I should choose Chston, but if I enter regularly into the service w'd of course go where I am sent. I am depending upon the acc't Johnson will write me of the state of things below.

The temptation has been strong to persuade myself that I ought [to] go at once to Ch'ston. I do want so much to see & talk to you about these matters. But I wish to do all I can to keep up the seminary until this first spasm of excitement passes over, & we are cool enough to see whether it is really necessary to break it up.

Your last letter came right in the midst of my greatest doubt & despondency, & it cheered & soothed me more than any other <u>human</u> influence at least could have done. I am not inclined to be despondent, I think, but inaction & reflection tempt us to look sometimes on the dark side of things. It is not only the cause of our country that I regard, but the cause of religion & the Church. However I am more trustful now; all this tries our faith & shows us our weakness.

I see, since I commenced, that Johnson has a letter to you from Miss Sarah, possibly inviting you up. I wish you could come, whether I am here or not. However hard it may be, I hope to decide upon my course independently of my mere personal ends—but I must confess that I w'd like duty to call me near to you. With love to the household.

I remain

Yrs most affectionately

W. P. DuBose

1. This probably refers to Thomas Fisher Gadsden (1839–91), who became rector of Grace Church in Anderson, South Carolina. He was the son of Bishop Christopher Edwards Gadsden (1785–1852). See Gadsden, *Gadsden Family Portraits,* 18; Thomas, *Protestant Episcopal Church,* 497; *WPA Cemetery Index.*

Holcombe Legion
Dec 17th 1861

I am afraid you are beginning to think my dearest Miss Nannie, that I never think of you in camp at all. On the contrary I am missing you more and more every day. Those sweet weeks in Charleston have spoiled me, and I begin now in reality to long for the time to come when the anxieties & distresses of war all over, we shall no more be separated in this world. As I can see so little of you, I am growing anxious now for a letter; do write as often as you can, & trust me for [wishing] to write much oftener than I do. From seven in the morning until eight at night & often much later I haven't a moment to spare & at night it is so cold in our tent without fire that our ideas as well as our fingers are stiff. I imagine that if it was warmer & I had a little more time I w'd take pleasure in giving you as graphic a picture as I could of our Camp life. As it is I know you will make allowances for the difficulties of my situation. I continue to work hard & to thrive [in it]. I have . . . [control] of the drill & have been yesterday & today [forming] an awkward squad, the performances of which, I feel confident, do credit to my judgment & discrimination.[1] It is amusing to see how independent they are of one another, & how firmly each one believes that he c'd keep step perfectly well if the others did not put him out. We continue to receive applications from companies & there will be no lack of men if we can get arms.

On Sunday night I reached the place of appointment a minute before & the Col. a few minutes after the time. We rode Camp, then visited the pickets & then went the Grand rounds & did not get to bed before 1 o.c.

Your sister Martha's present did me good service & . . . Thank her for it again. I find it [harder] than I expected to be regular in my religious duties & to keep up the spirit of devotion in Camp. It is so different from my former life & my time is so broken up. So much the greater necessity for you to remember me in your prayers. I am more than ever struck with the religious character of my Uncle;[2] it is felt wherever he is, & the more, I believe from the fact of his being a layman.

Give my love to Miss Sue & to your Mother & sister Martha & [kiss] the children for me. I used the papers you sent me & recd them with more pleasure because they came from you.

Mr. McCollough[3] [looks] as comfortable . . . as well as any. . . . I have not heard lately [from] home.

Good night & believe that you are always in my thoughts & my prayers.

Yrs affectionately
W. P. DuBose

If your Brother still has that sword [to spare] I think I will take it. The one I have does not suit me exactly. But if he has made or wishes to make any other disposition of it, I can do perfectly well without it.

1. An "awkward squad" denotes a military squad that comprises recruits or those undergoing training.

2. Octavius Theodore Porcher (1829–73) was the brother of William Porcher DuBose's mother. See MacDowell, *DuBose Genealogy*, 352.

3. John DeWitt McCollough (1822–1902) was chaplain of the Holcombe Legion. His son John Lane also served in the unit. See Thomas, *Protestant Episcopal Church*, 56; *WPA Cemetery Index;* Compiled Service Records, Holcombe Legion, M267, roll 377.

Charleston Dec 18th 1861[1]

Your letter was a delightful surprise to me Dear Mr. DuBose, arriving as it did when I was sewing busily, and amusing myself thinking how pleasant a visit from you would be!

Of course I knew you could not come, but the fancy was so harmless that I indulged it, and I think it made me enjoy my letter all the more. It was very good of you to sit up for so long in the cold. I hope you slept soundly enough afterwards to forget all discomfort.

Do not imagine that I am writing so soon, in order to encourage late hours, even in so good a cause. The reason why I cannot sleep just yet is that I am thinking of the possibility of your Legion being ordered to meet the enemy on John's Id,[2] and of course I long either to talk or write to you. I am trying to yield you Dearest, entirely to the will of our Heavenly Father, and I am sure He will give to both of us strength equal to our need.

His will has been very mercifully manifested to us of late; I trust that in view of this far more painful trial I may be ready to bear up with strong courage.

I suppose Mr. Stevens[3] was in town today in hopes of getting arms. Has he succeeded? The enemy is so near now that the crisis must come soon.

I am very glad you enjoyed the paper, tho' it was Sue who deserved your thanks for it. If you like, they can be sent to you frequently. With my note you will receive a few tracts Miss Ammy sends you. She thought you were quietly in Camden.

It must indeed be pleasant to have your Uncle with you. One of the greatest trials of a Christian soldier usually must be the want of sympathy, which his fellow soldiers have in matters of religion, and that you are spared. When you get to that pleasant parish to which we look forward, I do not think you will regret this unexpected lesson in the study of human nature. I feel that God is perhaps preparing you for great usefulness in the ministry. I suppose you have hardly time or opportunity for influencing your men in religious things, except by example.

Sue and I are very busy at present. She goes on a particular day to help Kate at the Soup House; my work is in the cutting-out department; clothing for the poor destitute creatures burnt out[4] last week.

Dec. 19th. There is only time for me to add a few lines today. Brother arrived last night and says he will be able to lend you the sword. One thing I must tell you that I fear will sadden you much. Miss Emma Means[5] is no longer a mover among these troubles and excitements. For her the change only for good; you have always described her as so pure and spiritual; but you will miss your sweet friend I fear. Your sister too must be sorrowful. The Miss Johnsons commenced to get to rights yesterday and two of them dined with us. They feel sadder everyday about their loss, and Miss Charlotte is almost

24

despairing about the future. Miss Catherine goes to Pineville today. Mr. Johnson's still at work surveying and very much interested.

Our household desires to be affectionately remembered to you. Sue says she tried to get some pine straw sent to you, but her effort failed. Miss Mary McCord[6] is going to spend some time at Mrs. Parker's place in St. Andrew's about five miles from you. Please remember me to your Uncle if you think best and

Believe me

Yrs most affectly

N. B. Peronneau

1. The envelope is addressed to Adjutant W. P. DuBose, Holcombe Legion, St. Andrew's.

2. Johns Island is a sea island located southwest of Charleston.

3. This refers to Maj. (later Col.) Peter Fayssoux Stevens. See Compiled Service Records, Holcombe Legion, M267, rolls 372, 379.

4. The great Charleston fire, the most devastating in the city's history, occurred on December 11–12, 1861, and consumed over 540 acres and 600 private homes. See Marie Ferrara, "Moses Henry Nathan and the Great Charleston Fire of 1861," 258–80; Long, *Civil War Almanac,* 148.

5. Emma Sarah Means, the daughter of Gen. John Hugh Means and Susan Rebecca Stark, died at the age of eighteen. See *South Carolina Genealogies,* 3:114. Her death date is given erroneously as December 10, 1860.

6. This is probably the stepdaughter of Louisa Susannah Cheves McCord (1810–79), widow of David James McCord (1797–1855), whose first wife was Emmeline Wagner. Mary McCord (1825–1903) later married Andrew Gordon Magrath (1813–93), a war-time governor of South Carolina. See *South Carolina Genealogies,* 3:83.

Brother has brought me the sword for you Dear Mr. DuBose, and I want to know whether I shall send it to you by Mr. Sage's[1] wagon, or keep it until you are prepared to take it. He says you are quite welcome to it as long as the war lasts if it can be of any use. It is not his property but has been lent to him indefinitely, otherwise he would gladly give it to you.

Hoping to see you tomorrow.

I remain

Yrs most affectionately

N. B. Peronneau[2]

1. William M. Sage was the assistant quartermaster in the Holcombe Legion. See Hewett, *South Carolina Confederate Soldiers,* 425; Compiled Service Records, Holcombe Legion, M267, roll 378.

2. This undated note is addressed to Adjutant W. P. DuBose, Holcombe Legion, St. Andrew's. See Hewett, *South Carolina Confederate Soldiers*, 425; Compiled Service Records, Holcombe Legion, M267, roll 374.

Christmas day

Dear Brother William,

I have only time to relieve your anxiety about our Va. Friends. Doubtless you saw Bev's & Mr. Edwards names among the wounded in the skirmish near Centerville.[1] Fortunately a telegram was received from them before we saw the battle had taken place. Both received slight flesh wounds. I do not know where, & the last telegram received yesterday reported them as doing well. Both were to have left yesterday for home, & I suppose will be here tomorrow, & in this case, sorrow will be turned into joy. You can imagine what anxious days Sunday & Monday have been, expecting another battle had been fought & dreading the [results]. It seems strange that one can . . . up through such terrible anxiety & trouble, & yet how wonderful has been God's mercy to us. Dr. Bratton & our other friends are well, having escaped unhurt. You saw Frank English's[2] death, a terrible blow to his poor Mother & feeble blind Father, who for years has been dependent upon this son.

I cannot help asking myself if this can be Christmas. It brings me such very sad thoughts. I long for it to pass away. My thoughts will revert to all I had during the last, to make me happy, & dwell upon what is lost forever [here]. Everywhere I go, reminds me that Emma was here, & everything I do recalls the loving hands that were ready to help in all things. Her loving words & ways only fill my heart & oh the missing dreary [loving] for her is so hard to bear.

Bettie returned yesterday from Yorkville, & she is looking & feeling very much better. It is a pity she could not have remained longer. Willie[3] was sick several times while she was away & is [looking] pale, but seems to feel pretty well. Johnny has grown a good deal & promises to be quite [merry]. Mother continues wonderfully comfortable. I cannot remember her as well at this season, but she will not admit this.

I am afraid there is no hope of your getting silk [handled] here, in fact, nothing is to be had. Father gave away his sash some years ago. There are stockings & several other comfortable [men's] articles to be sent to you. How & when shall they be sent? Do you wish a [compress] or any other article in that line?

Mrs. George Bryan[4] & H. Thomas have been with us since Saturday. . . . is here also. She returned home with Janie. . . . are to have services & it is time for me to get ready. Much love from all to Octavius & kind regards to Mr. McC.

Why did you not tell us what had become of the Johnsons, & if they saved much? You know how interested we are.

The children are all happiness over their little collection of gifts. What do you think [Jim] Stark was telegraphed for the very day after he reached Columbia, to go to his child in Va. which was extremely ill. I do not know which child. Love from all, & many warm wishes for the coming year.

Your affect. Sister

Annie

1. Beverly William Means (1833–62) was the husband of William Porcher DuBose's sister Jane. The couple married around 1859. Mr. Edwards was possibly William L. Edwards (1831–95?). Means served in Company C, Sixth South Carolina Infantry, and Edwards served in Company B of the same regiment. Means was wounded severely in the thigh at an engagement near Dranesville, Virginia, on December 20, 1861. There is no record in the Compiled Service Records of Edwards's wounding at Dranesville. See MacDowell, *DuBose Genealogy,* 13; Compiled Service Records, Sixth South Carolina Infantry, M267, rolls 206, 209; *WPA Cemetery Index.*

2. Franklin English of Charleston was born in 1844. He was a private in Company C, Sixth South Carolina Infantry, and was killed on December 20, 1861, at the battle of Dranesville. See *WPA Cemetery Index;* Compiled Service Records, Sixth South Carolina Infantry, M267, roll 206.

3. William DuBose Bratton (b. 1860) was the son of Dr. John Bratton and Elizabeth Porcher DuBose. See MacDowell, *DuBose Genealogy,* 232.

4. This possibly refers to Rebecca L. Dwight Bryan, wife of George S. Bryan (1809–95), a prominent Charleston attorney. See *Cyclopedia of Eminent Men of the Carolinas,* 5.

Dec 26th 1861

We rec'd orders this evening, My dearest Miss Nannie, to move in an hour & a half. Of course we have been busy preparing for it, but the time has passed & here we are still, packed, belted & waiting. Of course my thoughts turn towards you, but paper, ink & every convenience for writing, except a stump of pencil & this rumpled half-sheet, are beyond reach. We are going immediately to Adam's Run[1] by R.R. Where next, or what next, it is impossible to say. I have been too busy even to find out the exact nature of the news that renders our advance necessary. It may be that I may see the enemy before I have another opportunity of writing to you. I do not look forward, but hope that I may be prepared to meet whatever each day may bring forth.

I only regret that I cannot see you, Dearest, before I go. I know it will be a disappointment to you too, but you are brave & strong & know where to find comfort in this & any other trial that we may be called upon to bear.

You may be assured that, whether I shall be able to write or not you will be in my mind at all times & under all circumstances. Your letters are a great comfort & strength to me. Write whenever you can & direct to Adam's Run "until further orders."

I rec'd a delightful letter today from Mr. Trapier. When you write, do acknowledge it for me; I will answer it as soon as I can. Your sash has been much admired, & will do me good service. I forgot to thank your Brother for the sword. Please do so for me.

I will write as soon as I can, but oh, if I find could only see & talk to you once more before I go! I know you will remember me in all your prayers.

Yrs most affectionately
W. P. DuBose

1. Adams Run is a village situated about thirty miles from Charleston. It is located near the village of Willtown, in present-day Charleston County. See Smith, "Willtown or New London"; *Map of the Seat of War.*

Charleston Dec. 30th 1861

The opportunity of spending a few moments in a quiet converse with you Dear Mr. DuBose must not be thrown away, so I will at least commence my letter trusting for some other propitious moment for ending it. It was hard to believe that you really had gone, until Sunday had actually passed without bringing you. I could not help looking out for you altho' I knew you could not come, and you may be certain that your usual visit was missed by more than one member of our household.

Your move must have been very sudden and hurried. I long to hear something about it; are you twice as busy as ever? bringing even the awkward squad into fitness for immediate service? I suppose you have as much to do as you can possibly crowd into the day. Are the sentinels better skilled in their duties than they were? When you last described them they were scarcely fit to guard a camp exposed to real danger. Those heavy guns on Thursday last shook our windows and alarmed us a little but I never thought that they were likely to bring your Legion to John's Id until I was told you had actually gone.[1] Have you seen anything of the enemy as yet and do you feel that you have begun to live a soldier's life in real earnest?

We are progressing just as usual; all of us quite well and very cheerful. Yesterday afternoon a whole troop of children went with me to the Orphan's chapel[2] to hear Mr. Howe preach. He succeeded in interesting even little Lise, whose comments by the way were rather amusing. She said "Mr. Howe[3] told us that Jesus when a little child was lost, and that his parents hunted for him three days, but Susy just then there was just a coughing that I don't know where they ever found him."

The Marion Artillery are still in St. Andrew's. Carrie Pinckney paid them a visit on Saturday and had a delightful time. She has invited me to go there too this week. Is it not tantalizing that just as my prospects open for a visit in that direction, you should march away out of reach. Thomas and I were building largely on Carrie's equipage, to take us to see you, when to our great disappointment, we heard of your departure. Thomas and Jane Gadsden both went to see the Marions[4] with her. The carriage is only a recent acquisition of my sweet friend's; having been given to her since the fire by old Miss Pinckney. Carrie is so very lovely that I really want to know her. When . . . is quite an unanswerable question.

Monday evening

Your precious little note, written just before your departure for Adam's Run has arrived at last. I felt sure it was some where on its way to me, tho' it has taken a long time to find me. Thank you for writing under such disadvantages. It is doubly pleasant to be remembered when I know your duties crowd so thickly upon you as almost to engross your time & thoughts. You scarcely need the assurance that my thoughts are constantly with you, and that my prayers are often and often ascending for your preservation from all evil. I try to use the heaven-taught prayer that God's will may be done; perhaps we would never have realized how completely we depend on His free grace for every blessing, if He had not called you to expose your life in this way. Shall we not strive to commence the New Year in more humble, thankful faith than we have lived before. The year that is just closing has been crowded with heavy troubles, and yet through them all, great blessings have been strewn, and you and I both feel that we have special cause for remembering 1861 with thankfulness. At least I trust you for feeling as I <u>know</u> I do on that subject, and I feel quite encouraged therefore in wishing you a Happy New Year.

All the household send much love to you. Jimmie thinks it very hard that you did not send him a kiss. He has become very fond of you. The bulletin board today says that Mason & Slidell[5] have been returned. Of course you must believe as much as you think best of that. I expect to write soon to Sarah and will remember your message to Mr. T. The Johnsons are getting on pretty well, tho Miss Charlotte's sore throat lasted longer than she expected. Oh what an ungrateful man you were to put sugar of lead in the way of three unsuspecting friends in that house. It is well Mr John is so "knowing," or mischief might have followed. They have determined to hire a house in Meeting St. nearly opposite Water for their school. The house is small, containing only five rooms, at a rent of $400. It will suit them pretty well, but is not exactly the thing. Are you and Mr. McCollough any nearer the pine trees than at your old camp, or have you a still rougher bed? Sue sends her love particularly, and I remain

Yrs affectionately

N. B. Peronneau

1. From noon to 3:00 P.M. on Thursday, December 26, 1861, residents of Charleston could hear cannon fire between the Confederate battery on Cole Island, at the mouth of the Stono River, and a blockading Union vessel. See *Charleston Mercury,* December 27, 1861, 2.

2. This was the Orphan House Chapel, which was located adjacent to the Charleston Orphan House at 160 Calhoun Street. Designed by Gabriel Manigault, a noteworthy Charleston architect, the Orphan House Chapel was demolished in the 1950s. See Poston, *Buildings of Charleston,* 26–27.

3. This was probably the Reverend William Bell White Howe (1823–94), who became the rector of St. Philip's Episcopal Church in Charleston and was later consecrated as the sixth bishop of the Diocese of South Carolina. See Thomas, *Protestant Episcopal Church,* 708–10.

4. The Marion Light Artillery began as an independent artillery organization for coastal defense in 1861 and ended the war in North Carolina in Rhett's Brigade. Edward Lightwood Parker was a captain in the Marions. See Compiled Service Records, Capt. Parker's Co., Light Artillery (Marion Artillery), M267, rolls 103–4; Kirkland, *South Carolina C.S.A. Research Aids.*

5. James M. Mason and John Slidell were Confederate commissioners en route to London and Paris when Union sailors removed them from the British mail packet *Trent* and arrested them in November 1861. The British government demanded their return, and the United States released them to avert a possible war with Great Britain. This incident is known as the Trent Affair. See Ferris, *Trent Affair.*

Holcombe Legion
Near Adam's Run
Dec 31st 1861

The last day of the year! I think if I c'd spend this evening with you, Dearest, I w'd be tempted to welcome in the New Year in that Tradd St parlour by your side. However here I am, with no possibility of seeing you for I don't know how long. We have had quite a taste of camp life since I left you, some experience both of the reality & of the humbugging of a campaign in the face of an enemy. As I know you are interested in the Legion, I will give you an acc't of its movements since you last heard of it. Well, I wrote you a note at 6 ½ o.c. on the evening of the 26th inst. informing you that we were momentarily expecting a train to remove us to Adam's Run. We remained in momentary expectation until 3 o.c. that night, when the train did come & we succeeded in getting off by 4 ½, & arrived at Adam's Run depot, three miles from the village, about 7 o.c. A.M. We sent on a courier to Gen'l Evans'[1] Head Quarters & after a hasty breakfast took up the line of march for the Village. We had hardly gone a quarter of a mile before our courier met us with orders to remain & establish our camp at the Depot. We returned, laid off the camp, pitched tents & prepared to make up for the entire loss of sleep the night before. Mr McCollough & I had just made a comfortable bed of pine straw, when another order arrived to remove to Head Quarters (the Village) "as soon as practicable." However the Col. determined that it was not practicable to move until next day, & so we went to bed. Little after four o.c. next morning (28th very cold) there was a loud call for the Adj't, who immediately reported himself: "Mr Adj't, have the drum beat, collect the command & publish orders to get breakfast, strike the tents & be ready to march by 6 o.c." The enemy had landed on Slann's Island & might march in the direction of Adam's Run. We marched to Adam's Run & found it a false alarm: pressed waggons [sic] into service & brought on our baggage & stores: laid off & cleared up a camp in the thick woods: pitched tents & made ourselves comfortable.

Next morning (Sunday) I put on the socks you sent, for the first time, & got ready for service. Just before the time, Col Stevens sent me over to Genl Evans about some local matter. I had hardly been introduced to him before he said, "Tell your Col., Sir, to form his Legion immediately [&] march towards White Pt to the support of Maj. James.[2] Halt at Mrs Seabrook Jenkins' place & be ready when Maj. James attacks the Enemy to move up to his assistance" & c. Then he asked me about the drill of our men and other such matters, & concluded by saying he thought we w'd have a pretty little fight. While he was speaking, another courier rode up from Maj. James at White Pt. The enemy were passing him on both sides in steamers, shelling as they went. In a very few minutes we were on the march. I was green enough in the service to believe that we really were on the eve of a skirmish: I thought of you of course, & prepared myself for it. When we had marched about three miles, we heard that the enemy had retired, so we halted, took lunch, selected a camp ground, then marched back to Adam's Run & packed up for another move. I laid out the new camp before the companies arrived, then directed the pitching of the tents, which took a long time, as it was in a dense thicket which had to be cleared, then it was long after dark. I had the Col's tent pitched temporarily (until we could clear up the right place) for the staff, & then I lay down on two stumps & several rocks & slept soundly, after a pretty hard days work for Sunday.

Here we are now at Mrs Jenkins'—or near it, two miles & a half from Adams Run. Genl Evans paid us a visit this evening. He seems to expect a fight, & says that if it comes, we can't retreat under any circumstances, but must fight on until we get reinforcements. For my part I do not expect to see the enemy—they sail up, or steam up, every day or so, shelling every thicket & feeling for batteries, but I do not imagine they will land here. Our legion has now eleven companies. We are pleasantly encamped in the woods with plenty of pine straw at hand. Our Cavalry are near & will save us from a surprise.

I am anxious for a letter from you. The one I rec'd near Charleston is all that I have to go on until your next. I am very glad I was permitted to spend such a delightful Christmas day with you just before leaving. I shall live on the memory of that, & your letters together, until we meet again. The practicability of my leaving the service seems to be growing fainter & fainter. I cannot do so in the face of an enemy, with the legions so imperfectly drilled & disciplined. That puts further into the future my ordination, & another event, secondary only to that, one which I look forward to with Oh! so much happiness. My perfect confidence & trust in you make delay much easier to bear, but in spite of that it is right hard.

Give much love to all the household little & big & to my other friends when you see them, particularly the Johnsons & the Gadsdens & to them who are interested in me for your sake.

Some time ago Miss Sue gave me some money to pay the freight of that package of clothing. I wrote to find out what it was, [but] as usual, I suppose each thought someone else had answered my questions, & so I never did find out. But the more I think about [it] the more certain I am that I remember that it was $1.50. Tell her I will owe her $3.50 until I have an opportunity of paying it.

I forgot to say that when I expected a battle, I put on my sash too for the first time.

And now I must close. Don't forget that passage from Eph. III, [I think].

Good night. God bless you & keep you & reunite us in His own good time!

Yrs affectionately
W. P. DuBose

I send Mr. Trapier's letter. Keep it for me.

My Uncle begs to be remembered & says he is sorry he c'd not see more of you. My friend W. H. Cain[3] begs permission to present his regards.

1. This was Gen. Nathan George "Shanks" Evans (1824–68). See Warner, *Generals in Gray,* 83–84.

2. This was probably Maj. (later Lt. Col.) George Sholter James (1829–62) of the Third Battalion South Carolina Infantry (also known as the Laurens or James Battalion). See Compiled Service Records, Third Battalion South Carolina Infantry, M267, rolls 179–80; D. Augustus Dickert, *History of Kershaw's Brigade,* 175–76.

3. This probably refers to William Henry Cain (1834–1909). See MacDowell, *Gaillard Genealogy,* 87.

2

In Death's Shadow
1862

"I received what I at first thought a mortal wound on Sunday."
December 16, 1862

During 1862 DuBose and the Holcombe Legion experienced intense combat operations. Beginning with a raid on nearby Edisto Island, the Holcombe Legion then traveled to Virginia to participate in the battles of Second Manassas, South Mountain, and Antietam. DuBose would miss the latter, having been captured following the battle of South Mountain. He was imprisoned at Fort Delaware, was paroled, and then rejoined his unit in time to participate at the battle of Kinston. There he received his third and most serious wound of the year. Year's end found him once again convalescing at home.

Roseland 4th Jan 1862[1]

I have been meaning for some time past, My dear Miss Nannie, to write to you but what with company, school, & my own intolerable indolence, I have procrastinated day to day.

Immediately after the fire when I saw your Mother's name among the list of the sufferers, I was so concerned for you all, that I was just about to dispatch to you a letter of sympathy & condolence, when Willie's letter came, & turned our condolence into joy. I am too thankful that I was spared from witnessing the horror of that night; for I know that I never would have recovered from the effect that it would have produced upon me. As it is, when absent from those I love, I am always imagining all sorts of evils happening to them. I do not think that one ever recovers entirely from a sudden & violent shock, at least, I find it so in my case.

I do wish that I were near enough to join you in the works of charity in which you are, at present, engaged. I know that it would do one a great deal of good to be obliged to rouse myself for the good of others, & I would soon learn to take great interest in it. Yet in the present instance, I find that my sympathies are more keenly aroused for those who have lost what money cannot purchase back for them, & for those who, as a friend of mine expressed it, "cannot dig & to beg are ashamed." Perhaps, however, this is owing to the fact that so much is being done for the very poor, for I hear that those who have lost by the fire, are better off than they were before. We have had a most anxious time of it of late, hearing of the landing of the enemy, & expecting a battle at any moment, in which one or both of my Brothers may either be killed or wounded.[2] God have mercy upon us, & spare us from such a calamity! We have so many dear friends & relatives on the coast, that it is not probable that all of them will escape uninjured, tho' so far, we have been most signally blessed.

My Brother, Beverly Means, is the only one of our friends who, so far, has even been wounded; & his wound, tho' by no means the slight one that he represented it to be, is doing very well. His leg is very stiff now, & gives him much more pain than it did at first, but the Drs think it will be well in about 6 weeks. He was struck by the very first volley from the enemy, but fought during the whole battle, & marched 16 miles back to Centerville before he discovered the extent of his injury. The hole that the Minnie [sic] ball made is larger than a dollar, & had it gone an inch further, it must have severed the principal artery of the thigh. It is a black angry looking wound. Fortunately for him, his long march worked the ball out, so he was saved the cutting out which he would otherwise have had to undergo. He & James went up the day after his arrival to his Mother's, where they expect to be until next week.

Mother has been suffering considerable pain lately, I suppose from the weather. Bettie was sick again yesterday from cold, tho' she did not have a return of her chills. Sister Anne[3] is not at all well tho' it is nothing more than she often suffers. You see I have written you all about ourselves, taking it for granted that you feel the same interest in us, that we feel in you. We received a nice long letter from Willie yesterday. I expect he finds it quite tantalizing sometimes to be so near to the City, & yet not able to avail himself of his proximity, for he seems not a little to enjoy & prize those visits. I do wish that Robert was with him, for his company is to be broken up, & I am afraid he will be obliged to join the service for a year, without the privilege of choosing his company. Poor fellow. I think his heart is with his comrades in Vir. Remember us all kindly to your Mother & Sisters. All send much love to you. Do write whenever you feel disposed, for I shall always be very glad to hear from you. My hands are about frozen, for I have let my fire leave me.

Yours truly

E. M. Porcher

1. Roseland was a plantation near Winnsboro, South Carolina, owned by William Porcher DuBose's father, Theodore Samuel DuBose (1809–62). See MacDowell, *DuBose Genealogy*, 12.

2. On December 10–12, 1861, the USS *Isaac Smith* made a reconnaissance of the Ashepoo River, seizing a Confederate fort on Fenwick Island and firing at Confederate pickets near the river junction with Mosquito Creek. See *War of the Rebellion: The Official Records of the Union and Confederate Navies* (hereafter *Official Records Navy* and series 1 unless otherwise noted), 12:392.

3. This was Anne Stevens DuBose (1834–70). See MacDowell, *DuBose Genealogy*, 12.

Chston Jan 8th 1861 [1862]

Your letter & note have just arrived Dear Mr. DuBose. It is fearful to think of your being in the midst of bomb-shells, surrounded by dangers. But God has brought you safely thro' them all this time, and we will trust Him for the future. Sue is delighted with her letter and I very glad that you wrote to her. My little note is very nice too. Jimmie is elated by the kiss you send him. Mrs. Porcher has written me a nice letter wh[ich] I have answered already, as I was writing it before hers arrived. She said your Mother had not been well, neither had Mrs. Bratton nor Miss Annie been quite well. Mr. Means was improving. I wish I had time to write you a letter, but it is no use wishing. The Marions are pretty near you at Rantowles—quite out of our reach. As I must stop now, you must imagine all that I would like to write to you and

Believe me

Yrs with much love &

Many earnest prayers

N. B. P.

Holcombe Legion

Jany 23rd 1862

Your last letter, dearest Miss Nannie, was, if possible, more enjoyed than any of the predecessors, & yet it seems to me that I have taken a very long time to answer it. That last visit to which I still constantly turn for fresh supplies of enjoyment, seems like a month ago. I think you might at least have sent a few of those violets in your letter: we both seem to have arrived at the same philosophical conclusion in regard to that Monday morning disappointment.

You must never be afraid of not being agreeable enough to me. I am satisfied with being near to you, & w'd always prefer your acting in the most natural way; there is a great deal of eloquence in silence.

Tell Miss Sue I was delighted to get her letter, just as I was beginning to despair of ever receiving it. I am sure I appreciated it as it deserved. I will not wait for my next <u>battle</u> to answer it, particularly as the Col has refused me a place in the only opportunity that presents itself for one just now. He went off two mornings ago with one hundred & fifty men to "conquer" Edisto Island from the negroes & any Yankees that may be on it. Before going on the Expedition he sent three officers to reconnoitre the Island, who after traversing it in the guise of Yankees, came back & reported that there were none of the enemy on it, the negroes being in undisturbed possession. A day or two after, a party of negroes attacked a picket of six men, who killed one of them.[1] I begged the Col to let me go, but he very properly refused, as my duties certainly require my presence here. I don't think I sh'd have asked, as he evidently disliked to deny me.

The weather continues bad, but for myself I really do not mind it. I keep dry & comfortable & well. I am more sorry on my horse's acc't than on my own. My comfort has been very materially increased by the arrival of my servant,[2] who is a most excellent & faithful fellow, one to whom we are all at home very much attached. He is worth all the other servants in camp put together. He brought me a large box of real substantial things, including, besides the eatables, one item which I know will meet your approval, viz: a stout p'r of boots. In a word, I am admirably provided for both externally & internally and so, with the inexhaustible stock of sunshine within which you give me credit for, I don't think I am in danger of suffering. If the mode of life is not disagreeable to me, & my health improves on it, why of course it is all right. And if these are my sentiments tonight, they are apt to continue so, as this is about as bad a specimen of a night as we are likely to have.

As to the matter of the sermon, I promise the matter my serious consideration; I have not yet devised a plan of gratifying you. If anything sh'd happen to me, I bequeath to you all that I have written; with the exception of my last sermon which Mr Hanckel has, they are in a copy of the "Journal of the Art Union" on my Dictionary shelf in Camden. Johnson c'd find them, or Mr Trapier or anyone who knows my room.

You look to me for an "elevating, sanctifying influence"; if I can ever exert any such influence upon you of all others in the world, I shall prize the power as a most precious gift. And, in spite of our infinite deficiencies, why may we not benefit each other? Will not our daily prayers for each other, even the consciousness that each is solicitous for the other's spiritual welfare, be such an influence? We are to be mutually dependent in this more than any other respect & we should pray for each other's spiritual growth as for our own. I like to think of you as being all that I w'd like to be myself, & I see plainly that you have a very ideal conception of my character. I do not object to it, it only gives me an additional motive to become more nearly what you think me to be. I have been reading snatches of Robertson's[3] "Lectures on Corinthians" & it has stirred me a good deal, although I begin to feel the deficiencies of his views of the Gospel.

I have never read more than about a third of "Tom Brown at Oxford."[4] Johnson & I were reading it together when I left Camden. I did not get far enough into it to observe the likeness you speak of.

I have written to Johnson to bring Gadsden with him to see me. I do not think he ought to volunteer; I only expressed the opinion that camp life w'd do him no good.

You need not be afraid of the enemies' ever getting your letters; I carried them to Chston the other day & put them up with my valuables there; those that I have with me, I keep on my person all the time.

Much love to all & tell yr Sister Martha I <u>was not</u> mean; two kisses apiece for the Children that value them.

Dick Dwight,[5] with my permission, sends <u>love</u>. Mr. McCollough has returned. I gave your message to Capt Cain.[6]

Good night

Yrs affectionately
W. P. DuBose

My love to Miss Carrie.

1. From January 22 to January 25, 1862, Col. P. F. Stevens of the Holcombe Legion led a punitive military expedition to Edisto Island, which planters had abandoned after the battle of Port Royal. The expedition was intended to capture slaves who had fired on Confederate pickets on Jehossee Island on January 20. Stevens's force of 120 infantry and 65 cavalry captured 80 slaves and killed 3 who attempted to flee into the marsh. In addition, the Confederates captured a number of horses, mules, carriages, and wagons and destroyed corn that was being used by the slaves. A large number of slaves escaped to Botany Bay, where they were protected by Union gunboats. See *Official Records Army*, 6:77–82.

2. Stephen was William Porcher DuBose's body servant.

3. Frederick W. Robertson (1816–53) was an English clergyman. See Old, *Reading and Preaching,* 366–81.

4. This was a novel by Thomas Hughes (1822–96) published in 1861 as a sequel to *Tom Brown's Schooldays* (1857).

5. Richard Yeadon Dwight (1837–1919) was a physician. See MacDowell, *DuBose Genealogy,* 262.

6. William H. Cain was a commissary officer in the Holcombe Legion. See Compiled Service Records, Holcombe Legion, M276, roll 373.

Holcombe Legion
Jan'y 31st 1862

I was looking forward to a good long evening spent in writing to you, Dearest Miss Nannie, but an unexpected influx of business has deprived me of the pleasure. Whatever does not come definitely under anybody else's business (& a great deal that does) falls upon me, & the consequence is that I can rely upon no hour for my own use. However I ought not to complain, as this constant occupation is all that keeps me as contented & happy as I am. I am still reflecting on that sermon proposition of yours, but the practicability of accomplishing it seems very small on a busy day like this. I rec'd a letter from home today, giving me a much better account of Mother than Stephen brought me a week ago. I could not, as I never can, help feeling a little disappointed at not hearing from you, although I had no right to expect a letter.

We have made some changes in our domestic arrangements lately. In the first place, seven of us, the two Drs, Mr McCollough, Dick Dwight, Rutledge,[1] Mr Irwin[2] (another "first rate" fellow, the new Ass't Commissary) & myself have seceded from the Col's mess,[3] under the auspices of Stephen, & established a new one. The mess was too large & unwieldy & irregular, & though I disliked very much to leave the Col's table, I thought it best to do so. Then Mr McCollough has gone into Mr Irwin's tent—they are great friends—and I have taken Dr Porcher[4] & Dick in with me, using their tent for our baggage, stores & c. We made this arrangement to get all our mess together & it works admirably. We three have a great time; Dr Porcher says I must tell you that the only objection he has to me is an inveterate habit of pilfering—we have a standing feud over towels & lead pencils. The Dr has become a great favorite in camp, with everybody from the Col. down, or rather from the Genl down. He attended Genl Evans some time ago & they have become great cronies. The Genl has put him over the Medical Department of the whole Mil. Dist,[5] & between them they are concocting a Hospital at Adams Run of which the Dr is to have the control. My Uncle was not Com.; he came as Ass't Com. but was app'ted Aide de Camp; his place has been given to Mr Henry Stevens[6] of St. Johns who will be with us in a day or two. Mr Irwin is now Asst. Commissary, an admirable man. For harmony, sobriety, piety, & other pleasant qualities, I do not believe there is another such staff in the service. We get on better & better every day.

Feb 1st. I have not had an opportunity of continuing my letter until tonight. Meantime I have rec'd your letter & have only one fault to find with it, which is that you seem to imagine that you can write to me too often.

I expect that you have heard rather an exaggerated acc't of the Expedition to Edisto. Some things did happen that were very unpleasant, particularly to a man of such tender feelings as our Col really has. One negro, I believe, was killed; eighty were taken all together, several of whom were among those who fired upon the picket & these, I hear, Genl Evans is anxious to hang; the others I suppose will be restored to their owners. We have had a party on the Island ever since, sending over every day wagon loads of corn & c. The negroes have all congregated on Clark's Island, or Botany Bay & burnt the bridge connecting it with Edisto. There were a good many amusing incidents too connected with the Expedition but I have half forgotten them all. One of our men was accidentally shot in the foot, but has been doing well; the man who was so severely injured by the bombshell is doing tolerably well too, I hear.

The Savannah news proves to be not quite so serious as we thought at first. We are very weak here; if the Enemy should take it into their head to advance on us in force, I trust that we certainly will not owe our success to numbers. We are having a great deal of sicknesses, principally Measles, & the Drs are granting a great many furloughs. I kept perfectly well during all the bad weather—not even a cough.

I have succeeded in getting to see Elliott[7] only once, and it was as delightful a day as I have spent for a long time. Wiltown[8] is a beautiful place, & the delightful weather, the ride & the visit exhilarated me very much. I am afraid Mrs Elliott's health is very delicate; the baby is a very fine fellow, but is not very well either. Elliott took us to see Mr Manigault's place, which is quite the feature of Wiltown.

Stephen continues to be a treasure to us, and the boots, I admit, are a great improvement on shoes. As for a fire in my tent, I w'd not have it if I c'd; I am quite comfortable as I am. I have at last got a desk, which you certainly would not infer from the appearance of this letter. I have got a clock, too, & keep accurate time, not only for myself but for the whole Camp. In the day I hang it in a box nailed against a tree near my tent, & at night I take it in.

I have an idea that this is a singularly uninteresting letter, but I will have to wait until next time to do better. My hand is not "in." Of course the Col w'd be more than glad to get the Marions on any terms, but he can do nothing unless the Generals are willing to attach them to the Legion.

I forgot to tell you that Elliott preached a very fine sermon to the Legion last Sunday; he exchanged with Mr. McCollough.

Love to all, in proportion to their deserts & demands. I will not let so long a time pass without writing again. I wish you only knew how much good your letters do me.

Good Night Dearest.

Yrs <u>very</u> affectionately W. P. DuBose

1. Robert Rutledge held the rank of sergeant major in the Holcombe Legion. See Hewett, *South Carolina Confederate Soldiers,* 422; Compiled Service Records, Holcombe Legion, M267, roll 378.

2. William Irwin (1818–93), a native of Ireland, conducted a military school at St. John's College for boys in Spartanburg, South Carolina. See *Confederate Veteran* 31 (1923): 426; Wallace, *History of South Carolina,* 4:356.

3. In military usage, a "mess" is a group or company that eats together.

4. Francis Peyre Porcher (1824–95) was a physician and botanist. See *South Carolina Genealogies,* 2:84; Hewett, *South Carolina Confederate Soldiers,* 387.

5. In Special Order 17, December 10, 1861, Gen. Robert E. Lee divided the coast of South Carolina into five military districts. See *Official Records Army,* 6:344.

6. This possibly was Henry LeNoble Stevens (1827–62), a St. Johns Berkeley Parish planter. See Davidson, *Last Foray,* 252.

7. Rev. John Habersham Elliott (1832–1906) was ordained a priest in 1861; his first parochial charge was Christ Church in Adams Run. His wife Mary Barnwell Fuller died in May 1862. See Barnwell, *Story of an American Family,* 152.

8. The village of Willtown was located on a bluff overlooking the Edisto River. See Smith, "Willtown or New London."

Holcombe Legion
Feb 12th 1862

My dearest Miss Nannie

In spite of the delightful weather, I have come nearer to the Blues within the last twenty four hours than I have done since I have been in Camp, and all because I got my head (my heart is <u>always</u> turned there) turned toward Ch'ston yesterday morning & had to turn it back in the evening. Much as I wd enjoy a visit during Convention,[1] it had not occurred to me to apply for leave until Capt Cain, who particularly since your message of thanks, has seemed (only <u>seemed</u>) to be more anxious to get me to Charleston than I have been to get there myself, informed me that he had obtained the Col's consent to my going. The very idea was so delightful to me, that I c'd not resist harboring it for half a day, without reflecting whether, in the first place, [it was] right for me to go or, in the [second], whether I c'd get the Gen's consent, even with the Col's. By evening I had reached the painful conclusion that I had better not apply, but I have not quite recovered my lost equanimity. I wonder if you have been looking for me.

We kept very comfortable during the wet weather, but it was very hard on the sick. Four died in two days including the man wounded by the shell.

When I see you I will tell you about a rather amusing, & decidedly provoking expedition that the Legion took last Sunday in the rain against the enemy, who as usual did not appear.

I wrote to your Uncle Edward about the Marion Artillery; & informed him of my desire of paying him a visit. This evening I rec'd a note from him giving me credit for no other motive in writing than the desire of [making] a pleasant little arrangement to see you. Enclosed was a cordial & sweet note from Miss Clelia inviting me to meet you; which I hope to do whenever it suits you to accept their invitation; & Miss Sue too I hope. The Col has promised me a day, which does not require the Genl's consent, & I c'd start very early & have a good long day of it. I am afraid I have grown so shabby by work, exposure & wet, since you last saw me, that you w'd scarcely recognize me. I did not get to Uncle Dwights[2] last Sunday as I hoped. But Moultrie[3] came to see us on Monday. I have been read'g the Velvet Cushion[4] and like the old Vicar & his wife very much.

The news during the past four days has not been of a very cheering character; N. Carolina & Tennessee are beginning to foot up a list of reverses for the Confederacy, which I hope will not be a long one.

I forgot to thank you for the socks & to send word to Miss Sue that I have as many now as I can conveniently wear. Thank her for offer to knit me some more, & beg her to wait until next winter.

Jno. Elliott, I suppose, went to Town today; I saw him yesterday afternoon. His wife has gone to Aiken; I am afraid her health is very bad. My friends here accuse me of not wanting to go to Ch'ston, because I do not make the effort, but you know better, & so do they. The Col has just asked us in to prayers in his tent & I must say Good Night. Love to all.

Yrs affectionately

W. P. DuBose

Remember me to Mr. Trapier if you see him & tell him how disappointed I am not to be able to see him.

1. The seventy-third convention of the Protestant Episcopal Diocese in South Carolina was held February 12–14, 1862, at Grace Church in Charleston. See Thomas, *Protestant Episcopal Church,* 650.

2. Isaac Marion Dwight (1799–1873) married Martha Maria Porcher, William Porcher DuBose's aunt (daughter of Elizabeth Sinkler DuBose and Thomas Porcher). See MacDowell, *DuBose Genealogy,* 262.

3. William Moultrie Dwight (1839–77) was the son of Isaac Marion Dwight. He was born in Winnsboro and joined the Second South Carolina Infantry Regiment in 1861. He served as a private in Company A and as a first lieutenant in Company K. See MacDowell, *DuBose Genealogy,* 263; *WPA Cemetery Index;* Compiled Service Records, Second South Carolina Infantry Regiment (Second Palmetto Regiment), M267, roll 155.

4. This was a "controversial" novel about the Anglican Church by John William Cunningham (1780–1861) and first published in 1814. See Sadleir, *Trollope,* 47–48.

Roseland

Feb 17th 1862

I know, Dearest, how much you have been with me in spirit during the last few sad days. And my perfect trust in your sympathy and prayers has been very sweet to me. I c'd not talk to you during those few comforting moments that I spent with you on Friday, but their influence has not worn off as yet, and I feel that I can better express with my pen the feelings that I find it so hard to utter with my mouth, even to you.

Uncle Dwight came up with me on Friday night, having only heard of Father's[1] illness; & as I expected, we found the carriage at the station. I was glad to hear there that Dr Bratton was at home having arrived from Virginia two days before Father's death. He is a first rate planter himself and understands Father's affairs & business better than any one else, so that his presence was a great relief. Mr Roberts[2] & DuBose Porcher[3] were the only others at home besides the family. Bev. Means having left for Va the very day before, leaving Father, as he thought, not dangerously sick.

Oh the feelings with which I walked from the gate to the steps, on which my sisters were standing, & then into the hall where Mother was! The funeral had taken place the evening before & they had all become calm, but my arrival opened the wound afresh. When I saw Mother composed & quiet again, the relief was so great after that painful meeting, that I have scarcely been able to realize at all the reality of our great loss. It seems to me as if he were only absent, & I have so often come home to great afflictions that the quiet subdued appearance of everything scarcely seems strange to me. Oh the unspeakable comfort of a Gospel that can so soften the terrors of death & sweeten the bitterest cup of affliction! There is no joy so deep & inexpressible as that which the Spirit of God can impart in our moments of deepest distress. Yes it is the "love of Christ" & nothing else in the wide Universe, that can give real comfort & strength. I have seen so plainly the Grace of God at work in the hearts of the afflicted here, that so far I have felt that my poor words c'd add nothing to His works & so I have left all to Him, only attempting to prove by my manner & conduct my affection for them and my trust in our compassionate Saviour.

Sunday was a sweet day to us all. It rained so that we c'd not go to Church & Mr Roberts who has been a great comfort to us all, had service at home. His selection of prayers was so judicious & his read'g of the service so full of feeling, that I seldom remember to have felt such spiritual elevation, and I am sure I was not alone. When they sang "There is a land of pure delight"[4] (Oh so sweetly!) I gave way completely, and c'd not sing at all.

The change in Father's disease was a sudden one on Thursday morning, after which he was delirious most of the time. Once he became conscious & said "Goodbye to you all. May God bless & preserve you"—the very words with which he concluded his last letter to me. They were his last conscious words & the only ones that indicated any consciousness of his approaching departure, but blessed be God! we are troubled with no painful doubts as to his condition now.

He had been looking forward for a long time to attending the Episcopal Convention in Charleston, & one great motive was that he might see you & have an opportunity of knowing you. He was also to have gone to our Camp to see me, & had promised Mr Hutcheson to take him to call on you.

There is a great deal more that it w'd delight me to write to you about it but it is quite late & so I will reserve it until I write again or see you.

This stay at home is so full of rest & peace to me. In a worldly point of view there is much ahead of us that is dark and doubtful, but I feel now that I can trust all to God. He knows what is best & He can bring it to pass. I can catch a glimpse of that Divine Hope that inspired St Paul to say "I know Him in whom I have believed,[5] and am persuaded that He is able to keep that which I have committed to Him against that day." I am willing to commit to Him myself, my Country, & all who are near & dear to me, & to have no care & no fear for the future.

Give my love to your Mother, Miss Sue & all the family. I hope you have Miss Sarah with you still; I w'd like very much to see her. I think of leaving home on Friday, & remaining in Chs'ton until Monday when my leave expires. We have seven children in the house, only one over four. Father was devoted to them & they to him.

Good night, Dearest. Your love is very dear to me.

Yrs affectionately
W. P. DuBose

All send love. Sister thanks you for your note.

1. William Porcher DuBose's father, Theodore Samuel Marion DuBose (b. 1809), died in February 1862. Frederick A. Porcher wrote the following of him: "Traveling one day in a rail car he observed a sick soldier and sat by him ministering to his necessities. The soldier had measles, and in less than a fortnight his benevolent nurse fell a victim to the disease." See MacDowell, *DuBose Genealogy,* 12; Porcher, "Upper Beat of St. John's, Berkeley," 44.

2. Rev. John J. Roberts was the husband of Elizabeth Sinkler Porcher (b. 1822), William Porcher DuBose's aunt. See MacDowell, *DuBose Genealogy,* 352.

3. This was possibly Isaac DuBose Porcher (1832–66), William Porcher DuBose's uncle. See MacDowell, *DuBose Genealogy,* 352.

4. This is the first line and title of a 1707 hymn by Isaac Watts.

5. 2 Timothy 1:12.

Holcombe Legion
Febry 28th 1862

My dearest Miss Nannie

There was only one drawback to my perfect enjoyment of your letter today, and that was self reproach for allowing myself to be so much behind you in this only mode of intercourse that this cruel war has left us! When I reflect how near I would have been to my ordination, my parish & you, I am almost tempted to murmur, & yet in spite of all, I have been very happy & ought not to complain. If I had only faith enough to live in the present, to enjoy blessings as they come, & leave distant & future things to God, I am sure there w'd be no place left for repining. Even the late severe affliction through which we have been passing has given me more real spiritual joy than grief; I cannot feel that the death of one whose salvation we have an assured hope is hard to bear. How much his ardent & patriotic spirit has been spared already! It is true that those at home can never cease to feel his loss, but do I not <u>see</u> the chastening doing them good? "Tribulation worketh patience,[1] & patience experience, & experience hope, & hope maketh not ashamed."

And then our po[litical] troubles. Do you know that I find them much harder to bear than the others? And yet how much there is for us to learn from them. I will not preach a sermon on the subject, although I am not afraid of wearying my congregation. But imagine the worst. Suppose Charleston taken & yourself a fugitive. Might not God wisely & in love select such a method of teaching us that here "we have no continuing city,[2] but that "we seek a better, even an heavenly." No, that is not the worst. Imagine our great cause finally unsuccessful & our beloved country conquered & ruined. I do not apprehend any such fate, but it might be God's will, & if so, it would be right. I do not admit that because we are in the right in this particular strife, that therefore our cause <u>must</u> prevail. Our enemies might be more wicked than we, but the Bible teaches us that the "ungodly are a sword of the Lord," & history, both sacred & profane, teaches us that God often has used more wicked nations to accomplish his judgments upon those that were less so. That we are in the right is a presumption but not a proof of our final success. Imagine then the worst, whatever it may be. Our enemies can advance not one inch further than God wills, & His will is obliged to a righteous one: He maketh the [wrath] of man to praise Him & <u>the remainder of wrath He restraineth</u>. It is a comfort to reflect that our sufferings come from God Himself & not from the pitiful wrath of man.[3]

And then much as we ought to remember that we belong to kingdom that is above the kingdom of this world, & which <u>must</u> prevail no matter what their fate may be. There is a Divine purpose running through all, bending everything to the growth of this kingdom, to the glory of its King & the eternal interests of its citizens. Oh! that we could live more among these unseen realities, and learn to attach less importance to the transient and the changeable. The Christian life consists in the gradual withdrawal of our affections from things temporal & fixing them upon the eternal. If the dissolution of our earthly relations, the breaking up of earthly ties have any effect in advancing this result, then is the Kingdom of Christ promoted by these material disasters, & we, while we sorrow as patriots, ought to rejoice as Christians. I don't know what the future is to bring forth, but I find great comfort in the assurance that almost all of those whom I love best here, will pass safely through these "light afflictions which are but for a season"[4] & be reunited in that happier home which has been prepared for us.

Somehow, I feel more hopeful & cheerful in camp here, than I did when away; about any political condition I mean. Our Legion is improving fast in health, spirits & drill. We have been having battles between the infantry & cavalry, in which the former are always victorious.

This has been a glorious day; being Fast day & therefore one of comparative leisure. I treated myself this evening to a delightful ride to White Point with Dr Porcher, Mr McCollough & Dick Dwight.

But I haven't got to your letter yet. I [don't] think it could have been improved, but I protest against sharing all your joys & none of your sorrows. I w'd like to know everything that interests you. There is the Birthday, too, that I have not said a word about; & would you believe it, it is nearly twelve o.c. Dick, who has just got into bed very tired, says "Tell Miss Nannie I am happy, & give her my love." I know he says it to tempt me to bed, but I can't resist it, so Good Night.

March 1st I have only a few minutes this evening & may not have them uninterrupted. I will try to write on your birthday, [or] else put it off [for] a day or two. What are your plans in case you have to move? Tell your Sister M. I am quite curious to know what is to be the fate of that piano.

The Postmaster is after me. Give much love to the household & <u>our</u> other friends when you write.

Yrs most affectionately
W. P. DuBose

I hear nothing [now] of giving up our present lines.

1. Romans 5:3.

2. Hebrews 11:16 and 13:14. The heavenly "City of God" was also the theme of St. Augustine's *De Civitate Dei,* written in the fifth century A.D. after Rome was sacked by the Visigoths in 410. Augustine wrote it to assure Christians that the City of God—that is, the New Jerusalem—would ultimately triumph. See Augustine of Hippo and Bettenson, *City of God.*

3. Psalms 76:10.

4. 2 Corinthians 4:17 (King James Version): "For our light affliction, which is but for a moment, worketh for us a far more exceeding and eternal weight of glory."

Hol. Legion
March 4th 1862

And so, after all, dearest Miss Nannie, your birthday slipped [between] two letters. I would have postponed it until today, but this won't do for a birthday letter. If it will be any compensation, I will inform you that I spent all Sunday night dreaming about you, & very sweet dreams too.

It seems to me a very short time since my 21st Birthday, & now my 26th is at hand. Who can tell what the next five years will bring forth? I often indulge in pictures of the future, & am sometimes surprised at myself for allowing this fearful war with all its uncertainties to interfere so little with my anticipations. And yet the time has certainly come for us to be taking a more serious view of our situation. With our disparity of numbers & resources, the sooner we assume a sterner, more determined & more devoted attitude the better for our cause. I do not think we have been enough in earnest & we will not begin to be invincible until we have begun to realize more the necessity of self-devotion, & to make up our minds to the choice of death in preference to surrender or defeat. In all probability we have to come to this point sooner or later, & though the prospect does not commend itself to our natural feelings, yet these are the circumstances to bring out the manly & heroic qualities of individuals & to prepare nations for subsequent greatness. If these 12,000 men had all died at Fort Donelson[1] in a fruitless effort to cut their way through, that bloody defeat would have been worth to us many victories.

And yet while I endeavor to bring myself to a more serious view of the future, & if necessary, to a cheerful surrender of its bright visions of happiness, I am a strong advocate of not only "living in the present," but enjoying in the present all the daily blessings that come to us. I am not in favour of permitting the clouds of tomorrow to darken the sunshine of today. Those bright hours spent with you were unalloyed by any recollection whatsoever of the darkness that might be in store for us. If it is not God's will that we are to be spared to each other in this world, I am grateful for the happiness that you have already brought me, & not a bit ashamed of having been so happy under such adverse circumstances. War is a dreadful evil but, if a man will not [stand] in his own way, he can do <u>all his duty</u>, & yet feel its evils a very small proportion of his time.

They were all well at home at last acc't, as well as usual, that is. I got a sad letter from Sister today. I forgot to send you Charlie's letter in my last.

I will not [trust] the little daguerreotype to a [cleaning] yet. Dick went on Sunday to Mr. Seabrook's church[2] & came back perfectly [beside] himself because he had seen some ladies—your cousins among them.

Since I have come back we have been having singing occasionally in the Col's tent, & I have learnt a new tune to "Just as I am" which most of us like better than the other. I must tell you my last pun (I very seldom indulge in them): The other evening at White Pt. every thing was so calm & sweet & peaceful (though a gun-boat was in sight) that I could not resist the temptation of reading your letter which I had just rec'd. Dick called to me "to enjoy the view reading letters and do very well <u>for a tent</u>" to which I answered "I am <u>intent</u>, whenever I read these letters."

I have an idea that this is a right egotistical little letter. So excuse both egotism and brevity & believe me, with love to the household.

Yours with sincere affection

W. P. DuBose

1. On February 16, 1862, Brig. Gen. Simon Bolivar Buckner (1823–1914) agreed to surrender the Confederate garrison of Fort Donelson in Tennessee unconditionally to Union brigadier general Ulysses Simpson Grant (1822–85). Shortly thereafter Grant received a promotion to major general. See McPherson, *Battle Cry of Freedom,* 402; Long, *Civil War Almanac,* 172; Warner, *Generals in Gray,* 38–39; Warner, *Generals in Blue,* 183–86.

2. The Reverend Joseph Baynard Seabrook (1809–77) was preaching at Church Flats in St. Paul's Parish, Stono, "largely to soldiers. But the congregation being 'broken up and dispersed by the war,' he left on May 1, 1862, and went to Anderson. The chapel was burned by Union forces on February 22, 1865." See Thomas, *Protestant Episcopal Church,* 411; *South Carolina Genealogies,* 4:218.

Holcombe Legion
March 19th 1862

My dear Miss Nannie

The disappointment of not being able to see you this morning, almost swallows up all the enjoyment of yesterday.

The Colonel does not wish me to go this morning. He says he w'd prefer my waiting until Saturday, & though many days' delay makes it harder to bear, I expect I will have to comply with his wishes. You cannot conceive, or rather, I hope you <u>can</u>, how hard it is for me to have to wait so long. I feel so unhappy too about the sickness at home, that I am the more impatient to see you & have an opportunity of talking with you. I cannot have much hope now of the recovery of my dear little nephew.

Do you know that one thing that has attracted me most strangely to the idea of assisting my Uncle in Abbeville[1] has been the opportunity of assisting in the education, religious & intellectual, of those boys. Little Mack[2] was the one of all others that I thought we might with God's will, make a minister of one of these days.

Captain Cain sends you several messages, one of which is that he is very sorry that he did not see more of you yesterday.

Mrs McCord's bracelet has not been found yet—it is to be searched for directly & I have no doubt will be found if here. Thomas Gadsden has almost made up his mind to join the Legion. I have not advised him to do so, but will of course be very glad if he does do so. I am in hopes that Bruce Davis[3] will come back today & Jim too.

The Post Master will not give me another minute. I think I will come Saturday, barely possibly Friday. One of the two certainly (D. V.).[4] If you do not see me on Friday expect me Saturday, if not then, every succeeding day.

Yrs very affectionately
W. P. DuBose

Everybody concurs in saying that yesterday was a <u>great</u> day.

1. Octavius Theodore Porcher (1829–73) taught at Willington Academy near Abbeville, a school founded by the famous educator and minister Moses Waddell (1770–1840). Porcher was later ordained an Episcopal priest. See Luker, "Crucible of Civil War and Reconstruction," 68.

2. This probably refers to McNeely DuBose (1859–1911), son of William Porcher DuBose's brother Cowan McNeely DuBose (1831–60) and Margaret "Mattie" Ann Boyd DuBose. See MacDowell, *DuBose Genealogy,* 20.

3. Bruce and Jim Davis were the sons of Bishop Thomas Frederick Davis (1804–71). See Thomas, *Protestant Episcopal Church*, 706–8.

4. *Deo volente* (God being willing).

Holcombe Legion
March 24th 1862

I must write this morning, Darling, if only to bring the letter that is dependent upon this. I have just burned with my own hand every letter from you that I had with me; I know you will need no stronger proof of my regard for your wishes. It was very hard to do it, but I thought that you were probably right, & after a fruitless effort to discriminate between them, I destroyed them all. Now I want another in their place. I wish I could tell you how much happiness you have given me during the past week; I thank God for giving me this cup of joy amidst all that I have been called upon to suffer for some time past!

We will probably go tonight upon the expedition to Edisto of which I have spoken to you. I do not anticipate much danger to ourselves, if we manage properly. We hope to be back tomorrow morning, so, for fear of giving you unnecessary uneasiness, I think I will keep this note until we return. If I should not return (of which I hope there is no danger) I hope some one else will send it to you. I am sure you would like to know how much you are in my heart & prayers this day. Darling, I do not (& I know you do not) like too much profession & too much warmth of expression, but at times like this when I realize that at least <u>possibly</u>, this may be my last communication with you, I cannot resist the strong desire that I feel to let you know how much my dear you are to me.

That we will really meet the Enemy tonight at last, if we go, I think there can be no doubt. In what force we will find them, it is impossible to say; the Col. thinks that there are not more than one hundred & fifty at the point which we design attacking. We will carry about three hundred men, & will be able to retire before a superior force can reach us.

Is not this a time for us all to be prepared for any change that may be ordered for us? It is true that this uncertain & ever shifting condition of things which seems intended to detach our affections from our earthly treasures, has rather the effect of strengthening their hold upon us. I thank our Father in Heaven that the treasures which are dearest to me here, are such as will not remain behind, but will be more precious to me hereafter. Only, may He make Himself & His holy will more precious to me than they!

Give my love to Miss Sue, Mrs Peronneau and the young ladies. Those days at Dungannon[1] were sweet to me, and apparently nearly as sweet to Dick. (I expect he w'd object to the "nearly.") We got safely to Camp on Sunday night & feel no ill effects from the "dissipation." The Col did nothing more than laugh at me & "tell on me" in a letter he finished this morning to his wife. I wish we had staid an hour later.

Nothing more from home. I still feel anxious. I do hope that Mother will be spared to know you. And now I must close for today. We have just heard from our pickets that several of the enemies' boats are passing up Little Edisto R. between Edisto & Jehossee Islands. This may prevent or at least delay our expedition.

Dick gives a <u>great deal</u> of love to "Miss Annie & all," says he "thinks of them by day & dreams of them by night." I will add something further before I send my letter.

Monday Night. Well we are not on Edisto, & our project has become indefinitely postponed. I was sure that this time at least we w'd see the Enemy, as it depended upon us & not upon them. But several circumstances have altered our plans. And now shall I tear up my letter & write another one more suitable to the altered circumstances? No, I did not write more strongly than I felt & I will send it as it is; destroy it yourself when you have read it.

There is some exquisite music going on a short distance from my tent—violins, flute, & c. It is a very delightful feature of camp life, where it exists. Mrs McCord has a very sweet voice; I wish I c'd hear her oftener. You know one of the best proofs to myself that I am perfectly satisfied with you, is that I never regret you are not a musician.

Write & tell me your plans, when you expect to return to Charleston & c. I might go over on Sunday, but hardly before, however, do not remain longer than you think you ought on my account.

Please remember that I haven't a single letter of yours. Let me see, I will hardly hear from you before Friday, unless you are <u>very</u> good.

I slept very little last night & must go to bed. If your happiness depended solely upon my love, I feel as if you w'd be very unhappy. But it depends upon a love infinitely greater than mine, & possessing that, I rest assured that you have a source of happiness infinitely more abundant & more lasting than anything I can offer.

Good night.

Yrs affectionately
W. P. DuBose

1. Dungannon, a rice plantation, was located about eighteen miles from Charleston. Edward Charles Peronneau (d. 1878), Nannie's uncle, rented it for a time from its owner Judge George W. Logan. See Roos, *Travels in America,* 75; Patey, *Whaley Family,* 198.

April 1st 1862
8 O.C. P.M.

Your precious letter, Darling, has just been put in my hands, brought by Col Stevens from Adams Run, where I suppose it has been reposing for several days.

I will not attempt to express the anxiety with which I have expected it. I knew it had been written, and was trying in vain to reconcile myself to its loss. On Friday morning it was finally announced that the long delayed expedition to Edisto was to take place that night.[1] Oh how I did long to see one line from you before we left & how disappointed I was when it did not come!

You may have seen an account of our Expedition but you have not seen a true one, at least I have not. It is too long to write. I wish I could see you to tell you all about it. The Expedition went in two parties, the larger party under Col. Stevens were to engage the Enemy on Edisto Island, while Majors Palmer and Garlington[2] with two hundred & fifty men of the Holcombe Legion were entrusted with the really hazardous part of the undertaking. This was to cut across the fields from Watts Cut to the bridge connecting Big & Little Edisto Islands, pass on to Little Ed., burn the bridge behind them and shut themselves thereby on the Island with whatever number of the Enemy might be there, with no prospect of escape if defeated. When we had gained possession of the Island, a flat was to be sent to take us off, before the Enemy should have time to get over at us in superior [forces]. All this was effected; we moved on encountering . . . fire of pickets & driving them before us, burnt the . . . attacked the Enemy who were ready for us but . . . to be only eighty strong, took twenty prisoners, killing one & w'd have surely captured them all but for the dense fog which produced some [confusion].

We then crossed on to Jehossee in the flat sent for us, and had to wade through the marsh for over a mile, with the water up to our knees all the time & frequently up to our waists. The attack was made at daylight & we reached Camp at Midday Saturday after a very fatiguing march; besides which I had slept none on Friday night. Through it all, I had your letter ever before me, & you can conceive my disappointment when after all it did not come. If I had received it, I w'd certainly have gone on Sunday, but I was really in no condition to go on the uncertainty. And so I lost my last opportunity, and now Dearest when can I hope to see you again! If I only thought that there was any prospect of your still being at Dungannon, I would try & get off early tomorrow morning to see you. Although the beginning of the month is my busiest time.

I have been interrupted in my letter by some heavy guns south of us. We can see the flashes, & by the interval between them & the reports, make out the distance to be between five & six miles. It is nothing, I suppose, but the Enemy wasting some more shells. There seems to me less prospect of an advance on their part about here than ever; you need not feel in any immediate uneasiness.

Gov. Pickens reviews us tomorrow, & will probably present the flag. I hope we will gratify our much beloved & admired Chief Magistrate.

. . . Mack still very ill, although I cannot but hope . . . better, though the acc'ts do not really say so. The . . . are as usual, except that Mother grows daily . . . & weaker. I do hope that you will know her before she is taken away from us. It would be a double disappointment if she as well as Father sh'd . . . my own dear Wife that is to be, in God's good Providence.

I know you were disappointed on Sunday when we failed to make our appearance. That you sh'd have waited for nothing! Not for nothing either, for Dungannon is very sweet, and so are your Aunt and Cousins[3] & Mrs McCord too. And I am sure every additional day in the country must have done you good. And then too you saw Miss Mary McCord, which was a treat in itself. By the by who was the Miss Annie, with the "sad, beautiful black eyes." Dick is very curious.

Tell Miss Sue I am sorry she lost any sleep on our account. I do love Miss Sue! and not altogether on your acc't either. I liked her before I had begun to love you, and she has been a good friend to me ever since. I often look forward to her going with us on our first visit to Roseland, when I will give both you & her some new friends to love. I hope it will not be <u>very long</u>. You will receive a warm welcome when you get there.

Dick sends a great deal of love, & says (let him think so, poor fellow!) that he was as much disappointed as I was at not seeing you on Sunday. He says he certainly expects a visit again from the ladies.

I took too large a sheet to finish tonight, so good night my darling!

Wednesday Morning. I have no time to add anything this morning, but will write in momentary expectation of the M.C.R. (as he signs himself—Mail Carrier I believe he means). I am afraid you will not be satisfied with my meagre acc't of the Edisto Trip. It is hard to give you an idea of it, without a map & the use of my tongue instead of a pen. I accompanied Maj. Palmer but was not under fire. The companies engaged had three men slightly wounded, & were for a few moments under a hot fire. I had been [detached] with one company & hurried to the scene of action but got there too late. At one time we had the fifty or sixty men who escaped completely surrounded but could not distinguish friend from foe in the fog & so let them get away.

It is a sultry, disagreeable morning, and I am afraid that the Gov. & ourselves will not have a very pleasant day of it.

By the by, I nearly forgot to tell you that I have [received] my uniform, very much like Col Stevens' it is, with the braid on the arm (according to directions) as nearly invisible as possible. You w'd have seen me with it on Sunday, if I had gone. I hope it will not be as unfortunate as your dress.

I am glad Gadsden has joined the Marions; I believe it the best thing he c'd have done.

I suppose you are certainly in Charleston by this time. Give much love to Miss Sue and to your Mother & Sister Martha. And kiss all the children for me. The death of your cousin was indeed sad, certainly to her husband.

I w'd have written to you before, but was doubtful whether to direct to Charleston or to Rantowles.

And now I will get ready for the M.C.R. I see him coming. Write as often as you [sic] & never doubt that I am perfectly satisfied with you & your letters.

Good by Dearest. Continue to give me your prayers &
Believe me

Yours most sincerely
W. P. DuBose

1. On March 29, 1862, Confederate forces launched another expedition to Edisto Island, this time with the goal of engaging Union forces, which had moved there to protect the slave population from Confederate raids, such as the expedition of January 22–25, 1862. See *Official Records Army,* 6:113–20.

2. Their full names were Francis Gendron Palmer (1832–62) and Albert Creswell Garlington (1822–85). See *Confederate Military History,* 6:133; Bailey, *Biographical*

Directory of the South Carolina Senate, 1:544–45; Towles, *World Turned Upside Down,* 993.

3. Nannie's aunt was Mrs. Anna Smith Peronneau (née Coffin), wife of Edward Charles Peronneau. She was the widow of William McKenzie Parker (d. 1830), by whom she had two sons, William and Edward. The latter, Edward Lightwood Parker (1828–92), married Emma McCord (1830–50), by whom he had one daughter, Anna. The cousins mentioned are probably some of the children of Edward Charles Peronneau; they included Eliza, Anna Coffin, Clelia Finley, and Mary Coffin. See Patey, *Whaley Family,* 198; Parker, *Genealogy of the Parker Family,* 30, 49.

April 4th 1862

Twenty minutes to Eleven! but principles & Dick to the contrary notwithstanding, I must at least begin a letter to you tonight, Dearest Miss Nannie. "Principles" says it is wrong, & Dick says it is humbug, but I don't care for Dick, & I will compromise with "Principles" by stopping very soon in the hope of finishing tomorrow morning.

I was about starting to write to you an hour or two ago when I remembered that I was obliged to write home this very night. I have not heard since my last to you, but I still go on the principle that "no news is good news."

I am both gratified & grieved that my non-appearance at Dungannon was taken so much to heart. You see I give you credit for any am't of disappointment, & imagine that the others were disappointed with you, on the Bible principle of bearing one another's burdens. That part of your consolation which was drawn from the contemplation of my disappointment was certainly well grounded. I have been reproaching myself with not having gone anyhow, but in my low state of spirits consequent upon the non-reception of your eagerly looked for letter. I had persuaded myself that you could not be there. However I do have too much, to repine at what I have not; & so I will accept that disappointment & bury it in the enjoyment which is still fresh in my memory.

We are beginning to have real Spring; the trees are growing green & the sandflies troublesome. Other kindred nuisances too are beginning to make bold inroads upon the pleasures of camp life. While I speak, I pause to make an ineffectual grab at a passing mosquito, & tomorrow morning I anticipate an exciting hunt for fleas in the blankets. There is another advantage of blankets; I couldn't catch them in sheets. Excuse so elevated a topic as fleas. Taste must yield to Truth. I cannot give you a true picture of camp life, without mentioning this element in it which is becoming more & more prominent every day; besides, all knowledge is useful, if you want to catch a flea, drive him on a blanket & you have him.

But "Principles" has called in an ally (one too, that knows exactly how to manage me—I am sure he ought to; he has been doing it every night for the last twenty six years "come next Friday") and I yield to superior numbers & lay down my pen. Good night, Dearest. I consign you to the loving care of Him who never slumbers nor sleeps. Oh, that we could realize more the love of that Father for us his unworthy children! "As for me, I am poor & needy, yet the Lord careth for me"—"Knows us yet loves us better than He knows."

Saturday Morning. I hope your garden is having some of these refreshing showers that are passing by us. It must be getting pretty. I am going today to see Miss Ammy at Adams Run, & tomorrow I want to pay Uncle Dwight a visit which I have already delayed too long. This country will be beautiful in a few days. I must contrive to take some rides, & only wish I could enjoy the sweet pleasure of having you with me. Don't you wish there was peace & we could pay a visit to the French Broad together. That exquisite little valley recalls the most delightful associations to me.

The M.C.R. is upon me and business is accumulating. Love to the household & a kiss for the children.

Good bye & write soon.

Yrs most affectionately
W. P. DuBose

"As for me, I am poor & needy"—Psalm 40:17

My feet are worn & weary with the march
Over the rough road and up the steep hillside
O city of our God! I fain would see
Thy pastures green where peaceful waters glide

My hands are weary toiling on
Day after day for perishable meat;
O city of our God! I fain would rest—
I sigh to gain Thy glorious mercy seat

My garments, travel-worn and stained with dust
Oft rent by briars and thorns that crowd my way
Would fain be made O Lord my righteousness
Spotless and white in heaven's unclouded day

My eyes are weary looking at the sin
Impiety & scorn upon the earth
O city of our God! within thy walls
All are clothed upon with thy new birth

My heart is weary of its own deep sin—
Sinning, repenting, sinning still again;
When shall my soul Thy glorious presence feel,
And find, dear Savior, it is free from sin?

Patience poor Soul! the Savior's feet were worn;
The Savior's heart and hands were weary too;
His garments stained, and travel-worn, and old;
His vision blinded with a pitying dew.

Love thou the path of sorrow that He trod;
Toil on & wait in patience for thy rest;
O city of our God! we soon shall see
Thy glorious walls—home of the loved & blest![1]

1. This is a hymn entitled "The City of God." It is in the handwriting of Nannie
Peronneau. See Hedge, *Hymns for the Church of Christ*, 624.

Holcombe Legion
April 19th 1862

Your letter of the 17th Dearest Miss Nannie was received yesterday evening,
and I have only twenty minutes this morning to acknowledge its receipt &
thank you for it. I am quite concerned that you should not have heard from
me for so long a time. On Monday morning (14th) Mr. McCollough mailed
a letter to you in Charleston, together with me from Dick which has since
been acknowledged. I was feeling badly on my Birthday & wrote on Sunday
instead. I hope it will reach you yet. I wrote again a day or two ago, in answer
to your letter of the 14th.

I went yesterday to Church at Wiltown and enjoyed the service very
much indeed. Elliott preached an admirable sermon. I called on him afterwards & paid a short visit; he says his wife is better, but I very much fear that
she can never be well again.

I have not been very unwell, never too much so to write, although I confess that a very marked feature or consequence of indisposition is a decided
disinclination to writing.

I am anxious to go to Mr. Seabrooks' Church and Dungannon tomorrow (Easter), but am not sure that I am quite well enough yet for so long a ride. You may be sure, though, that wherever I may be in person, I will be frequently with you in Spirit. I enjoy these stated periods of the Church year very much, particularly Christmas and Easter; they suit my intellectual tastes as well as my religious feelings. I have never enjoyed more elevation & exhilaration of spirit than at these two delightful seasons, coming as they do too, I think, at such appropriate periods of the year.

I have been interrupted a dozen times, and have been keeping the M.C.R. fifteen minutes past his time. I cannot send another letter before Monday & so prefer to send this note.

I have seen not much of the Col's wife; she is staying at Adams Run & I have been unwell.

Much love to all. A happy Easter to you Dearest.

Yrs most affectionately
W. P. DuBose

Holcombe Legion
<u>Nearer</u> Adams Run. Apr. 23rd

The mosquito nets reached us this morning dearest Miss Nannie & in the absence of a letter, I will answer <u>them</u>. Dick seems really to value his as much as I do mine; he insisted on taking the one with the direction pinned on it, which, in compassion, I permitted him to do. I wrote you a note on Saturday morning, mainly to tell you that I had written you a letter on the 13th which had not reached you on the 17th. The mail is getting unreliable. I wrote to your Mother on Monday, not much to my satisfaction, though, in consequence . . . of interruptions & [other]. . . . I hope she . . . her consent. I am indulging strong hopes of a furlough in May, if she does. Stephen arrived today from home and gives a more favorable account of the condition of things there than I have yet received; they do not write but I am inclined to receive his report as he exhibited a decidedly somber tone of mind on his first arrival. Little Mack is, I trust, actually getting well, for some wise & useful purpose I hope.

I got your likeness by him & have transferred it to the new case successfully. I was right glad to see you again. Talking of birthday presents, ask Miss Sue what she thinks of my not having tasted the pickles she sent me; they came just as I went on the sick list & went before I came off of it; it was a daily temptation to me, the successful resistance of which probably did me more good in the way of discipline than the enjoyment of them could have done.

And talking of that indisposition, do you know how I cured myself at last? After ten days of rice diet to no effect, I spent a charming Easter at Dungannon, so much so as to forget I was an invalid, & to begin dinner on Pepper pot & end on [curds] strawberries & cream. [I] came back . . . well. That Easter . . . delightful to me . . . the sweet weather, the buggy ride (we borrowed a buggy) the services, the Communion, and then the ladies, the flowers & the sweet thoughts of you! Everything conspired to raise me above the world, & to transfer me to one more peaceful & spiritual. Its influences have not worn off yet, in spite of the rather depressing contrast of our new pine woods camp "nearer Adams Run" to which we moved yesterday.

[Letter not signed]

Holcombe Legion
April 28th 1862

Your letter of last week, Dearest, reached me in due time. I will not deny that it was a great disappointment to me, yet I would not have you act against your convictions of duty. I would be unwilling myself to take any steps in this matter without your Mother's approval. I may have regarded the subject too exclusively from my own standpoint, & too little from yours. There were several reasons besides those I gave you which made me anxious for it, some of which, however influential with me, would not I suspect have had any weight in deciding you.

Certainly, however unwelcome your decision was, I have had no reason to be disappointed in you or in the evidences you have always given of the love which I prize more than any earthly blessing. Possessing that, I ought not to be dissatisfied that your sense of duty forbids you to give me more. I received your last letter yesterday; I am glad you received the lost letter, as I would have disliked it falling into the hands of another & less appreciative reader.

Much to our relief, the General decided finally I hope, that the field officers not having been originally elected, could not be reelected in the reorganization. The election for company officers has been going on yesterday &

today, & has resulted in a good many changes, some of them for better, & as many or more for worse.[1] We are in for the war . . . for general defence, under the same field officers. You ask me whether I would consent to be treated as Dr. Bratton was. I hope I would not, under any circumstances. I don't believe I am fit for an independent command. The disposition, occupation & habits of a student are not the best preparation for such a position. The world requires two different classes of laborers to carry on the operations of society, men of thought, reflection & study, & men of action. I belong to the former class, & now is the time for men of action. I am too contemplative, too absent minded, & can never remember the points of the compass. Besides that, after having so long trained myself to regard myself the "servant of men" I w'd find it hard to become their master. I would make a very good captain, or possibly major. I think I have a knack of gaining attention & obedience without often appearing to command it. I believe I can, when I try, exercise discipline without giving offense, and in this way am more accessible and popular than some others. But this is all I can boast in the way of qualifications & this is not all that is required. I think my present office suits me better than any other; as a constant thing it is more important than any other except the Colonelcy, & keeps me constantly occupied. I know I am a pretty good Adjutant, that I give general satisfaction, that being out of the regular line of promotion I stand in nobody's way & interfere with no one's aspirations. And so on the whole I congratulate myself that I am, I hope, permanently fixed in a situation which can beget no ambitions desires to be succeeded possibly by failure, disappointment or harassing cares & responsibilities. Providence has given me a place where there are no temptations, or few, to selfish or earthly aspirations; and it is very much better for me that it is so, for I am not unambitious of worldly distinctions.

The prejudice against the Colonel was unfounded & I hope short lived. The reaction has begun already. Destroy that letter in which I spoke of it.

I have heard nothing more of Col Bratton and his Regiment. The Enemy has produced quite a stir among us today. A gun boat came up the Dawho River, shelled our men out of a little battery of two guns, landed & destroyed the guns (I don't mean that the gun boat landed) and went off before we could get to the scene of action. After dark, though, she passed near six or eight field [pieces] that had been hurriedly sent to White Point, all of which crashed into her at that range, doing some damage, I have no doubt.[2]

To console ourselves for the loss of the guns, Dick & I came back with exquisite bunches of flowers, moss rose buds & c. We generally have them; we brought elegant bunches from Dungannon.

Apr. 30th. Give much love to the household, and tell Miss Sue that it is my present intention to give her the next letter I write; it is not fair to give you all.

Dick sends love; but says he thinks the Language stands very much in need of another word less commonplace & <u>cold</u>. He has received another mosquito net from Miss Nannie C. I have not got to the Marions yet, & was prevented by the weather from going to Wiltown last Sunday. Yesterday morning before starting to meet the Enemy, I burnt all your letters. I heard from Johnson yesterday, expected to be in Ch'stn by May 1st.

Yrs affectionately

W. P. DuBose

1. On April 9, 1862, the Confederate Congress passed a conscription act dictating that, among other things, elections would be held for all company, battalion, and regimental officers. See Matthews, ed., *The Statutes at Large of the Confederate States of America,* 29–32.

2. *Official Records Navy,* 12:789–92; *Official Records Army,* 14:13, 339–40.

Holcombe Legion

May 2nd 1862

Your letter, dearest, reached me today, and the prospect which it gives me of seeing you so soon again is as sweet as it was unexpected. As it is out of the question for me to think of going to Charleston, even with the additional inducement of seeing Johnson, I will proceed at once to make arrangements for the visit to Dungannon. I hope you will not be prevented from coming on Monday. I have no doubt I can get off on Tuesday or Wednesday. I think I had better fix the latter day, as my letter may be delayed or something else may prevent your coming on Monday. Besides I shall be safer from a press of business on that day. Let us say Wednesday then, unless you have any reason for preferring Tuesday, which, by the way, I w'd have no means of finding out. If by any means I sh'd be prevented from going on Wednesday and you can spare the time, try me again on Thursday. I cannot describe the happiness I feel at the prospect of a day with you at that sweet place.

We have been intending to go there again before the family leave, but the last of the month is a particularly busy time with me.

I would like very much to see Johnson; I think he might call by here on his way back. By the by, I wish I knew what day he is to pass. I w'd go to the R.R. to see him.

The probable fate of Charleston and Savannah is too serious a subject for only a few lines, which is as much as I have time for tonight. I am glad to hear that Mr Barnwell is interesting himself in the matter. I should think that if it should be the policy of the C.S. to give up Charleston the State should undertake its defence. It would be sad to see our beloved City in the hands of the Enemy, but so far as our course, & the policy of the war are concerned, I am fast becoming reconciled to the surrender of every place accessible to gun boats, and falling back into the country.

It was not our men who were in charge of the guns destroyed by the Enemy. The officer <u>took a tree</u> "to see the effects of his balls," and the men left for safer parts. The fact is our men here will not fight these big guns. They cannot stand this thing of being "bombed."

Our reorganization is completed & we are in for the war. I am pretty sure no further changes will be made. Capt Sage has resigned and though we will never get as good a Qr Master again, yet we have no Yankees now, & that is something gained.

I would like very much to know your friends the Barnwells, or rather to meet Miss Leila again & become acquainted with Miss Mary. I think on the whole, I very decidedly <u>approve</u> of your friends.

And so after all you have contrived to make me write to you again before writing to Miss Sue. However this is only a business letter, in order to make it more so, I think I will not turn over to the next page. It is getting very late, & I don't think I will have time tomorrow morning to add anything.

So Good night, Darling, with the sweet hope of seeing you very soon.

Yrs affectionately
W. P. DuBose

Dick begs you to deliver the enclosed letter.

Holcombe Legion
May 9th 1862

I hope, Dearest, that the mail will prove as propitious this Saturday as it did last. I would like you to hear from me once at least before the memory of last Wednesday begins to grow faint. That day was such a bright spot in my life that it has seemed to me ever since only a sweet dream of fairy land. I can scarcely believe that so much happiness was real. I don't know when, or whether, I will ever see Dungannon again, but my recollections of it will always be most delightful. Your Aunt may well enjoy the generous satisfaction of having been instrumental in conferring a great deal of happiness during the last six months. But to return to that day (I don't know that I have anything else to write about)—could it have been sweeter? It was equal, at least, to any other day we have spent there, plus the music, which I did enjoy exceedingly. No, it was sweeter than that even, by the increase of my love for you, Darling, since we last met. May it ever be so, each day in your company sweeter than the last, as long as my love is susceptible of increase! I must not forget the small difference of the strawberries too, particularly the second saucer.

But there was one thing to be subtracted from the superior enjoyment of the day, & that was Miss Sue's absence. I am sure you must have told her already how much she missed; tell her for sure that happy as I was, I was not too happy to miss her or to wish for her. Miss Sue's unselfish love for you & sincere interest & sympathy in your happiness are a source of real enjoyment to me; I hope I may have abundant opportunity of witnessing & enjoying it. Tell her I am very sorry that I will not be able to see her again before she leaves the City. Do tell the Johnsons the same thing; I really long to see them before they leave. Who knows what may take place before we ever meet again in Charleston.

I heard yesterday from home. All as well as usual, & send much love to you. Mattie had gone to Clarendon with little Mack continuing to improve. Dr Bratton's Reg't is full, & he is Colonel.

They had heard of your sister Martha's letter to Mr Robertson & were hoping that you <u>might</u> go there. I wonder when it will be practicable for you to pay them a visit. I know they would enjoy it above all things. Would not that furlough of thirty days come in nicely sometime this Summer? You would be surprised to see me walking into your shop some morning to buy a pound of sugar. I will promise, if possible, to seize a more appropriate opportunity & catch you in the garden, when the customers won't be in the way.

The General is publishing sanitary rules & suggestions which does not look like abandoning this country. I suppose we will remain here until the Enemy compels some other disposition of us. Col Stevens has written to request that we be transferred to Genl Capers'[1] command, if the exigencies of the service permit it; but I don't suppose there is any prospect of it. Don't say anything about it. Genl Capers is near Savannah.

Our flowers are fast fading; I am touching mine now, & the odor is still sweet enough to remind me of Dungannon & you. I believe some philosophers say that the sense of smell recalls associations more strongly than any other. Excuse repetition, but I find myself constantly living over the events of that day. Sometimes I stand & look at the sunset over the Reserve, by your side; sometimes I sit & listen to the music & remember how much sweeter even that was after you came in & sat by me; and sometimes I am with you, & am quite happy enough, without any extraneous aids to happiness.

I have no time to write more.

Love to your Mother & all.

Yours affectionately

W. P. DuBose

1. In 1861 Francis Withers Capers (1819–92) was commissioned as a brigadier general of the Georgia militia. He served as superintendent of Georgia Military Institute and the Citadel (1853–59) and was the brother of General/Bishop Ellison Capers. See *South Carolina Genealogies*, 1:359.

Holcombe Legion

May 21st 1862

I am anxiously expecting, Dearest, to hear of your safe arrival in Anderson. Amo Coffin[1] whom I saw one or two days ago told me that he had seen you safe as far as Branchville, and Mr. Hume took great pleasure the other day in informing me that he had heard of your safe arrival in Columbia. So you see that I have followed you part of the way at any rate. I have heard nothing since then though, and am anxious to receive your first impressions of your new home.

I paid a very pleasant visit to the Marions on Monday. I only spoke to the Captain[2] who was just starting to meet the Johns Island faction of the Company which is at last reunited; but spent the day with my other friends there, who gave me a warm welcome. Gadsden told me that his mother & sisters had gone up & seemed as anxious as I was to hear something further. We concocted half a dozen pleasant little excursions to Anderson together, but could come to no more definite arrangement than the mutual promise to give each other timely warning of any attempt at a furlough.

Amo came to form the Company the day I was there. They are pleasantly situated and seem to be having a good time.

We are expecting to be ordered to Loganville. I am indifferent about the change now that Dungannon is deserted; if we go, I promise you an occasional rose leaf from the garden, as a memento of "the days that are no more."[3]

By the by, I wish this Court Martial[4] had come off when you were, or might have been, at Dungannon. While I am "in detached service" I am relieved from duty here, & could spend every night away if I wished.[5] How sweet it w'd be to spend every evening at Dungannon with you without the prospect of a fifteen mile ride after 11 o.c.

But the idea of indulging in such fancies with you in Anderson! I wonder what you are doing up there. Be sure & tell me all about yourself, the unpleasant as well as the pleasant things of your situation. Tell me too how fast you are improving; I don't think you were looking perfectly well when you left.

I wrote to you some days ago & directed as you instructed me. You must excuse my letters during the session of the Court Martial; it is new to me & gives me a good deal of trouble. Fortunately I have received an admirable sectry [secretary], who relieves me of most of the writing of wh[ich] there is a great deal.

Sunday May 25th

I would commence a new letter to you, Darling, but wish to prove to you that I have at least made an effort to write to you during the long interval since my last letter. The Court Martial of which I am a member did not get fairly to work until Wednesday (not having a quorum), since which time I have had scarcely a moment of my own. Besides the most incessant & trying work in the Court from 10 to 3 o.c. daily, which of course is very exhausting, think of having between eighty & one hundred pages of foolscap[6] of Proceedings to copy in four days; and then arranging cases, summoning witnesses, &c & c. Fortunately, as I said, I have an admirable clerk who does the greater part of the writing, but I have to be with him when it is done in the afternoon & at night & I am generally writing and helping until 1 o.c. at night. This may last several weeks so you must make allowances for me. And beg Miss Sue's pardon for defrauding her so long of her promised letter; don't let her think I don't wish to write to her. I would almost prefer her believing me an advocate of drunkenness, I believe.

Today is a sweet day of rest to me, in spite of a cold gloomy rain which is lasting the day out. We have had services notwithstanding. We are encamped near a church which we use every Sunday.

But I am talking about nothing but myself. Your sweet letter came to hand on Thursday & is a great comfort to me. I am glad your journey was accomplished so successfully & that you are as comfortable as you represent yourself. I know you have been working hard and hope you are beginning to rest now. The letter you wrote me on the eve of leaving Charleston was quite a cheerful one, although it was written at that unlawful hour. I will have to issue "orders" against such hours in future—your health & strength are more to me than letters. The fact of your going, & the sweet, affectionate Goodbye were what made me sad, together with the knowledge that you were very far sadder than your letter indicated.

The thought of your love for me becomes sweeter to me every day—until sometimes I feel that I would be dwelling too much upon it, if it were not that I believe that God in his mercy daily opens my eyes more and more to His own infinitely greater & more gracious love. "We love Him because He first loved us."[7] How, as the Christian life progresses, does God's love for us swallow up every other thought! It is the one thing that never changes, and the thought of which <u>must</u>, under all circumstances, give strength & comfort.

Remember me to the Gadsdens. I am glad they are settled at last, and that Thomas knew nothing of their troubles until they were over, as he could not help them. Is Miss Carrie Winthrop with you; if so remember me to her as warmly as she will approve of. With her & the Gadsdens, I should think you & Miss Sue would not lack society. What other friends are with you?

I feel a strong & constant longing to spend this day with you. It is just such a gloomy day, as I like to spend in a comfortable room in good company. When the cheerlessness without, like a dark background, brings out in strong relief the peace & comfort within. I have no doubt you are enjoying a fine today in your Northern latitude, if there is such a thing to be had in the general scarcity. However whether you have one or not, I suppose I am at liberty to put a fire in the picture which <u>will</u> come up to me of a cozy room somewhere, with you, the fire, and a vacant easy chair for me. May the day soon come, Darling, when peace shall be restored, and with it, free scope for the realization of all such happy dreams or fancies! By the by, I had a sweet dream about you last night, which I cannot recall now.

I am going to evening service.

It was raining too much to go to the church, so we had a smaller service in the Col's tent, and then sang until it is too late to write anymore by daylight. Mr. McCollough is going to leave us; his congregations in Union & Spartanburg have grown so large and are so anxious for him to return he thinks it is his duty to do so. Mr. Irwin has also determined to leave & resume his school. The loss to our mess will be a very great one. I have heard nothing more of moving to Loganville.

Dick sends a great deal of love to you, begs to be remembered to Miss Sue & sends "most friendly regards" to the Seabrooks.

You had better steal a little piece of that rye patch and make a flower garden out of it, if you have time for it. You might bring some roses to your cheeks, even if you fail to raise them on your beds. As for the lawyers shop, now that I am turning lawyer, it would be the pleasantest place I can think of to hang my shingle.

John Taylor[8] was defeated by one or two votes for a Lieutenancy in his Company. It was a very ungrateful thing on the part of the Company, for which they had no excuse, as I have no doubt his opponent is an inferior man. I see very little of him, but have no doubt he finds it lonesome without his Father & other friends who have left.

And now, Darling Goodbye. I hope you will not have so long a time to wait for the next letter. Give much love to your Mother & Sister Martha & the children. Write as often as you can. Do as you would be, not as you are, done by.

Yours most affectionately
W. P. DuBose

Tell Miss Sue I advocate the case of drunkenness tomorrow. Give her a great deal of love.

1. Amory Coffin Jr. served as a private and sergeant major in Captain Parker's Company (Marion Artillery). He was probably the son of Dr. Amory Coffin (1814–84). See Compiled Service Records, Capt. Parker's Co. (Marion Artillery), South Carolina Light Artillery, M267, roll 103; Waring, *History of Medicine in South Carolina*, 215; Hewett, *South Carolina Confederate Soldiers*, 96.

2. This likely refers to Capt. John Gadsden King (1831–1906), Company F, First South Carolina Artillery. See Compiled Service Records, First South Carolina Artillery, Regiment M267, roll 61; DeSaussure, *Lowcountry Carolina Genealogies*, 611.

3. This is a line from the poem "Tears, Idle Tears," by Alfred Lord Tennyson. See Gardner, *New Oxford Book of English Verse, 1250–1950*, 647.

4. This is a military tribunal, especially for the trial of soldiers or sailors.

5. DuBose was assigned to serve on a local court-martial case.

6. This is a standard sheet of writing paper sized thirteen by sixteen inches.

7. 1 John 4:19.

8. John Taylor (1842–1912) was the son of Capt. Alexander Ross Taylor (1812–88) of the Congaree Cavaliers. He "joined his father's company, then Co. B (cavalry), Holcombe Legion, afterwards Co. D, 7th South Carolina Cavalry; was successfully corporal, first sergeant, lieutenant, and first lieutenant." In 1870 he married Eliza M. Coffin. See *South Carolina Genealogies*, 4:273–74, 281–82; *WPA Cemetery Index*.

Holcombe Legion
June 1st 1862

The trial, Darling, of which I wrote in my last letter, & . . . have so long dreaded to think of at last come. God has not seen fit to spare me this last affliction. Our dear Mother, after having been so long in mercy spared to us has been at last called to her reward, & I have enjoyed neither the privilege of receiving her last blessing nor the [sad] satisfaction of mingling my tears with those of the bereaved ones at home. You too, who [would] . . . sympathize so deeply with me, are far away beyond my reach.

And yet I cannot but [forget] myself in the thought of the affliction of my sisters, who have in so short a time been deprived . . . presence of two such parents. It is [too] painful to attempt to realize the . . . that has come over our happy home & the feeling of desolation of [those who] are there to miss the loved . . . taken from their midst. Oh [darling], you never knew our home as it used to be, but I know you can sympathize with those who have been so suddenly deprived of all upon whom they have been accustomed to lean, & for whom they had learned to live. Write to [them]. They do not doubt the sincerity & depth of your sympathy, [and] will value your letters. Write to Sister Anne too, even if she does not write to you first. She has suffered deeply during the past few months: the three persons upon whom her happiness mainly depended have all been taken from her, and I know she feels very desolate. You have read or heard several of her letters and need not be afraid of intruding upon her grief. If you do write to her, tell her I begged you to do so. You might write to Sister first & her afterwards. I hope [Darling] I am not asking too much of [you] but I know better than you do how much they would value your letters.

I wrote to you about the first information I got of Mother's sickness. Yesterday morning I got a letter saying that she was no better & [suffering] a great deal of pain. In this letter . . . told me to write & tell you about [her] sickness & to beg you to write to her; they all send love to you. Yesterday afternoon I received the telegram which I enclose. I am anxious to hear further particulars, but am afraid they will be expecting me at home & will not write. Situated as I am, I . . . grateful that I did not hear of Mother's extreme illness before I received the news of her death. How much harder would it have been to [accept] a call to her dying bed! . . . calls us a deeply afflicted [family]! But God has vouchsafed us His blessing which alone outweighs all His chastenings. And that is the blessed [assurance] that all whom he has . . . us, no matter how sudden [and] painful the method of his visitation, . . . has taken to Himself. May we who survive all [join] there in those . . . mansions which they now inhabit.

I go to the Court Martial again tomorrow morning.

Good bye my own Darling. God bless & keep you.

Yours affectionately
W. P. DuBose

Holcombe Legion
June 18th 1862

My dearest Miss Nannie

Miss Sue's letter & your own note reached me yesterday. I was anxious to answer hers immediately but haven't time for it tonight. I am still busy with the Court Martial, which we hope will be dissolved about Monday or Tuesday. Thank Miss Sue for me until I have time to do so for myself.

I don't know whether I told you the circumstances of my Mother's death. She was quite unwell on Friday morning, as she had been for some time. Sister Jane was to have gone that morning to Columbia to have her likeness taken for Mr. Means, but had given up the idea on account of Mother's sickness. When Mother found it out she insisted upon her going, which she did to return on Saturday. On Friday night Mother told sister who was sleeping in her room not to have her waked next morning, as long as she continued to sleep. Sister had the room darkened, & lay awake most of the night. During the night Mother asked for a glass of water, thanked her for it, & when she had drank, placed the tumbler on the table in reach of her. Towards morning Sister fell asleep & did not wake until after daylight. The room was dark & Mother seemed to be asleep. She waited & waited and after a while becoming alarmed at the stillness went & touched her hand. It was cold. The spirit that had occupied that frail tenement had taken its departure apparently without an effort or a struggle. "The earthly house of this tabernacle"[1] was discarded. She had gone to inhabit the "house not made with hands, eternal in the heavens." Before many days the mourning of the sad survivors was changed into gratitude that she had been spared the heavy trials that were even then at the door.

Beverly Means died on the field of battle the morning after his wound— a triumphant Christian death.[2] Truly God does take His own way of answering our prayers. The Chaplain, I have from another source, said it was the most remarkable deathbed scene that was ever witnessed on a field of battle.

He was not a man for such displays—it was a reproof to our ignorance & blindness from our Heavenly Father.

Col. Bratton's[3] fate is still wrapped in mystery. He had an artery cut & left by himself after the fighting was over to look for a hospital. Nothing is known of him, though diligent search was made for him. He has never been mentioned among the officers taken by the enemy. We can only wait in patience, & trust in Him who has never yet failed us. I believe that our prayers for him have been heard, & that in some way or other God will manifest to us his love & pity in this as in other cases.

Never in all my life have I suffered such anguish, sometimes torture, of mind as during these past two or three weeks. What must they have suffered at home.

I must go to bed.

We have not left our summer camp yet, but must in a very short time now expect to meet the enemy. For the sake of those I love, may God spare my life!

Good night Darling. Do not [antedate] the day of woe. When it comes, I know you will have strength to bear it. Love to all, including the children.

Yrs affectionately
W. P. DuBose

1. 2 Corinthians 5:1.

2. Sgt. Maj. Beverly Means, Sixth South Carolina Infantry, died on June 1, 1862, of wounds received at the battle of Seven Pines. See Compiled Service Records, Sixth South Carolina Infantry, M267, roll 209.

3. "Dr. John Bratton was temporarily in command of Jenkins' Brigade at the Battle of Seven Pines (31 May 1862), where he was wounded and captured by the enemy. Bratton was held prisoner at Fort Monroe in Chesapeake Bay until 1863, when he was exchanged and rejoined his regiment." See Bailey, *Biographical Directory of the South Carolina Senate,* 1:180–81.

Charleston S.C.
June 18th 1862

You will be surprised Dearest, to see me writing from Charleston. Nevertheless I am. I came yesterday to bring to Genl Pemberton[1] the proceedings of our Court Martial which adjourned sine die on Monday last, very much to my relief and gratification. I will return to camp tomorrow morning and resume my duties as Adjutant, which are certainly much pleasanter than those of Judge Advocate. You must excuse me, Darling, for having neglected you so much during the past few weeks. I do feel very grateful for your love, & for the pleasure which my letters give you, but I have had much to occupy me during that time.

One strong reason which induced me to bring instead of sending my papers was the fact that Johnson is in town. He is waiting for orders & keeping batchelors [sic] hall with his brother Joseph. I am here with him & enjoy it very much of course.

The city is mourning today for loss of many valuable lives in the late gallant fight on James Island.[2] We seem destined to be the last troops ordered to the scene of active operations. I think the main reason is that our cavalry is needed where we are.

Charleston looks very desolate, & this house especially looks dreary. I have not ventured to go round to Tradd St. Oh for some evenings there such as I have spent! The very idea of spending an evening in town anywhere else is painful.

My sister did not go to Richmond. Poor girls! I hear they have borne their trials nobly, but are looking very badly. It seems that Mr. Means did not die before his friends left him. He was incapable of being moved & so they fixed him comfortably in one of the enemies' tents, & when they retired, left him to their tender mercies. He must have died very soon after, though, although they say that he revived a good deal at the last & the surgeon even thought that there was a faint hope of his recovering. So his fate is still in suspense.

There are reports that the Burnside fleet[3] is soon to appear before Charleston to cooperate with the land movements on James Island. Prisoners say that they have been expecting the attack on the fort to begin everyday.

I must go now to attend to some business & get my passport[4] for tomorrow morning. I will write again in a day or so. Give much love to Miss Sue, & all the family, including the children.

I am afraid my visit to Anderson is indefinitely postponed by this movement upon Charleston. It is a great comfort to me to know that I am so constantly in your mind & prayers.

I don't believe I even told you that we had heard by flag of truce that Col. Bratton was a prisoner & doing well.

Yours very affectionately
W. P. DuBose

1. Gen. John Clifford Pemberton (1814–81) was commander of the Department of South Carolina, Georgia, and Florida. See Sifakis, *Who Was Who in the Confederacy,* 220–21.

2. DuBose is referring to the June 16, 1862, battle of Secessionville on James Island, at which Confederate forces stopped a Union advance on Charleston. The battle resulted in 683 Union casualties (107 dead) and 204 Confederate casualties (52 dead). See *Official Records Army,* 14:41–104.

3. Union forces under Maj. Gen. Ambrose Everett Burnside (1824–81) captured New Bern, North Carolina, on March 14 and Washington, North Carolina, on March 20, 1862. On July 6, 1862, Burnside sailed with reinforcements for the Army of the Potomac on the James River. See Long, *Civil War Almanac,* 184, 187, 237; Warner, *Generals in Blue,* 57–58.

4. The "passport" to which DuBose refers is actually a pass, a written leave of absence from a military post or station for a brief period.

Camp Hope
July 13th 1862

The tin box made its welcome appearance a few days ago, Dearest, but not until Mr. Seabrook had already started on his return to Anderson. Much to my disappointment I did not see him at all. I was very anxious to hear his account of you & your surroundings in Anderson. I think he left earlier than he had intended. Dick saw him for a little while & says that he was in high spirits, quite enthusiastic about Anderson & its attractions. By the by Dick has been detached temporarily as a surgeon to a Virginia Battery stationed on Mr. Seabrook's place;[1] [I] hope it will not be very long as I feel quite lost without him—helpless, he would say. The contents of the box were all very nice, particularly your sister Martha's cake, which was especially admired. The apples were quite ripe by the time they arrived. Tell Miss Kate that the hand she had had in the gloves did not make them a particle the less welcome. I value such evidences of her remembrance; and however sweet such tokens are from you, I certainly do not <u>need</u> any additional proofs of yours. They came in very good time, as I wanted a cool pair, and are not as much too long as you imagine. I have been long intending a visit to the Marions and Miss Sue's package revived my resolution, so Rutledge & I went down on Saturday & spent a delightful day with them. My fellow students were all well & seemed delighted to see me. Their mess is composed of five seminary students, Stuart, Willie Martin & Simmons—a very congenial crowd. Tom

Gadsden looks well & cheerful; how I wish I could have him with me. It does me good to be with him for even a few hours. He & I, of course, talked over our visit to Anderson together, and, distant & improbable as it may be, were happy in the very contemplation of such happiness. I wish I could foresee the speedy realization of our desires, but it is hard to see a day ahead. If we are ever to have furloughs it seems to me that this is the time, when everything is so quiet along the coast & there is so little probability of any movement on the part of the enemy. Tell Miss Sue if furloughs were to be had for the asking, I would find no difficulty in pocketing my principles & begging for one. The Col. went off a day or two ago for twelve days, the happiest man you ever saw, or will see until you see me in Anderson. He had had a severe cold & cough for some time, which assisted him to get off. It is the first leave he has had for over a day.

But to return to the Marions. The Capt. was absent most of the day, returning in the afternoon, so that I saw very little of him. I did not see Lt. Lowndes[2] myself, but Gadsden delivered the package safely. On my way back I met your Uncle Edward, the first time I have seen him for a long time. He does not seem to think that the family are very well satisfied at Clarkesville; I wish they were in Anderson. Dick got a very pleasant letter from Mrs. Peronneau some time ago, which he valued very much. Do remember to give my love whenever you write. I am glad that your Mother has gone to your aunt & cousins. I know what they must be suffering.

Capt. Bratton, Col. B's only brother, was killed in the Battle of Richmond.[3] He was very kind in sending us information about his brother & Bev. Means. We [have] heard more of the latter; in fact, I [feel] so confident of his death that I never look for news from him. We will probably never hear anything more of him, & the very place where he has been buried will remain unknown. Such is war! Oh for a perpetual end of it! I do not like to realize the fact that I am engaged in a profession whose avowed object is to destroy my fellow man, & create widows & orphans throughout the land. I feel no desire to be in a battle, and would be perfectly satisfied for peace to come before I win my laurels. If fighting were ever justifiable though, certainly that in which we are engaged is so.

Amo Coffin has been made Sergt. Major of the Marions. I hear he is very highly thought of. When the appointment was to be made, the majority of the Co., fearing that the Captain might be deterred from appointing him by the connection between them, signed a written request that he should do so. I saw him & he sent much love to you all.

I have not heard from home since my last letter to you; I would like very much to be there if only for a few days.

I think we have done with Edisto now—if the enemy are content to let us alone from that quarter. It is too late in the season to risk the heat, fatigue, & exposure of an expedition there after this. Please remember me particularly to the Gadsdens and to any other friends of mine in your neighborhood. I received sister Anne's letter enclosed in yours. It expresses nothing more than I know they all feel. You will not be allowed to feel like a stranger long when you go to Roseland; they are all prepared to receive you as a sister. I wish you could be there now for a while. I think the pleasure of becoming acquainted with you would be a relief and recreation to them. I wish you could have known Miss Emma Means; before we were engaged, she used to tell me I must be sure to make Miss Nannie love her. Good night, Darling. God bless & keep you, & grant that in His own good time this painful separation my end! Much love to your sisters, a kiss for Margie & Lise.[4]

Yours most affectionately

W. P. DuBose

1. The battery is probably the Turner Light Artillery, which was stationed in the Second Military District. See *Official Records Army*, 14:576.

2. This was Bvt. Second Lt. Henry Deas Lowndes (1829–95). See Compiled Service Records, Capt. Parker's Company (Marion Artillery), South Carolina Light Artillery, M267, roll 104; WPA Cemetery Index.

3. First Lt. William M. Bratton, of Company B, Eleventh Alabama Infantry, was killed at the battle of Frazier's Farm on June 30, 1862. See Compiled Service Records, Eleventh Alabama Infantry Regiment, M374, roll 25; Bratton, "Letters," 35, Southern Historical Collection, University of North Carolina, Chapel Hill (hereafter SHC).

4. Margie was probably Margaret Peronneau (1849–80), the daughter of Nannie's brother William Henry Peronneau, and Lise was likely her sister. Margaret Peronneau married William Edward Breese (1848–1917). See Patey, *Whaley Family*, 198.

∞

Camp Hope

July 16th 1862

As I am alone tonight Dearest, I will have recourse to this infallible cure for loneliness, which has never yet failed me. Not that I am really suffering under that malady, nor that I take my pen as I would medicine. I disclaim both.

I write so irregularly that I think it must puzzle you as much to antici-pate the arrival of my letters as it does astronomers to compute the periodi-cal return of most comets. If it produces the same effect upon you as it does upon me, you expect a letter everyday and are disappointed every time that one fails to arrive. I don't know how often I write, but I hope I treat you as well as you do me.

I think if I could get to Anderson for a few days, I would not find it hard to join you on your morning walks. I would have to economize my time, & under such circumstances hope that I would be able to sacrifice even my morning nap to the pleasure of being with you. I don't think it possible though to sleep better than I do here. My bed is a plank, or several of them, with half a dozen blankets on it, and a harder bed to get up from I never slept on. We have been getting more & more comfortably fixed, so that all I can find to complain of now is the impossibility of seeing you. By long use I have become accustomed to the absence from home, and since the painful neces-sity of having to remain here when I was really needed there, I have become reconciled to it again, sweet as it would be to see my sisters even now. But I do not find that use accustoms or reconciles me to separation from you. It is natural for a man to give up the home of his youth, & make a new one for himself amid other scenes & associations; and Nature prepares him for it, even though that home be as sweet as mine has been. But the relation be-tween us is one which makes separation abnormal & unnatural, and hard to be reconciled to, except on the consideration that it has been ordained by the same Providence that first brought us together.

Dick Dwight was detailed to act as surgeon to a Virginia company, but was released by the arrival of the regular physician, and availed himself of the opportunity of running over to St. Johns. On the way he met Dr. Logan coming to get him to go to the Washington Artillery, so he is to return on Monday & leave again on Tuesday, for I don't know how long a time. They accuse him of having an object in going to St. Johns, but I don't know that he can be convicted of it, as his home is there. He & I are very intimate, but he has never made a confidant of me, and I never invite confidence on such subjects. Don't say anything about it.

I have not heard from Johnson lately. I hear he is on James Island.

It looks as if Lincoln is going to succeed in raising his 300,000 more men and the struggle may become greater & fiercer than ever, but still I have a feeling that peace is not very far off. [Intervention] is obliged to come soon, & the war is too large already to be very long. However I do not waste much time speculating on the future. "Sufficient unto the day is the evil thereof"[1] is especially true of these evil times. The visit to Anderson is the only future thing in this world that I allow my mind to dwell upon. When I have attained that of which there is no immediate prospect then maybe I will indulge myself with anticipations of peace & its joys, of which that will be the fore-taste.

July 17th. As a visitation for calling myself lonely last night, several friends came in and so retarded my letter that I was unable to finish it. This evening we march down to Wiltown nearly four miles & let the men go in bathing. Seven miles on such a warm evening (so called) over a dusty sandy road is no joke. Wiltown is a charming place for bathing & I have gone there several times lately for that purpose. The Bluff & the view from it are beautiful & the water fresh & of a delightful temperature with something of a beach. I have often wished that I could sit with you on that bluff at sunset and look at the exquisite scenery. It reminds me of poor John Elliott; no doubt he often sat there with his sweet wife, happy & unconscious of the sad bereavement in store for him. I have been several times on the point of writing to him & have not done so yet. No doubt this blow has done much to wean his affections from the things of this world & to fix them upon things above. He is a man to be affected thus by affliction.

I am afraid Mr. Trapier's scheme will not succeed. In the first place I hope that the war will be over before he gets it through Congress; in the second place I don't think he will get it through Congress if the war isn't over. The difficulties after that need not be considered, as he will never get to them.

I have never read Dr. Arnold's Life,[2] though I have had the book a long time, & have been familiar with & a great admirer of the Dr.'s character. He is one of the characters that it "pays" to make a study of. The Life of Bunyan[3] of which I spoke was not his autobiography "Grace Abounding," although composed in great part of extracts from it. Tell Miss Sue that the reason Dick enjoyed the "Reveries" so much is that, though they were those of a batche-lor [sic], yet they were all "dreams of fair woman." I will testify to it, that he will be a model husband. Dick is a rare fellow. Strangers do not appreciate at once his strong sense, sound judgment, warm affections, elevated & unflinch-ing spirit, unflagging energy, and—I might make the enumeration still longer, but that will do. He is a great politician & student of newspapers, takes decid-ed views & can hold his own against any officer on our line. He glories in victories & is not cast down for a minute by the most serious reverse. He is the most universally cheerful man you ever saw, incapable of being cast down by the little troubles that annoy most men. But the characteristic of the man is his pure, enthusiastic & unchanging admiration for women. Besides all this he is one whose character & life are pervaded by genuine Christian principle.

There is another man here whom I have gradually learned to admire & like more & more and that is Rutledge. He is candid & blunt to a fault, but he is a high toned, generous, modest gentleman. Though I have so many good friends, I have but few intimate ones, & have had very few I think. I could almost count them upon one hand.

I feel very grateful to Miss Carrie Pinckney for her sympathy; I feel a strong desire to know more of her & hope that I may do so one of these days. I have known many persons to last a long time whose health is no better than hers. Remember me affectionately to Miss Carrie Winthrop, the Gadsdens & our Georgia cousins when you write. I saw several notices of Hayne's gallantry.[4] Tell Margie I am very much obliged to her for her offering, but for the present at least I am in no need of a mosquito net. Where we are we are perfectly free from all winged insects. I have several times almost regretted that I had had no occasion to use your helmet. I have never told you that before I had read the book Miss Sue gave me, "Cause & Contract," it was borrowed by a friend & ruined so that he threw it away & tried to get another but failed. I was very sorry to lose a present from her. You need not tell her.

I have heard quite lately from home. They are as usual. Sister Jane had not yet returned home. Poor girl. I expect that the hope to which she clung so strongly is fast fading.

We find no difficulty in keeping our table tolerably well supplied—have been very far from coming down to parched corn. I [am] afraid you find great difficulty in this respect. You tell me all the pleasures & none of the difficulties or inconveniences of your situation.

But I expect you are getting tired of this long drawn out epistle (that is a story). Give very much love to Miss Sue, your sister Martha & Mother if she has returned. Kiss Margie & Lise for me. And believe me Darling

Yrs most affectionately

W. P. DuBose

1. Matthew 6:34.

2. This is the biography of Dr. Thomas Arnold (1795–1842), British schoolmaster and historian, "portrayed as a leading character in the novel, *Tom Brown's Schooldays.*" See Stanley, *Life and Correspondence of Thomas Arnold.*

3. This possibly refers to *The Life of John Bunyan Written by Himself,* published in 1845. John Bunyan (1628–88) was a Christian preacher and author of *The Pilgrim's Progress* and an autobiography, *Grace Abounding to the Chief of Sinners.*

4. Pvt. Edmund T. Shubrick Hayne (1843–62) was a member of the color guard of the First Regiment of South Carolina Infantry when he was killed at the battle of Gaines Mill on June 27, 1862. See Compiled Service Records, First Regiment, South Carolina Infantry (McCreary's) (First Provisional Army), M267, roll 129; *South Carolina Genealogies*, 2:325.

Camp Hope
July 18th 1862

I have just time for a hurried note, Darling, to tell you that we leave for Virginia on Sunday morning.

The order came this morning just after I had dispatched a letter to you. Gen. Evans is to go on with a Brigade consisting of the Legion, Means,[1] Gadberry's[2] & Benbow's[3] Regts., Leake's (Va.)[4] & Bryce's Batteries[5] & the Rebel Troop.[6]

I am going to try to get off tomorrow & join the command as it passes through Winnsboro, as we are to take that route. In this way I will have [a] day at home and be able to tell . . . [goodbye] at least. I am by no means [certain] though that the Genl. will permit [me] to do so.

I wish we could have had a little more time to prepare, and unfortunately too Dick is away. Still more unfortunately for the Colonel. Besides that, a considerable no. of our men had just received furloughs for which they have been sighing for the last six months; these have been recalled.

And so we have at last been called from our quiet retreat into the active scenes of war & are about to taste some of its hard realities. Well I am ready I trust for the change, even though it thrusts our longed for meeting still further into the uncertain future. Nothing short of peace, or a state of things preliminary to it will bring me back, I suppose. Well, the reunion will only be the sweeter when it comes, if God spares us to experience its joys. If He does not He will bestow the strength requisite for the trial of a little longer separation.

Tell all goodbye for me, particularly Miss Sue, & kiss the girls for me. I will see some of my friends I trust in Richmond. What our exact destination is I do not know.

And now Darling, I must say good bye. I feel very grateful that [you] have strength and courage, so have. . . . May God bless you & . . . that every change may serve [to] draw us nearer to Him.

[Letter is not signed.]

1. John Hugh Means (1812–62) was a signer of the Ordinance of Secession from Fairfield District. His wife was Susan Rebecca Stark. "He enlisted in the 17th South Carolina infantry and was made colonel of the regiment. He was mortally wounded in the Second Battle of Manassas . . . died on August 28, 1862." See May, *South Carolina Secedes*, 183.

2. James M. Gadberry (ca. 1817–62), a signer of the Ordinance of Secession from Union District, raised the Eighteenth (Infantry) Regiment, South Carolina Volunteers. He was killed in action at Second Manassas. See May, *South Carolina Secedes*, 147–48.

3. Henry Laurens Benbow (1829–1907) of Sumter District and Clarendon County was colonel of the Twenty-third South Carolina Infantry. See Bailey, *Biographical Directory of the South Carolina Senate*, 1:127–28.

4. This was named for Capt. Walter Daniel Leake (1813–73). See Compiled Service Records, Captain Leake's Company, Virginia Light Artillery (Turner Artillery), M382, roll 33; *Official Records Army*, 14:586; Tyler, *Encyclopedia of Virginia Biography*, vol. 1, 105.

5. This should be "Boyce's" Battery, which was named for its commander, Capt. Robert Boyce (1825–63). See Compiled Service Records, Macbeth Light Artillery (South Carolina Light Artillery), M267, roll 99; *Official Records Army*, 14:586; WPA Cemetery Index.

6. This was an independent cavalry company commanded by Capt. John Jenkins (1824–1905). It later became Company I, Third South Carolina Cavalry Regiment. See Compiled Service Records, Third South Carolina Cavalry Regiment, M267, roll 15; WPA Cemetery Index, 166.

Roseland
July 23rd / 62

You will be surprised, Darling, to see that I am still at home. While it is of course a great satisfaction to have been here so much longer than I expected, my visit has been a very sad one, besides being very unsatisfactory. I attended this afternoon the funeral of one of my little nephews, Col. Bratton's youngest son,[1] nearly a year old. He was sick only two or three days. The other is far from well too. They were both remarkably fine fellows.

The day after my arrival we sent for Sister Jane, who was still with Mrs. Means, and she arrived on Tuesday evening, looking badly, but not worse than I had expected. Her long & distressing suspense was ended some days ago by the positive & final intelligence of Bev's death, from the Confederate surgeon who remained with the wounded & was afterwards, liberated. It is wonderful with what tenacity she had clung to hope even up to that time.

She says that comforting as was his dying testimony, she did not need it to assure her of his readiness to die; he had been writing in the same way for months. And others bear testimony to the same fact. All the others are pretty well.

When I reached Columbia, I heard that the Legion would scarcely pass for three or four days, as there were several Regts ahead of it awaiting transportation. Of course, I regretted at once that I had not remained one day longer in Anderson.

On Tuesday I heard to my surprise that they had gone by the N.E.R.R. This has left me quite in a quandary, as I find it impossible to get transportation for my horse. I wrote yesterday to a friend in Columbia to make arrangements for me if possible, but I have been disappointed in hearing from him today. I am in doubt whether I should go on tomorrow without the horse, or try it one day longer. It was a great pity that the Legion could not come by this route, as hundreds of wives, mothers & friends had come to Columbia & other points to bid their goodbye, & bring provisions &c for the journey.

I have lived over & over again that sweet visit to Anderson, & feel very grateful that I was enabled to see you before leaving for Virginia. It would be ungrateful to regret its shortness. I was very glad to meet your brother & sister Martha at Belton, & to be able to see so much of them.

I will write next from Richmond. You had better direct there to the care of Col. Stevens.

I wish you could have come with me & spent some time with my sisters; they are all anxious to know you.

I have heard nothing of our destination, but am inclined to believe that we will remain near Richmond. I have a great many friends there so that there will be no danger of falling into the hospitals in case of wound or sickness. Give much love to all the family and kiss the girls for me.

Excuse brevity, and believe me, Darling

Unchangeably & affectionately yrs

W. P. DuBose

All send much love.

1. This was probably John Bratton, Jr., who is buried at St. John's Cemetery in Winnsboro, South Carolina. See Bratton, "Letters" [ii], SHC.

Richmond
July 29 1862

It is past 10 O.C., Darling, and we are to be up and preparing to march by 4½ O.C. tomorrow morning, so I have but little time to give you any detailed account of myself. I left home on Friday morning and reached this city last night in a rain. On my way to camp I passed by my friends the Dudleys,[1] & was taken violent possession of & detained through the night. This morning I went to church, where I encountered about a dozen of my old University friends & was again pounced upon & captured. Mr. & Mrs. Haskell[2] are at Mr. Dudley's nursing their two sons John & Joe[3] former recovering from the amputation of his right arm at the shoulder joint and the latter from Typhoid fever. At church I met Genl Kershaw,[4] Moultrie Dwight & others.

This afternoon I reported for duty. We are a little way out of Richmond, but expect to march early in the morning about eight miles to join Gen. Longstreet's Division.[5] So there is no immediate prospect of joining Jackson.[6] You had better direct to the Holcombe Legion, Evans' Brigade, Longstreet Division, near Richmond.

I received two letters from you this evening, one directed to Richmond, the other to Adams Run dated 17th. I believe there is one missing still, but I am very happy to have these two. I am very glad that I saw you, Darling. It would have been hard to have had to come away without telling you goodbye, and the recollections of that one evening are a constant source of enjoyment to me. This evening Tom Dudley & I rode to a beautiful place that his father has bought him, just out of town & not very far from our camp. But instead of occupying it with his wife, she is away off in Loudoun County within the enemy's lines with her two little children. She is with her parents & he cannot get to her. He himself is engaged in the Commissary Department in this place. As we sat in a sweet cool room of the deserted cottage, he told me to send you his love & tell you what a happy picture he had drawn of a visit at some future day for you & me to his wife & himself. He was assistant professor at the University when the war broke out, but has made up his mind to study for the ministry, as a good many of my Virginia friends now in the service expect to do when peace is restored.

I did not speak to the Seabrooks[7] at all in the cars, but did so & told them goodbye in Columbia. The cars were very crowded. Between us, I was not struck with Mr. Seabrook's attention to his wife. I would be sorry to think that the day could ever come when I could travel on the same train with you & spend so little time by your side as he did, and then his manner to her is very provoking I think. However a stranger has no right to judge such matters. She understands him I suppose, & is no doubt satisfied. I wonder if anyone will ever accuse me of indifference to you.

Dick has come since I commenced writing & taken away a good deal of the little time I had to spare. He went out to look for me & has just returned after Sunday visits. I enjoyed the service very much this morning in St. Paul's Church, with which I have many delightful associations. I did not forget you in my prayers, you may be sure. I pray for you now Darling, as I pray for myself. May we indeed have strength for our appointed trials! I could not but be touched the other day with a sentiment which Sister Jane expressed, & which I have felt myself. She said she could not help being hopeful all the time, because she felt as if God was trying to see how she would receive the chastening, and that if she would only take it in the right spirit, He would spare her in the end.

I have heard nothing new here. Saw Pres't Davis today in church. There are no end to the Confederate uniforms in the street. They are by far the commonest dress. I am very tired & sleepy & dull so I think I must come to a close. Thank Miss Sue for her affectionate little note & tell her that her handwriting is always a welcome sight. Give her much love, as also the rest of the family & other friends.

I will try to write as often as possible.

Goodbye, Dearest.

Yrs very affectionately

W. P. DuBose

1. Thomas Underwood Dudley (1837–1904) became an Episcopal bishop and chancellor of the University of the South after the war. He was the son of Thomas Underwood Dudley, a prominent Richmond merchant. See *Appleton's Cyclopaedia,* 2:244; Haskell, *Haskell Memoirs,* 145.

2. Charles Thomson Haskell (1802–74) and Sophia Lovell Cheves (1809–81) were from Abbeville District, South Carolina. Seven of their sons served in the Confederate army, and two, William and Charles, were killed in action. John Cheves Haskell (1841–1906) lost his right arm at the battle of Gaines Mill in late June 1862 and later returned to full duty. Joseph Cheves Haskell (1843–1922) joined the army at age seventeen and became an adjutant for E. P. Alexander's Battalion of artillery. See *South Carolina Genealogies,* 1:381; Haskell, *Memoirs,* 103–20; Davidson, *Last Foray,* 208–9; Ferguson, *Abbeville County,* 50.

3. Reference here is to First Lt. John C. Haskell, Company D, First Regiment South Carolina Artillery, and Captain and Asst. Adj. Gen. Joseph C. Haskell, general and staff officers. See Compiled Service Records, First Regiment South Carolina

Artillery, M267, roll 60, and Index to Compiled Service Records Raised Directly by the Confederate Government and of Confederate Officers and Nonregimental Enlisted Men, M818, roll 11.

4. In February 1861 Joseph B. Kershaw was promoted to brigadier general of the First (Kershaw's) Brigade, and in May 1864 he became a major general, commanding the First Division of the First Corps of the Army of Northern Virginia. See Bailey, *Biographical Directory of the South Carolina Senate,* 2:868.

5. Lt. Gen. James Longstreet (1821–1904), a native of Edgefield District, South Carolina, commanded the First Corps of the Army of Northern Virginia following the Seven Days Campaign. See McPherson, *Battle Cry of Freedom,* 471; Warner, *Generals in Gray,* 192–93.

6. Lt. Gen. Thomas Jonathan "Stonewall" Jackson (1824–63) commanded the Second Corps of the Army of Northern Virginia following the Seven Days Campaign. See McPherson, *Battle Cry of Freedom,* 471; Warner, *Generals in Gray,* 151–52.

7. "The Seabrooks" are probably the Reverend Joseph Baynard Seabrook and his (third) wife Martha Catherine Beckett Seabrook. See *South Carolina Genealogies,* 4:218.

Camp Clover
Aug. 7th 1862

The last letter from you, Dearest, was dated July 25th but finished I think on the 26th. I wish you would keep the dates of all that you write, so that we may know if any are lost. I mailed a letter on Friday or Saturday I think giving you some account of our present position. We have been remarkably fortunate so far in losing so few letters. I received a day or two ago the last you wrote me at Adams Run, and am very glad that it was not lost, in spite of your indifference as to its recovery. I went to Richmond to church on Sunday and enjoyed the communion more than I can express. It reminded me forcibly of two previous communions in the same church; one was on the 1st Sunday in October 1856, my first service in Va. sick & a perfect stranger in the state; the other was on Christmas Day 1858, in a great snow storm. They both made a deep impression on me. Mr. Minegerode[1] on Sunday preached an admirable sermon from the text in the history of Gideon in Judges "Faint yet pursuing." When I remember how faint & weak I have been many times during these long intervals, I feel that it is through the grace of God alone that I am "yet pursuing." I felt profoundly humbled & grateful at the recollection of my own wanderings, murmurings & rebellions, & God's forbearance & continued help.

During the communion service a friend, whom I most wished & least expected to see, walked down from the chancel &, without waiting for the conclusion of the service, left the church. His name is Preston,[2] you may have heard me speak of him. I was much disappointed in not seeing him as I don't know where to find him.

We went yesterday to work in the trenches, but had scarcely begun when we were ordered to throw aside the tools & occupy them with more murderous weapons to resist an advance of the enemy. The enemy had taken Malvern Hill[3] seven or eight miles off and might advance further. However they did not, and after occupying the works all day we returned to camp. This morning troops have been going in large numbers down the road, and an attack on our part may be contemplated. We have rations cooked a day ahead but have received no orders to move. All day yesterday the roads were filled with returning exchanged prisoners shouting for Jeff Davis, Dixie, &c., a fine looking set of fellows and happy as they could be. I heard from some of them that Col. Bratton was behind with the officers. I was anxious to go to Richmond today to hunt him up, but cannot go while there is any prospect of our moving. I conversed with some of the exchanged men; they say that there is a great deal of sympathy for us in Baltimore & Washington, but that they were not well treated by the Yankees.

I had the sweetest dream a few nights ago—about being married, a subject on which I do not suffer my mind to rest much in these uncertain times. Generally such dreams, when they do come, which is not often, are marred by some ridiculous inconsistency; but this was a complete & charming little tableau of a scene after the wedding, the next day probably, the impression of which has clung to me through all the heat & distractions of the past two days. It has been very warm for two or three days & today is particularly so. A battle such a day as this would be no fake [sic]. If you could only spend a day in camp, even when a battle is most imminent, you would be effectually cured of anything like excitement or nervousness on the subject. Everything looks so calm & indifferent that war & concomitants are banished from the mind. Not there is any prospect of a battle here. I don't think that there is the slightest probability of one, unless a small part of our forces undertake to dislodge the enemy from Malvern Hill, in which case we will hardly become involved, as there are a great many troops ahead of us.

7th. I had scarcely written the above when orders came for us to move in the direction of Malvern Hill. The orders should have come in the morning but failed to do so, so that the rest of the Brigade was six or eight hours ahead of us. We marched about six miles to New Market where we expected to find Gen. Evans, but other regiments had rested & marched on half an hour before us. We pushed on the men hot & weary, overtook the [command] at a place near which we now are, drawn up in line of battle, with some companies deployed as skirmishers. Our delay [threw] us in the rear of the brigade instead of the front, which is our [proper] place. In this order we advanced a mile or two & halted at dark, Means & Gadberry's regiments ahead on the [two] sides of the road. . . . Dick & I who were riding together took a prisoner. A big Dutchman came riding innocently up a byroad armed with a sabre [sic], a carbine, a pistol, a turkey & a duck. Dick had no arms at all, and I, a little pistol not much bigger than my thumb. "Do you know where Co. L is" he asked. "Just down the road," I said, fishing for my pistol. He turned to go with one of us on each side of him, and as I drew my pistol Dick grabbed his arm on the other side & said, "you are my prisoner, sir." The fellow seemed delighted to hear it, & [kindly] surrendered his arms. Another had been taken a few minutes before. About this time a large body of Cavalry came galloping up the road & were fired into by Means & Gadberrys. They galloped back after one volley . . . found four killed . . . Gen. Evans ordered. Col. Stevens ordered [Lt.] Stevens to take them . . . reconnoitre one mile towards Malvern Hill. The Col. had me take a company of skirmishers & lead the way, which I did, deploying them through the woods a hundred yards ahead of the column. I could distinctly hear the enemy around the bend of the road a hundred yards ahead of me. However they retired as we advanced for about half a mile, when whiz came a ball down the road followed by others in quick succession. We could not see anything but [the fireworks] & I could perceive that the enemy was retreating by the sound of the discharges, which still continued. The Col. then ordered us to retire as there was a sound of [wheels] ahead.

But as the artillery of it was such, came no news . . . advanced until we could see the light on Malvern Hill when we returned, having accomplished all . . . was intended for us to do. The object was not . . . storm the Hill, to take it from some other direction and this task was, or is, . . . entrusted to some [other] portions of our forces, the [location] of which I am [well] acquainted with. We were only to deal with [such] of the enemy as were situated between us & the Hill. The only casualty on our side was a flesh wound through the leg received by one of my skirmishers, unless I include the loss of my cap, knocked off by a branch of a tree where we were under

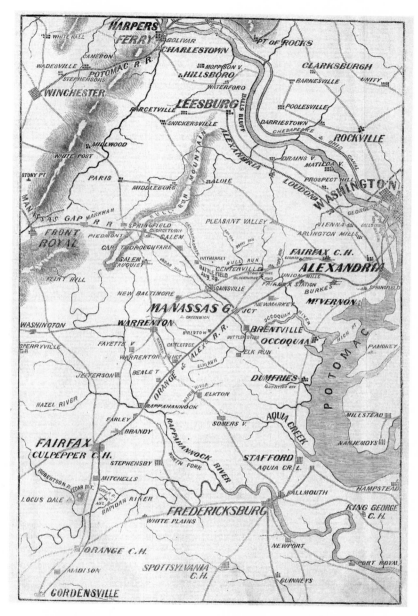

The Holcombe Legion participated in several important battles in Virginia during the summer of 1862. William Porcher DuBose was wounded at the First Battle of Rappahannock Station and at the Battle of Second Manassas. From *Frank Leslie's Illustrated Newspaper*, September 13, 1862

fire. I am now wearing a Yankee hat. We are now about three miles from Malvern Hill. I had only a few hours sleep last night on a horse blanket with my saddle for a pillow. We [have been resting all the morning though] & I have wandered off some distance to read & finish my letter. The little birds are singing around me and everything looks & feels peaceful as if war were not in the land. [We were] awaiting further orders, possibly to renew our attack tonight, but I have this moment heard that M. Hill has been evacuated & that our troops have taken possession. If it is so I suppose we will have nothing further to do & may be ordered back to camp.

... last night I had captured a Yankee ... but it found an owner in one of our camps.... horse has not come yet, and I am living upon the [generosity] of my friends.

I have not heard from home since I left. I expect to hear in a few days of the arrival there of Col. Bratton.

Give much love to the household & kiss the girls for me. I don't think there is much prospect of a general engagement at this point, in fact from what these prisoners say, I don't think McClellan's army is in fighting condition or spirit.

And now Darling, goodbye. I will write as often as I conveniently, or inconveniently, can.

Yrs affectionately
W. P. DuBose

I am away from my stamps.

Morning of the 8th. We are safely in our old camp again, having arrived late last night. It is as well to have scared as to have fought the Yankees away. More of their dead have been discovered. I had no opportunity of sending my letter from our yesterday's bivouac. I found here your letter of the 4th; I am sorry my letters have to be delayed.

1. Dr. Charles F. E. Minnegerode (1814–94) was the minister at St. Paul's Episcopal Church in Richmond. See Moore, *Civil War Guide to Richmond,* 28.

2. This was Samuel Davis Preston (1834–88) of Virginia. See Preston, *Preston Genealogy,* 50.

3. Federal forces reoccupied Malvern Hill on August 2, 1862, and withdrew on August 7. See Long, *Civil War Almanac,* 246–49.

1862

Anderson
Aug. 16th 1862

You have been so good in writing to me Dearest, that I cannot resist the temptation of stealing a half hour this sweet cool afternoon to spend with you. The extreme heat of the past ten days has been dispersed by a storm of wind and rain, and this whole day has been as sweet as October weather [c'd] have made it. I hope yr faithfulness to theory until the last extremity has been rewarded by a similar respite. You have had enough to break down the theory I do think, but I believe the Va summer is not as long as Charleston summers, and therefore I hope for better opportunity for yr improvement in camp. Your last letter arrived yesterday. I cannot help regretting every step you make nearer the enemy; and to be with Jackson is synonymous with being in constant action, wherever there is most to dare and most to win. I pray, Darling, that all the dangers surrounding you may only serve to sanctify and purify you for future labor in the Savior's cause, but often and again the sweet words of the hymn

> E'en if again I ne'er should see
> The friend more dear to life than me,
> Ere long we both shall be with thee—Thy will be done[1]

Come across my mind, and linger there, mingling comfort with all the sorrow they suggest. It is hard to prefer God's will to our own hopes, but He has power to teach us the lesson.

I never meant my strictures against Sunday writing to apply to you for you are so pressed for time frequently as to make it necessary, besides in your Sunday letters I can so often trace the holy influences of the day, that I love to receive them more than any others. With me the case is generally quite different. I write in distraction, and in so much publicity, that for the sake of example alone I ought to avoid it.

I think the descriptions in the Improvisatore[2] are exquisite & Cousin Mary McCord, who read the book (I believe) in Italy, pronounced them the most truthful she has ever seen. The story is rather unnatural to American minds but I enjoyed it. I am going to read an old novel, Villette,[3] to draw my thoughts a little while from the war. I believe I live too much in the present. Sue is taking excellent care of me. You need never fear that my physical wants will ever be neglected—the mental are in a pretty bad way, but Sue does her best there too. I have finished Dr. Arnold. It is beautiful to see how in his later years the roughnesses and asperity of his character are harmonized by the all pervading element of Christ. He died in the prime of life, 47 years old, vigorous and in the full employment of every faculty in the work of infusing truth into every mind that he could approach, yet there was a mellow ripeness for this entrance into a higher sphere, which makes his death harder for the survivors to bear while it assured them of his peace. How I would have liked you to read it with me and tell me something more about many of the subjects he discusses in the letters.

Aug. 18th. I heard last night, my own dearest Friend, that Jackson's forces were engaging the enemy near Gordonsville,[4] and there is little room for doubting that you too have been in battle. Words are cold to tell how eagerly I shall watch for this evening's papers, longing to hear that you have passed successfully thro the conflict. My prayers too, Dearest, have been ascending for you, and shall still continue to seek blessings for the army and the cause so precious to us all, as well as for yourself in whom my affections find so much to cling to. But it is useless to attempt writing now. I only send this letter that you may see how I love to think of you, and be in imagination with you, whether I know you are in danger or not.

Sarah Trapier wrote me a sweet letter the other day. She asked affectionately after you, bidding me tell you that you are frequently in her thoughts and prayers. Mr. Trapier is clinging more hopefully to his scheme for the students, as the Sec. of War[5] has determined to recommend it to Congress. If you men of Stonewall's army do all that the nation expects of you, I daresay the students will be spared from the army, tho' I am hoping that you will win such victories that peace will follow very soon.

Mr. Pinckney never [came] to [preach] and his congregation were in consequence subjected to a very awkward necessity. Most of them went to the Pres. Church where it was their communion Sunday. Many of us had never seen the form of that sacrament in that Church, and altho' we were kindly invited did not wish to remain. The minister did not dismiss the congregation but went right on with the communion service, while the strangers arose and went away without a blessing being pronounced, and while the members were seating themselves at the table. It was a painful scene, and I was sorry I came away. There was nothing in the preparatory service that c'd in any way compare with the beautiful solemnity of our service. They seem to dread more than they love the sacrament. In our service the thoughts presented are so full of love and comfort, with the solemnity, that I love to turn to it whenever my heart longs for the encouragement of simple Gospel truth. And now my own darling Good Bye. Sue sends much love to you, and Lise is puzzled to know how to send you a kiss in return for those she likes to receive from you. Margie sends love. Remember me to the Dr. and Believe me Yrs with sincere affection

Nannie

1. The words are found in selection no. 135 of a hymn book published for Confederate soldiers. See *Soldier's Hymn Book,* 133.

2. The work referred to is *The Improvisatore, or Life in Italy* by Hans Christian Andersen; an English translation from the Danish appeared in 1845.

3. This is *Villette* by Charlotte Brontë, published in 1853.

4. There were no significant actions around Gordonsville from August 12 to August 16, 1862. See Long, *Civil War Almanac,* 250–51.

5. This was George W. Randolph (1818–67), a Richmond lawyer and a member of a prominent Virginia family. Born at Monticello, he was a brigadier general in the Confederate army when he agreed to serve as Confederate secretary of war in March 1862. He served in that capacity until he resigned on November 15, 1862. See Foote, *Civil War,* 232–33; Warner, *Generals in Gray,* 252–53.

Anderson

Aug. 30th 1862[1]

I have just been reading some of your old letters, Dearest, refreshing myself with them, and trying to forget for a while how far away you are; and now I will further indulge myself by commencing a letter—an act of faith tho it be, for I don't know how to direct until you can tell me. I am not getting impatient to hear from you but I cannot help longing to know what have been your fortunes during the past week. The papers have told us of Long-street's having had to fight its way across the Rappahannock and specified Anderson's Brigade as engaged. As you are not or were not actually connect-ed with Artillery, I have been hoping you were still absent from the contest; tho' I daresay you have seen and done plenty of the same sort of work since that day, of which news has not yet reached us. Thank you for the sweet lit-tle note you wrote me near Orange C.H. It came quite safely, and tho' com-ing from the very atmosphere of war, breathed the sweet spirit of peace, underlying all cares and annoyances, which God only c'd have given to you. Your letters always do me good, for they shew me how much better it would be if my thoughts dwelt where you suppose they do, and my will had ceased to struggle for what is dear to it. And then, darling, I love to read of your own Christian faith and hope, both seeming ever to grow stronger and purer. I always feel that the influence of them must be very happy on all within their reach. Just at present I am missing you dreadfully, but I have determined to be patient and brave, and I am quite as cheerful as even you wd think desirable.

I hope you have not been obliged to dine a second time on quarter of a cracker and molasses. Gen'l Stuart's capture of the enemy's stores was splendid, was it not? Enough I hope to supply our poor, hungry army for some time. It w'd have been glorious to have quite taken Pope, and punished him in person for his barbarity, but we must be content without him this time.[2]

There is the strongest confidence felt in our army and generals in Va. I do not doubt that they will accomplish a great victory, and perhaps be in Washington before many weeks elapse. The great dread seems to be lest the victory should not cost as much as that before Rd. [Richmond] did. The enemy however can scarcely fight as well, after their disappointment there, so we are hoping and trusting for great results. Morgan is again winning laurels for himself; by rapid movements and daring adventure cutting up the forces sent to Gallatin to take him.[3] Affairs all thro' the West seem brightening too; when I look at the tone of the army and its position all round our borders, I hope a great deal, but the North is so obstinate and virulent in its temper, that one glance there [just] knocks down hopes of speedy success.

It has been my turn to go with Kate Gadsden this week to the depot to see after sick and wounded soldiers, and what do you think of my proceedings yesterday on recognising Capt. Frank Miles[4] among the number. Instead of offering him refreshments I shrunk back, because I knew him, and not until he came into the room tired and thirsty and asking for water, did I remember he might want it. Was that not a pretty piece of management? The poor fellow was looking miserably, having had an attack of jaundice, besides country & typhoid fever and his wound. He is recovering now.

Sep 1st. I have kept my letter till this evening Dearest in hope of hearing from you, but I will now complete the act of faith and despatch my letter to Rd. I do hope you are quite well and as brave and strong as your last letter describes you. We have a beautiful view of the stars from our square, and whenever I look up and admire their glorious beauty, I think of you and of the proficiency you attained to last year in astronomy, then I wonder whether you are not now in the best possible place for astronomizing, encamped upon the hills of Virginia. Do you improve your nights in that way? If you go stargazing you must have noticed the comet which lives in the great bear, or is at least sojourning there awhile. It is a little thing but pretty I think. I have just finished a letter to your sister Annie, and have told her I w'd come and see the Roseland folks some time when it shall suit them to have me. Do you know the Mrs. DuBose up here thinks I look strikingly like your Mother? I sh'd like to resemble her in character as well as in face. The book I told you I had been reading "Counterparts,"[5] has made me melancholy in one respect—it shows how music is almost as life itself to those who love it, and I never can make music for you.

There was a very imposing execution on Sullivan's Id last Thursday. One corporal of the Reg't of Artillery in which Brother is, designed to desert to the Fleet and attempted to persuade others to do the same. He was shot on the beach not far from Moultrie House in front of his own Reg't, Keitt's & part of Dunovant's, and the provost marshall's guard. Lieut. Col. Gaillard superintended. The prisoner was calm as he marched to the stake to the music of the dead march. He was killed almost instantly. This was done in full view of the blockading fleet, which not long after fired several shots upon the Beauregard battery. No harm was done however. The fort returned the fire and the vessels retired before long. There are many rumors afloat here, that Charleston is to be attacked within two weeks, but I do not think they have adequate foundation. Our gunboats are both launched and will be ready for anything in a few weeks unless the Yankees come just too early.

Brother is not well enough for duty yet. We expect him in Anderson in a few days. Aunt Wilkes[6] has got so tired of us that she has gone to town. And now for fear you will be tired I will say Goodbye.

Hoping my own darling to hear a good report of you 'ere another day has passed, and trusting you this night to the care of Him who never slumbers,

I remain,

Yours most sincerely,
Nannie

1. The envelope is addressed to "Adjt. W. P. DuBose, Holcombe Legion, Evans's Brigade, Longstreet's Division, Richmond, Va." The last three address lines are crossed out, and a forwarding address of "Winnsboro SCa" has been written.

2. On August 22, 1862, Maj. Gen. (later Lt. Gen.) James Ewell Brown Stuart (1833–64), cavalry commander for the Army of Northern Virginia, led a raid into the rear of the Union Army of Virginia with the goal of burning the railroad bridge over Cedar Run. Instead, Stuart attacked the headquarters of Maj. Gen. John Pope (1822–92), who was away on an inspection. Stuart captured Pope's dispatch book of

orders, personal baggage, and a payroll chest with $350,000. See Foote, *Civil War,*
608–9; Warner, *Generals in Gray,* 296–97; Warner, *Generals in Blue,* 376–77.

3. On August 12, 1862, Confederate cavalry under the command of Col. (later
Brig. Gen.) John Hunt Morgan (1825–64) captured Gallatin, Tennessee, and its
Union garrison. See Long, *Civil War Almanac,* 250; Warner, *Generals in Gray,* 220–21.

4. This was probably Capt. Francis Turquand Miles (1827–1903), a Charleston
physician. Miles commanded Company B of the First Battalion South Carolina
Infantry and later served as a surgeon. His brother, the Reverend Edward Reid Miles
(1824–85), was the husband of Nannie's cousin Mary Peronneau (b. 1842). See
Compiled Service Records, First (Charleston) Battalion South Carolina Infantry
(Gaillard's Battalion), M267, roll 150; Waring, *History of Medicine in South Carolina,*
267–68; *South Carolina Genealogies,* 3:186; Patey, *Whaley Family,* 199.

5. Most likely this is the novel *Counterparts, or, The Cross of Love* by the English
author Elizabeth Sara Sheppard (1830–62), which was published in 1854. See
Sutherland, *Stanford Companion to Victorian Fiction,* 571–72.

6. This was probably Clelia Lightwood Wilkes. See Patey, *Whaley Family,* 210.

Occoquan River
Sept. 22 1862

Madam,

It is with a very sad heart and a deep sympathy for yourself that I address
you this morning to inform you of the misfortune which has befallen my
beloved friend Willie your brother.

Yesterday a week ago we went into battle at the mountain pass near
Boonesborough Maryland.[1] Through God's mercy both Willie and I escaped
the dangers of the battle tho compelled with our troops to fall back from the
field where we had fought against greatly superior numbers. Late at night, in
accordance with Gen. Lee's orders Willie, then in command of my Legion (I
being in command of the Brigade) was directed to return cautiously to the
battlefield and ascertain whether the enemy had retired as was supposed.
Despite of the caution repeatedly impressed upon him, my dear friend with
that self devotion and utter fearlessness which ever characterised him, preceded his men and upon arriving at the designated point a single shot was
heard in the advance, followed immediately by an exclamation. In accordance with their orders the men fell back a short distance and waited for
Willie to return. After some hour or so they were recalled and the entire
army withdrawn. From that morning I have been unable to learn anything
of my friend. The exact nature of the exclamation I cannot fix—some say it

was one of pain some of surprise &c. My own strong hope and faith in God is that he had gotten within the enemies lines and was captured perhaps wounded.

God assures us in his word that he chastens those whom he loves. Large must be his love for your bereaved family with whom my constant and heartfelt sympathy has been during the last few months. But I know in whom you trust and from whence cometh your help. The physician of souls our blessed Saviour who wept over the loss of his own friend has balm for every wound and Heaven is the brighter and dearer the more dreary is Earth. Our Father in Heaven takes no pleasure in afflicting us but his chastening is always for our good. May his Spirit be with you all!

I shall inform you whenever I hear anything more positive about your noble and lovely brother, one of the purest men I ever knew. I am sorry to say that Major Means[2] was badly wounded and left in the hands of the enemy on the same field. God may have taken Willie to be his nurse and spiritual guide. I hope so.

Most respectfully
Your friend to command
P. F. Stevens

1. This was the battle of South Mountain, September 14, 1862. See Sears, *Landscape Turned Red,* 134–43.

2. This was probably Lt. Col. (formerly Maj.) Robert Stark Means (1833–74), son of Gen. John Hugh Means. Means was lieutenant colonel of the Seventeenth South Carolina Infantry Regiment and was shot through the thigh and captured at the battle of South Mountain. See *Official Records Army,* 19(1):945; Compiled Service Records, Seventeenth South Carolina Infantry Regiment, M267, roll 294; *South Carolina Genealogies,* 3:118.

Mrs. Marion Porcher
Fort Delaware. Del. River[1]
Sept. 24th 1862

My dear Sister

You will be surprised to hear of me, as I am surprised to find myself a prisoner of war at Fort Delaware. I was taken at South Mountain (or Middletown Heights) on the night after the battle of the 14th, while engaged on a reconnaissance—reached the place on the 21st, and am quartered here with sixty seven other officers. What disposition is to be made of us we do

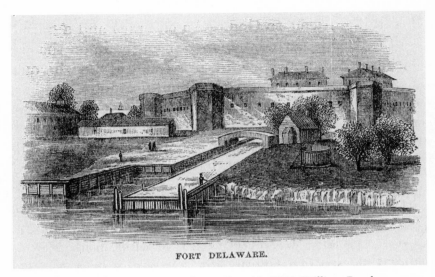

FORT DELAWARE.

Captured at South Mountain on September 13, 1862, William Porcher DuBose was released from Fort Delaware on October 6, 1862. Fort Delaware later became notorious as one of the worst Union military prisons. From Benson J. Lossing, *Pictorial History of the Civil War* (Hartford, Conn.: Thomas Belknap, Publisher, 1874), 3:79

not know of course, but our situation has an ominous air of permanency. We are rather closely confined but well treated & well fed—in fact have nothing to complain of & do not complain. Among my fellow prisoners are two old University friends (Gayles & Leitch)[2] Capt. Miller of Columbia, and Capt. Grimes,[3] a brother of my North Carolina friends who sent me the sermon cover you remember.

Our most pressing wants, underclothing &c have been supplied by charity from Baltimore—something to be read is my main desideratum now.

My last letter from So. Ca. was dated Aug. 16th; how many things may have occurred since that time! However I trust that all in whom I am interested are well, and will wait patiently until I can hear from you all again. Send this note to Anderson, with much love for my friends there. It is a long time since they or you have heard from me. I have been through [three] battles, & have been three times . . . twice running very narrow escapes. The great battle of Antiedam (or Sharpsburg) on the 18th, I did not participate in of course. I have not heard of Dick since he was left with the wounded at Bull Run. I have heard nothing of Col. Bratton.

May God, who has so wonderfully preserved me, keep us all in body & soul & restore us to each other in His own time.

Your aff. Brother
W. P. DuBose

Stephen will be taken care of by the Col. & others.

1. Built by George B. McClellan while he was with the Corps of Engineers in the 1850s, Fort Delaware was relatively new at the time of the Civil War. It was a granite, pentagon-shaped fortification situated at the southwest corner of Pea Patch Island, a mud shoal in the middle of Delaware Bay. It was a prisoner-of-war camp beginning in July 1861 until the end of the war. See Speer, *Portals to Hell*, 46, 87, 143–47.

2. First Lt. John H. Gayle, Company C, Sixteenth Virginia Infantry, was captured at Crampton's Gap on September 14, 1862. First Lt. Samuel G. Leitch, Company F, Nineteenth Virginia Infantry, was captured on September 15, 1862, at Williamsport, Virginia. See Compiled Service Records, Sixteenth Virginia Infantry, M382, roll 21, and Nineteenth Virginia Infantry, M382, roll 33.

3. Capt. John Gray Blount Grimes was assistant quartermaster of the Fourth North Carolina Infantry Regiment. See Compiled Service Records, Fourth North Carolina Infantry, M230, roll 15.

Roseland 2nd Oct. 1862

You have . . . been out of our thoughts . . . this terrible, wearying . . . about Willie. We heard about . . . telegram from Capt. Means that our dear Willie was missing, but, hoping . . . day to hear one thing more definite of . . . we did not have the heart to inform [you] what was making us so miserable.

Yesterday Stephen (Willie's servant) returned home, bringing me such a nice letter from Col. Stevens, that I immediately determined to send it to you, as I know you would rather know all the <u>truth</u> that it is in our power to hear for some time to come, than to be tortured by the many rumors & conjectures which, I suppose, you have already heard. Besides, I know that you will value such a letter as much as I do, so I have sent it to you to keep, that you may, one of these days, I most sincerely hope, have the pleasure of sharing with Willie himself.

I [must say] that Col. Stevens' letter, unsatisfactory [as it] . . . , has given me a great deal of [hope] & comfort . . . I had pictured my precious [Brother] as [wounded] . . . falling from his horse, . . . probability . . . [trampled] upon by advancing [columns]. Now, even if wounded, he surely was cared for, & I [know that] God will raise up friends to him even [among] his enemies. In fact, if he is not dangerously [wounded], I would prefer his being . . . Yankees, than lying among our [wounded] without even a clean shirt to put on for weeks, as our poor wounded at Warrenton & elsewhere are now doing. It is too depressing, too heart rending, to read Miss Victoria's account of the destitution, filth & sufferings of our brave men. I try to prepare myself for the possibility of having all my hopes prove delusive; for I know that it is very possible for that shot to have hit him in some vital part, & to prove fatal, but still, there are so many more chances against such a fearful event, that I am determined to hope for the best, until I am forced to do otherwise. But when will this wearying, depressing suspense [end.] And yet, when we have so much to [comfort] . . . Willie's case, it seems ungrateful to murmur. I have [felt] that whatever is best <u>for Willie</u> will be, & I know that wherever he is, & in what condition so ever . . . be, it is well with him. Oh! that we could [feel this] about all of our brave soldiers. How many hearts [that] are now breaking, would feel [comforted], & even thankful, after the first shock of their [grief] is over.

Stephen has not seen Willie since he . . . his food, & filled his canteen for him [preparatory to his] going into battle. He was quite well then. Stephen looks miserably, & has been quite sick. He could not stand those dreadful marches at all. He says he was too weak to bring on the saddle, papers, letters &c &c that Col. Stevens gave him to bring to us, so he put them into a wagon which was to have overtaken him that night at some little town, but of which he has never heard since. He told the Quarter Master, however, of his trouble, & he promised to see about the things for him, & have them sent on after him.

I am glad to be able to tell you that Jane is safely & happily over her troubles. Her little daughter (Jane DuBose), was [born on] . . . morning of the 29th, between 3 & 4 o'clock. She had a . . . Palmer it is hoped, is improving, tho' slowly. [Richie] Dwight is with him & looks & feels very badly himself. . . . Dr. . . . was here on Tuesday on his way from [Virginia] . . . he heard that Kershaw's staff were all safe after the battle. But when he got here, he heard [through] a letter [from] Franklin Gaillard[1] that he had [received] . . . from his horse on the battlefield & had hurt his back so much that he had . . . the rear, & one of the Gaillards with [him] to attend to him. Nothing further having been heard of either. Uncle D is perfectly wretched, & imagines that Moultrie is a prisoner. [Lessie] Dwight had just recovered from typhoid fever, but I suppose all this anxiety will make her sick again for she has fever for two days past. All here send a great deal of love to you, with our kind remembrances to your mother & sister. Hoping soon to send you good news, or hear good news from you, I am, my dear Nannie,

Yours truly
E M Porcher

You must excuse this careless hasty letter.

1. Franklin Gaillard (1829–64) was born in Pineville, South Carolina. In 1853 he married Catherine Cordes Porcher (1832–56), cousin of William Porcher DuBose. He was lieutenant colonel of the Second South Carolina Infantry and died at the battle of the Wilderness on May 6, 1864. He is buried at Fredericksburg, Virginia. He edited the *Fairfield Herald* (Winnsboro) and the *South Caroliniana* (Columbia) until the beginning of the war. The Gaillard family member attending him may have been Dr. Edwin Samuel Gaillard (1827–85). See MacDowell, *Gaillard Genealogy,* 38, 43.

Richmond Oct. 8th 1862

My dear Sister

As soon as I reached Richmond yesterday, I telegraphed to you to inform you of the fact, with a request that the dispatch should be forwarded to Anderson, as there is no line to that place & a letter from you might reach its destination earlier than mine. I had a faint hope of coming home for a few days, while the commissioners were engaged in effecting our exchange, but I have lost it this morning. We may be detained several days more in Richmond, but will soon leave for the army & in the meantime are not permitted to leave the City. I have limited time (as I wish to send this by hand) and limited paper (with me just now) & so, instead of a sketch of my adventures which w'd be necessarily very meagre, I will enclose a note written in the hope of an opportunity by flag of truce, which I have found in my packet. It was written to be approved by the Yankee authorities. It is true though with regard to the officers at least. The privates had more to complain of a great deal, but the treatment of prisoners at Fort Delaware has been exaggerated.

I was pained to hear of the rumours of my death & to learn how much pain the uncertainty of my fate had caused those at home. I will find time I hope to write you full particulars of my capture &c. From what I have heard from Mr. Dudley, I judge that you are at least partially acquainted with circumstances under which I was <u>lost</u>. A shot upon which I suppose my men based their report of my probable death was fired <u>by me</u> & not <u>at me</u>. But it is a long story & I shall have to reserve it for another time.

I hope Stephen & my baggage are all safe with Col. Stevens. If so I don't know anything I shall want for the winter, except my two thick shirts & something in the way of knitted articles which you have, such as caps, night caps, . . . , including a pr of gauntlets that sister Anne knit for me—just the things that I had last winter & left at home. Send them if you can to Mr. T. U. Dudley near the corner of 7th & Franklin Streets, and if you have an opportunity send Mrs. D., in return for <u>parental kindness</u> to me, something like eggs butter &c which are fabulously high here.

I have written to Anderson of course, but not as many particulars even as this letter contains. I will write again tomorrow, but in case my time sh'd be limited I wish you would send this letter there. Don't expect reciprocity though.

I have heard today for the first time of Col. Bratton, & was grateful to hear of his safety &c. My time & paper are out. Much love to you all.

Yr aff. Brother
W. P. DuBose

[Note in pencil:]

I have just had the intense gratification of meeting [Willie or Willis] and am going with him now to see Miss Victoria. Ask Anne to send on my knitted vest. Eddie Gaillard carried it home I think.

Richmond

Oct. 8th 1862[1]

It is many weeks, Darling, since I have had the sweet satisfaction of writing to you, and in the painful interval I do not know what you have been called upon to suffer on my account. I reached Richmond yesterday from Fort Delaware, & went at once to the Telegraph Office to telegraph to Winnsboro & Anderson, forgetting that there was no line to the latter place. I sent a dispatch home with directions that it sh'd be forwarded to you, as a letter from there might reach you sooner than mine. I have delayed writing so many hours myself under the fruitless hope that I <u>might</u> go on in person. We are paroled & <u>they say</u> are to be exchanged & ordered to our commands immediately, but official processes are always liable to delay & I was anxious to take advantage of that fact & steal a few days, but it is "no go."

I was shown my obituary this morning, much to my surprise & pain. The circumstances under which I was missing might have caused serious mis-apprehensions, but could not have justified the statement of my death. The history of my adventures I shall have to reserve for tomorrow as I am anxious to get this off by a safer & more expeditious channel than the mail.

It is not impossible that I may be detained some days in Richmond, long enough possibly to hear from you. At any rate direct to the care of Mr. T. U. Dudley & it may be forwarded to the army if I am not here. My last letter from you & from So. Ca. is dated Aug. 16th. But I have thought of you only the more, my own Darling, for the long deprivation of the letters which used to be such a comfort to me. The 1st Oct. I spent almost literally in recalling & living over the events which it commemorated. My imprisonment gave me much leisure for such occupation, as well as for the still more profitable one of prayer, meditation & thanksgiving for the innumerable & wonderful mercies of God during the past year. I am quite well. My <u>wounds</u> never gave me much trouble. I want to write home by the same opportunity by which I send this, & in order to secure time, have limited myself to half a sheet. I will write immediately by mail. Very much love to all, & believe me, Darling

Yrs with more affection than ever

W. P. DuBose

[Two newspaper clippings are with this letter:]

"Adjutant W. P. DuBose.—We have been informed that by a letter received from Col. P. F. Stevens, of the Holcombe Legion, all that is known of Adjutant DuBose is that he is missing, not having been heard from since the battle of Boonsboro' Gap. The report of his being wounded or killed is without any foundation, and it is reasonable to hope for favorable accounts from him before very long, even if he be in the hands of the enemy."

"We are more than gratified in hearing, from a private dispatch received in this city from Richmond, of date 8th instant, that Adjutant W. P. DuBose, of Holcombe Legion, had returned well from Fort Delaware."

1. The cover is addressed to "Miss N. B. Peronneau, Box No. 3, Anderson C.H., So.Ca."

Cokesbury Oct. 9 '62

Dear Miss

As a member of the military family of Col. P. C. Gaillard,[1] I often heard Capt. R. Press Smith[2] speak of Adjt. W. P. DuBose, & of the fact that nothing definite had been heard of him. On Monday last, at dinner, he passed a letter to Col. G, and as I understood from Mr. D, in which he spoke of his wound. Not being acquainted with the gentleman, I did not read the letter, but I am perfectly satisfied that it was <u>very satisfactory</u> to Capt. Smith.

That he is safe, & I think within our lines, there is no doubt. I am sorry I can't be more particular in my information, but trust you will soon have all your fears relieved.

Very respy

Wm. E. Howland[3]

1. Col. Peter Charles Gaillard (1812–89) of Berkeley County, South Carolina, commanded the Twenty-seventh South Carolina Infantry Regiment. See Mac-Dowell, *Gaillard Genealogy*, 32; Compiled Service Records, Twenty-seventh Infantry Regiment, M267, roll 356, 357.

2. This was probably Capt. Robert Press Smith (1839–99) of Berkeley County, South Carolina, who served as quartermaster of the Twenty-seventh South Carolina Infantry Regiment. See MacDowell, *Gaillard Genealogy*, 288; Compiled Service Records, Twenty-seventh Infantry Regiment, M267, roll 360.

3. William E. Howland was commissary sergeant for the Twenty-seventh South Carolina Infantry Regiment. See Kirkland, *South Carolina C.S.A. Research Aids;* Compiled Service Records, Twenty-seventh South Carolina Infantry Regiment, M267, roll 358.

To Miss Peronneau
Richmond
Oct. 9th 1862

I intended, Darling, to write you a full long letter last night or this morning, but circumstances too numerous to mention have brought me to eleven o.c. tonight with the letter unwritten. Among other things last night I stumbled against Charley Dwight who took me at once to see Miss Victoria Murden, neither of whom I had discovered before. Charley had heard of me before he saw me, but the amazement & emotion that Miss V. exhibited when I addressed her, unannounced, have made me realize, as I had not done before, the <u>fact</u> that I have been some time dead to you all.

While all who love me are rejoicing & giving thanks for my restoration to life, my gratitude I am afraid has been almost drowned in the comparatively petty disappointment of not being able to see you. I would not mind it quite so much if I could return to the army, but the process of exchange may languish for days or even weeks without my being able to get away. As a sort of price for the privilege of remaining in the City, instead of the "camp of paroled prisoners" two miles off, I go each day to the latter place to assist in making out payrolls for the men there.

I shrink from the task of giving you the detailed account of my capture & adventures which I know you will expect. It is too long a story for paper, and it would be so much pleasanter to tell it by word of mouth. If I have time to tell the story in this letter, I will do so on another sheet & get you to send it home, which will save me the trouble of repeating it to them. Miss V. informed me of the birth of another niece,[1] for which I feel very grateful, something to occupy the thoughts & affections of its bereaved Mother.

Oh that I could get even a letter from you! I was told tonight that if I had telegraphed "to Anderson via Columbia," the dispatch would have been forwarded & have reached you earlier. I sent a letter to you yesterday by an acquaintance going most of the way, but I hope the dispatch which I sent to Winnsboro reached you before that.

10th. My health is as good as it ever was. Exposure & hardship have done me much more good than harm, and I have seen a good deal of both. They are monsters though that lose much of their hideousness on close inspection— the world has grown very self-indulgent, & men will always be surprised to discover how much they can endure when forced to it. I cannot tell you how often I have read your last letter. Several times I was on the point of destroying it but it always escaped to give me more comfort. It went into battle once, but w'd not have done so if I had not got into it very unexpectedly. I did not dream when I was reading the words "Een if again I never should see &c" in prison how much more deeply you were feeling them at home. Your daguerreotype is safe with me too.

I am staying at Mr. Dudley's, but spend all day at Camp Lee where I am writing now in the interval of my work at muster rolls. Give much love to Miss Sue & tell her I have thought often of her. I suppose there is scarcely a moment of that little visit to Anderson that I haven't lived over many times. I have even thought over the breakfast some mornings when I had none other to occupy my attention. Give my love to your mother & sister M. & aunts & the Gadsdens & all friends & kiss Margie & Lise for me. I hear that my servant has gone home, having given me up. I am going to write to Johnson & Mr. Trapier if I have time, but in case I do not have time for both, give my love to all the Trapiers & tell Mr. T. I met at Fort Delaware the Rev's J. B. Tustin[2] & Benjamin Franklin. The former, who once lived in Charleston & preached in the Huguenot Church (then a Baptist minister), was acting temporary chaplain & was very kind to the prisoners. He charged me to remember him to his friends in C. I heard both preach good sermons.

And now my own Darling, goodbye. I wonder where all the letters are that you have written from the 16 Aug.

W. P. DuBose

1. This was Frances Beverly Means (born September 29, 1862), daughter of Jane Porcher DuBose and Beverly W. Means. See MacDowell, *DuBose Genealogy,* 13.

2. The Reverend Josiah Philips Tustin (1817–87) left the Baptist denomination to join the Episcopal Church in 1859. He was the pastor of the French Huguenot Church in Charleston from 1854 to 1859. William Porcher DuBose incorrectly gives his middle initial as "B." See *Historical Catalogue of Brown University,* 179; "Memorial Tablets in the French Protestant (Huguenot) Church," 59.

Anderson Oct. 10th 1862

How sweet it is to write once again to you Dearest. Since last I undertook such a thing, the days have passed slowly enough, each one seeming long and weary with the burden of anxiety and fear it brought. But tonight your telegram has made me so happy that I must send you a little note of welcome home again. Annie enclosed me the joyful tidings that you are safe in Richmond, and I am rejoicing in thankfulness to Him who has heard our prayers and restored you to us. I feel in the first flush of gratitude that I would like to give some tribute to His love and mercy; I trust this will not wear away, but that rather my life may show my acknowledgement of these blessings.

We have all been longing for you very much and yearning to know where and how you were. Think of our actually hoping you might be a prisoner, yet so it was. After the first two days of suspense, I took courage and believed that you must be one, and have ever since felt strongly hopeful. Sue has been sadly distressed for your sake, but I will not dwell on that—it is pleasanter to tell you of her perfect sympathy with my gladness and of the strong attachment she feels toward you. Indeed all of our household have proved themselves your warm friends, as well as many, many others of whom I will tell you all when we meet again. And how, Dearest, have you fared in

Yankee hands? I wonder if they had the miserable cruelty to treat you badly; or if, as we fondly hoped and prayed, friends were raised up to meet your needs. I have hundreds of questions to ask and only restrain them with the assurance that there is a letter for me on the road, telling all I want to know. I had concluded you were wounded, but the telegram seems to contradict that, for which I am very thankful. It seemed so desolate for you to be suffering and helpless, and among enemies, when so many at home would have given all they possessed to have the privilege of comforting you. I suppose you are waiting in Richmond to be formally exchanged, but are you coming on to see us for a little while? Please come if it is possible. I have so much to tell and so much to ask you, and I want so very much to see you, to satisfy myself of your actual identity. Our anniversary, the 1st of Oct., was not spent by either of us as we had hoped. It was to me most miserable, the most hopeless day of all. Please if you cannot come to answer all my questions, write me every single thing that has happened to you from, let me see when—the commencement of your advance towards Manassas. The 17th Aug. was the last day on which you gave me anything like an account of yourself, except the welcome little bulletins after the battle. And I am so anxious to know how you fell into the hands of the enemy, and every little thing. Fort Delaware is under Gibson[1] is it not, a real brutal wretch. But my dear friend, I can tonight feel nothing but joy at your escape, not even suffering with your trials. Will you forgive me?

I have the Col.'s letter to shew you, and some one or two (among many others) which I would like you to see. You would be gratified, tho' I hope not surprised, to see how many friends you have among mine. Sue sends her love to you and her congratulations at your first visit north of the Potomac being made in such company. Mattie also sends her love, while vowing vengeance against you whenever you come in her way. Mamma and Aunt Eliza welcome you warmly to Southern soil, and hope to see you soon. And now good night my Darling. May God spare us another such trial as we have just endured and may He ever be your Comforter, and Guide. Yrs most fondly,

Nannie

1. Capt. Augustus Abel Gibson (1835–93) was the first commandant of Fort Delaware at the time of the war. See Fetzer, *Unlikely Allies,* 31; Heitman, *Historical Register and Dictionary of the United States Army,* vol. 1, 453.

∞

Oct. 12th 1862

I send you Darling, a portion of my last letter which was not written in time for the mail. I am still here, & still as uncertain as ever with regard to my exchange. I have received no letters yet from So.Ca. but must do so tomorrow. How eagerly I looked for them! I am expecting Col. Bratton too, who I heard was to leave home on Friday, but could not have done so. We had a sudden change in the weather yesterday, since which time I have been more homesick than ever; it is cold, raw and raining, just such weather as I love in the house with those I love, & no where else. Charley Dwight[1] is making preparations to go in command of a large surveying party to survey Culpeper [sic] & the adjoining county. In the meantime he is here & I see more or less of him every day. I see Miss Victoria Murden too quite frequently, & as they are representatives of home & give me letters to read, it is a great satisfaction to me. But it is hard to keep staying here in suspense when it w'd be so easy to go home. Many of the officers who were paroled with me have left but they can only have done so by indirect means which I w'd not like to descend to. Some of them procured passports by changing their dress and applying as citizens. I suppose the object of keeping us here, besides assuring our earlier return to the army after exchange, is to prevent capture by the enemy from becoming too desirable a thing. I will not go off into a letter until I hear from you which I hope will be tonight (Monday). I don't know what is being done about our exchange. I am not particularly anxious to return to the army as I hear nothing is doing up there, and I am very comfortably domesticated with my friends the Dudleys, who constantly assure me that I stand on the same footing as their son Tom & who w'd be distressed if I were to leave them. But in these hard times & in this hardest of places, I do not like to impose so long upon the hospitality of even such friends. And then there is the constant temptation to homesickness. Much love to all. Remember me to our Georgia cousins when you write to them & their father & mother. Also to any other friends that you may write to.

And now my own Darling good bye. Continue to direct to Richmond care of Mr. T. U. Dudley until further orders. I hope the Fall weather in that fine climate is doing you good, and Miss Sue too. Give her a special share of love. Tell me about Gadsden & what you know of Johnson & other friends. I see Dr. Johnson's death announced in the papers. The old gentleman was constantly ripe for the grave. How are the sisters?

Yours affectionately
W. P. DuBose

At Fort Delaware I sent for some envelopes and they had the impertinence to send these. I have them & must use them.

1. This was Charles Stevens Dwight (1834–1921), brother of Dr. Richard "Dick" Yeadon Dwight. Charles Stevens Dwight served as a corporal in Company I, Second South Carolina Infantry (Second Palmetto Regiment). He was born at Somerset Plantation (Berkeley County, South Carolina) and was an engineer and planter. He married Maria Louisa Gaillard (b. 1847) in 1871. See MacDowell, *Gaillard Genealogy,* 130–31; Hewett, *South Carolina Confederate Soldiers,* 142; Compiled Service Records, Second South Carolina Infantry (Second Palmetto Regiment), M267, roll 155; MacDowell, *DuBose Genealogy,* 262.

Oct. 15th 1862

Dear Nannie,

This letter should have been sent to you yesterday, but if you could have seen who was absorbing my mind & forgive, you would not think strangely of my not remembering until too late, later than this letter was to be sent. As soon as Brother W. letters reached us, with only two days for preparation, a servant had to be selected, & I fit him out entirely, besides getting up winter clothes for Brother W. I have no idea he will find any of his things when he reaches the Legion, as Stephen actually started with them, but never took them from the wagon.

Miss V has seen Brother W. in Richmond & thinks he is looking thin. Janie is not well, threatened birth [risings?].

Excuse this note, as I really can do no more. Yours very affect,

A. S. DuBose

Stephen is too distressed at not being allowed to return, though he is very feeble & sick. Dr. B. will take on the servant & clothes & keep them with him, until he either joins Brother W. or can safely send them to him.

Anderson Oct. 16th 1862

Almost a month has passed Dearest since the sight of a fresh letter from your loved hand, so that you may imagine how impatiently longed for and eagerly welcomed was the one that came last night, all dressed in Yankee livery tho' it was. Alas for frail human nature! In spite of conscience loudly reproaching me for unthankfulness, and all the precious anticipations of the improbability of your getting home, I was so bitterly disappointed at hearing it from your own lips, that I could feel nothing else, except perhaps still further disappointment at hearing so little of your late adventures. Letters cannot take the place of the long conversations I yearn after—my heart is very full and I long to pour out its fullness to your indulgent loving self in a way that pen and paper will not accomplish. I feel so weak and fearful, so very unwilling to have you plunge again into danger and endure hardships and fatigue, that I am positively frightened at my own ingratitude and faithlessness. The only thank offering for your precious life that God demands of me is that I should trust you again to His omnipotent arm and infinite love, and I, weak and sinful, rebel against His will! Oh may He work in me that which is well pleasing in His sight!

I daresay it is a disagreeable task to write a full history of all that has befallen you, but as your Col. says you have <u>courage</u> I hope you will not shrink from it. Fearing you may forget anything Sue threatens to write you a catechism which you must answer patiently, to make up for all she has suffered from love to you. Her fear is that you may be bound to secresy [*sic*], as we see the prisoners from Lafayette[1] are. I wonder if you have had to endure all that they hint at? We were never stout hearted enough to suppose you escaped without being badly wounded; I am glad to think you had not, as you letter infers, that pain to bear. It must have been pretty desolate as well as very provoking to find yourself in no worse condition than that of a prisoner. I have concluded at last that your daguerreotype has one claim to resemblance that was not foreseen when it was given to me. It looks as I am sure you did the first moment you appeared before your captors when there was light enough for them to scrutinize you. If you have time in Richmond, will you not have another likeness taken for me, in uniform, which shall represent the prisoner, restored. You could have yourself photographed on cards and send them by mail. I would judiciously present one or two of them to appreciative friends and the rest I will put carefully away when I am not looking at them—they shall not be carelessly exhibited to the public. You will not refuse me this one gratification I know. I want also another piece of your hair when it is longest; think of my fancying to have an ornament made out of it. I find Anderson furnished with a skilful hair-worker.

We were quite delighted to hear of Mr. Tustin again. He ought to have been kind to you for he had warm friends when in Charleston, tho' many were afterwards very angry at his becoming an Episcopalian. One of his old congregation is our friend, Miss Harriet Washington,[2] who gladly received his message of remembrance. Both you and I ought ever hereafter to rejoice at any opportunity of obliging Miss W. for we have unwittingly caused her the greatest sorrow. Old wounds which I for one had thought quite healed by time were laid bare, and new poignancy given to their pain. She was once engaged to Mr. Hume. Every preparation for their wedding was made and the time at hand, when he was taken ill of country-fever [sic]. They did not tell her of his danger till very late, nor take her out to see him until his consciousness had gone forever. He died, and she, in the first flush of youthful joy and hope, with a temper perfectly undisciplined, a heart knowing no higher love, nor the priceless value of the Comforter from above, was almost crushed to the ground. Her health failed entirely, and the light of her existence for many years put out. At last she was gradually won over to Christianity and resignation. But on the very anniversary of his death, I discovered in the papers a tiny paragraph stating you were "wounded, supposed to be dead or a prisoner." Her heart was already full of sad memories, and when a like calamity seemed to have fallen upon me, and you, at best, were in pain and loneliness, she gave me her fullest sympathy, and shared all my sorrow. Even then I had to acknowledge, her trial many times worse than mine. The grief of it had not passed away yet. Oh darling, it was such an inestimable blessing to know that no earthly trial could shake your soul's eternal safety. I felt then that no sacrifice was too great to yield to Him who had provided such infinite happiness for you. Patriotism sunk into the most obscure corner of my heart, utterly unable to compensate for your absence, but I was strengthened and consoled by Christ's love. I felt that many prayers were ascending for me, and they bore me up. I know darling, that if I was so supported, fully and numerous were the prayers that ascended for you, that friends and supports might be given you, and comfort from Christ himself, and I trust you were upheld.

You scarcely can know of all the friends you have. From every quarter I have received letters of intense sympathy, so that I in my turn have grieved for the authors. Carrie Pinckney, Cousin Nannie, Sallie Lowndes, Aunt Ravenel, Mary Jervey, Clelia Gibbes, Sarah Trapier, Catherine Coffin, my Brothers and Sister and others have lavished loving sympathy, measured by the knowledge of your worth, upon my insignificant self. I w'd give a great deal to shew some of their letters to you. Carrie's more than others, because I feel certain you will never know her in person.

I have written you a great many times since the 16th of Aug. but they will be no loss to you—it is better that you should not have them all. Many were written under the saddest feelings when I did not know whether you were even living. If they do accumulate upon you I hope you will put them into the fire unhesitatingly. I wish to run no further risk of tiring your patience than this long letter will cause. It is a perfect age since you have written anything longer than a note. I fear you have tiresome work at the camp, tho' I feel very thankful for anything rather than you rejoining the Legion for a while. Besides I know you enjoy being at the Dudleys, and sharing their hospitality after the life you have lately led. I am sorry Stephen has deserted you. He did not strengthen on hard work as his master has done. Your stock of health will I trust last thro' the winter. Has the sunshine retained its brightness even in prison? How I would revel in some of its genial rays. I suppose you were not allowed much writing material in Fort Delaware, otherwise you might have made a thrilling story of your Va. campaign. I am sure, with all the fortitude and resolution of the bravest officer, if endowed with deep feelings also, a man's very soul must be tried by the scenes of such battles as you have witness [sic]. God spared you from the awful field of Sharpsburg. Anderson life goes on as usual. The Gadsdens have shed many tears both of joy and sorrow on your account. Mrs. G. and Anna are both unwell. Poor Stuart Hanckel's[3] sad fate has depressed Anna a good deal. No one knows yet what has become of him. His family are distracted by contradictory reports. You were fortunate to stumble against such a cousin as Charley Dwight, and I am very glad to hear Miss Victoria is safely out of Warrenton. Do give my love to her. Is it not a blessing that her brother has been spared? And now dearest it is time for me to stop. Please be as egotistical as you possibly can whenever you write. Remember that I have no imagination and must be told everything I ought to know. The dear old Bishop is to be here on the 21st to confirm. I hope T. Gadsden may be here to meet him. You must enjoy Dr. Minegerode, tho' there is little doubt of your being willing to come to us a while. Sue is so good to me. I was very glad to hear of Janie's little daughter. She must have been a bright spot in the household when all were wondering where you were. Mamma Mattie and Aunt E., Sue and the children send much love to you. Did you know that Mattie had been sick and bruised and rib-broken? She is almost well again. Most affctly,

Nannie

1. Fort Lafayette in New York served as a prison for Confederates and political prisoners. See Faust, *Encyclopedia of the Civil War*, 275.

2. Harriott M. Washington of Charleston died in 1905 and is buried in the churchyard of St. Philip's Episcopal Church. See WPA Cemetery Index.

3. This was possibly James Stuart Hanckel, who died on September 25, 1862, at Sharpsburg, Maryland. See Kirkland, *Broken Fortunes,* 147.

Richmond
Oct. 20th 62

I leave for home tomorrow morning Darling, on a short furlough. I will go on in a very few days to Anderson. Cannot you & Miss Sue come back with me & pay my sisters a visit at Roseland? Otherwise I don't know how I can divide my time which is only 20 days with five or six to be spent on the road, or more, if I have to go to Winchester, 90 stage miles from Staunton. I would not make the proposition knowing your Mother's strict ideas, but when I rejoin the army there is no knowing when or whether we will meet again. And I do want to see you, my Darling, more than words can express. Of course I w'd stay several days in Anderson even if you return with me. Miss Victoria will be going to Greenville & will take you back home.

I am particularly anxious that Miss Sue sh'd come with you if possible. I wish my sisters to know her with you, and they are as anxious as I am. Please write to me at once to Winnsboro as my plans will depend upon your decision. Tell your Mother that these are peculiar times and peculiar circumstances.

I received your letter today enclosing Miss Sue's. How much I value them, I cannot begin to estimate.

I have not a moment to spare. Am trying to get off tomorrow morning, but have to make great exertions to do so.

Yrs most affectionately
W. P. DuBose

[In pencil:]

Roseland. Oct. 22

I have brought the note with me to help it on its way, but forgot to send it on by the cars today. I arrived at 2 o.c. P.M. & find all pretty well & hoping that you will come with. I leave here for Anderson as soon as I get your answer.

Richmond Nov. 14th

I did not think, my own Darling, that I could have allowed a whole day to pass after reaching Richmond without writing to you, but the disagreeable journey, added to the pain of our late parting, made me right sick yesterday; & today visitors & business have not left me a moment for myself or you, until just now when I have barely time to save the mail. After leaving you on Tuesday evening I felt perfectly stupid & insensible. Slept well that night & the next day on the cars. Had to ride on the platform most of Wednesday night on acc't of the crowd. Lost both of my keys & nearly lost one hand of the gloves you knit me (to say nothing of the connection in Petersburg & my breakfast, the latter of which I lost by nearly losing the former & quite losing the key of my saddle bags), and finally arrived in Richmond after a journey which was disagreeable from beginning to end. Yesterday I felt quite badly, but today I am perfectly well again.

I got this morning the little package of socks &c. Thank you for the peach leather which has not lost its flavour. Tom Dudley is in town, with several other friends. My exchange was published on the 11th Nov. accompanied by an order to report immediately for duty. I thought of leaving tomorrow but have made up my mind to wait until Monday. Our brigade is somewhere beyond Weldon, its exact location I find some difficulty in ascertaining.

And now Darling, what shall I say about missing you? I am barely beginning to collect my faculties sufficiently to feel the pain of being separated from you. I have been too dull & stupid for several days even to attempt to recall the joys of the preceding weeks, or to lift up my soul in gratitude to the Giver of all blessings. I am afraid I rested too much in my happiness & gave God too little of my precious time at home. And when I was obliged to leave that happiness, instead of being filled with Him, there was an aching void in my heart which all must feel who rest too much on the best & purest of Earth's treasures. But do not think Darling, that I mean this as an answer to the question you asked during that last sweet walk, "Whether we might not rest too much in our present happiness instead of helping each other on to something better." You have helped me on, Dearest, more than you think, & I thank God for it. You have been more serious & earnest and faithful than I have. I have begun long ago to rest & rely upon you to help strengthen and comfort me in the straight path which God, we trust, has ordained that we shall walk together.

Give a great deal of love to Miss Sue & remember me affectionately to your Aunt & cousins. And now good night my own Darling. God bless you for your love to me.

Yrs affectionately W. P. DuBose

My friend Miss Anne Johnson sends love to you. She & I are great friends.

Richmond
Nov. 16th 1862

I wrote to you, Darling, to Columbia, but if you left there on Monday, my letter may not have reached you. I am afraid that I too shall leave tomorrow without receiving the letter which I know you must have written. However, in both our cases, the disappointment of not hearing in time is much softened by the assurance of the letters' having been written. Maybe our confidence in each other, so dear to us both, is strengthened by these occasional little trials.

You see I am writing on Sunday, and that too when I could have written on another day. But I do want the influence of the day to pervade this epistle, & bring us into closer & holier communion than my hurried, disconnected letters generally do. My unsettled & eventful life during the past six months has rendered me almost incapable of calm, connected & sustained thought or reflection, and I have to struggle against impatience & restlessness in sitting down to a long slow letter even to you. But what is harder & more painful still, I find that the same difficulty has grown upon me in my intercourse with God. I find it hard to be still, & rest in His presence, to rejoice in dwelling quietly in the light of His countenance, as I sometimes used to do in my more favored hours. Restlessness & impatience have taken possession of me & have robbed my devotional hours of much of their joy & peace. This morning after service I came to my room & tried in vain to settle down quietly to reading and meditation & prayer. At last I turned to the text which you have written in this little Testament you sent me, and prayed that my mind might be calmed from its restlessness & "stayed on Him,"[1] from whom alone c'd come that "perfect peace" which I longed for. And, Darling, it came, as an answer to your prayer, inscribed there in your own familiar handwriting. May your prayers be always thus answered in my behalf, when <u>mine</u> fail by their unworthiness to bring the promised answer. Often when

I am faint & weak in spirit & cannot pray, I turn for hope to the prayers which I know are reaching the throne of Grace from faithful hearts that love me, oftenest of all, to the intercessions of Him whose love changeth not & whose prayers must prevail.

Tell Miss Sue that there is a copy of Miss Muloch's[2] poems in this house, the first piece in it is "Philip, my King." I have been looking for the book in all the stores to send to her but it is not in the city. I w'd beg for this copy but it is a present to Mrs. Dudley. I had a tooth pulled yesterday; are you not sorry for me? I have been thinking of having my likeness taken & w'd have done so if I had had a decent uniform coat, although I know it be no satisfaction to you when it is done. No better likeness can be taken of me than the one you have.

I don't know how to tell you to direct to me. I hear our Brigade are at Kinston, near Weldon, but I don't know whether Kinston is the P.O. or not. Give much love to Miss Sue and remember me particularly to your friends. I hope you are enjoying your visit & that you will continue to improve & you began to do at Roseland. And now, my own Darling, Goodbye.

Yrs affectionately

W. P. DuBose

1. Isaiah 26:3: "Thou wilt keep him in perfect peace, whose mind is stayed on Thee."

2. Dinah Mariah Muloch Craik (1826–87) was an English novelist and poet.

Camp Evans Brigade
5 miles from Kinston
Nov. 19th 1862

I arrived here yesterday evening, Dearest, & write this morning more to give you my P.O. than with the hope of accomplishing a letter. I will wait for that until I have had a day or so to form impressions & see ahead. Gen. Evans is here alone with his brigade; the legion has improved wonderfully in health & numbers, but is lamentably off for officers having lost all the best. To tell the truth I would dislike very much to go into action under Gen. Evans & with our present officers. The enemy are apparently quite active fifteen miles ahead of us, but whether there is any prospect of their advancing I cannot judge yet. I suspect that Gen. Evans is drinking a good deal,[1] & have no doubt he will be having us out on all occasions to meet imaginary enemies on sensational reports, but do not speak of this.

What do you think of my saddle bags being stolen almost out of my very hands as I passed through Petersburg. I put them down for a moment to pay my omnibus fare & when I looked again they were gone. Among other valuable contents were the Testament you gave me and my Fort Delaware Prayer Book. The former I had put in by mere chance, my pockets being unusually full the morning I left Richmond. I find too that my saddle & bridle, valuable oil cloth &c &c were lost near Winnsboro. My valise was saved & I have read a little of your Tennyson this morning to compensate in part for having used a borrowed Testament.

And now let me tell you where I am. Kinston is on the Neuse River, about twenty five miles from Goldsboro, on the R.R. from that place to Newbern. Direct to <u>Kinston</u>, Holc. Legion, Evans Brigade. I got your letter before leaving Richmond, and most refreshing it was to me, like a draught of fresh air from Roseland freighted with love from you. How vividly it recalled all the events of those sweet days we spent there as I had not been able to recall them before. I spent all the time from Weldon to Goldsboro reading the old letters which you & the girls tried to cheat me out of at Roseland. You w'd all have injured yourselves, as well as deprived me of much pleasure, if you had succeeded in persuading me to destroy them. This country is not unlike Adams Run, and I would not object to spending some months quietly here, as we did there, with time for reading, writing &c, but as I remarked above, I am not in the company I w'd like to fight with. I found Rutledge just gone off on furlough much to my regret. Dr. Russel[2] is the only one left of the old field & staff & he & I are together. My servant & horse at last acct were at Staunton.

I hope you are enjoying your visit at Graniteville. I w'd like to drop in on you sometimes & share, perhaps add a little to your enjoyment. Give a great deal of love to Miss Sue & remember me particularly to Miss Lila & to any others you please. You have taken more of my time than I intended to give you today. I hope you have received both of my previous letters.

Good bye Darling. God help you, & me too, to live as we pray to be enabled to do.

Yrs ever W. P. DuBose

1. One historian wrote that Evans was "much too fond of liquor and was always accompanied by his Prussian orderly, who bore on his back the famous 'barrelita' containing a gallon of whiskey." See Stone, *Wandering to Glory,* xvii.

2. William T. Russel (b. 1827) was surgeon of the Infantry Regiment of the Holcombe Legion. See Compiled Service Records, Infantry Regiment Holcombe Legion, M267, roll 378; Hewett, *South Carolina Confederate Soldiers,* 421; *Confederate Military History,* 6:820.

Dismal Swamp
Near Kinston Nov. 23rd 1862

Sunday again, Darling, & this time no church in reach, & no chaplain to preach for us. Still the day has passed pleasantly & I trust not unprofitably. More time to myself is what I have long needed, & what I have plenty of now. I lay down in my tent this morning & read & thought to my heart's content. A volume of Robertson's sermons which I found in my old valise adds another to my list of treasures. I think Tennyson & Robertson a good deal alike in many respects. There is a purity & refinement, an ideality, about them both which is very attractive to me, while I recognize the theological faults of both of them. There is good deal of religion about Tennyson, of the Robertson kind. I found another book in camp too which will prove an acquisition, "The Wit & Wisdom of Sydney Smith."[1] These will last me for some time. I have had to write seven or eight letters since I have been here & have half a dozen more on hand, with no convenience whatever for writing, as you may judge by my handwriting. The night after my letter to Miss Sue our leaking fly gave us a nocturnal bath, so like rats, which abandon a leaking vessel, we transferred ourselves to a tent, which is at least dry. I have received only your first letter, & not one from the people at home. Am expecting some to be forwarded to me from Richmond.

I read a beautiful & admirable sermon of Robertson's this morning on the text, "Eye hath not seen, nor ear heard &c." As often happens with me, that was sent to me which I most needed at the time. There was much in it calculated to comfort and encourage me in the state of mind in which it found me. We are all too much dependent upon circumstances for happiness & contentment. He who loves God truly, for whom have been prepared the "things" spoken of in the text, ought to be altogether independent of earthly surroundings. The sermon contends that the "things prepared" are not the happiness that awaits us in the next world, but that which is attainable here by all who truly love God, no matter what their situation or circumstances. With you amid the beauties of nature, or by myself within the borders of the Dismal Swamp, if I but truly love Him, I have within my reach, around me

& above me, inexhaustible treasures of peace & joy. He is equally everywhere, & the soul that realizes its possession of Him must be happy anywhere. This solitude of which I have a taste here is, you know, what I think we all need at times. The frequent occasions on which our Saviour went on the lonely mountain or in the desert place apart to pray, have for a long time been a subject of thought with me. I have often upon my knees endeavoured to picture him there at midnight, communing with the Father as no other man has ever done. Oh for such prayer as went up from the heart of that only man who has ever known & loved God perfectly! When we are lifeless & cannot lift up our souls to God, it is always of advantage to us to turn to the man Jesus & contemplate him under circumstances similar to our own, & where can our experience extend where he did not reach. He came here to put us in the same relation to God with himself, as I have always thought indicated by those words after his work was finished. "I go to my God & your God & to my Father & your Father." As much to say "What God is to me, He now is to you." Therefore it should be our aim to be to the Father what Jesus was, to aspire to the same intimate filial communion, to pray for that same "grace without measure" which was given to him & finally to hear applied to ourselves the words "this is my beloved Son, in whom I am well pleased." God sees us in His Son, in proportion as we see ourselves in Him, & the only relief for us in our hours of bitter self-condemnation & self-abhorrence is to look away from ourselves infinitely unrighteous in ourselves to ourselves perfectly righteous in Him.

Pray for me, my Darling, that I may improve this opportunity which has been given me of increasing my faith by prayer & meditation, of this identifying myself more & more by faith with the Son of God, acquiring his mind, his Spirit, his intimate communion face to face with the Father, & finally preparing myself to go forth in his Spirit & in his strength to do His work.

I have very little to do just now, & do I am afraid less than I might find to do if I felt more interested. I wrote to Col. Stevens a long letter yesterday. I was sorry to see the death of his eldest child, a sweet & interesting little girl, in the papers some days ago. I hear that Dick Dwight has been appointed a Lt. in the So.Ca. regulars, but don't know whether he has accepted.[2] I will find no man to take his place with me. He has an amount of hard common sense & judgment and manly independence united with enthusiasm, freshness & buoyancy of spirit, which was of great service to me.

And so you think I am fortunate in my sisters. You know how well I agree with you. I wish I were more to them than I am. You know the peculiarities & the needs of each now, & can do much to supply my deficiencies.

If anything should happen to me I want you to feel always as a sister to them. It will do them more good than it will you, & they w'd be glad to be enabled to regard you in that light. I have always told them that I wished them to look upon Miss Sue as a part of yourself, & to treat you both the same, and am very glad that they found it so easy to love her, though not at all surprised. Give much love to Miss Sue & remember me to Miss Lila & all other friends. Send my love to your Mother & Sister Martha, Aunt Eliza & the children when you write.

And now Good Night, my precious Darling. God bless & keep you & bring you daily nearer to His Son!

Yrs affectionately
W. P. DuBose

1. Sydney Smith (1771–1845) was an English writer and clergyman.
2. Richard Y. Dwight probably served as a second lieutenant in the First South Carolina Regulars. See Compiled Service Records, First (Butler's) South Carolina Infantry (First Regulars), M267, roll 112.

Kinston N.C.
Nov. 29th 1862

Your letter of the 24th reached me day before yesterday, Darling, bringing with it also the truant of the 18th. I readily forgave the latter for its dilatoriness both on its own acc't & for the good company in which it came, & enjoyed the double treat with more relish than a dinner after a day's fast. (A hard experience has made me practical, you see, in my choice of illustrations.) I had set apart a portion of yesterday to give them a speedy reply, but it was taken from me by other business.

I hope you succeeded in reaching Augusta before the convention[1] adjourned, & were rewarded for the early hour you gave me by a pleasant day, though I suppose you did not, as your subsequent letter made no allusion to the fact. I am somewhat interested in the result of the Lay. reading discussion. If the old batchelor was overruled, and ladies are to enjoy the privilege Mr. Trapier contended for. I wish you would begin at once to strengthen your voice by constant practice, preparatory to relieving me occasionally in the reading desk. I have not seen a word in the papers of the proceedings of the Council.

I am glad to hear that you are enjoying your visit so much. My contribution to your happiness, Darling, is a subject of deep gratification to me, &

thankfulness to God. Every night I read & talk by the fire until the Dr. my tent mate, retires. Then I poke up the fire to a cheerful blaze, & gaze into it for an hour or so by myself, conjuring up every conceivable image of happiness. You of course are always with me in these hours of joy, but then we have other visitors. Sometimes my sisters come up one by one, & I think over the particular disposition, trials & needs of each, and of my debt to them for their quiet & thoughtful goodness to me. Everything that I love comes up before me in these moments of sweet reflection, but it is you after all that monopolizes most of my thoughts. I do indeed pray for you, Dearest, that all your heart may be given to Christ, & all His Grace imparted to you. Much as I prize your love for me, it is much sweeter to think of your love for Him. Human love is so dear to us, that I for one am often tempted to rest too much in it. It is only sometimes that I can share Sir Galahad's higher transports.

> "More bounteous aspects on me beam,
> "Me mightier transports move and thrill."[2]

I am living comfortably now, and am really enjoying it exceedingly. I am the last one left of the old <u>appointed</u> field & staff. The command of the Legion has passed into its own hands, that is into the hands of one of the elected officers. The senior Captain commands, & he will be promoted if Major Palmer does not return. My peculiar position gives me consideration & influence without responsibility, an enviable popularity without odium or envy, and, what is of most value to me, peace of mind undisturbed by ambition or disappointment.

The only thing that will induce me to leave will be a prospect of having to go into battle without some improvement in the Company officers. I know by experience the effect of this need in battle.

I am appointed Judge Advocate of a Court of Inquiry to sit at Kinston on Monday. I hope it will not prove a repetition of my Adams Run experience in that capacity.

I am very cheerful & hopeful on the subject of the war, but w'd find it difficult to give my grounds for being so. I am happy to hear that Mr. Barnwell is so. It must be distressing to them to be so unsettled. I hope the search for another horse was satisfactory in its results.

Miss Anne Johnson is Tom Dudley's half sister. She is very fond of me & is very anxious to know you. In spite of my losses, I am well protected against the cold, of which we have been having some experience.

I am very glad to hear of your Cousin Nannie's confirmation. A person of her depth of character, sincerity & humility cannot take such a step lightly, & is therefore most liable to those peculiar trials. But she will triumph over them with God's help, & be proportionably [*sic*] more deep & earnest in her faith & love.

Much love to Miss Sue and all friends. Goodbye my Darling.

Yrs in love

W. P. DuBose

1. The first formal convention of the Protestant Episcopal Church in the Confederate States of America was held in Augusta, Georgia, on November 19–21, 1862. A Southern Bible Society was organized at this convention. See Thomas, *Protestant Episcopal Church,* 60.

2. This is from the poem "Sir Galahad" by Alfred Lord Tennyson. See Tennyson, *Poems and Plays,* 189.

Hospital Goldsboro

Dec. 16th 1862

I hope this note will reach you, my Darling, before any other acc't of me, otherwise my neck will be sure to be wrung the next time I see your sister Martha. I received what I at first thought a mortal wound on Sunday, but it has disappointed me very much in the same way that DuBose Porcher's did, and my recovery to perfect health will be only a matter of a few weeks' time, I trust. The ball (musket) made seven holes through my thick clothing before it reached me. It entered near the hip & stopped short of the intestines. I was carried three or four miles in a litter & in a blanket when the ball was extracted, & I then traveled twenty miles in an ambulance to within twelve miles of this place where I took the cars, & arrived here yesterday. I was very sore & painful [*sic*] when I first arrived, but feel perfectly easy this morning, sufficiently so to be propped up for writing. In fact, now that the pain has passed off, I call my wound a slight one. We made a pretty vigorous resistance to a vastly superior force the other side of Kinston. The Holc. Legion left Greenville on Friday, reached Kinston on Saturday & was put immediately into position after a march of thirty five miles. On Saturday we held our ground for three or four hours & were the last to retire & cross the bridge, having to do so through the flames.

Reinforcements are being rapidly hurried through but they may not be in time to save this place, as the enemy are very strong. We will probably be

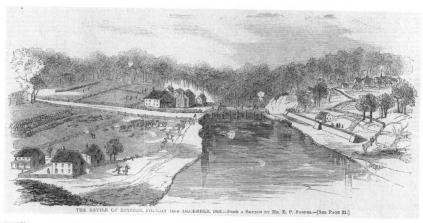

THE BATTLE OF KINSTON, FOUGHT 14th DECEMBER, 1862.—From a Sketch by Mr. E. P. Forbes.—[See Page 21.]

William Porcher DuBose was seriously wounded while in command of the Holcombe Legion during the battle of Kinston in North Carolina. *Harper's Weekly* 7 (January 10, 1863): 20

sent to Raleigh today, & if I can get home I will do so. They are fighting now in hearing of this place.[1]

I have no time to write more now, my Darling. With much gratitude to God for this additional proof of His guardianship & care, and with much love to you & your household, I remain

Yrs affectionately
W. P. DuBose

I hope this will find you at home.

1. From December 16 to 17, 1862, Union major general John G. Foster's troops engaged Confederate forces near Goldsboro and attempted to destroy the bridges over the Neuse River. See Barrett, *Civil War in North Carolina,* 145–47.

Dec. 1862?
Dearest Nannie, I have been trusting to the good nature of Miss Sue & yourself, to excuse my not answering your letters which I assure you gratified me intensely. You can imagine the turmoil of mind & body I have been enduring for some time. Moving here, sending [Brother's] things home, & fixing [Brothers] at the same time, which literally gave me not one minute's leisure. I promise very soon to make amends for past remissness. Now comes a request dear Nannie that seems too much to ask of you, yet we cannot resist

making the attempt. There seems but one thing needed, to make of our grateful joy [perfect], that is to have Miss Sue & yourself again with us. I could not tell you how delighted, how very grateful we would be if you could come to us. I do not ask this through form dear Nannie, but because our hearts are set upon this. We all feel that you are a part of ourselves & crave another [re-union]. Tell Miss Sue, with a kiss, I say the same to her. You have made us love you & now must pay the penalty. We tell Brother W, he only thinks & wishes for you, & leaves no time or thought for us. You should have heard his laments all last evening.

He is thin, & looks as if he has been suffering, but is much better than we dared hope. There seems no end to the mercy showered upon us. He ought to keep very quiet, moves about badly, & is obliged to wear a dressing gown.

Do write as soon as possible & relieve our suspense about your coming. We are at last fixed, & [just] ready to give you a [little] corner.

I will try & write in a day or two, & tell you something of ourselves. The [lamp] arrived safely, answers beautifully, just what I wanted. What was the express bill. I will send the money very soon but would like to pay it in person. A cheering Christmas & peaceful New Year. Best love to Sue.

Yours A. S. D.[1]

1. Anne Stevens DuBose.

Charleston, S. C. Dec. 23, 1862

My dear friend,

Your wound puts a stop to my procrastination, and I now hasten to answer that letter of yours you wrote me from Kinston, soon after getting there. I had hoped and prayed, that after so many hair breadth [*sic*] escapes you would get through the war without any serious wound, but, to judge from the list given in a Fayetteville paper, you must be hurt severely in the groin. I say, severely, only because I can't conceive of a wound there being a slight one, of course I hope and shall keep hoping for the best, until I hear from you, or of you from someone at your hospital. Perhaps this letter like some of its predecessors may miss you, in case, as I half wish, you may have already started homewards to recruit. Whether it does or not, I want to write now, and tell you once more how often you are in my mind and in my prayers, for I look to Him who has given you to your friends and His Church

to be your safeguard and defence through all these dangers, I look confident-
ly, and believing, shall not I receive? Your Brigade deserves the thanks of the
country, special thanks, I mean, for their brave and protracted resistance to
superior numbers; and I expect, for the time it lasted, the fight must have
been as fierce and exhausting as any you have yet been through. Oh, how
disappointed I was at not being able to get off from duty, when you were in
Fairfield, and run up to see you. I had so many questions to ask, so many
things to talk over. Ever since that time I have been kept so busy I could
scarcely find time to read a newspaper (you know how busy that must be).
Soon after adding to my St. Andrews Map the change of works on E. James
Island, which I told you of, the powers that be ordered by way of extras two
extensive Reconnaissances & Reports: one of the Altamaha Riv. Ga., which
took me, with preparation of sketches report &c ten days close work, the
other of the Stono and back by land through Evans old Dist., the Adams
Run and Rantowles country, which involved a map and 20 letter pages of
Report. In the cause of this latter reconnaissance I paid a very pleasant visit
to the camp of the Marion Artillery near Simmons Bluff spending two
nights and part of one day with them. It so happened that, riding into their
lines after dark, I was challenged by our friend Salt, and we stood confronting
each other in the most formal and military manner for some time before a
light was brought and my pass read by the Corporal of the guard. I found the
theologs all looking extremely well and they and the officers did everything
in their power to make my time pass agreeably. With the Cpt. I found I was
renewing an old schoolboy acquaintance or rather intimacy, and Wilkins and
Lowndes among the Lieuts. were also old acquaintances. Gadsden's mother
& sister Cath. I see in the city again, and shall by all means call and tell them
how well I left Thomas. Although it is so near Christmas I am yet unable to
promise a visit to my sisters in Sumter. After disappointing them three times,
the most I can say is that I hope to get off before New Year. They hardly ever
write without inquiring when I last heard from you and how you were. I
have given them from time to time your messages and can assure you they
are valued and reciprocated.

You must have heard 'ere this of Mr. Dehon's[1] death here in the city after
a short illness with Typhoid fever. He had never been well since last winter
and must have been overtaxing his strength all the time. He was a devoted
man and had attached many of the congregation to him. Mr. Howe will
probably succeed him. Last week brot [sic] me a letter from Tom Dudley in
which he makes mention of several of our friends. C. L. C. Minor[2] is an
Ordnance Cpt. I have heard also at some length from our friend Lantz B.,

who writes from Lynchburg where he's on detached service as clerk to a surgeon, and seems to be enjoying the change. Hoping, my dear DuBose, to hear favorable accounts from you in your handwriting and not ceasing day & night to think of & to pray for you, I remain as ever yours

Truly & affectionately

Jno. Johnson

1. The Reverend William Dehon (1817–62) was rector of St. Philip's Episcopal Church. See Thomas, *Protestant Episcopal Church,* 258; WPA Cemetery Index.

2. Charles Landon Carter Minor (1835–1903), a native of Virginia, served in the Second Virginia Cavalry and was later an ordnance officer in the Army of Northern Virginia. After the war he became a well-known educator and writer and is best known for his book *The Real Lincoln,* an unfavorable assessment of Abraham Lincoln. See Tyler, *Encyclopedia of Virginia Biography,* 3:188.

Winnsboro

Dec. 26th 1862

I was distressed, Dearest, to learn by your note to Sister which reached her yesterday, that neither of my notes from N.C. had reached you as late as the 23rd. I wrote in Goldsboro on the 16th & in Raleigh on the 19th, I think, both in bed. The letter from G. was sent before the list was made which was published in the Raleigh papers, & which you saw copied in the S.C. papers, and I was sure that you w'd receive the first acc't of my wound from myself. I am working hard, you see to save my neck, but besides that I am too sorry to be so constantly causing you unnecessary pain. You have been called upon to practise all your faith & I trust Darling that you will be rewarded for it. Sister A. says that the reason they did not write to you was that my letters failed . . . them too in time, & they were sure that you had heard more than they.

The Chief Surgeon at Raleigh is the son of an old & dear college friend of Father's & was more than kind to me. I staid [sic] with him several days & was delighted with his wife & himself. One of our men who was taken prisoner & paroled was detailed to take care of me, which he was glad to do as I got him a furlough & paid his way. With his assistance I got home very comfortably and am improving rapidly. The wound gives me little or no pain, although it may take some time to heal & keep me at home in the meantime. If you were here I could bear it very philosophically, but it gives me some trouble to practise patience without you. Sister Anne & myself wrote to you yesterday to beg you & Miss Sue to come, but I don't set my heart upon it. It w'd be too . . . a disappointment if you did not come. I will not dwell upon that subject for fear of raising my hopes. Sister B. says you must come if only to see how the baby has improved. She says she was feeling so badly while you were here that she does not feel as if she had become acquainted with you. Sister Jane is with Mrs. Means, improving slowly. She told them to send for her if I came but as I am likely to be here some time we will not do it yet. I found them all . . . well here, except little Porcher [who is] very thin & unwell.

Mrs. Sass'[1] death was very distressing to us all. She was a rare woman. Mr. Gadsden's notice of her in the "Southern Episcopalian" is very just. There is an acc't of Octavius Porcher's school in the same no. of the S.E.

Dick Dwight has had charge of a hospital in Warrenton, but left after Major Palmer's death to accept a Lieutenancy at [Fort] Moultrie. He is going on a . . . visit to Abbeville on Monday & expects to return the same week. Tell Miss Sue that I not only lost the socks she seemed so concerned about, but have had the additional & greater misfortune of losing the red ones she gave me. I am not bankrupt yet though as I had in reserve the two prs you sent me.

Mr. Hutcheson[2] has just been paying me a visit, which has lost me today's mail, so I will not quite finish my letter yet.

I am reaping some of the advantages of being wounded. Oysters have been sent to me from two different sources, ladies too. Besides that I am not expected to pay visits, or to rise from my chair when visitors come, which saves a great deal of trouble for a lazy man. I have not said a word about Christmas. I hope you heard from me in time to lift a shadow from your enjoyment of the day. It is very quiet with us. Good bye my Darling. May the next Christmas be a happy, peaceful one to us both.

Yrs with much love
W. P. DuBose

Much love to the household. [Give a] Christmas kiss [to the] girls.

1. Octavia Murden Sass (1813–62) was the wife of Jacob K. Sass. See Tison and Stoney, "Recollections of John Safford Stoney," 209; Jervey, *Inscriptions in St. Michael's,* 242.

2. The Reverend James Theodore Hutcheson was the rector of St. John's Episcopal Church in Winnsboro. See Thomas, *Protestant Episcopal Church,* 182, 625.

Winnsboro, S.C.
Dec. 30th 1862

Your letter, Darling, reached me on Sunday & did not disappoint me enough
to prevent my enjoying it. In fact I knew what your answer w'd be & refused
to set my heart on your coming. The girls say they did not know how much
hope they had, until your letter came. As for my going to Anderson you may
rest assured that I will go as soon & stay as long as I can. My furlough was
for 30 days from the 23rd but I promised to return sooner if possible; that is
not likely to be though, as my wound has only lately begun to suppurate. As
soon as it is sufficiently healed to enable me to dress properly & do a moderate amount of walking without risk, I will start for Anderson. The sooner
that is, the longer I will be able to remain. I promise to keep still & hurry up
the time.

Frank & Edmund Gaillard are at home, both slightly wounded at Fredericksburg.[1] Moultrie Dwight rec'd an injury which though slight in itself
has brought back pains in his back.[2] He will probably come home this week
& may be for a long time or even permanently incapacitated for service. On
the whole our family have been signally blessed in this war, considering the
no. of men in the service.

You ask about my Raleigh friends. While I was in the hospital the Grimes
could not come very well to see me, but they sent me constantly little delicacies &c, and before I left I went out into the yard & saw them. Their brother invited me to his house, as did also another gentleman of the town, but I
was afraid it might delay my getting off. The latter part of the time I stayed
with Dr. Hill to whom & his sweet little wife I took a great fancy. Our fathers
were dear friends as boys at the North, and it made great friends of us in a
very short time.

About the battle & other matters connected with it I promise to tell you
everything when I see you. I will not be as disobliging as I was before. To satisfy you though in the meantime I will give you a brief sketch of our part
in the affair. We reached Greenville on Wednesday, remained there Thursday
& were ordered back on Friday. We marched back to Kinston (33 miles) by
midday Saturday & were ordered in at once to meet the enemy. The skirmishing had ceased when we reached the ground, & we were put into position in the immediate centre with the expectation of an attack at daylight
next morning. You may imagine how much sleeping was done by our 2000
men awaiting the advance of 20,000. About ten o.c. on Sunday came one
shot from our advanced picket, then another and another, each nearer than
the last. Words cannot express the feelings excited by those isolated reports

falling at last upon ears which have been listening for them for hours. The man who has been through battles & knows what they are must have strong nerves to keep a constant pulse & a steady hand at that trying moment. That is the time for cool officers. A command given in a trembling voice just then might produce a panic or even a stampede, where such odds are expected. We were not kept waiting long. The roar of artillery & musketry soon became deafening & the men soon warmed up with work & then really behaved well. We were growing quite enthusiastic about one o.c. having successfully resisted them at every point up to that time, when at the very crisis of the engagement and at the very pitch of the excitement & enthusiasm I was shot & immediately borne off the field in a litter. As I passed by the General he enquired who it was & when he was told came & grasped my hand & said "You always were a gallant man, sir." He then gave me a drink & made me bathe my face in brandy which revived me very much. He was very kind to me afterwards, sending his Chief Surgeon to see me & speaking in rather flattering terms about me. How c'd I help feeling better towards him, to be treated in that way when I believed myself mortally wounded.

Dr. Robertson has come to see me & I must stop. Much love to all & all send love.

Yrs affectionately
W. P. DuBose

1. Lt. Col. Franklin Gaillard of the Second Regiment South Carolina Infantry was wounded on December 18, 1862, near Fredericksburg, Virginia. Cpl. Thomas Edmund Gaillard (1840–63), Company I, Second South Carolina Infantry Regiment, was wounded on December 13, 1862. See Compiled Service Records, Second South Carolina Infantry Regiment (Second Palmetto Regiment), M267, roll 155; MacDowell, *Gaillard Genealogy*, 23.

2. First Lt. William Moultrie Dwight was listed as detached as acting assistant inspector general on General Kershaw's staff. The editors could find no record of his being wounded at Fredericksburg, Virginia. See Compiled Service Records, Second South Carolina Infantry Regiment (Second Palmetto Regiment), M267, roll 155.

3

A Change in Vocation
1863

"With regard to my views of the Chaplaincy, I would not have you imagine that I underrate the importance & necessity of the office."
April 9, 1863

By the spring of 1863 DuBose was once again in combat with the Holcombe Legion, this time in Mississippi. From there the unit moved to Mobile, Alabama; then to a sea island near Savannah, Georgia; and finally back to Charleston. By the end of 1863 DuBose had received a commission to serve as a chaplain in Kershaw's Brigade and had begun his vocation as a military minister.

Winnsboro Jan. 7th 1863

It is nearly a week, Darling, since I sent my last letter to you in consequence of constant company which has left me scarcely a moment to myself. My Uncle Edward DuBose[1] came up on Friday and paid us a delightful visit until Monday. Besides that, in the interval Major Means & family have paid me a visit, Mr. Roberts & Chassie[2] are still with us and Dick Dwight left last night. All this besides morning & evening visits. As I am in the house always I have done little reading, writing or thinking. I regret this the more as I really wished to say something in connection with the theological questions you proposed to me, which I cannot do now for want of reflection as well as time, as we go to Church directly. I will write to you again in a day or so.

Dick came back to see Moultrie who is not looking or feeling well. I was glad to hear from Uncle Edward that Col. or Mr. Stevens[3] is giving great satisfaction in St. Johns. He, Mr. S., is very anxious that I sh'd leave the service now and join him in a different work. He has so many negroes [*sic*] under his charge that he needs an assistant and has written not only to me but to the B'p on the subject. I have not answered yet, but have little doubt what my decision will be. The Col. writes very affectionately.

I see you have prevailed upon Personne[4] to publish me at last. I don't know who or what else could have produced the effect, and I know it was a favorite plan of yours. How did you bribe him?

I hope to get to Anderson next week. I think I will be able to go by Monday without risk but may not go for some days later to give you full time for your Pendleton visit. I am very glad you went to Miss Carrie. Her case is a very different one from mine, & you might have regretted not going to her. If this letter finds you in Pendleton, remember me affectionately to her. I got a long letter from Thos. Gadsden a day or two ago, and have rec'd so many others that I despair of answering them.

Sister Anne says she is ashamed of not having written to Miss Sue & yourself & wants me to write for her, but I refuse. They are all well except Porcher who does not thrive. Augusta began school on Monday and seems delighted; her teacher writes that she "does <u>nicely</u>," which in connection with the underscore Daughter interprets to mean "very nicely," and is gratified accordingly.

I am afraid our Tennessee victory has ended as all other western victories have done.[5] There seems to be a fatality about them.

Chassie Roberts plays very sweetly on the piano & I have been enjoying her music. You know she is engaged to Thos. McCrady who is at home wounded.

I am glad of course that I am to have the additional pleasure of seeing John Elliott in Anderson. I hope I will hear him preach.

I suppose we are to have more fighting in No.Ca. I hear that it is well ascertained that Foster has now 50,000 men at Newbern.[6] And they say that a portion of our army at Fredericksburg is to be sent to No.Ca. I wonder if I will get there in time.

I have no time to write more. Give much love to your Mother, Miss Sue, your Sister Martha & Aunt Eliza. Remember me particularly to Miss Harriet and kiss Margie and Lize for me.

Yours with much love
W. P. DuBose

1. Julius Edward DuBose (1829–96) of St. Stephen's Parish, South Carolina, was the half brother of William Porcher DuBose's father. See MacDowell, *DuBose Genealogy*, 9, 14.

2. Mary Charlotte Roberts (b. 1844), the daughter of the Reverend John J. Roberts, married Thomas Nightingale McCrady (1843–82) in 1867. He was the son of Edward and Louisa R. McCrady of Charleston. See McCrady, *Mrs. Edward McCrady*, 49ff.

3. Peter Fayssoux Stevens resigned from the Confederate army in October 1862 to return to his ministry as an Episcopal priest. He "returned to his pastoral charge at Black Oak, and there finding a large negro [*sic*] population without ministerial service, he devoted much of his time to labor among them." See *Confederate Military History,* 6:861.

4. This is the pen name of Felix Gregory DeFontaine (1834–96), a native of Boston, Massachusetts, and the son of a French nobleman. He was a congressional reporter in Washington and a member of the New York press before the war. He moved to Charleston in 1860, and in 1861 he became a military correspondent with the rank of major, providing reports for the *Charleston Courier.* In 1862 he founded the *Daily South Carolinian,* a newspaper published in Columbia. See DeFontaine, *Army Letters of 1861–1865;* Stone, *Wandering to Glory,* 57; Wakelyn, *Biographical Dictionary of the Confederacy,* 168.

5. The battle of Stone's River, December 31, 1862–January 2, 1863, began with the Confederate general Braxton Bragg's Army of Tennessee driving back the forces of Union major general William S. Rosecrans's Army of the Cumberland. Rosecrans, however, formed a stable defensive line, which repelled further Confederate assaults. Faced with an enemy who refused to retreat, Bragg withdrew his forces after declaring "victory." See McPherson, *Battle Cry of Freedom,* 579–82.

6. Union major general John Gray Foster (1823–74), commander of the Department of North Carolina, returned to New Bern, North Carolina, following his December 1862 raid on Goldsboro. See Barrett, *Civil War in North Carolina,* 147–48; Warner, *Generals in Blue,* 157–58.

Winnsboro S.C.
Jany 10th 1863

On the day on which my last letter was dispatched, Darling, I rec'd most unexpectedly by R.R. another visitor, in the shape of John Johnson. He came up to spend [29] hours with me, my share of eight days furlough, which of course I enjoyed no little, short as it was. He had just completed his map & reconnaissances, and got this furlough by way of reward I suppose. He left night before last at 2 ½ A.M. and the consequence was that I spent all day yesterday unprofitably for want of sleep, instead of writing several letters which I sh'd have done.

I rec'd yesterday your letter from Pendleton. I suppose you will have returned by the time this reaches you. I talk of leaving for Anderson about next Tuesday although I have not yet tried the experiment of dressing myself presentably. I wear a loose cloak which, if it w'd pass muster in other respects, has grown rather too shabby for general exhibition. My furlough expires on the 23rd and I think from present appearances I will have no excuse for pro-longing it beyond that time, while at the same time I will enjoy little or no margin of perfect health as I will scarcely be able to walk [freely] before that time. Robert says he is going back with me; he has made up his mind positively to enter the service somewhere & no one opposes him.

Mr. Roberts left on Thursday taking all his children with him on a visit. Sister A. will go for them when I leave & pay a short visit also. If I can do so, I w'd like to take the Wilmington route & spend a day or so in Camden on my way back to N.C.

I have been quite disturbed by the rumours of the fall of Vicksburg, and am by no means satisfied that they are well grounded.[1] I suppose that the threatened movements in N.C. will hardly take place before my return, although I am by no means ambitious of getting back in time. The North does not seem to be relaxing its efforts, and bright as our prospects have been for some time past we may soon be plunged again into the uncertainties of another struggle for Richmond. Still the past should give us more hope, & what is better, more faith, for the future.

Inactivity and the want of exercise, while my general health is pretty good, tells a little upon my spirits sometimes & predisposes me to despon-dency. You must make up your mind to find me most uninteresting, and take credit to yourself for the change, if it should be otherwise. There are several letters requiring some exertion which I ought to have written ere this and I have not yet been able to stimulate myself to the task. One to Mr. Sass,[2] for example, who in the midst of all his trouble has not been unmindful of his interest in me, and has sent me several messages. Miss Malvina is much bet-ter, quite out of danger I hope.

Sunday. 11th. You ask me for some scriptural proofs of the divinity & per-sonality of the Holy Ghost. If I were in reach of my books or had even a concordance with me, it would not be difficult to give the usual arguments or to make a collection of the texts usually adduced in proof. But really, to judge by my own experience, I do not think that mere logical argument, even when based upon Scriptures, has much effect in settling these painful religious doubts. I remember early in my religious life being much troubled by the texts which seem to deny the divinity of our Saviour. They kept con-stantly recurring to me, and all the other texts of Scripture did not seem to me sufficient to counterbalance them. I knew however that I was not capa-ble then of settling such a question, and all I could do was to pray to be led into the truth. After a while it ceased to trouble me, and the subject never confronted me again until comparatively lately. When one has sounded the depths of the Gospel, has been led by the Spirit of Truth into the mysteries of redemption & been taught the riches of the grace of God in Christ Jesus, he knows that the Son of God is divine. The Gospel loses all of its meaning, all its warmth, its power, its life without this doctrine, & consequently we see that those who begin by denying it are obliged to go on to the denial of the atonement and all the most fundamental & essential truths of the Gospel. Many a man who, upon the mere comparison of texts & weighing of testimony, has decided in favor of Unitarianism, has, in his deeper and humbler seeking after truth, been brought back to Trinitarianism by the Heaven-inspired want of a personal Saviour and the felt necessity of this doctrine to the fullness & power of the Gospel. He is willing to believe Jesus only a man until he feels how cold & inoperative & unsatisfying a thing is a Gospel based upon this hypothesis. He finds then that he must go back & remodel his foundation before he can rise high enough to share the transports of St. Paul. The most tender & affecting testimonies to the truth that we have had, have been from men who having been kept out in the cold & darkness of Unitarianism until late in life by the pride of reason, have at last been subdued & humbled by the Spirit of God to an acknowledgement of faith in a divine Saviour.

Therefore I say that I never feel like arguing such questions even with proofs drawn from Scripture. I feel the profoundest sympathy with anyone who is painfully seeking after the Truth and can only say to them, "Study the Word of God with humility & with prayer & you will be led into all Truth." There are only two ways by which we are ever brought to a belief in the Trinity. The first is to receive it on the authority of the Church until we come to a practical knowledge of it for ourselves. The second is so to study the Gospel and accept its teachings as to be taught of God all that it contains. The 2nd chapter of 1 Cor. teaches us that the Spirit of God alone can teach us the mysteries of the Gospel, and surely there is no greater mystery nor any which more requires the teaching of that Spirit than the doctrine of the Trinity. When we begin to argue on the subject we plunge at once into metaphysics.

With regard to the divinity of the Holy Ghost there is & can be no question, the doubt is concerning His personality, and here a very great part of the difficulty arises from the indefiniteness of the term used. The word "Person" is a very vague one, and we only employ it for the want of any other to express more nearly the sense of the original (Greek). It is used in this connection not in its popular but in its metaphysical sense, and even then there is no word in theology which is so unsatisfactory or so difficult to define precisely. Personality does not mean here, as in popular languages, separate existence. We do not mean to say that the persons of the Trinity exist separately & distinctly, on the contrary, though they are to be distinguished from each other and are actually so distinguished in Scripture in their persons, offices, &c, yet they are <u>one</u>. We may speak of the Sun, its rays & its heat and distinguish these three without affirming their separate existence, or the mind, the intellect and the affections &c. Not that these objects bear exactly the same relations to one another that the persons of the Trinity do. What that precise relation is we don't know, because it has not been revealed to us. All that we know is that Jesus Christ is God and that the Holy Ghost is God and that they are one with the Father, and yet that in the Bible they are distinguished in their persons & in their offices, and as this distinction is useful one to the proper comprehension of the Gospel we express it by the term Trinity. Now let one read the New Testament & see if the Holy Ghost is not distinguished thus throughout from the other persons of the Trinity. See for example John 14:26, 15:26, 16:7–15 &c where the Father is spoken of as sending the Holy Ghost, & the son is spoken of as sending Him, and His peculiar office & mission is described. We are told elsewhere not to blaspheme, and not to grieve, not to resist the Holy Ghost &c. In the benediction "The Grace of our Lord Jesus Christ, & the Son of God & the fellowship of the Holy Ghost" the three persons are named together. I say nothing of 1 John v. 7 because there is some doubt of its genuineness.

I mention these passages which are some that occur to me at the moment. Whatever is intended in Scripture by this consistent keeping of the distinctive characteristics of the nature & office of the Holy Ghost we try to express in the term "personality" and no more. In the work of redemption each person of the Trinity has his peculiar office, & this distinction of offices is kept up consistently in the main, with just sufficient blending & interchange occasionally to exhibit the cooperation of the three persons & the unity of the whole work. The deniers of the Trinity contend that the H. G. is only the influence, the agency, the power of God exerted in the heart of man, but the Bible in describing His operation &c uses language which can only be applied to a Person intended to be distinguished from the other Persons of the Godhead, & so following the Bible we keep up the distinction by giving it a name.

It is very late & I am afraid my extempore ideas on the subject are neither very clear in themselves nor very clearly expressed. However I may fail in this respect though, I promise my constant prayers that the Holy Spirit will testify of Himself as He has testified of Jesus to every earnest seeker of the Truth.

Give much love to Miss Sue & all the household, and believe me Darling as ever

Yrs most affectionately

W. P. DuBose

1. On December 29, 1862, Union troops under Maj. Gen. William T. Sherman were defeated at the battle of Chickasaw Bluff as they attempted to capture Vicksburg. See McPherson, *Battle Cry of Freedom,* 578–79.

2. Jacob Keith Sass (1813–65), a Charleston banker, was an active layman in the Episcopal Church and served as the treasurer of domestic missions of the Protestant Episcopal Church of the Confederacy. See Thomas, *Protestant Episcopal Church,* 56, 493, 670; Sass, *South Carolina Lowcountry,* 3:936; Jervey, *Inscriptions in St. Michael's,* 241.

Winnsboro, S.C.

Jan. 28th 1863

I reached home yesterday, Darling, without any further mishap than missing the connection in Columbia and being obliged to spend the night there in consequence. I met Dr. Jervey[1] on the cars, and Wm. Haskell[2] in Columbia; you predicted that I w'd find acquaintances. Poor Mrs. McCord, Haskell told me, is in great distress for her son.[3] The intelligence came to her very suddenly & with great shock. I saw the Misses Blake in Newberry & delivered the messages; they did not look as happy as they did in Anderson. I left the bundle at [Janey's].

All are well at home, except that Willie looks a little thin. Porcher is improving by last acc'ts. [Mrs. Sams] is with us & will be until next Tuesday. She is quite agreeable. It has been snowing all day today but melts as fast as it falls, except on the trees & housetops. I wonder if it has extended to Anderson & if it reminds you of me. You w'd have a more satisfactory answer than I gave you in words to the question you asked me Sunday night, if you could read my heart now. I wish you could do so, Dearest, not that I think you doubt my love, but that you might know how great it is. When I think how much you have given up & will give up for me, how freely & unreservedly you have given me your love & confidence, I feel with how much right you could say that you w'd not be satisfied with anything less than a great deal of love from me. You are entitled to all the love I am capable of, Darling, and may I always fulfill my obligations in this respect with as much ease & happiness to myself as I do now! Do not imagine that you are ever uninteresting to me. Your simple presence, when I seem most unconscious of it, gives me happiness, and I long for the day to come when I shall be no more deprived of that presence in this world.

I came home to find Robert[4] engaged & crazy on the subject. He declares he does love the girl too much; and what is more he seems equally charmed with himself for being capable of such unparalleled devotion. He says he is a changed man since last Saturday, that such a depth & tenderness of feeling he had never believed himself susceptible of, &c. When he gets there he cannot get away, goes for two hours & stays for nine or ten. She is a sweet girl, not eighteen, somewhat young and wild to the world, but modest & full of depth of feeling in reality, according to Robt. I believe I told you about her, Miss Minnie Boyce. Don't say anything about it yet, except to Miss Sue. R. has written to Mr. Boyce in Richmond & does not want it known until he gets his consent.

Now for another piece of news. We hear today that Dick Dwight[5] is engaged to Nina Ravenel, a cousin of ours. I believe I have told you about that too. We have only heard the bare fact, indirectly. She is a fine girl. Are not engagements growing common?

I still expect to leave for camp next week. Robert will follow the week after, I think. I have not seen the Dr. yet, but will consult him, in obedience to your orders. The newspapers today indicate more strongly than ever decided movements in Va. & N.C. It has grown quite dark & a fragment of candle which is all I have in my room has burned down in the socket. So I will stop, for the present at least. Much love to all & a kiss for the girls.

Yrs with much love
W. P. DuBose

1. This was probably James Postell Jervey (1808–75), a surgeon in the Confederate army. See Waring, *History of Medicine in South Carolina,* 251.

2. Capt. William Thomson Haskell (1837–63) of Company H, First South Carolina Infantry (McCreary's First Provisional Army) was the son of Charles T. Haskell and Sophia Cheves Haskell. He was killed in action leading his men at Gettysburg in 1863. William Porcher DuBose wrote a biographical notice of Haskell, whom he characterized as a "Christian hero." It was published in 1871 in *Biographical Sketches of Alumni of the University of Virginia Who Fell in the Confederate War* (q.v., 456–64). See Compiled Service Records, First (McCreary's) Infantry, M267, roll 129; Ferguson, *Abbeville County,* 50; WPA Cemetery Index.

3. Capt. Langdon Cheves McCord of Company H, Holcombe Legion, was wounded on August 29, 1862, at the battle of Second Manassas. He died of his wounds on January 23, 1863, in Virginia. He was the son of Mrs. Louisa S. McCord.

See Compiled Service Records, Holcombe Legion, M267, roll 377; *South Carolina Genealogies,* 3:85; WPA Cemetery Index.

4. William Porcher DuBose's brother Robert Marion DuBose (1841–1907) married Mary Pearson Boyce (b. 1845). See MacDowell, *DuBose Genealogy,* 13; WPA Cemetery Index.

5. Dr. Richard Yeadon Dwight married Rowena Elizabeth Ravenel (b. 1837), daughter of Dr. Henry Ravenel of Pooshee Plantation and a cousin of William Porcher DuBose, in 1863. See MacDowell, *DuBose Genealogy,* 262; Ravenel, *Ravenel Records,* 166.

Winnsboro Feb. 3rd / 63

What with having to go to Farmington and Roseland, paying & receiving visits, and settling up scores with less attractive correspondents than yourself, Darling, I have delayed this letter longer than I intended. I might have received another letter tomorrow if I had kept you more definitely informed as to my movements. I expect to leave tomorrow night for Camden & will be there until Monday so that if you have not already directed a letter to me there, you have yet time to do so. Direct to the care of the Bp. Your letter came in time. As you have so good an example as Hopeful's[1] to appeal to I shall have to forgive the despondency which you make a confession of. But remember that Hopeful was never caught but once, and was ever true to his name after that. I am sure you w'd cut Mrs. Diffidence's[2] acquaintance for good, Dearest, if only you knew how settled and immovable, and satisfied, I feel in my love. It is a part of my nature now, and cannot be eradicated so long as I feel secure of your love. I am glad you see in "Lucy"[3] what attached me to it; those little readings were very delightful. You must learn to read Scotch, as you will have to do the reading when we "settle down," and we will be sure to renew our acquaintance with the Ettrick Shepherd.[4]

We had a more successful snow last night, covering the ground completely. Today it all melted, but tonight is very cold. I hope tomorrow night will be more moderate, as I leave at 3 A.M.

Some evenings ago, Mrs. Cain and Miss Maria Horlbeck spent the evening with us and the latter sang for me to my heart's content. We spent yesterday evening with them & renewed the treat. She has a glorious voice.

Hurrah for our gun boats! What glorious exploits, to reanimate old Charleston.[5] We are growing quite brilliant on the water; Galveston has aroused our youthful navy.[6] Matters seem quiet in N.C. & I think they are weather bound in Va. Genl. Evans is now being tried by a court martial in

Goldsboro.[7] I am curious to see how it is to terminate. Mr. Boylston[8] has gone on to defend him. Col. Bratton came very near being made a Brigadier the other day. McGowan[9] had the advantage of being in the brigade in which the vacancy occurred besides having political influence, & was appointed.

You ought to see how devoted Willie Bratton[10] is to me. He repeats over & over "dis is <u>my</u> Uncle," throws his arms around me & squeezes me & says "dis is a big huggin." Every morning he mounts my knees & says "Now what shall we have?" "Let us have Yankee Doodle, or Dixie or Wait for the wagon or Bobtail horse or Bonnie Blue Flag, or There is a Happy Land &c," according to his taste. And he knows the names of them all & can recognise them immediately. The children are all well, and Porcher was improving when last heard from. Mr. Sams came today & he & his wife will leave on Thursday. Sister Betsey goes with them to Yorkville, to see her sisters Mrs. McLean & Mrs. Noble.[11] I like Mr. S. very much. I did not know that the omnibus driver had gone either to your house or to my room the morning I left. I had gone out long before he came and was sitting in the office of the Hotel when I was informed that the omnibus was ready. I am sorry he disturbed your household; I told him distinctly that I was staying at the Hotel. However it is a satisfaction to know that you were proof against all disturbance.

Thank Miss Sue for her note & tell her I will be very prudent. I don't think there is any further danger from my wound. I have not seen the [Dr.] yet, but will do so today. Robt. Wilson has a little daughter a few days old. Give much love to Miss Sue, your Mother & each of the members of the household & remember me to all other friends including Jno. Elliott.

From what I hear an attack on Charleston seems imminent, and may come in a day or two. Sunday was Communion day, and you may be assured that you were remembered Darling, as you always are in my prayers. The weather is very cold. I will write from Camden. All send love. Goodbye Dearest.

Yrs with much love

W. P. DuBose

1. This character in John Bunyan's *The Pilgrim's Progress* is the companion of Christian, the title character.

2. This character in *The Pilgrim's Progress* is wife to the giant named Despair.

3. DuBose refers here to "Lucy Gray," a poem by William Wordsworth.

4. James Hogg (1770–1835) was a Scottish poet.

5. On January 31, 1863, the CSS *Chicora* and CSS *Palmetto State* attacked Union naval ships blockading Charleston and forced them to retire from the mouth of the harbor for a brief time. See *Official Records Army,* 14:204–10.

6. On January 1, 1863, Confederate forces under the command of Maj. Gen. John B. Magruder recaptured Galveston, Texas, which Union forces had captured on October 5, 1862. See *Official Records Army*, 15:199–227.

7. Brig. Gen. Nathan G. Evans commanded Confederate forces during the battle of Kinston. After defending the town from Union attacks, Evans's command was forced to retreat. Following the battle, four of Evans's regimental commanders, led by Col. William Fitz McMaster of the Seventeenth South Carolina Infantry Regiment, and thirty-four company commanders requested a transfer from Evans's command. Evans responded by bringing charges of "misconduct before the enemy" against Colonel McMaster and Capt. M. V. Bancroft, of the Twenty-third South Carolina Infantry Regiment. Col. Spartan David Goodlett (1831–74), of the Twenty-second South Carolina Infantry Regiment, charged Evans with drunkenness, incompetence, unbecoming conduct, and cowardice. Evans arrested Goodlett for cowardice. McMaster was acquitted on all charges except one, and no records could be found of Bancroft's trial. Goodlett was convicted and cashiered in April 1864. See Stone, *Wandering to Glory*, 97; Goodlet, *Links in the Goodlett Chain*, 163–64.

8. Robert Bentham Boylston (1822–65) was a Winnsboro attorney and president of the court-martial. See *Cyclopedia of Eminent Men of the Carolinas*, 212.

9. Samuel McGowan (1819–97) of Abbeville, South Carolina, was promoted to the rank of brigadier general in January 1863. See Warner, *Generals in Gray*, 201–2.

10. William DuBose Bratton (1860–97) was the son of Dr. John Bratton. See MacDowell, *DuBose Genealogy*, 232.

11. They were the sisters-in-law of Elizabeth DuBose Bratton. See Bratton, "Letters," 10, SHC.

Holcombe Legion
Febry. 24th 1863

I have just remembered, Darling, that we are to move our camp tomorrow (about six miles nearer Wilmington) and that it may be inconvenient to write until we get settled. Particularly as we will have to give up our house now & have not yet secured tents. I would have written to you anyhow tonight, but remembered that I had not yet written to Minnie Boyce, & my conscience w'd not permit me to enjoy the pleasure of writing to you until I had performed the task (I must say it) of writing to her. This has brought me quite late, but I will at last begin. We were in hopes that Gen. Evans' return would be the signal for us to leave for Charleston but it has proved otherwise. Still, I have no doubt we will get there by the time the [ball] actually opens.[1] Oh how much depends upon the defence of our old City! And how glorious it would be to end the war there where it began! We have had rumours of

Jenkins' Brigade[2] & other portions of Longstreet's Corps coming down to So.Ca.[3] You have no doubt seen in the papers the decision of the court in the case of Genl. Evans. Col. Goodlett was the author of the charges against him. It was quite enough to have acquitted him, I think, without going on to denounce the prosecution as the court has done. I suppose the Genl. will retaliate now upon the Cols. who have prosecuted him—he has two of them under arrest.

My Lent fasting is not as compulsory as you imagine. Our board is always well spread with delicacies often, as well as substantials. We have been feasting upon the little cream that this country affords, while our men starve about every other day. In fact we live much higher (pecuniarily & gastronomically) than I care to do. However this is only temporary. We have a compound mess & therefore a large one, and large messes are always extravagant. When we move, we dissolve copartnership, & then we can take the liberty of being economical & frugal.

I trust however, that the close of this season of self-examination and self-denial and prayer will find me somewhat more spiritually minded than the beginning. You must not imagine that I live always or constantly in the presence and enjoyment of spiritual realities. My soul is often dark & heavy. Sometimes for days my daily prayer is "turn us again, Oh Lord. Show us the light of thy countenance & we shall be whole!" Light and life are not vouchsafed us in this world without intervals & periods of darkness and spiritual lifelessness, as tests & trials of our faith. When these forty days of penitence & prayer are over, may we rise with our Saviour to the freedom & glory of the sons of God!

Robertson's lecture on Wordsworth is very fine. His spiritual perception is as clear and strong & true as any man's I have read. More orthodox men might learn a great deal that is useful from him, I think. And yet that very capacity of enjoying the ideal & the spiritual, rendered him peculiarly susceptible of pain. I have read also three plays of Shakespeare, The Merchant of Venice particularly I enjoyed very much. I hope always to have time & the disposition to cultivate the ideal & poetical part of my nature. The poetic & the religious faculties are very closely allied, if not identical. I do not think the religion of Christ is meant to exclude the religion of Nature; on the contrary it should interpret & elevate it. Every faculty is meant to be cultivated, the imagination as well [as] Reason & faith.

25th. I did not finish my letter last night and today another of your letters has reached me. I am glad Jno. Elliott still continues to preach such good &

useful sermons. Has he ever called upon you for criticism, as he threatened? I hope he has a comfortable room & that he appreciated those violets. You did not say whether [Miss Minnie] C. had arrived. If so give her my love, & tell her I w'd like very much to see her in Anderson.

As today was probably our last day in this neighborhood, I rode down with Rutledge to see the sound & get a nearer view of the ocean. The weather was charming & I experienced the exhilaration you describe at the sight of the sea. I would not like to be drowned in it though. I must request you not to go to Graniteville again if you have gone so far as to select a place to be drowned in. We shall have to avoid Scotland & [Switzerland] too in our European tour for fear some of those beautiful lakes might tempt you.

I have heard of the Scarlet fever at home & will feel very uneasy until it is past. Sister Betsey was fortunate to have left home just when she did. Sister Anne has written to me in the same strain as in her letter to you. This time last year was a sad time to us all. I wish you could see something of them while I am away. My sisters w'd all be glad to accept you as my representative. It has added very much to my happiness to see how thoroughly satisfied they all are with the sister that I have selected for them. I hope Robert's choice will give satisfaction too. I will not say as much satisfaction—that w'd be expecting too much. We do not know [whether] she is fit &c, how well she will . . . , yet have no reason to doubt that she will prove satisfactory.

When Miss [Sue] returns tell her I will not be satisfied until I receive that long and egotistical letter she promised me. I hope she has had better luck this time in her visit to Graniteville.

Remember me to Miss Carrie Winthrop when you go to your next [reading]. Also to the Gadsdens & to Mr. Ravenel, and to all my friends especially Jno. Elliott. My wound is [extremely] well. I did consult the Dr. before I left home. Who are the teachers to assist Miss Sue if she resumes the school?

And now I must leave at least two pages of my letter legible by coming to a conclusion on this. Remember me to each member of the household and kiss your scholars for me. I was very much pleased with Timrod's Ode[4] on the opening of the Richmond theatre. Have you his Christmas Ode and his Ode to [Charleston]? I w'd like to [preserve] them. Good night my Darling. God bless & keep you.

Yrs with much love

W. P. DuBose

1. DuBose means before the beginning of combat.

2. This was Brig. Gen. Micah Jenkins (1835–64). See Warner, *Generals in Gray,* 155.

3. The rumor probably originated from Special Order 30, issued January 30, 1863, which authorized Brig. Gen. Micah Jenkins to proceed to South Carolina to procure conscripts and volunteers for his brigade. See *Official Records Army,* 25(2):600. Instead of moving to South Carolina, on February 18, 1863, two divisions of Longstreet's First Corps were ordered to move from Fredericksburg, Virginia, to take position east of Richmond to guard against Union attacks from the east or south. See *Official Records Army,* 25(2):632.

4. Henry Timrod (1828–67), a native of Charleston, is known as the "Poet Laureate of the Confederacy." See Faust, *Encyclopedia of the Civil War,* 756–57.

Holcombe Legion S.C.V.
March 1st 1863

I write once more from a tent, Darling, and in weather not particularly favorable to life in so frail a tenement. We came here in the rain on Friday & have had rain ever since until this morning when it has been succeeded by a March wind. However we have been pretty well protected although Capt. Cain, Rutledge, Dr. Michie & I occupy one tent. You must think I suffer for want of companionship. Our little mess of four is a very agreeable one. You know how fond I am of the Captain. Dr. Michie is a very gentlemanly fellow, whom I am learning to like very much. He is younger than I am. Dr. Ravenel[1] has been on furlough for a month. Rutledge is naturally my most constant companion & I become more & more attached to him the more I know him. It is refreshing to see such a straightforward, candid man. He is blunt to rudeness sometimes, but never to me, and in everything that involves principles, is always fearlessly on the right side.

Our mess connection with the officers of the 23rd is of course dissolved, although they are not too far off to deprive us of the pleasure & privilege of attending Dr. Girardeau's[2] services.

I suffered a great disappointment this morning. I had determined to attend service in Wilmington as it was Communion day, to hear Bp. Atkinson[3] who I believe is there. My horse was saddled & I had mounted when an order came to prepare a report by two o'clock, which w'd take several hours. Accordingly, I spent my morning over report books, four miles from Bp. Atkinson & the Communion almost in hearing of Mr. Girardeau's voice. Was it not hard? I will go to hear Mr. G. tonight.

This neighborhood is no improvement upon the one we have left. I have not explored it yet though & may find something of interest not visible from our camp. I am unfortunate in the matter of horses. I bought another at home which Robert was to have brought on for me, but when the attack on Charleston seemed so imminent sometime ago, he gave up for the present the idea of coming to me & went there. He may yet come on.

Some sad things happen in this war, which the public never hears of in the absorbing interest of more important events. Do you remember that silver watch that I wore in Anderson? It belonged to our drummer Givin, who put it in Dick Dwight's keeping during our Va. campaign. Givin was a good-looking, happy tempered fellow, quite a favorite in camp and under my immediate supervision by virtue of his position. He was newly married & devoted to his wife so much that in his separation from her, he undertook to learn to write so as to communicate with her. We used to give him copies & in a marvelously short time he acquired the accomplishment sufficient for his purposes. He was always anxious to go home to see her but never succeeded in getting a furlough until a few weeks ago. When he received it he remarked that he c'd not be happier if he were going to Heaven. A happier man, under happier circumstances & with happier anticipation never [entered the cars]. A few hours later there was a R.R. collision & Givin was instantly killed, the only man injured I believe. The strange part of it was that his wife died the same day before it was possible to hear of his death.

You may have seen a notice in the papers of a body in a metallic coffin marked "[Gentry], Holcombe Legion"⁴ lying unclaimed at Richmond. The history of it is this: when the body reached Richmond, the father, a respectable, steady old man from Spartanburg, [to receive it]. A few mornings after his arrival there, his body was found in the James River. No one knows how it came there. There's another son here who is applying for leave to go for the bodies.

You ask what sort of a girl Dick Dwight is engaged to. She is a half first cousin of ours, a very fine girl, a little older than he is. Her father & sister are so distressed at the prospect of losing her that I hear it has quite subdued her. Dick is going to try to get married very soon.

Do you remember what I told you about a ring. Both before & since I have been trying to get one, & can neither find such a thing nor have one made. I wish very much I had got it at first. Not that I would care much under ordinary circumstances, but at such a time you should have one. I will continue to try when I have opportunity.

I have just come back from Girardeau's service. He gave us a clear & admirable discourse on faith. His style of preaching is very happy, high enough for the highest and not too high for the lowest. Sometimes I think it will not be long before I can with propriety leave the service, and then again

142

when I see notices of Yankee Conscription Acts,[5] retaining the 300,000 men in service, whose time is about to expire, & putting at their disposal three million, I feel that the period of release looks further off than ever. For a long time after the organization of the Legion the drilling was entirely in my hands. I drilled both officer & men. Then I felt that I was of use to the cause. But now I am no longer of any use in that capacity & never meddle with it. The consequence is that my work has diminished very much & is of such a nature as to be easily performed by many who c'd not have filled my place at first. I have time now to read and employ myself in that way. But sometimes the thought comes to me, whether I am not thrusting aside too lightly the claims of the ministry, without duly weighing and appreciating its great needs, particularly in such a parish as this. There are two dangers which I strive to avoid. One is the temptation to mistake personal & earthly motives for the dictates of conscience & duty, [&] to construe an increasing distaste for the service & a natural longing for a more congenial occupation (to say nothing of less worthy motives) into a sense of duty leading me to exchange the one for the other. The other is the danger of remaining indefinitely in the service simply from neglect to institute a comparison between the contending claims of the service & the ministry, or from a depreciation of the spiritual in comparison with the temporal claims upon me.

When the proposition came to me at home from so many sources I felt that I could not indulge the idea while my very brigade was daily threatened by the enemy. I feel so now, while Charleston is in such danger, and as long as this continues to be the case, will not think of resigning, but if Charleston sh'd weather the storm, or if she sh'd escape it altogether & leave us [becalmed] here, I may give the subject of leaving a more serious consideration than I have hitherto done. Pray for me though, Darling, that in this as in all things I may be led by God's Spirit to do that which is right. And do not hesitate to give me your views candidly on the subject. You can give me no better proof of your love than by helping me to do right, even if it sh'd be against my own inclination.

It is past my bed time and I must stop for tonight at least. You are always in my prayers. Much love to your Mother, Miss Sue and all the household.

Yrs with much love
W. P. DuBose

1. This was possibly Edmund Ravenel (b. 1840), son of the physician and naturalist Edmund Ravenel (1797–1871). See Ravenel, *Ravenel Records,* 64, 158.

2. The Reverend John Lafayette Girardeau (1825–98) was a popular Presbyterian minister from James Island, South Carolina. He pastored the Anson Street Chapel, a

mission church for blacks in Charleston, South Carolina, which became the Zion Presbyterian Church. He became famous for his preaching and was known as the "Spurgeon of America." See Gist, *Presbyterian Women of South Carolina,* 276–78.

3. Thomas Atkinson (1807–81) was the third Episcopal bishop of North Carolina. See *Appleton's Cyclopaedia,* 1:115.

4. This possibly refers to Pvt. Patrick C. Gentry, who died of wounds at Harrisonburg, Virginia, at age nineteen. See Kirkland, *Broken Fortunes,* 128; Landrum, *History of Spartanburg County,* 706.

5. On March 3, 1863, President Lincoln signed the Enrollment Act, which required that all males between the ages of twenty and forty-five, whether citizens or immigrants who had filed for citizenship, be enrolled for military service. Federal agents thereafter established a quota of new troops that were to be conscripted from each congressional district. See McPherson, *Battle Cry of Freedom,* 600–601.

Holcombe Legion
March 4th 1863

To think, Darling, that after looking forward to your birthday for a month beforehand I should after all have let it slip by unnoticed. I keep very little acc't of hours or days but take them as they come, and I did not realize until this morning that the 2nd had come and gone. The years are slipping by very rapidly, and I long to be released from the painful necessity which this unnatural war imposes upon us, of spending so much precious time in an occupation which seems to us so senseless and inhuman. And yet God knows what the world needs better than we do, and if He permits it we must submit cheerfully. I confess that after indulging the hope of peace this summer for so long a time, I feel a little disappointed at the recent indications which the North has given of a still unwavering purpose to prosecute the war indefinitely. In spite of all this though, I will express and indulge the hope that your next birthday will find us settled down in peace and quiet to a more congenial and lifelong work. After all our probation here consists in working out our salvation in the midst of circumstances of God's appointment & not of our selection. Hope so long deferred is a sore test of faith & patience, but God appoints it & is willing to give strength to endure it. Your birthday was a beautiful day with us. What a walk we might have taken! I would willingly have given up "The Tempest" for so sweet a pleasure but the latter being out of my reach, I took the former for a solace. I had read it before but never enjoyed it as much. It is a wonderful creation of imagination, an exquisite blending of the natural & supernatural. I am going to read the "Midsummer

Night's Dream" next, which is quite equal in a different way. I never enjoyed Shakespeare before as I ought although I heard delightful lectures on some of his plays at the University of Virginia. I have only six with me, and wish I had brought more. I have almost [read] through my little pocket library. I often wish that I could employ my leisure in some more . . . way, but living four in a little tent, subjected to the multitudinous interruptions of my position, it has hitherto proved impossible for me to do so. I have had to learn to be independent of the presence of others in my devotional reading and exercises, but have not succeeded in extending my independence any further.

I don't know how the impression got abroad so generally in So.Ca. as it did, that our Brigade had gone to Charleston, unless it was produced by the announcement in the papers of Genl. Evans' arrival in Columbia. He passed through on furlough. Genl. Evans & his staff occupy in Wilmington when they are there, a fine house nicely furnished and containing an elegant library which with the servants &c was lent to them by a rich refugee from the City. I called there the other day & saw one of his aides reclining on a luxurious lounge, reading a book with a most perfect air of elegant leisure.

We are rather disagreeably situated just now. Our camp is on a hill where the March winds have a clean sweep. The weather attracts us to the fire, but the smoke, like the flaming sword at the entrance to the Garden of Eden, turns in every way and prevents our approach. Our fuel too is decayed pine, the smoke of which blackens us almost beyond recognition. You would be ashamed of the hand that writes this letter, if you could see it. There are very serious doubts whether you w'd [shake] it.

I am convinced that Sister slanders me about writing. I wrote to them the very night I reached the Legion & got an answer back dated the 15th from Sister Anne. I must really write to Miss Malvina; I haven't done so since her illness.

Has Miss Sue resumed the school and if so who are her associates? I hope the pleasant visit to Greenville has strengthened her for the task. Give her much love and tell her I shall continue to expect her letter, but will not be too impatient if she has taken the labour of the school upon herself. I am glad you find pleasure in your teaching. It is a pleasure which depends very much upon the scholars & I should say that you are very fortunate in that respect. Give them my love & a kiss. I hope Miss Nannie C. is still with you, as her presence seems to give you so much enjoyment. I wish I could share it with you, as I certainly would if I were there. You must not forget always to remember me to your Aunt Eliza & Miss Harriet, though I do not always mention their names. How much I would like to enjoy some of your Lent services. Mr. Girardeau has gone on furlough so that for some time to come we will not have his services. I will try to go into Wilmington sometime.

Todays [sic] papers report the gunboats at Fort McAlister again.[1] Probably the attack on Savannah has begun in earnest this time. They do seem to hesitate to attack Charleston. Whether they are waiting for more gunboats, or have declined the issue there altogether, remains to be seen. In the meantime, we are as quiet here as possible. Everyday or two a vessel runs the blockade, & sometimes we hear the heavy guns firing upon her as she runs the gauntlet of the fleet. Daughter was well again when I last heard, & Sister Jane's precautions had so far succeeded in keeping her baby from the fever. Sister mentioned having received a letter from you, one of your "sweetest" she said.

With much love to your Mother, Sister Martha and each member of the household

I remain

Yours with much love

W. P. DuBose

1. On February 28, 1863, the Federal monitor *Montauk* moved up the Ogeechee River, which is located south of Savannah, and destroyed the CSS *Nashville,* a Confederate cruiser that had run aground near Fort McAllister. See Long, *Civil War Almanac,* 324.

Holcombe Legion

March 9th 1863

I am sorry, Dearest, that my letters have taken to lagging by the way. I think you will find by consulting the dates, that I write pretty regularly twice a week. That of the 25th though was delayed several days with me for want of an opportunity to send it. The violets were a present from Rutledge who found them in the neighborhood & persuaded me to open my letter after it was sealed to put them in. The first or second Sunday in Lent last year I spent at Dungannon, my first visit there. On our way from church your Aunt Annie gave me a little bunch of violets which I put in my prayer book by the collect for the day, and there they are still. There is not much freshness or odour left in them now, but their association with Dungannon & its inmates and our happiness there makes them quite precious enough as they are. As Spring draws on once more I recall more vividly than ever those sweet days of love & flowers. How we are scattered now, who used to meet there a year ago! In three different states, to say nothing of districts. Dick Dwight is in

Charles Haskell's company at Battery Marshall on Sullivans Island.[1] He seems pleased with his new situation & happy in his St. Johns letters. He has not written to me yet, since I left home.

I had a most delightful day yesterday, enough to compensate for the disappointment of the Sunday before. Rutledge & I rode to church & attended morning and evening services. Bishop Atkinson read and preached both times, which was a treat in itself, but the simple pleasure of being in a church once more, & hearing the service & the music would have been happiness to me without any addition. I will go as often as I can and think I will call on the Bp. & renew my acquaintance of 1860. The music in his church is very fine, better than any I have heard in Charleston. It is beginning to rain & I must go in & put off my letter for tomorrow.

In the tent. I believe I will go on writing, for fear I may not have time tomorrow morning. The rain is coming down in earnest, with thunder & lightning. We feel quite secure & comfortable in our tent, & enjoy the contrast between this & other stormy nights that we can remember.

Mrs. Frank Winthrop[2] has a brother, Rutledge Parker, in the 23rd Regt. encamped near us.[3] I hear he has been a very dissipated man, but that he has been steady for one or two years. He certainly is so now, & I observe that he takes a great deal of interest in Mr. Girardeau's preaching. He comes to see us quite often and I like him. I told him the other day that I had a correspondent in Anderson who knows his sister well, and he begged me to send word to her that he was well &c.

Robert has joined or is going to join the Charleston Light Dragoons, with DuBose Porcher.[4] I do not know how to get my horse. I have promised an orderly that I have, one of our men, to get him a furlough on condition that he come back by Winnsboro & ride my horse to Wilmington. It is impossible to have him brought on the cars, and I am very much in need of him.

I am very glad to hear of Miss Carrie Pinckney's improvement. I w'd like very much to know her in health. Remember me to her when you write, & tell her how glad I am to hear that she is so much better. Give my love to Miss Sarah Trapier too when you write.

I have just received a letter from Sister Jane, the first I believe that she has written me since Bev's death. Poor girl! It is a trial to her to recall the correspondence in which she used to find so much joy. I have written home regularly, the only long interval having been caused by Robert carrying off one of my letters to Charleston without showing it to the girls. I think

Minnie had determined to go to school before she became engaged. I commend her very much for adhering to her intention, but do not think you need feel tempted to follow her example. She is not educated yet & I have no doubt will go more seriously to work about it than she has ever done yet. She is intelligent enough naturally.

I am obliged to go now. If I have time before the mail leaves to finish my paper I will do so.

Yrs with much love

W. P. DuBose

I forgot until I was concluding my letter this morning that I had promised to drill a company, & the drum brought me to a sudden end. The weather has grown quite warm & if we had any flowers to bud or any trees to grow green we might begin to see the evidences of approaching Spring. I wonder if we are to be ordered back to So.Ca. this summer or to active service in any other direction or are to remain in quiet summer quarters. You need not imagine that we are, any of us, anxious for [stirring] service, or that it is a disappointment to [be] kept out of it. We take when it comes, and are not sorry when it does not come. [They say] Rosencrantz[5] has been heavily reinforced. What w'd you think of [our going] to Bragg?[6] Give much love to your Mother, Miss Sue &c, also to Miss Nannie if she is still with you.

Yrs &c

W. P. DuBose

1. This was Company D, First South Carolina Infantry Regiment (First South Carolina Regulars). See Compiled Service Records, First (Butler's) South Carolina Infantry (First South Carolina Regulars), M381, roll 9.

2. Francis Winthrop (b. 1832) of Charleston had a brother-in-law named Charles Rutledge Parker (1822–64). See Mayo, *Winthrop Family,* 389; Parker, *Genealogy of the Parker Family,* 28–29.

3. Rutledge Parker served as a private in Company D, Twenty-first (not Twenty-third) South Carolina Infantry Regiment. See Compiled Service Records, Twenty-first South Carolina Infantry Regiment, M267, roll 47.

4. The Charleston Light Dragoons was a prominent militia company that later became Company K, Fourth South Carolina Cavalry. Robert DuBose never joined the Charleston Light Dragoons, though DuBose Porcher did join the unit. See Compiled Service Records, Fourth South Carolina Cavalry, M381, roll 6; Emerson, *Sons of Privilege,* 1, 117, 124, 134.

5. Union major general William Starke Rosecrans (1819–1902) was the commander of the Army of the Cumberland. See Warner, *Generals in Blue,* 410–11.

6. Confederate general Braxton Bragg (1817–76), a North Carolina native, was commander of the Army of Tennessee. See Warner, *Generals in Gray,* 30–31.

We are to make another move tomorrow, Darling, near to the river, three or four miles below Wilmington, but not yet to Charleston. Gen. Evans, I hear, says that he expects to be transferred from this brigade to the Department of Tennessee, but I do not know whether this is so. He says also that he wants to take Holcombe Legion with him, but I hope very sincerely that he will not succeed in this, if he does succeed in transferring himself. The Gen. is now on furlough, & the Brigade is under the command of Col. Benbow of the 23rd. Our troops are in fine condition & excellent spirits. From dark until taps there is a perfect din in camp, from the shouting, singing, laughing &c. Last night their spirits fairly overflowed & we had one of the most novel & amusing scenes ever witnessed in a military camp.

A few of the men began it by carrying each other on their shoulders, & then seizing an officer who was passing & riding him through the camp. The idea took like wildfire & in a few minutes every officer that c'd be found was captured and elevated. Then the spirit of fun became perfectly irresistible & broke down all barriers. The two Drs. & I were seated at our fire reading & talking, when a mass of men poured in around us & carried us off on their shoulders. We were finally deposited in a bower of bushes in the midst of the camp which soon became filled with officers. After the crowd had exhausted themselves shouting, they began to call upon us for speeches. It was very evident that it was better to swim with the current than to attempt to stem it, so I set the example in a little speech which was followed by several others, after which the excitement subsided & all dispersed quietly.

While our men though are lively in a lawful way, they show their training by being remarkably manageable & orderly ordinarily.

I received your letter yesterday and prize it even more than usual & not only because it was unusually long, although that was a great recommendation to it. I will excuse your Mother for thinking your letters too long, but I will not excuse you for falling into such an error. I will not undertake to answer it tonight, because for several reasons, I will be obliged to make my practice inconsistent with my preaching. I promise you a longer letter than usual on Saturday or Sunday to pay.

I am very glad Jno. Elliott continues to sustain himself so well; I would give a great deal to have heard his Thanksgiving sermon. The more I see & hear of his success as a preacher, the more I hope & pray that he may be spared to the church. We need all the life & power we can get in the ministry. The walk to Silver Brook too I would have enjoyed after the sermon. I hope we will yet have the pleasure of taking it together. I wonder if the memory of the walks we have taken as far back as that to Hoxad's Falls gives you as exquisite pleasure as it gives me.

I have got through my little portable library & have taken to studying Anatomy & Physiology. I have only got "<u>skin</u>" deep into it yet, having just finished that first subject.

I promised you a note & I must adhere to it. Give much love to the household. I am very glad that you have a pastor & minister who understands so well the wants of his people, & is able to satisfy them. I am glad too that my friend has found a congregation capable of appreciating him & of arousing him to the extent of his powers. Give him my love when you see him.

Good night, Darling.

Yrs, W. P. DuBose

Holcombe Legion S.C.V.
March 15th 1863

I succeeded in getting to church again today, Darling, & was quite repaid for the warm walk of three miles there, & back. The service was sweet & soothing as usual, although the effect of my walk interfered a little with my enjoyment at first. The B'p preached on the subject of the training of children, text, "Train a child in the way he sh'd go &c." Probably you might have got some ideas if you had been there, which would have improved Lise's education, but I think the sermon applied principally to less conscientious teachers than Miss Sue & yourself. He spoke with a good deal of strength & feeling, as he said the subject was one of peculiar interest to him. I have not spoken to him yet, but still intend doing so. I recognized in church, or after church, two young ladies that I know, Miss Moore & Miss [Foissin], cousins of the Davis' in Camden, where I met them. They chant in the Bp's church at the Benedicite (instead of the Te Deum); I did not know how beautiful it was before; how much of the religion of nature there was in the piety of David and all the Bible. Christians! The spirit if not the words of the Benedicite is David's. The two last verses come in so beautifully after the enumeration of the objects and powers of nature. Mr. Farrow the missionary to the soldiers has been spending some days with us so that what with Mr. Girardeau's & his ministrations, the Legion has not suffered lately for religious instruction.

We are now on the river, three miles below Wilmington. Still no improvement in the country, except that possibly we may get fish a little more easily. We have been living on bacon for some time past. We have come down to pretty plain living, but thrive remarkably well on it.

Your last letter reached me on Friday, and must have found me in an unusually impossible and appreciative mood, or else have contained some hidden spell of unusual potency, for it gave me peculiar pleasure. It may be that the "motions of Spring" are stirring within me, quickening my susceptibility & increasing my power of enjoyment, or it may be that you succeeded a little better than usual in touching the chord of sweet associations, or both. You know that I have often been surprised with the frequency with which our letters, crossing each other on the way, have contained allusions to the same associations or events. I don't know whether you have observed it, but it has often been so. During the comparatively short periods that we have been together, the same objects & events have produced the same impressions upon us both and by some subtle & incomprehensible sympathy between us they are often recalled to us simultaneously. At least that is the way I explain it. I think it a more satisfactory as well as a more probable solution of the phenomenon than the plausible one that "Great minds always think alike."

I used to feel so enervated and "dissipated" in Spring that I was utterly incapacitated for enjoying its beauties. I ought not to regret these former ills though, as they finally culminated in the ill health which sent me to North Carolina & to you. Since that time I have never been afflicted in the same way. I don't know whether to ascribe my freedom from them to improved health, or to the fact that since then I have had a mental vent to the Spring feelings which until then used to exhibit themselves in physical maladies. My last candle has given out & I must put off my conclusion for tomorrow. Good Night Darling.

16th. Miss Nannie has I suppose left you by this time. I wish she could have remained longer. Has she returned now to Georgia? I wonder if we will ever pay a visit together to Dungannon after the war, & renew the pleasant times we once enjoyed there. I think we owe it both to the place & to the people if it sh'd be practicable to do so. What is of more importance to us, though, is whether the simple presence of each other will ever cease to cast the glow of beauty & joy over everything we enjoy together, which it has hitherto done. What transforming power Love exercises! And I often wonder why it is that, while human love possesses such a potent & magical charm, Divine love is so weak and inoperative. If we only knew & loved God with the same reality & earnestness with which we love some of His creatures, how beautiful this world could become to us! I wish I could look forward to our visiting together, not only Dungannon, but Wilbrook (Uncle Dwight's[1] place) and St. Johns. This is just the season I would select for our visit & I would warrant you a full enjoyment of them. Then a little later we should go to North Carolina, & revisit the scenes of our first acquaintance. Would it not be a pleasant programme for a few months holiday?

I have never told you how near I came to promotion sometime ago, although I fully intended doing so. After the death of Lt. Col. Palmer, and while Crawley,[2] who had been regularly promoted to the majority, was believed to have been permanently disabled by his wound at Manassas, we were left without any field officers, and with very few company officers. The Legion was consequently in a very disorganized state, and under these circumstances I believe that there was a very general desire that I should, if possible, assume and command. But as I was, from my position, not entitled to promotion I never allowed such a suggestion to be made to me, nor indulged the idea for a moment. Until just before the battle of Kinston, the Senior Captain who was entitled to promotion, Zeigler,[3] came to me & offered to waive his right to promotion if I would accept the Colonelcy. The proposition was so unexpected that I declined giving any answer & begged him to reconsider the subject. He urged me to decide at once & spoke to Gen. Evans about it that very day. The Genl. approved the suggestion at once, & went so far as to tell me to take command of the Legion in line of battle that evening. This I declined to do (although I did practically assist with the command, & this was the way in which Personne came to report me as being in command). The next morning I was wounded & separated from the Legion. A day or two after I reached home, Capt. Zeigler wrote to me to say that he had again spoken to Gen. Evans and arranged the matter about which we had spoken. I then wrote to him that if he continued to be of the same mind, I w'd accept his offer, but that it w'd be some time before I could return to camp, & in the meantime I would mention the subject to no one, so that he need not feel any hesitation to change his mind if he felt so inclined. I then banished the matter from my thoughts during my stay at home. On my return to camp, I learned that Crawley had written to say that he hoped to be able to return in a few months. He would then be entitled to the Colonelcy for which he is quite competent and I knew that the other officers, however willing they may have been to resign to me the Colonelcy, would not be willing to give up the [lower] field officer. Under the circumstances I requested Capt. Zeigler to say nothing more to me or to anyone else on the subject & so the matter was dropped. I hear that Gen. Evans has said that he still means to recommend me for a field officer. But I have said to the officers entitled to promotion that I w'd not accept it if it were offered to me. It is a satisfaction to know that both officers & men have looked to me as the most eligible man to command them. But I am satisfied that the affair should have resulted as it has, and am glad to be able to say that I have never made one effort direct or indirect to advance my claims. Zeigler is now in command & does very well. He is the next best man to Crawley. The Legion is pretty well organized now & in good condition, and I doubt whether he would be willing again to relinquish his right to the chief command, even if Crawley c'd not return.

I wish you would keep this but say nothing at all about it to anyone. I have never spoken on the subject except to those who had heard it from other sources. I hear that Jenkins[4] wants to get me in his staff, but he has not written to me on the subject, although he had told Col. Bratton & Sister & others that he was anxious to do so. I am not desirous of change, & have not made up my mind whether I would accept. Do not say anything about this either.

I am sorry Miss Sue has not got the school, if she desired it. Give much love to her & to each other member of the family including Margie & Lise.

[Letter is not signed.]

1. Isaac Marion Dwight (1799–1873) of Cedar Grove was the husband of Martha Maria Porcher (1807–42), who was the sister of William Porcher DuBose's mother. See MacDowell, *DuBose Genealogy,* 262.

2. This was Lt. Col. William J. Crawley (1835?–1902). See Boyd, *Boyd and Connected Families,* 253.

3. This was Maj. Martin Govan Zeigler (1830?–88). See Compiled Service Records, Holcombe Legion, M267, roll 380; WPA Cemetery Index; Kirkland, *South Carolina C.S.A. Research Aids.*

4. Brig. Gen. Micah Jenkins (1835–64) was born on Edisto Island, South Carolina, and was both a brigade and a division commander in the Army of Northern Virginia. See Warner, *Generals in Gray,* 155–56.

Holcombe Legion
March 20th 1863

My last letter, Darling, was written in Spring. Since then we have been plunged back into Winter—cold, wind, & rain. I am trying to write with gloves on, the first consequence of which is that I see I have begun on the last page of my sheet. A more disagreeable day for camp could not be imagined, but I have so much to warm me up within, that I am superior to the combined opposition of the elements. Not that I always take the same pleasure in overcoming obstacles that I do when I am with you. You trained me so well in that exercise before I overcame you that your simple presence ever since has always nerved me with the spirit of resistance to opposition. I hope it will be so through life, in spiritual as well as physical things. We have an old tent which Capt. Cain & myself occupy until we can get another. It keeps off wind & rain though, & we are quite comfortable in our less crowded quarters. Rutledge went off this morning on a three weeks furlough. They are gradually furloughing the troops of this district, giving them fourteen days at home. If this continues a month or two longer I might be tempted to apply for my turn. By that time however, I am afraid we will have entered upon the summer campaign, when all furloughs will be at an end. A week in Anderson & one at Winnsboro would be very sweet, would it not? Then we will take that walk to Silver Brook.

Your letter reached me yesterday, and I cannot tell you how shocked I was to hear of the disclosures about Mr. & Mrs. Morse.[1] Drunkenness, and other crimes even greater, we can palliate if not excuse on the ground of the weakness of human nature & the strength of temptation, but deliberate & persistent cruelty, it is hard to find even that slight palliation for. I can well understand what a shock the revelation must have given you all. What effect has it had upon his ministry? Does he still continue his pulpit duties as usual? As for your conduct to the family that should depend mainly upon the ground he takes and the spirit which he manifests—whether he proudly & stubbornly justifies such unchristian & inhuman conduct, or whether he "sorrows after a godly sort"—"unto repentance." It is indeed a grievous blow to the Church of Christ. Alas, that it should suffer often & grievously from its professed & cherished champions!

But to turn to more agreeable subjects. There is no danger I suspect of our being sent to the West. Genl. Evans came to Wilmington several days ago, but has gone on since to Richmond, possibly to try to get himself promoted or transferred or something of that sort. I hear the Genl. is quite a friend of mine but I cannot learn to admire him. Gen. Jenkins is at Blackwater which is I don't know exactly where, in the upper part of this state I believe or low down in Va. He is in command of all the troops there so that Col. Bratton still commands the Brigade. I have just heard from Sister Betsey who has lately returned from Yorkville. She speaks a good deal of you & seems a little concerned [lest] you or I sh'd think that she takes less interest in you than the others do. She says she is so reserved, & therefore seemingly cold, in her letter, that she cannot demonstrate her true feelings in that way & despairs of accomplishing her object before she comes to know you well. Her apology is very unnecessary to us who know her, & I hope equally so to you. I think Sister Betsey's character a very rare & lovely one. I have never known more modest & unconscious charms than she possesses. Before she was married, when she was very much admired, I have often looked at her at the piano, the centre of attraction, and felt my heart swell with pride at her perfect unconsciousness and indifference to the admiration she attracted. She never cared much for company and I don't believe to this day ever dreams that she has ever been regarded otherwise than as a perfectly commonplace person. Her love for me used to be intense & romantic, and though, as she says, she is very reserved & undemonstrative now, I would never doubt her love for anyone who was dear to me. I do wish you could see more of the girls. I know it w'd be a great pleasure to you both. Willie has not forgotten me & can never forget that I came away in the dark & in the snow. He is a great boy.

You wish to know my favorite pieces in Tennyson.[2] It is hard for me to decide; the poems I like the most now I was least attracted by on first reading. The small pieces at the beginning I have never appreciated fully. Of his female portraits in these I admire "Isabel" most & more, the oftener I read it. In some moods, not very deep or thoughtful, I like the "Talking Oak," "Gardener's Daughter" & some other sweet love stories like them. After a good deal of study though, I enjoy best his larger poems, "Locksley Hall," "The Princess" and "In Memoriam" &c. "St. Agnes" & "Sir Galahad" are favorites with me. I never read "Maud" until the other day & enjoyed it much better than I expected to do on the first reading. I would like to have Wordsworth now, since reading Robertson's admirable lecture on him.[3] The tent in which I am writing, a sort of public one, has been taken possession of by Qr. Master who is transacting business at my ears. Capt. Cain begs to be remembered.

Give much love to Miss Sue and the other members of your household. Miss Clara Glover[4] is a good friend of mine, whom I have never met. She &

Miss Emma Means were very intimate & my sisters like her very much. I have often wished to know her.

My orderly has got his furlough & I hope will bring me my horse, if we are not out of reach when his leave is out. I wanted to go to church today, but the weather has prevented. I hope to go on Sunday. Remember me affectionately to John Elliott. Goodbye now, my darling.

Yrs with much love

W. P. DuBose

1. This was possibly the Reverend Albert A. Morse (1819–94), a Presbyterian minister, who is buried at Abbeville. See WPA Cemetery Index.

2. Alfred Tennyson (1809–1902), First Baron of Aldworth and Freshwater, was an English poet who is considered to be the chief representative of Victorian-age poetry.

3. William Wordsworth (1770–1850) was a major romantic poet and poet laureate of England. See Robertson, *Lectures on the Influence of Poetry and Wordsworth*.

4. This was probably Clara Glover (1836–69), the daughter of Thomas Worth Glover (1796–1884) of Orangeburg, South Carolina. She was the secretary and treasurer of the Orangeburg Aid Society, a relief organization for soldiers. See Glover, *Colonel Joseph Glover*, 75, 141.

Holcombe Legion S.C.V.

March 25th 1863

Three letters from you, Darling, on three days in succession, including the note in Miss Sue's letter, was such a treat that I was half tempted to propose a daily correspondence. I have met several instances of such constant communication since I have been in the service, but would distrust my ability to make such a correspondence either beneficial or interesting. I think however, from that short experiment that you c'd successfully sustain the practice & w'd not object to your continuing it, or repeating it as often as you please. Unfortunately though for the precedent, I don't think the letters were written on successive days.

I endeavoured to show my appreciation of Miss Sue's letter by answering it as promptly as I could. The toothache under which I wrote still annoys me a little. It was a cold in the tooth, which never troubles me except in such weather & after such exposure. I congratulate you on your exemption from dental difficulties of any description. For one who has generally as sound & strong teeth as I have, I have had a pretty good share of trouble from them.

I have made my arrangements to get my horse by the 8th or 9th of April. He is to be ridden to Kingsville & there take the cars under the care of my orderly. I hope my usual ill luck in that respect will not pursue me any longer.

Gen. Evans has once more resumed command. There is a rumour that he has been made Maj. General, but I do not believe it. He seems bent upon crushing Col. McMaster[1] if he can, but I have no idea that he can injure him.

I have had to suspend my studies in physiology for want of a book. The one I was using having been returned to the Surgeon of the 23rd from whom it was borrowed.

I want to speak now, Dearest, on a subject which I have been tempted before to write about, but could not quite make up my mind to do so. Do you not think that your Mother might be induced to relent with regard to the duration of our engagement? I have not allowed my mind to dwell upon the subject until lately. I am sure I am quite grateful for you under any circumstances, Darling, to be perfectly willing to wait patiently any length of time. I submitted very cheerfully before, & am ready to do so again, if you think it best.

But to say that we are to wait until this war is over, or until I am ordained, is to postpone it to a period which may not come for a much longer time than we now anticipate. It is in fact to postpone it indefinitely. I really cannot see that our marriage w'd make any practical change in your relations to your home & family, as long as I am in the war, & when that is over we would be married anyhow. And whatever be my fate in the future of this war, I cannot express to you with how much more satisfaction I would be prepared to meet it, if we were married. I don't think it would add much to your anxiety & it w'd add a great deal to my happiness.

Think of it, Darling & let me know as soon as possible your decision. I have so much confidence in you, that I promise that either answer will satisfy me. But if it can be done at all it must be done quickly. For a month or so to come, furloughs are possibilities. After the summer campaign opens, everything is dark & uncertain. It is this consideration, combined with the apparent hopelessness of speedy peace, that has induced me to urge this matter once more. And I wish I had done so earlier.

I should think that very few preparations w'd be necessary. Even if it were not for the peculiarity of the times, a perfectly quiet & private wedding w'd be more congenial to all parties. Therefore please decide quickly & if my wishes can be accomplished, fix as early a day as possible. I am sure I can get the furlough as long as we remain here, and there is every prospect of our doing so for some time to come. Fourteen days is the time allowed, but for so laudable a purpose I am sure I c'd get longer. Having been at home so much, I would not apply for a leave without a strong excuse. If your Mother consents, fix a day in April, the sooner the safer & better. I expect you will think me hasty & violent, but these are times to which we cannot apply ordinary rules. We must take them by the forelock or they leave us in the lurch.

It is too late to write about other things, and besides this one possesses me just now. I told Capt. Cain some days ago that as the war showed no signs of ending, I believe I w'd try to get married. And he told me to tell you that he has always hitherto opposed me, but that he is now a convert to my views. The Captain is very generous & unselfish & very much interested in the happiness of his friends. I know he will ask whether I sent his message.

Good night now, Darling. Do not let my request trouble you, if you do not think it right to accede to it. Much love to the household. May our Father guide, strengthen & comfort you!

Yrs with much love
W. P. DuBose

1. Col. Fitz William McMaster (1826–99), a native of Fairfield District, was the commander of the Seventeenth South Carolina Infantry Regiment. McMaster and General Evans exchanged charges of misconduct, and the colonel's court-martial resulted in an acquittal on all accusations except that of a charge of conduct prejudicial to military discipline. McMaster was an attorney, businessman, and state legislator who maintained a lifelong antipathy to Evans. See Bailey, *Biographical Directory of the South Carolina Senate,* 2:1017–19.

Holcombe Legion
March 31st 1863

The weather, Dearest, is a pretty serious obstacle to writing, so much so as to check effectually all my correspondence except with you & home. March having come in as a Lion refuses to go out as a Lamb; and I for one am happy to get rid of him on any terms. Yesterday it rained, blew & was cold all day, so as to preclude the possibility of church. After my other reading, I was inclined to write to you, but spent the time instead, in reading over letters which I have rec'd during the past few weeks from you. They were as fresh & interesting as though they were quite new, and served as an admirable appetizer for the one which was handed me from the office, by the time I had got through with them. I will never object to the dissipation in which you indulge but w'd like to go home notwithstanding, to encourage or restrain you, as you please. It w'd be quite sufficient for me that I got there, & I would consent very cheerfully to adapt myself to your mood. While I am with you, I am quite satisfied with you as you are, while I am away I am happier to hear that you are enjoying yourself in any dissipation which c'd furnish you enjoyment. I hope John Elliott enjoys his dissipation. Does he seem to do so? Miss Sue says he is quite cheerful sometimes & not above an impudent joke occasionally, of which she gave me an illustration which you may remember. Has his address come off yet? And how did the Presbyterians like his sermon?

I attended service on Friday, as you hoped & enjoyed it very much, although the Bp. did not officiate. The Rector of the church has resumed his place, which the Bp. seems to have been filling temporarily. I have not learned his name, but recognized him as a man who visited the Hospital at Goldsboro while I was there, & with whom I conversed without knowing that he was an Ep. clergyman. He is by no means an ordinary man, but not as attractive a preacher as the Bp. I will go to church as often as I can this week & certainly, I hope, on Friday. I have never walked to town since the day I wrote you of. I can generally get a horse & hope to have my own by the 9th.

Col. McMaster is now under trial, Gen. Evans acting as Prosecutor. Gen. Martin (Wm. E.)[1] is Col. M's Counsel; he sent word by Capt. Cain that he w'd like to make my acquaintance, mainly on your account, in whom he professes much interest, so I am going to call on him.

Gen. Jenkins has never written to me about the staff appointment which he spoke of offering me, or at least I have never received any communication from him. I do not often think of military changes, and am quite contented as I am. I have no doubt I w'd see much more hard & dangerous service with Jenkins than with Evans, so you had better not wish me with him. With regard to leaving the service I have ceased to think of that, since I have grown less hopeful about the speedy termination of the war. I did think sometime ago, that we were pressing through the last throes of the struggle, but am inclined to believe now that it will last as long as Lincoln's Administration. I would feel justified in leaving, if I thought, or had reason to think, that the tug was over & that nothing was left but the lingering preliminaries to an armistice [&] final adjustment of terms, but we have something more serious than that ahead of us I fear, & so I dismiss the prospect of anything more congenial than arms for the present. An experience in [frustration] of over a year w'd make [me hesitate] very long under any cir-cumstances to try a chaplaincy, with my ministerial inexperience at least. It would be a trying beginning to my ministry. No one not in the service can realize the difficulties of such a position. I really have known but one chap-lain worthy of the name, Mr. Girardeau, & his labours have been almost fruit-less apparently.

I am afraid you may have thought me hasty & impetuous in the propo-sition contained in my last letter. I expect that you must but don't let it worry if you find any difficulty in [acceding] to it. One thing only I would feel inclined to contend strongly against, and that is the necessity of waiting until peace, no matter how long it may be delayed. I trust though that you can arrange matters for the latter part of April.

We get quite enough to eat and have had a great deal of fish [lately], [shad] &c. I am in as good health as I ever was. Give much love to all the household & remember me to all friends. Goodbye Darling.

Yrs most affectionately
W. P. DuBose

1. This possibly refers to Maj. Gen. William Thompson Martin (1823–1910). See Warner, *Generals in Gray,* 214–15.

Holcombe Legion
April 7th 1863

Your letter of the 1st has just reached me, Dearest and I have waited for it a day or two longer than I w'd have done otherwise. I wish more than ever that the letter which I have written to your Mother had been sent earlier so as to save you the pain of broaching the subject yourself. In spite of your assertions, I was not as considerate as I might, & should have been. The dif-ficulties in our way from your peculiar situation & circumstances, I hope, Darling, will not be allowed to have too much weight. We can dispense with a great many things in these times, that w'd be considered quite essential under better circumstances. The . . . that objection . . . only you & nothing . . . it seems to me that a furlough . . . & the consent of all parties are all the preparations necessary. However you know better than I do, and I do appre-ciate fully, Darling, the inconveniences and self-denial to which Refugees are subjected.

With regard to one other consideration, it <u>may</u> be that Charleston is about to be attacked. The [reasons to which you refer] proved groundless, but within the last day or two others have taken their place. It may be that I may fail to get my furlough. But I don't expect to see the day during this war when it will be possible to make arrangements which may not be deranged by possible or even probable contingencies. It seems to me best under the circumstances to act as though there were nothing in the way & then to submit as cheerfully as possible when our plans are frustrated. And, Darling, I do not [propose] it simply for my happiness or your happiness but because I believe it to be right. That it w'd add to our happiness, does not make it wrong. Chston may not be attacked for now however. And furloughs may never be as accessible as at present. And if I fail now, . . . forward to the first . . . opportunity & not to the. . . . The more I think of it the less [reason do I] see for waiting. However I leave it to you [&] am willing to abide by your decision. I don't know about that either; one thing I do know though, that nothing can shake my love for you, or my perfect trust in your love for me. That is fixed, Darling, beyond all power of change; as much as though the vows were already uttered which are to give us to each other.

I am very much obliged to you for the Wordsworth, which [came] quite safely. I have not read a great deal of it yet. My reading has at least the merit of variety. I have taken to Latin lately & am reading Ovid.

I attended a most delightful service on Easter Day, & enjoyed the day very much [indeed] so much so that I have been happier every day since for it. I remembered you frequently and particularly during the Communion service. The singing was very fine [&] everything conspired to impress even the careless spectator. There were a great many officers at church, but very few remained to the Communion. Among these few was Genl. Whiting[1] who commands this post, & who is a very constant & devout attendant. I rec'd a long & interesting letter from Johnson some days ago, which gave me a better idea of the condition of things [there] than I had before.

I want to send this note tonight & must come to a close. Love to all, and believe me, Dearest

Yrs with much love
W. P. DuBose

1. This was Maj. Gen. William Henry Chase Whiting (1824–65) of Mississippi. See Warner, *Generals in Gray,* 334–35.

Wilmington Apr. 9th 1863

Your letter reached me yesterday, my Darling, and has given me much happiness. It is all that I wanted, and I feel very grateful for it. I hope you have long ere this received the note to your Mother, enclosed in one to you. I will enclose another in this. I never suspected that others had used their influence with her in our behalf. Very few had any right to know from me that I have ever made any effort to get married, and still fewer, if any, to know that her objection was the obstacle. However all that makes but little difference now that I have her & your consent. All that remains to complete our arrangements & my happiness now is to be able to fix definitely the date of my furlough, and that Dearest just at this juncture I cannot do. The demonstration against Charleston seems to be in earnest at last, & the attack has actually begun.[1] We have orders to hold ourselves in readiness to go there if we are needed, & may do so in a day or two. We have nothing later than the acc't of Tuesday evening's engagement, & do not even know whether it was renewed on yesterday. The news so far, if reliable, is cheering & encouraging. Two vessels injured in so short a time & at so great a distance may discourage them from a more serious assault, or may be the happy beginning of a successful & glorious repulse. In this case we will most probably be kept quietly here, as we are the only infantry troops in this neighbourhood, & it seems to be the disposition of those in authority to keep Genl. Evans by himself in a safe place.

In this case I apprehend no difficulty in getting off, & in being able to apprise you very soon of my definite plans. Of course I can do nothing while this uncertainty lasts. The great issues at stake in Charleston swallow up in great measure all minor interests, but as I said in my last I am going to act precisely as though the way was all clear, & hope that all obstacles great & small, public & private will be removed, & that the end of the month will see me in Anderson. If I am disappointed in this hope, we will only have to defer it a little longer, which will be the more easily done as the exact time has not yet been definitely fixed.

The prospect of such a step brought so unexpectedly near, seems to have startled & disturbed you anew. You need not fear for me, Darling. I am going advisedly into the "hornet's nest." As long as I have your love, I am not afraid of anything else; if love & sympathy on my part can strengthen & comfort you, you need not fear for yourself either. My happiness is to make you happy, and I long for the time to come when it shall become a holy & sacred duty as well as a labour of love. Oh my Darling, may the God of love bless & sanctify our union to His glory & our mutual help & comfort! It makes no difference what we are in ourselves. He can make His strength perfect in our weakness. All we need is faith & grace, and prayer can bring us these without measure. I am glad that Easter brought so much joy & peace to us both. The prayers & chants & whole service for the occasion was inexpressibly elevating & comforting.

I will not begin in my other half sheet for fear of not having time to write to your Mother. I see that Beauregard in his official dispatch says that the Keokuk was certainly sunk. If such is the case, I have strong hopes that the Monitor experiment, of which I confess I rather dreaded the result, has proved a failure for the Yankees. I will not be precipitate in my judgment however. I only pray that my hopes may not prove groundless. If these Monitors fail, my hopes of peace will be considerably [revived]. The fate of Charleston interests me beyond expression. The very idea of the Yankees taking possession of her makes me shudder. I am glad your articles arrived safely from Nassau. It will make me very happy to drink some of your coffee before the end of the month.

With regard to my views of the Chaplaincy, I would not have you imagine that I underrate the importance & necessity of the office. The salary has been lately nearly doubled & I hope that more competent men will be able to afford to accept the office. What I meant was that in active service the influence of a non-combatant, even though he seems to possess every qualification for the sacred office, is sadly & inexplicably small. Even Mr. Girardeau a few months ago could not explain his utter failure to produce any effect, except on the ground of personal unpopularity or denominational prejudice. He underrated his influence & labours, but it is enough to make a younger man whose power is yet to be tried, hesitate to undertake such a responsibility. And yet our men are steady, easily managed & not irreligious. I would not venture though to leave the prestige of a combatant for that of a non combatant, and I believe that the [silent] & imperceptible influence of the right sort of officers is very great. One principal reason that w'd deter me however, is the fact that several of the students in the Marions have been desirous of being ordained as chaplains, & the Bishop after discussing the matter with many of the clergy disapproved of their doing so. Johnson & I agreed with him in his decision & I would not now make the same application. Although I am further advanced towards the ministry, my case w'd be somewhat different.

Think of my being again unfortunate about my horse. After making the most careful & minute arrangements for having him brought. He was to have been sent to Columbia on Tuesday to meet my orderly who was to bring him on the cars from that place. I wrote home about ten days beforehand minute instructions as to their part of the programme. Yesterday I heard from the orderly that Tuesday & Wednesday had passed & no horse had appeared. I wrote to him immediately to go to Winnsboro & make other arrangements, but I don't know when to expect him now. Of course there was some reason for the failure. Sister A. never fails except when there is sufficient reason.

We have pleasant Spring weather at last. It made me a little unwell for a day or two but I am quite well again, and capable of enjoying the pleasant change. I wish, Darling, you would continue to make your preparations as for the last week in April, say the 27th or 28th. If all goes well my next letter may announce my plans. If a precise day is not fixed it will be easier to accommodate ourselves to circumstances. I hope your Brother's trial is over; it must be particularly annoying at this time.

Give much love to Miss Sue & all the family & kiss the girls for me. And now my own Darling, God strengthen & comfort you, & prepare the way for our speedy union.

Yours with much love
W. P. DuBose

1. On April 7, 1863, nine Union ironclads under the command of Flag Officer Samuel Du Pont attacked Fort Sumter at the mouth of Charleston harbor. Confederate batteries on Fort Sumter and Fort Moultrie returned fire, damaging several of the Union vessels and forcing them to retire. The worst damaged was the USS *Keokuk,* which was hit ninety times by Confederate guns and sank the following morning. See Long, *Civil War Almanac,* 335–36.

Wilmington Apr. 11th 1863

We took the cars this evening for Charleston, Darling, where I suppose you will next hear from me. I have already a furlough of 25 days to begin whenever I choose to leave. Before that time comes I may have very different scenes to pass through, from those which I anticipate in Anderson. The same power which has so far preserved me, will continue to do so, I trust, & enable me to see you by our appointed time. What the movements of the enemy are near Charleston, I have not heard. God I trust will carry me safely thro' all that awaits us.

I rec'd your letter this morning, my birth-day. We have indeed been blessed in the midst of many doubts & uncertainties & dangers during the past year. Let us trust & hope that the next will bring its blessings too.

I have no time to write. We march for Wilmington in five minutes.
God bless & keep you, my own Darling.

Yours with much love

W. P. DuBose

Direct to me in Charleston, & if you can enclose a ring of the size you will
need. If you have none measure the circumference with a slip of paper &
enclose it. The many arrangements you allude to was [sic] just what you sh'd
have done.

Charleston

Apr. 14th 1863

Your Sister Martha's letter has no doubt already informed you, Darling, of
my arrival in the city. We arrived at 10 o.c. Sunday night, and several of us
walked immediately down. I was fortunate enough to meet Mr. Sass ringing
his own doorbell, as we passed by on our way to the Chston Hotel.[1] Yesterday I was equally fortunate in meeting friends & acquaintances, among
them your brother & his wife. Your brother promises to go to Anderson if
can possibly do so. I hope he will succeed. We were ordered immediately out
to the 4 Mile House[2] where we are now situated in hourly fear of being sent
back to Wilmington. It seems that after we left W. orders arrived there coun-
termanding those upon which we came here.[3] We are the only Regt that
came safely through, the others having been recalled before reaching Florence. We were at first ordered immediately back, but at Genl. Evans [sic]
urgent request, have been reprieved until further orders.

I was rather surprised to find your Sister Martha in town, although you
wrote me she was to come. I met Harry DeSaussure on the St., quite joyful
at the prospect of graduating tomorrow. I was on my way to see his Mother
when I met your Brother & went . . . to see your Sister Martha, which consumed all my time. I will go to see Mrs. DeSaussure if I have time or rather,
another opportunity.

Everybody here seems to feel personally secure from further danger. The
Monitors have disappeared and the troops been withdrawn. No one knows
what to expect next. How can we be sufficiently grateful for this last proof
of Divine favour towards our city? It has been a privilege for me to be
thrown even for a day with Mr. Sass. The faith & the prayers of such men as
he have had no [little to do] with the salvation so far of our beloved city.

Since his great affliction, his light seems to burn more brightly than ever. The [influence] of such laymen is powerful in its influence; the church would suffer an irreparable loss in him.

I was very much afraid I would not be able to get a ring, but I have secured one which will answer our purpose. After my failure in Columbia & Wilmington & what I was told there I scarcely expected to succeed in beleaguered Charleston. The time is rapidly drawing near, my Darling, to which I have so long been looking forward. Everything seems to favour us so far. If nothing occurs to alter my plans, I expect to leave from here about next Friday [week] & go up to Anderson about Monday, Tuesday or Wednesday (28th or 29th). We had better appoint [more] probably Tuesday. My furlough is for 25 days. I long to see you, and am anxious for the time to come.

Robert determined to bring my horse to me & stay with us for a time at least. He was to arrive at Wilmington Saturday evening, the evening we left. If [we] go back I expect to find him there; if we stay here, he will come with one of the other Regts. Sister A. wrote to my orderly but he did not get my letter.

I must close now, my love. I hope to get a letter from you very soon.

Yrs with much love
W. P. DuBose

1. The Charleston Hotel was located at 200 Meeting Street between 1838 and 1960. See Poston, *Buildings of Charleston,* 200.

2. This was a tavern built circa 1750 north of Charleston. The building was placed in the vicinity of the four-mile stone, which marked the distance from the city along King's Highway. See *Charleston News and Courier,* October 14, 1969.

3. On April 13, 1863, Union troops began a series of expeditions from New Bern, North Carolina, to Swift Creek Village. At the same time, Confederates under Maj. Gen. Daniel Harvey Hill were attempting to recapture Washington, North Carolina. See Long, *Civil War Almanac,* 338; Barrett, *Civil War in North Carolina,* 159–62.

Charleston
Apr. 17th 1863

We are still here, Darling, and still in suspense as regards our destination. It is a pleasant visit to me as I come into the city everyday & see a great many friends. The only thing I mind is that my . . . deranged our correspondence so that . . . no letter since the . . . which seems to me a very [long time].

Another thing is that Robert [is in] Wilmington with two [horses] & [doesn't know what to do]. The . . . Wilmington [to this place] . . . nothing but smoke & Pine trees. Here everything is green, beautiful & Spring-like. Spring never appeared so charming to me except at Dungannon; and [it all] makes me long more for you.

The prospect of spending several weeks with you, and of having you more to myself than ever, seems almost too joyful to be realized. The girls are delighted with the prospect of receiving you [so soon] and will not be satisfied unless we go immediately to them & spend my furlough there.

I rode by the house in Tradd St. yesterday evening and was very glad to see it again. It will always be dear to me for your sake & for the happiness I [had enjoyed there]. Mr. Sass has [bought a house on Legare St. next door to Mr. Gadsden's]. . . .

Has your [ubiquitous] Sister Martha arrived safely at home? She will tell you what a talent we have for meeting. The last [thing she said] I believe, was "Well this is the last time I hope." Give her my love & tell her I will be as successful in meeting her in Anderson as I was in Charleston. I was sorry to hear from her of [the sudden] death of Mrs. McPherson.

I . . . to go directly to Fort Sumter, having failed to do so [hitherto]. I spent a night with Johnson in the city & have seen all my friends, I believe, who are [here]. The people seem to feel . . . & secure, although Yankee acct's call the late engagement "a successful reconnaissance." Yesterday we had a thanksgiving service at St. Philips . . . met your Sister there . . . going to call on her this afternoon. I think she is looking remarkably well. I have seen [the Dr.] several times too on the streets.

Give much love to your Mother, Miss Sue & the household. Excuse the brevity of my note. I am writing at Mr. Sass' &. . . . With much love, my Darling & the hope of seeing you very soon, I remain

Yrs affectionately
W. P. DuBose

Winnsboro
Apr. 25, 1863

I arrived safely today, Darling, and must fulfill my promise to write by tomorrow's mail. But the cars were so crowded last night that I did not sleep with my usual facility, and the consequence is that tonight I feel somewhat used up & not equal to anything but a note. We have had quite a musical soiree, Miss Maria Horlbeck, Chassie Roberts and Sister B. being the performers, and it has brought us to 11 o.c., up to which hour coffee & music have saved me from disgracing myself. My first day at home has been a sweet one. What will it be when I have you here in addition. Sister Betsey cannot go with us and we have tonight succeeded in persuading Sister to take Augusta with her. She and her Mother find it so hard to be separated, & it will no doubt do her good. I wish Sister B. could have accepted your Aunt Anna's invitation. I rec'd your note before leaving Charleston. Of course I never expected invitations to be sent. I have requested a few of my elderly friends to go up, as Uncle Dwight, Octavius Porcher & a few others, but I don't know whether any of them can do so. Of course they w'd stay at the Hotel. Of the girls & daughter, you can make what disposition you please, between Miss Kate & your Aunt Anna. I will leave you to determine what day we shall leave for Winnsboro, whether the same week or on Monday. We hope to be in Anderson on Wednesday evening. I would not be surprised if I have neglected several things that I should have done—I generally do.

I saw your Sister just before leaving, & am sorry she cannot go up. I fear too that y'r Brother will find difficulty in getting off. Good night my own Darling. This may be my last note until I see you. God bless & prepare us for what we are about to do! Love to all.

Yrs with much love
W. P. DuBose

Near Jackson
June 1st 1863

I succeeded at last in reaching Jackson, my Darling, yesterday evening without further inconvenience except from the weather, which has become very warm. The cars stop five miles the other side of Jackson & the Brigade is one mile this side, west, so we had to walk six miles, as conveyances were not to be had. The Brigade had been encamped beyond the Pearl until the morning of the day we arrived when it took its present position. I passed through Jackson at 9 o.c. last night and have not seen it yet by daylight. Gen. Evans is in command of the place for the present with his own brigade and a portion of Gen. Breckinridge's.[1] Johnston[2] is said to be moving from Canton with the remainder of the troops. There is nothing said yet of our moving, but we may do so with Breckinridge's division when the whole of it arrives. This country is not particularly prepossessing in any respect so far as I can judge, but is particularly deficient in the matter of water which is a very serious consideration. Even at this early season we are entirely dependent upon cisterns, and I don't know how it will be later in the summer. Grant is said to have fallen back upon the Big Black for want of water, & my hope is that the Yankees will suffer more than we will.[3] Having got back into the Army I have got once more out of the reach of news from any point. You would be surprised to see how perfectly quiet & secure we are. We know less of Johnston's movements than you do and are probably less interested & excited on the subject. I hope we will have rain before we have to march as the dust is very distressing, added to the heat. The feeling here is by no means despondent now with regard to the result of this campaign. There is little doubt that Rosencrantz's whole army is moving to this department & Bragg's I suppose will follow. In fact the impression is that everything is to be staked upon the issue of this attempt upon Vicksburg.

So much for the position of affairs in these parts, which I have no doubt is much less than you have already gathered from the papers. With regard to myself, I am in fine health, and have so far recovered from my torpor that I have not taken a nap in camp, in spite of the fatigue of the past week. You will not feel complimented I am afraid to learn that our parting should have had the effect of restoring me to myself, but you know that adversity or affliction is the most effective instrument to bring us back to the straight & narrow path, & you must judge the depth of my affliction by the good it does me. And you need not fear, my darling, that your presence will not influence me for good. In nothing have I ever so plainly recognized the undeserved goodness of an all controlling Providence to me as in the bestowal of you, my precious wife. And the few weeks which we were permitted to spend together have made me more than ever satisfied that my choice was directed by Him who has ever delighted to bless me, at the same time that they more than ever convinced me of my utter unworthiness of such blessings, & my inability to use them gratefully & humbly. During this painful absence which renders dearer day by day the happiness from which I am separated, my daily prayer shall be that I may have grace & strength to be better prepared for a more holy and godly enjoyment of it when it is restored to me. Sometimes my only hope before God is my utter wretchedness. I say in my soul, "If all these numerous & great earthly blessings which are so dear to me cannot give me happiness without the favour of God & the presence of Christ, may I not hope that this very misery is given to me as a most gracious gift to drive me to the comfort I need, and as an assurance that I must find it at last?" Sometimes when everything seems to conspire to complete our happiness, God appears to withdraw the light of His countenance & the help of His grace as if to show us that all things without Him are but dust & ashes. I felt this at times when I was at home, and at the same time seemed utterly incapable of the spiritual exertion necessary for the recovery of my strength. I was often afraid that my manner might lead you to believe that I did not enjoy as much as I should the privileges and blessings that surrounded me, especially your love and the affectionate kindness of my sisters. The same feelings often caused me to assume an appearance of lightness & even indifference which were infinitely at variance with the reality. Your love & that of my sisters are inexpressibly dear to me, & I feel that God will yet so fill my heart with the higher & holier love to Himself as to enable me to feel all the happiness which he has bestowed on me.

I have to stop now, my Darling, and send my letter. I am hoping daily to hear from you. Give much love to Sue & all the household, and to all my friends. I hope my letters do not take too long to reach you. This is my fourth letter since I left you. The last was written from Meridian, the others from Montgomery.

Your affectionate Husband
W. P. DuBose

1. Maj. Gen. John Cabell Breckenridge (1821–75) of Kentucky was vice president in the administration of James Buchanan and a presidential candidate in the election of 1860, finishing second to Abraham Lincoln in electoral votes. By 1863 he was a Confederate major general and a division commander in the Army of Tennessee. He later would serve as Confederate secretary of war. See McPherson, *Battle Cry of Freedom*, 194, 232, 580; Warner, *Generals in Gray*, 34–35.

2. Confederate general Joseph E. Johnston (1807–91) on May 9, 1863, was placed in command of all the Confederate defenses in Mississippi. See McPherson, *Battle Cry of Freedom*, 629.

3. Maj. Gen. (later Lt. Gen.) Ulysses Simpson Grant (1822–85) was in command of Union forces besieging Vicksburg, Mississippi. Contrary to DuBose's information, Grant had encircled Vicksburg in a vise and was slowly starving the city and its defenders into submission. See McPherson, *Battle Cry of Freedom*, 626–36; Warner, *Generals in Blue*, 183–86.

1863

Near Jackson Miss.
June 7th 1863

I have been hoping anxiously for a second letter from you, my Darling, but it has not come yet. I hope my letters by the way were not dilatory in reaching you; your first from Camden was only five days, I think, on the road. I find it hard to realize that this is Sunday. I have been hard at work all the morning on reports which might just as well have been made on any other day, but the military makes no distinction of days, unless it is to double work on Sunday. I find it very hard to recover from a morning spent in this way, and I have to confess that I feel this evening little of the peace & rest that should belong to the day. However it disposes me more to a proper state of feeling to turn my thoughts to you, & to remember that you at least have not been debarred the precious privileges of the day, & that your mind has had full leisure both in church and at home to recall your absentee and offer up your petitions in his behalf. It is probably your Communion day too, and I can picture to myself the little body of privileged worshippers who a few hours ago united with you in that holy feast. It is hard to realize that at the last communion I was by your side in that same church. And now I am in the woods out of reach of a church and many hundred miles from you. I have no doubt, my darling, that you would be glad to share all my hardships but I am very glad that you cannot. It is often a relief to me to reflect that one half of me at least is tranquil and quiet. At the same time I think that yours is the hardest part to bear. Our hardships are easily described and much exaggerated—yours are not so apparent but much more trying and wearing. Ours are more physical and yours more mental.

We are still very quiet, and it is fortunate for us, for the weather is very hot & dry. I can bear heat but dust and redbugs are a great trial. It is rumoured that pontoon bridges are building, and I would not be surprised if, when all things are ready, instead of joining Johnston, we are thrown over the Big Black immediately west of this place, either for the purpose of reinforcing Vicksburg by cutting our way into it, or for the purpose of attacking Grant conjointly with Johnston from a different direction. Johnston is certainly taking his time, and no one seems to be in a hurry. In the meantime we hear, I do not know how reliably, that besides their immense losses before our fortifications, the enemy are suffering terribly from sickness. At the same time they are being constantly reinforced from Memphis. We are two miles from Jackson but are not allowed to go there, otherwise I should have made an attempt to go to church. I have had my hair cut within an inch of my head so that I am relieved for a time from the labour of a brush & comb. I

Forces commanded by Gen. Joseph E. Johnston, including Evans's Brigade, unsuccessfully attempted to relieve the besieged Confederate defenders of Vicksburg, Mississippi. Johnston's army retreated to Jackson, Mississippi, after Vicksburg surrendered. From F. V. Greene, *The Mississippi* (New York: Charles Scribner's Sons, 1882), 134

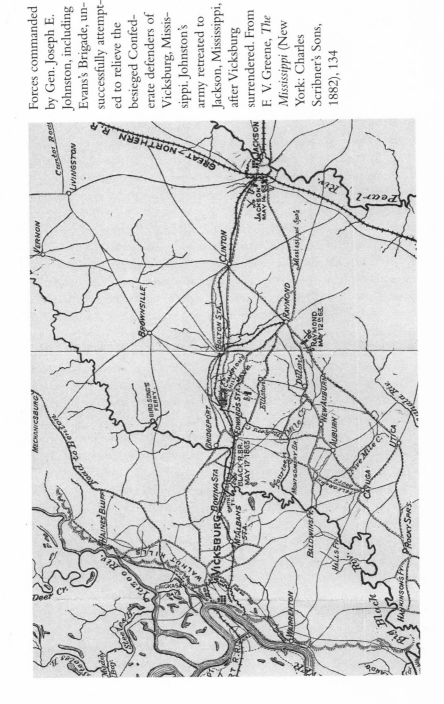

wash my head as I do my face, and find it a great convenience. The only objection is that I look like a convict, whereas I am nothing more than an exile.

Monday evening, 8th. I was fairly beaten out yesterday by the heat and concomitant discomforts, and for the same cause have not had the heart to resume today. This evening we have moved our tent to a more comfortable spot and tonight I am burning a piece of my last candle to finish my letter. I have been considerably revived by a swim in the Pearl River this evening. I succeeded in swimming across the river, no very great exploit except for a novice in the art, as I am. I hope I will succeed as well as I did in the accomplishment of whistling. No news again today, & no letter from you. Tomorrow will be a week since you first & last reached me. I think this is my sixth, and I know that you have written at least several times. I am the more anxious to hear, because I may be placed any day beyond the reach of letters. I like to think of you in your daily routine of occupation, so different from my own, and a letter from you is like "Sabean odours from Araby the Blest."[1] I have not heard once from home yet. You must not think that I mind as much even as my letters would indicate the discomforts of our present situation. The heat of Summer is more endurable to me than that of Spring. I do not object much to honest, straightforward heat, and now we are out of the dust, and I hope out of the reach of redbugs.

There is so much monotony & so little incident in our life that I am afraid you will find my letters very dull, in spite of the fact that this one is written in the same dignified and elegant posture in which the one from Gordonsville was written, which you pronounced interesting. William is quite sick tonight, but I hope it is nothing serious.

The bombardment at Vicksburg is immensely heavy while I write—the city must be entirely destroyed by the continuous cannonading of the past few days & nights.

Give much love to your Mother & all the household, also to my old Auntie and my cousins there, and tell them I w'd be delighted to accept their invitation now. Remember me also to the two Miss Carries and all other friends.

My candle is about to desert me and I must draw to a close. To compensate for all the other deficiencies of my long & dull letter, I will end by assuring you of my ever increasing love, and of the joy which it gives me to look forward through all the uncertainties of the future to our final & permanent reunion, my own precious wife. Till then may He who has been so good to us, continue His gracious protection to you & me and fit us more & more fit for His service on earth & His glory in Heaven.

Your loving husband
W. P. DuBose

1. This is from *Paradise Lost* by John Milton (1608–74).

Jackson Miss.

June 11th 1863

Your second and third letters, from Camden and Columbia, have both reached me, my Darling, since my last was written, and have been all that I longed for. I have had little to complain of from you, as I belong to a mass of husbands who have not heard half so often as I from their wives, some of them not at all. Of course they lay all the blame on the mails, & complain that the latter are partial to me. They are afraid to make use of the old adage "New brooms sweep clean"—for fear that it may reflect upon their own conjugal experience. Our mess consists of Lt. Col. Crawley—an old Citadel classmate of mine—Maj. Zeigler, Capt. Cain, Drs. Russel & Michie, Rutledge & Robert & myself. We have too old tents among us, enough to eat so far, and on the whole are now as pleasantly situated as we could expect. The long drought was "put to the rout" yesterday by a heavy rain, which ended last night (if it has ended) with a magnificent thunderstorm. The grandeur was somewhat abated by the fact that it was all we could do to keep our tent from blowing down, and that the rain besides beating freely in the door found but little obstacles in the roof, but fortunately it stopped in time to give us a comfortable night's rest. Nature seems much refreshed today, but I am afraid the rain is not over yet. Your remarks on the "perversity of human nature" are very true. I have by nature considerable equanimity, & capacity of adapting myself to circumstances, but I confess that I have been fairly "beaten out" on several occasions of late. Being shuttlecocked in the rain between the cars & the boat did, I acknowledge, unsettle me for a while even beyond the remedy of memories of you & of higher influences still. I can keep cool with the thermometer at 90 or 100, but redbugs do get the better of my patience sometimes, & so on that occasion it was not so much the big inconveniences that unsettled me as the indescribable little perplexities & petty annoyances of my situation. It is hard to recognize these little trifles as a part of the trials & discipline of life, and therefore of the Divine government, and yet they are, probably on that acc't, the hardest to bear. I

1863

remember that when I was taken prisoner, I succeeded tolerably well in bearing with Xtian [Christian] patience the fatigue, exposure, hunger, thirst, heat, dust, dirt, confinement & even the pain of separation from you & home, until one day in Ft. Delaware I found on me a body insect, the first I had ever seen. I believe I could more easily have prepared myself to be shot for one of Pope's officers, than have reconciled myself cheerfully to this last affliction. It was the straw that broke the camel's back; from that moment I pined for freedom and found it almost impossible to resign myself to God's will. Unless we can learn to sanctify even such trials by accepting them as a part of His discipline, we have a large & important class of troubles for which there is no relief. I hope this is one of the lessons I am to learn by my present life. Besides His direct grace, comfort & strength, God has given me blessings in this world which I am sure would counterbalance a multitude of trials, if I could but always avail myself of them as He designs. The chief of these, my darling wife, & the one of which I do avail myself the oftenest, is yourself.

You wonder whether I realize what I anticipated from our marriage, or whether at this distance it gives me any comfort. I will not undertake to say how it gives me comfort. What has a woman to do with reasons? That it does do so, I am ready to give you all the assurances you need. At least I am quite satisfied now, and I was not so at all before. I feel fixed, settled & better prepared for the exigencies of the future.

Lastly, for the Bp's proposition, in which no doubt you are more interested than in anything else. I will write to him today or tomorrow, when I have given it a little more consideration, and will also write to you more fully in my next, or else send my letter to him, as you request. If the thing can be effected, I do not know that I can refuse. I would a thousand times rather be engaged in the work of the ministry than in my present occupation, but I shrink from such a position in proposition as I know its difficulties & my capacity & qualifications for it. If you knew them as I do, you would shrink too. Still if it comes without my seeking, I do not see yet how I can refuse the responsibility. I can only trust that I may be fitted for any duties to which I may be called. I will say no more on the subject yet. Nor must you until my mind is fully made up.

Our deserters have generally returned & the Legion is in good condition & health. Give much love to Miss Sue & all the family, in both houses, & remember me to all friends. Rutledge begs to be remembered. Robt sends love.

Your aff. Husband
W. P. DuBose

175

Jackson. June 15th 1863

I would have written to you yesterday, my darling wife, but had the good fortune to spend the day in a more appropriate way, and in one which was the more delightful for having become so unusual of late. I got permission to go into Jackson in search of a service, & was eminently successful. The weather was quite pleasant and everything combined for my enjoyment, that is the services were delightful, the sermon admirable, the music fine, and last, but not least, I was in a frame of mind to enjoy them all. Oh how I do so yearn after a more constant & <u>reliable</u> capacity of spiritual enjoyment! Sometimes when I least deserve it, from previous prayerfulness & earnest seeking, I have a relish for the truth & grace of the Gospel; and at others, when I least expect it, my ears are deaf & my heart dead.

In the evening at 8 P.M. I attended service again, when Bp. Green[1] preached and confirmed a young lady. She was very pretty in her pure white dress & by gas light, and the ceremony was very attractive. After the service the Bp. gave an impressive & touching little address on the crisis impending in the immediate vicinity, in which he said that it was by no means improbable that "within a week, or even a few days, our soil might be abundantly moistened with the blood of friends & of foes." His gray hairs, evident infirmity, and solemn manner made it very impressive & made me realize more than I had done, that in spite of our present quiet & security, we are probably on the eve of important & dangerous events. The indications are that our preparations, whatever they are, are drawing towards completion, and that we are likely to move very soon. All extra baggage is being sent to the rear, arms & ammunition inspected &c &c. My baggage is reduced to three or four pounds & is contained in my book bag. My valise I have sent to the house of a gentleman over the Pearl River whom Robert has been visiting, Mr. Birch. There is still talk of Pontoon bridges, but we have no idea of the plans of the Genls. You see I tell you candidly all that is happening or likely to happen among us; I know that you will not allow yourself to be troubled by possible & future dangers. I am sure we ought to have learned by this time to rest in the present & leave the future with its contingencies to the disposal of that Providence which has so wonderfully preserved me, and blessed us both. It strengthens me very much to see that you have so little weakness in this respect.

Your letter of June 7th has just reached me. It seems to me that by that time, my note from Meridian or even my first letter from Jackson should have reached you. In order that you may know whether all my letters reach you I believe I will number them on the top of the first page. I will call this the 7th as I have written that many since leaving you. I wish you would adopt a similar plan. This letter represents you as once more in Anderson. The little marriage episode is over, & you have resumed the thread of domestic life so rudely broken by me a month & a half ago. Thank you, my own darling wife for the loving memories which you have of me & of the blessed weeks which we spent together. To think that I have conferred happiness upon you, & to be assured that I have still the power of doing so, present or absent, is the source of the sincerest joy to me. May God enable me to add, more than I am worthy of doing, to the usefulness and happiness of your life!

I am glad you have found sufficient occupation to interest you, & of so congenial a nature. Arithmetic seems such a hobby to you that I will have to appoint you financier of our firm. I am glad that your Sister Martha is to be so long with the Capt. I cannot but think regretfully of the housekeeping arrangements we were to make. Capt. Cain & I sometimes speak of what we have lost by the removal from James Island—how we were to have come over to Town in the 7 o.c. boat every evening and return in the 7 o.c. boat next morning. But all that is past, and I cannot look forward to the time of our reunion.

With regard to the Bp's message & its possible consequences I don't very often think since writing my answer, except to pray that God's will in connection with it may be accomplished, whatever it may be. There is so much immediately before us, that I cannot very well see beyond it. I do know the spiritual destitution of the army, & if the way is opened to me by Providence, will not hesitate, as much as I may be tempted to shrink from the difficulties of the work. We have two chaplains in our brigade, Mr. Girardeau & a Mr. Dill,[2] the latter as ignorant and ranting as the former is the opposite. They have both preached to the Legion, so that we are not entirely destitute. The Bp's opinion of me gratifies me of course very much. I only wish I was more worthy of it. I am glad my Camden friends treated you so cordially. The Kershaws are remarkably affectionate, & seem, or I should say are, very fond of me. It was pure accident that I failed to send the letter to John Elliott from Camden, & I regret that I did not, although I have written to him since. I am afraid that my [Ovid] is out somewhere. I have several books lent out, and I am sure that if it had been on the shelves, I would have recognized it as the one I had promised to send.

I took a very pleasant ride about the country on Saturday & saw some very pretty places. We rode by a common looking little house in the woods, where I saw five little children in the piazza, plainly but neatly dressed. I stopped & spoke to them & felt quite a home feeling. They said the Yankees had stolen from them a horse & two mules, all they had in that line, & so they treated everybody else about here.

Give much love to all the household & to my Aunt & cousins in the other house. My candle is flaming so much that I must stop. I was interrupted today by an order for a Brigade inspection which has brought me tonight. Good night, my own Darling wife.

Your affectionate Husband
W. P. DuBose

1. William Mercer Green (1798–1887) was an Episcopal bishop of Mississippi. See Batterson, *Sketch-Book of the American Episcopate,* 159–60.

2. Edward Dill was a chaplain of the Twenty-second South Carolina Infantry Regiment. There was a Baptist minister of Greenville District named Edward Dill (1836–86). See Compiled Service Records, Twenty-second Infantry Regiment, M267, roll 326; Kirkland, *South Carolina C.S.A. Research Aids;* WPA Cemetery Index.

Jackson. June 19th 1863

Your fifth letter, my darling wife, reached me a day or two ago. I believe I neglected in my last to thank you for the Quinine,[1] of which I have received both instalments. I will promise to use it as soon as the Dr. says that I have the slightest excuse for doing so. This country seems healthy enough & I could not be better. Possibly before long we may be nearer Vicksburg & in more danger from fevers. Then your neat little package will come into requisition, and I have no doubt the association with you will do me as much good as the medicinal virtue of the powders. At present there are no indications than there have been of a speedy move. Gen. Johnston is here inspecting troops, batteries, &c, but no reinforcements are arriving & we are as quiet as ever. We hear this morning of Gen. Ewell's exploits at Winchester;[2] if all is true, no doubt it is part of an important movement on the part of Gen. Lee. But I will not anticipate until I see something more than first reports.

The Northern papers do not seem disposed to let Charleston alone yet. They still point to the possibility at least of further operations from Folly Island.[3] The inhabitants however must feel very secure as so many families are returning, or thinking of doing so. The Gadsdens & Ravenels will be a great loss to your society; I am sorry they are going to leave. It is a good thing that you are fixed for the year as you might be tempted to follow their example, an act which I would be apt enough to approve if we were on James Island or the Battery, but which at this distance would seem to me a little imprudent. I think you would find the city the most unpleasant place to spend the summer in its present condition. If I were there I flatter myself I could make some amends for its numerous inconveniences, for you individually, by the same secret that has converted Castle Pinckney into "a pleasant home."

It makes me sad to hear your account of Jno. Elliott.[4] I do pity him sincerely, and yet I do not know how much he is to be pitied. Affliction in this world seems to be constantly & inseparably connected in the Bible with glory in the next, and prosperity is so full of temptations & snares, that I have no doubt the time will come when he whom the world has called most afflicted will see that he has been most blessed. Jno. Elliott has been by Providence, as he was by Grace, "Separated unto the Gospel of God."[5] When health & friends (the nearest & dearest) are taken from us, we learn what it is to say "Whom have I in Heaven but thee."[6] I am sure that Adversity & Prosperity have both been brought to bear upon me, and I will not despair of being enabled more & more to value the latter & not above the former. I am glad you attend the Bible Class. You must give me some acc't of it & tell me how you like it.

Robert is with us and seems pleased. He is quite a favorite with officers & men. I am glad of seeing something of his disposition & character, & of becoming more intimate with him. He is fond of me & our intercourse is of the pleasantest & most cordial nature. He offered to give up his horse to me on the march when I c'd not get one, but with great difficulty I have succeeded in getting, for $480.00, an old horse that I would not ride in Peace times. Horses are not to be had here at all & I only got this one by getting permission to buy him from the Government.

I am glad you have some of my books with you. Even if you do not succeed in reading them, I hope the books will do you as much good as they did me. As for the little picture which got broken, even if it cannot be repaired, it will not make much difference. If that is the extent to which my wife is to be a trial to me I do not think my temper or disposition will suffer materially. I would like to look at the "Guardian Angel" with you and hope to have the pleasure of doing so in time. I am glad to hear that my friends remember me. Do give my love to my Cousins Nannie & Mary and all the family who are at hand, as well as to your own household. I am glad

Sue has had one ride at least on horseback & hope she has repeated it. Give her much love & tell her to enclose a note sometimes. Remember me to all friends including Miss Glover & Miss [Taller].

I am very happy to hear that all my friends have been so affectionate to you. I will show you a community one of these days in St. Johns, I hope, where they will be affectionate to you & will not flatter you.

Rutledge begs to be remembered. Did you see his sisters & how did you like them? Robert sends love. I think if you read a little of Leighton[7] daily, devotionally, you will like it. Jno. Elliott's wife used to be fond of it. Do give him my love. Regimental Commissaries are to be dispensed with after the 21st July & Capt. Cain will leave us then.[8] He will be an irreparable loss to us. And now Darling goodbye. May God keep you under the protection of His good Providence & grant you the continual help of His grace.

Your affectionate Husband
W. P. DuBose

1. This is a bitter crystalline alkaloid produced from cinchona bark and used as an antipyretic or antimalarial medicine.

2. Lt. Gen. Richard Stoddert Ewell (1817–72) was appointed commander of the Army of Northern Virginia's Second Corps after the death of Lt. Gen. Thomas J. "Stonewall" Jackson. At the second battle of Winchester, his corps captured thirty-five hundred Union troops at Winchester and Martinsburg. See McPherson, *Battle Cry of Freedom,* 648; Warner, *Generals in Gray,* 84–85.

3. From June 12 to 16, 1863, Confederate batteries on Morris Island engaged Union naval vessels and Union batteries on Little Folly Island. See *Charleston Mercury,* June 12, 1863, and June 17, 1863.

4. William Porcher DuBose may be referring to the death of Rev. John H. Elliott's son John, who was born in October 1861 and died in May 1863 in Greenville, South Carolina. See Barnwell, *Story of an American Family,* 152.

5. Romans 1:1.

6. Psalm 73:25.

7. This was possibly Robert Leighton (1611–84), a Scottish clergyman and scholar whose writings were published posthumously.

8. A May 1, 1863, Confederate statute dictated that the position of regimental commissary was to be abolished and responsibilities assumed by regimental quartermasters. See *Statutes at Large of the Confederate States of America,* First Congress, session 3, chapter 61, 1863, 134–35.

I write from the same spot, my darling wife, from which my last letter was sent. No developments have taken place since that time and we have relapsed into the state of quiet & security from which our recent move temporarily awoke us. If a soldier halts one minute on the march he settles down on the ground as if he had a day's rest before him, & if he goes into camp for a day or two he forgets that he is on a campaign, even in hearing of the enemy's guns. The heat of the last two days has contributed still more to our immobility & we congratulate ourselves that we have been able to keep quiet.

Gen. Johnston possesses the faculty of keeping his own counsel & no one even attempts to fathom his intentions, but we cannot help feeling that it cannot be his purpose to attack Grant with his present force. Grant has near 100,000 men & is powerfully fortified in his rear. Johnston has only about 30,000 men, Loring's, Walker's, Breckenridge's & French's division (we are in the latter).[1] There are two ways of accomplishing our purpose without a battle. One is so to supply Vicksburg with provisions & ammunition as to enable it to stand an indefinite siege, & then let Grant wear his strength out by fruitless assaults or waste away with useless waiting. The other is in some way to cut off his supplies & compel him to a change of base. Whether either is feasible I cannot say, but I am content to keep quiet & trust the Generals.

In the meantime I am perfectly well, have enough to eat (at big prices), a horse & a pair of saddle bags, & get my letters pretty regularly, so I am quite independent of the world. I am happy enough too generally, although sometimes (not very often) I feel a little disconsolate & unsettled.

Your sweet letter of the 17th reached me late last night and was particularly refreshing to me. We are sending twenty one mules to Jackson for our mail & it is therefore more irregular than it was. Still it is a blessing to get it at all, especially when its contents are as satisfactory as they were yesterday. I feel very grateful that during my absence you are so happily situated. I am afraid that my return will not improve your condition, in this respect at least. We may for a long time be almost entirely dependent upon each other. I who have been thrown so much upon myself will find it easy enough to be satisfied with one, who is a second self. You will be satisfied too, my Darling, I know, but it will not be easy to give up so much that you now enjoy. I am very glad that you have had an opportunity of bestowing upon your friends the tokens of remembrance of which you write, besides the fact that your friends are mine & that I take the same pleasure that you do in seeing them gratified, you may be sure that I enjoy best what gives you most pleasure, & I am happy to believe that that is the giving of pleasure to others. We went out today and enjoyed a vegetable dinner at a neighboring farm house. Bacon & beans, green corn, squash & cucumbers composed our bill of fare. There were some more civilized dishes such as beef &c, but we did not touch them. It was quite a pleasant variety to our invariable beef & bread.

I am writing by candlelight & have to carry my letter some distance tonight to ensure its going off early in the morning. Give much love to the family, & to all who have remembered me, including Aunt Eliza & Miss Harriet, Mrs. Ravenel, the Winthrops &c.

I am willing that you should reserve the Metaphysics[2] for our reunion. I hope we will one of these days be able to read them together. My portable library I left at Jackson, so that I am without reading matter now. I will have to give up quoting poetry, as I never can do it from memory. Goodbye now, my Darling. May God's Spirit give you constantly the joys of His presence.

Your aff. Husband
W. P. DuBose

1. Maj. Gen. William Wing Loring (1818–86), Brig. Gen. Henry Harrison Walker (1832–1912), Maj. Gen. John C. Breckinridge, and Maj. Gen. Samuel Gibbs French (1818–1910) were all division commanders in the Army of Northern Virginia. See Warner, *Generals in Gray*, 93–94, 193–94, 318.

2. This is a philosophical work by Aristotle.

Near Livingston
June 29th 1863

Your letter of the 21st reached me yesterday, My Darling Wife. One week is the time they generally take to reach me now, and I am happy in the enjoyment of a regular mail. You look forward more hopefully than I have done to my transfer to the chaplaincy. I trust that it may be that we are to meet in a few months or weeks, but there are so many obstacles in the way that I do not often indulge in the hope. Would not a few weeks at home be sweet, in transition from here to Virginia? The Virginia army, however, is by this time, I suppose, out of my reach.[1] The latest rumour that has reached us is to the effect that Lee was entrenching at Hagerstown, just below the Penn. line. If it is so I would dislike to undertake the task of working my way to the army.

With regard to the duties of a Brigade Chaplain & the amount of preaching he should do, you must remember that there are four or five or six regiments, each of which, I think, should have at least one service a week. At the same time physical strength & endurance impose a limit upon all labour, however necessary, and I do not think I would be inclined [to] overtax nature & sacrifice permanent usefulness to a hasty & mistaken zeal. That the life of a chaplain with all its difficulties will prove a more satisfactory one to me than the comparatively pleasant & easy one I now lead, I have no doubt. I believe that the work of the ministry is the only thing that can impart reality & earnestness to my life. It is the only thing in which I feel a permanent & self-supporting interest. But I do dread sometimes the effect of discouragement upon me, the loss of interest, freshness, enthusiasm, the gradual decay of zeal, energy & hope will occasionally rise before me like a phantom. Lifelessness in religion is such utter wretchedness to the private Christian even, that I can conceive what a lifeless & hopeless ministry must be. However with God all things are possible, and there is one certain remedy which His Spirit can impart against the approach of discouragement, the Spirit of self-renunciation & forgetfulness. Obedience is its own reward & the indifference or opposition of men should not weigh in the balance against the favour and encouragement of God. I will tell you another thing which has been a trial to me in any effort I may have felt disposed to make for the spiritual good of the soldiers. There have been men exerting themselves in this way, well-meaning & zealous, but ignorant & incapable (in my opinion) of imparting instruction or [profit]. Now to cooperate with such men in a thing I cannot do, _heartily_. I have respect for their zeal & even for their piety but they do no real good, because they don't know the Truth themselves. On the contrary to ignore their labours & work independently of them altogether, has not a good effect upon the men, who don't understand it, & many of whom value preaching in proportion to its loudness, or because it comes from a preacher of their particular denomination. I give this as a sample of a class of difficulties which are greater & more numerous than you would suppose. These things have had more effect upon me than they should have done, & my irregular & unsatisfactory exertions have been a subject of bitter self-reproach. It has been a hard struggle to me to make up my mind to the course which I have finally, within a few days, decided to adopt. With the approval of [three] of the officers whom I cared to consult, I have determined to accept the position (without the _office_, of course) of Chaplain of the Legion while I am with it, that is to perform as far as is compatible with my other duties the function of a chaplain. I have discovered that if I am to do anything at all I must do it regularly, with the sanction & warrant of a definitely & professedly assumed duty. I consulted with Mr. Girardeau on the propriety of taking this step & he agreed that a well defined position of this sort would give me a great advantage. I was further encouraged to do so by Bp. Green's remarking to me the other day that at the last General Council of the Church it was decided that each B'p could licence his theological students to preach in the Army. I was to have held a service yesterday afternoon & announced my intention, but several preachers from neighboring regts volunteered their services & I went to hear Mr. Girardeau by invitation. I will do so this week if nothing prevents. Say nothing of this for the present. Of course this is only an informal & temporary arrangement & will not interfere with any other plans.

Several ladies attended Mr. Girardeau's service yesterday morning. Among others Gen. Evans carried some relatives of his who live in this neighborhood, & to whom he did me the honour of introducing me, & I was invited to visit them. In this neighborhood lives the Rev. Mr. Fontaine, father of the "Hero on crutches."[2] He has lately married a fortune here I believe & has one or two churches. He held service yesterday but I did not know that there was an Episcopal church in reach until last night. We have moved our camp a few hundred yards to a more breezy & comfortable place, water not very convenient but pretty good.

If I am to exchange my present position for that of a chaplain, I will see the hand of Providence more plainly in the obstacles which have prevented my military promotion. Nothing but informality & the irregularity of the thing seems to have prevented it. Even Crawley who graduated in my class at the Citadel & who is now in command, says that he never would have opposed me for the Colonelcy & that he would be perfectly willing to have me over him. General Evans says that he urged my promotion when he was in Richmond, but that the War Department was unwilling to act irregularly. I would not have refused it, but still less would I have sought it & I am glad it never came. Capt. Cain is to leave us at the end of this month, much to the regret of everyone. I don't know where he will be able to secure another position.

Give much love to Sue & all the family & remember me to all friends. Robert sends love & Capt. Cain & Rutledge beg to be remembered. I am sorry to hear that Miss Sarah has been sick. I am afraid she never will enjoy good health. What a misfortune it would be if their house were to prove really unhealthy.

And now my darling Wife, I must close. Give me your constant prayers that particularly in the matter which interests us most just now, I may be guided by the Spirit of God to act as will best promote His service & glory, & that His Providence will make the path of duty straight before me.

Remember me to Jno. Elliott. I hope he has the book.

Your affectionate Husband

W. P. DuBose

1. On June 29, 1863, Lee's Army of Northern Virginia was operating in Pennsylvania as part of the Gettysburg campaign. See Long, *Civil War Almanac,* 373.

2. Lamar Fontaine (1841–1921), a native of Texas, was the son of Rev. Edward Fontaine. He served in the infantry until his foot was injured in battle, and then he was transferred to the Campbell Rangers, Second Virginia Cavalry Regiment. He continued in active service, carrying a pair of crutches with him on horseback. He was the author of "All Quiet along the Potomac" and several other famous war poems. See *Confederate Military History,* 9:351–55.

4 miles from Brownsville

July 1st 1863

We are once more on the move, my darling Wife, with a strong probability this time of crossing the Big Black.[1] We left our last camp at 5 O.C. this morning & have come eight miles through heat & dust enough to suffocate novices in the art of marching. Our veterans stand it well enough, but the 26th Regt., a recent acquisition to the Brigade from the coast of So.Ca., to which their experience has been limited, seem to suffer a good deal, to judge from the am't of straggling they do. Tomorrow we reach the Big Black, & next day we will cross if we are to do so. Johnston's plan is still in mystery, but I still do [not] anticipate a direct [attack] upon Grant. He is not accessible in his [present] position, and his army is too [large] for our forces. You see [many] of the conflicting rumours which [perplex] us here. Vicksburg is provisioned for only two weeks more, according to some, & for as many months, according to others. Kirby Smith[2] is, & is not, opposite the city. Grant is sometimes undermining our fortifications, & sometimes preparing to get away, &c, &c. I suppose in So.Ca. Lee's movements are sharing public interest with our own.[3] I wish we could hear something more definite of him. I am afraid the Big Black, like the Potomac last summer, will prove a barrier to our correspondence, but I hope for the best.

Remember, my dearest wife, that I never hesitate to tell you precisely what I think is ahead of us, because I know that if any important movement really takes place you will be apprised of it by telegraph, & I rely upon you not to attach any importance to my prognostications until you see them verified. I am afraid I am not careful enough to save you unnecessary anxiety.

While I write, I am enjoying the music of an excellent band belonging to a brigade near us. At this moment they are playing "Sleeping I dream Love, dream Love of thee" & under its transforming power the realities around me do seem to fade away, & leave in their stead a bright & soothing dream of which you are the centre & the charm. Now they have suddenly changed to the Fishers Hornpipe, & my mind runs off to Willie, for whom I used to whistle it, & who had a variety of names for it, such as the "Fish Horn," "Horn Fish," "Fish Pipe," &c &c. And now they have stopped, & my dreams are dispelled & the grave reality resumes its place & its sway. But you need not complain, my Love, [for] I think of you, waking, much oftener than I dream of you, sleeping. Day dreams are very sweet, . . . amid these remorseless realities, & the imagination, when it does escape its fetters, brings home sweet joys.

You must be satisfied with a short letter. My time is limited and I want to write a few lines home. I am as well as ever, and well prepared for a march. My horse does well, & Wm. saves me much trouble & anxiety. Give much love to the family & remember me to all friends. Do not forget the Charleston members of the family. I hope to get a letter this evening.

May God bless & keep you, my precious wife, and answer all your prayers!

Your loving Husband
W. P. DuBose

1. The Big Black River and Brownsville are in Mississippi.
2. Gen. Edmund Kirby Smith (1824–93) commanded the Confederate Trans-Mississippi Department from 1862 to 1865. Smith was supposedly moving his men toward the Mississippi River to help relieve the siege of Vicksburg. See Warner, *Generals in Gray,* 279–80.
3. Lee's Army of Northern Virginia was engaged in the Gettysburg campaign. See Long, *Civil War Almanac,* 374.

1863

July 5th 1863

[I] write from the same point, my darling wife, from which my last letter was sent, but we have orders to march at 1 o.c. tonight. I thought at first from the hour, that the intention was certainly to cross the Big Black, but I hear it is not so & our early start is probably to avoid the heat & dust from which the men have suffered so much. The rumour is that we are going to Edwards Depot on the R.R. from Jackson to Vicksburg, & further from the latter place, I believe, than we are now. For remarks, see observations in my last on "Maneuvering." I have commenced regular services in the regt. Held one this morning, & Mr. Girardeau preached for us this evening. I trust that God will bless whatever efforts He may call upon me to make for his glory, but the responsibility & magnitude of the work & my immeasurable distance below the standard of an effective ministry weigh heavily upon me. I know there is a great deal of pride & want of faith mixed up with my feelings on the subject, & I pray that I may regard self less & trust more to the grace & strength of the Holy Spirit, but the battle has to be fought over & over & I cannot feel that the temptation grows weaker. However it is my trial & discipline, & I will try to work on over all opposition & discouragement.

6th. My letter was arrested yesterday afternoon by darkness & the departure of the mail. I began it in fact with the expectation of finishing it today at leisure at Edwards Depot. I little thought what developments were to be made in the next few hours, & how fearful a shock to our faith & hope was impending. By the time this letter reaches you, the telegraph will have informed you of the fall of Vicksburg.[1] We formed for marches at 1 o.c. this morning & to our consternation were there informed for the first time of the real object of our [march]. Grant with a large portion of his forces was endeavouring to cross the river & surround our little army. We remained in ranks for [several] hours waiting for the development of the Enemy's plans & uncertain whether we were to advance against him or retreat. About sunrise we began a retreat which was continued until 1 o.c. This has been the severest day upon troops that I have known since entering the service. The heat has been intense, the dust most oppressive & the men have been almost literally without water. I was afraid that the effect w'd be fatal in many cases, but I have heard of no serious consequences yet. I have seen men use water today which a horse w'd not touch ordinarily, stagnant, muddy & hot. But I have no time for details this evening. You can imagine the depressing effect of the sudden & unexpected blow upon us. Although the enemy are no doubt pressing upon our rear we cannot realize anything but the one dis-agreeable fact that engrosses our minds. We "die hard" as the saying is. We cling to every straw of hope that presents itself, & many refuse even now to believe the report even on Johnston's authority.

A storm is coming rapidly up & the rain is falling. Goodbye my Darling Wife

W. P. DuBose

The storm is over, quite a violent though brief one & I avail myself of a stump of candle to extend my peroration. I would not have you think I am despondent in consequence of our heavy reverse, or that I distrust the power of Providence to bring good to us out of this evil. Your & Sue's letters & one from Jno. Elliott reached me today & brought me considerable relief from the many adverse influences of the day.

Your letter, my Darling, I need say nothing about. It . . . as all your letters are, full of comfort to me. So was Sue's. Thank her for it & tell her I hope circumstances will soon enable me to answer it. I wish you would tele. Jno. Elliott that his letter gratified me very much & thank him for writing to me so freely & at length. Give much love to all the household and remember me to all friends. Our retreat may terminate at the Pearl River, or we may have to give up the whole state & fall back to the Tombigbee.[2] Do not be dis-heartened under any circumstances. We must meet with reverses sometimes & the result may not be as disastrous as we have anticipated.

Through all my precious wife you may be assured of my unchanging love & constant remembrance.

Once more your loving Husband
W. P. DuBose

1. On July 4, 1863, Confederate lieutenant general John Clifford Pemberton (1814–81) surrendered the city of Vicksburg, Mississippi, and its defenders to Maj. Gen. Ulysses S. Grant. See Long, *Civil War Almanac,* 378–79; Warner, *Generals in Gray,* 232–33.

2. The Tombigbee River runs through Mississippi and Alabama.

Raymond Road. 3 miles fr. Jackson
July 8th 1863

My last letter, my Darling, was written on the first evening of our retreat. It was resumed yesterday morning (the retreat I mean) and continued to

Jackson, which place we reached early in the afternoon, having marched in the two days about twenty five miles. The men gave way completely yesterday under the effect of the heat, dust & [drought]. The little storm of the preceding evening laid the dust for a few hours, but the burning sun & the incessant tramp of the army soon made it as bad as ever. Three fourths of the men broke completely down by the wayside, & crept up after dark, as many as were able. Two such days I have never seen since I have been in service. We settled down near Jackson for the night, and after refreshing myself as well as I could in a puddle, I prepared for as sound a night's rest as circumstances would permit. A fierce thunderstorm came up about dark, and a heavy rain commenced falling, in the midst of which, under the imperfect shelter of an oil cloth, I had just fallen asleep, when an order came for the Legion to march immediately to the above point in the Raymond Road, on Picket. It was a severe trial to the exhausted men, but there was no remedy, & so through rain & mud & darkness we trudged out here & stopped at about 2 o.c. I lost no time in getting to sleep on the wet ground with the rain falling steadily upon me, & did not wake until a late hour this morning. When I arose, the sun was shining bright & hot, & today we have another severe day, but fortunately no marching to do. The enemy is said to be advancing but it must be very slowly as he is not very near. If he comes in force we will fall back to the lines around Jackson where I suppose we will make our first stand. The paroled prisoners are beginning to come in from Vicksburg. Several have passed us today, among them Pemberton's[1] chief of staff.[2] I have had no conversation with them. The real cause of the surrender was, I believe, want of food. You will probably see full details in the papers, so I will leave the painful subject. I am not disheartened & do not intend to be. It is a great & painful reverse, but we have no right to expect uninterrupted success, & I believe it will be overruled for our good.

We hear what I have no doubt are vastly exaggerated reports of a victory in Pennsylvania.[3] I trust that our successes there will in some measure counterbalance the loss of Vicksburg and keep our people in heart. I think there is much more buoyancy & elasticity in the army than there is among those at home.

I am writing now at a house near the road, where we are allowed the use of the piazza & where we have just finished a dinner of corn bread, butter, milk & [beets]. The family is away & a servant is in charge of the premises. Robert is quite unwell & remained in Jackson. He always sends love. He hears quite regularly from Minnie. William is well & a great help to me. My horse has improved & turns out a fine old fellow. In every respect I am well prepared for the future & am not likely to suffer. Give much love to all the family & remember me to all friends. May the grace of our Lord Jesus Christ be with you, my darling wife, & strengthen & comfort you!

Your loving Husband
W. P. DuBose

9th. We have fallen back to the works around Jackson. The whole army is in the trenches awaiting the enemy. Before this reaches you, you will probably have heard of a battle. If not you may know it has not been fought. I will telegraph if possible if anything happens.

1. This was Lt. Gen. John Clifford Pemberton (1814–81). See Warner, *Generals in Gray*, 232–33.

2. This perhaps was Lt. Col. A. M. Foute. See Crute, *Confederate Staff Officers*, 182.

3. On July 8, 1863, Lee's army was in Maryland and retreating south from its defeat at Gettysburg. See Long, *Civil War Almanac*, 381.

Jackson. July 10th 1863

I wrote yesterday morning, my darling wife, that we had occupied the trenches and were awaiting the approach of the enemy. This morning before daylight we were startled prematurely from sleep by the firing of the pickets about a quarter of a mile in advance of the works. That turned out to be nothing, but about 8 o.c. the ball opened in earnest. It is now 4 o.c. P.M. and a desultory fight has been kept up all day, sometimes between batteries, sometimes between skirmishers, & sometimes with sharpshooters. We (the Legion) are supporting a battery which commands the Clinton & Vicksburg Road. The enemy advanced by this road & the main attack has been at this point. Balls, shot & shell have been passing over our heads the whole day, but not often in dangerous proximity. Very few men have been killed, one from the Legion. A minnie ball struck the ground less than a foot from me as I was lying down, threw dust over Rutledge & passed between him & Crawley, who were almost touching each other. I had just finished reading your letter of the 2nd which had been handed me a few minutes before, so that whatever tremor was produced by this undesired renewal of an old & disagreeable acquaintance, did not interfere with my full enjoyment of that sweetest of pleasures. At dinner, for which we had to wait a very long time without the support of breakfast, the tree was struck under which we were sheltered, but we had become somewhat accustomed to it by that time & it did not disturb our meal. The balls are still flying but I am pretty well protected and have nothing to do but wait, unless I write which I find a pleasanter task. We are in a large fine yard belonging to a Judge Sharkey. Genl. Evans occupies it as his H'd Qrs as did also Genl. McPherson,[1] the commander of the Yankee Corps immediately in our front when they occupied Jackson. It is a fine establishment destined I suppose to be ruined before friends & foes are done with it. I was a little unwell yesterday, but was brought up again by a couple of glasses of claret given me by Gen. Evans. He had received a present of a basket, and as the enemy was expected before he would have time to finish it, he was generous enough to make me a present, in addition to the drinks of a bottle, which I still have.

The other evening as we entered Jackson I stopped for a little while at B'p Green's, just out of town on the Clinton Road. I used to know his daughters in Camden, where they lived with Mr. Tom Davis & went to school. The Bp was very infirm & unwell at the time, but he packed up as rapidly as possible & left yesterday. The house, a very fine one, is about a quarter of a mile immediately in front of our works. For a long time it was not injured, but the enemies' sharpshooters have availed themselves of it to [annoy] us, and our battery is now playing into it.

We hear the most confused rumours of events in the East. I suppose there can be no doubt of a great victory in Pennsylvania, but I am anxious for details. The "Jackson Mississippean" our main dependence for news has "changed its base" & we are thrown upon the mercy of Rumour, which if it is not much more unreliable than the Mississippean is at least much more uncertain. I am afraid my motto is getting fast to be "News, good or bad, and good news, true or false"! I have grown quite voracious.

I will telegraph if I can, when the issue is decided, or if anything happens to me. I don't know, my darling, what dangers may lie before me before this affair is over. The enemy has been very slack in his operations today, but there can be no doubt that he intends more serious work. May God spare my life for His own work and for the sake of those who love me! I know that I do not realize as I should the solemnity of my situation as I stand thus, face to face with death. If I should be suddenly summoned to the presence of the Judge, it would not be in the frame of mind in which I should be prepared to meet Him. But I believe in the saving Grace of Christ, and I know that it is sufficient for me just as I am.

I will close my letter in case I may not have time to continue it, leaving space to do so if I can. Give much love to the household & receive my assurance, my precious wife, of the deepest & most earnest love.

Your affectionate Husband
W. P. DuBose

11th. 11½ A.M. The fighting was resumed by times this morning and has continued steadily up to this hour, rather more briskly than yesterday. Our line of skirmishers alternately advance & retire before those of the enemy without accomplishing anything on either side that we can see. The balls & bullets whistle around us, & occasionally we shift our position to get out of range, but no one has been seriously injured today in the Legion. I have seen the litters at work occasionally at the other parts of the line. A good many houses in front of our line have been fired to dislodge the sharpshooters. Among them the house I spoke of yesterday as Bp Greens, but I do not believe it is his after all; his house is a little more to our right & out of sight so that I do not know what has become of it.

We are in a beautiful lawn with forest trees for shade, and this morning the birds were singing and everything looked as peaceful as though there were no such thing as war. It so happened too that I read for the morning the Collect & Epistle for the 5th Sunday after Trinity, the spirit of which is so exactly the reverse of that of war, that I could not but shudder more than ever at the systematic & deliberate way men go about murdering each other. When will this thing end, and [sacred] peace be restored to us!

This morning a man, followed by a good looking young fellow, passed by Gen. Evans on his way to the trenches & said, "Well General they detailed me off in the [shop] but I got away & come back. This young man wants to try 'em a few too." An hour or two afterwards the young man passed back with his Sharpe's carbine, & I asked him what he had done. He said he had shot away his 40 rounds and as much more as he could borrow; that he was sure of three or four sharpshooters & believed he had killed more. He was a cavalry man of Gen. Jackson's escort, a mere boy, but he said he could "fetch a squirrel every time, & did not see why he could not bring a Yankee."

I believe there is no regular mail now from Jackson, but I will try to send my letter off by the cars. We had a rumour yesterday that there had been fighting at Charleston, but I don't know whether to believe it.[2] The campaign seems active everywhere now. Oh how I do pray for a speedy & honorable peace!

Once more my Darling, Goodbye.

Yr loving Husband W. P. D.

1. This was Maj. Gen. James Birdseye McPherson (1828–64). See Warner, *Generals in Blue,* 306–7.

2. On July 9, 1863, the mayor of Charleston warned the people of South Carolina that Union troops were preparing to land on Morris Island. The following day Union troops landed on the south end of the island and advanced against Battery Wagner. On July 11 Union troops launched their first assault on the fort but withdrew under heavy Confederate fire. See Long, *Civil War Almanac,* 382–83.

Jackson July 14th 1863

I sometimes think, my Darling, that it is inconsiderate in me to write so openly of the dangers which surround me, as it must increase your uneasiness for me. But on the other hand I know that the truth is not half so formidable as the misrepresentations of it which reach you from other sources, & besides that you must remember that by the time my letters reach you, their contents have passed into the history of the remote past. If anything occurs to me I will try to apprise you of it more expeditiously. I am afraid I will have to capitulate to my ink, although it turns darker after a while, it is so pale at first that my writing is scarcely legible, which besides making writing very unpleasant, must account for the above omissions and any faults which may hereafter occur.

Yesterday & today have been repetitions of those my previous letters have described, with this exception that today we had a most refreshing little truce of three or four hours. What the object was I have not been able to discover, although I suspect it to have been for the purpose [of] removing the insane inmates from an asylum which is now within the Yankee lines & of which they availed themselves to make observations from, relying on our unwillingness to fire into it. I heard that Johnston was going to demand the removal of the inmates [on] this account. As soon as the truce was assumed the Yankee sharpshooters emerged from their hiding places, and our men exhibited much more of their persons than they have ventured to raise above the parapets from some days.

The firing has just been resumed as fiercely as ever. What is to be the end of it, it is impossible to predict. I have been a little unwell today, just enough so to take away the relish from my [book] and to make writing somewhat of a task. I don't know what could have caused it unless it is the intensely sedentary life I have led for half a dozen days, and sleeping several nights in a house. I w'd not mention it, except to excuse a very dull note. I long for news from the East, from Charleston, from Lee, & from you. We have had no mail since that which brought me your letter of the 2nd, I believe. The P.O. has changed its base too, but I am in hopes that our letters will be forwarded from Meridian tomorrow. You need not number your letters. I can generally tell whether there are any missing, & I have discovered that it is some trouble always to remember the number. [Just] in my present situation regular letters from you w'd be particularly acceptable, and here I am, cut off from even the daily hope which it is so sweet to indulge. However, I know the letters are somewhere, & that whatever else they contain they are full of the love which is the most precious part of their contents.

I hold little meetings for prayer almost every night. It has to be after dark, without singing & without light. Give much love to the family and believe me, my darling wife, with much love & many prayers in your behalf

Your affectionate Husband
W. P. DuBose

July 15th 1863
While I am waiting for an opportunity of sending off my letters this morning, my darling wife, I will add a note to say that today has brought forth nothing new. All last night the enemy has been shelling the town, without much damage as the town is pretty well deserted. It has had this effect however, that our boys, who have to pass through it on their way to us, have not ventured up since yesterday morning, & thus we are effectually cut off from our base of supplies (as I wish Grant had been before Vicksburg starved out). However Robert has been enterprising enough to run the blockade & keep us supplied. There is much more noise than danger, but a negro does not distinguish easily between the two, and however well "loyal" negroes fight for the Yankees, the rebel ones like to keep their skins whole. Our establishment having grown rather warm, Genl. Evans, who had himself abandoned it some days ago for a safe locality, ordered us away from it yesterday evening. It was hard to exchange our elegant accommodations for our present position where the ground is destitute even of grass & dust & dirt prevail. Oh for cleanliness once more, & easy chairs!

I wonder what reports have reached you from us, and how you have been bearing the suspense. I am grateful that I have been enabled to write so regularly & only wish that my letters could reach you more expeditiously. We are digging trenches now to protect us from the balls to which we are still somewhat exposed.

My latest accts from Charleston are favorable, but still very indefinite. About Lee we can hear very little, except that he is at Gettysburg. Just over where we are working, in a little tree, there is a nest with two young doves nearly grown. The old couple hover about in great solicitude uttering the most plaintive notes, what we call "mourning" (although I believe it is the sound they make when they are courting, which, while it is certainly very trying, can scarcely be considered a "time for mourning"). It makes me sad to see the old folks so sad, & it is just now quite a question whether to end their suspense by broiling their young hopefuls for dinner, or to seek to relieve their anxiety in some more humane way. It is a case in which mercy, & the want of a frying pan are arrayed against a good appetite & perplexity as to how else to offer relief. The old birds are pathetic, but I am hungry & the boys are blockaded. However R. has just consented to go for dinner & letters & so I will spare the doves & close my letter.

Much love to all.

Your loving Husband
W. P. DuBose

July 16th 1863

Seventh day of the fight, my Darling, and still no change in the programme. There have been several hot skirmishes on the right in which the enemy were of course repulsed, I suppose, but I have heard nothing of them, except the rattle of the musketry which was very battle-like. I have become very hopeful, from principle. If a battle is fought, I assume it to be a victory, if one side cheers & we cannot see which it is, I cannot be convinced that it is not ours. I believe all the good news & laugh at the bad as unworthy of credence. Therefore I still believe Lee took 40,000 prisoners (unless it was 70,000) & that the enemy have been finally whipt off from Charleston. I hold it treasonable for any man to say that the enemy have, or are likely to have, the advantage of us at any point, or that we may have to retreat from Jackson, as some think, or any other discouraging thing. Despondency, I think, ought to be severely punished wherever found or in whatever form. Not that it is always a crime, for with some unfortunate people it is more a misfortune than a fault, but then it is a dangerous thing, and the good of the country requires that it should not be countenanced. When bad news comes, I take so long to believe it, that I have time to nerve & prepare myself for it. And then I avoid thinking of it so studiously that I soon forget it. In this way the fall of Vicksburg is as old to me as if it had happened when I expected it to happen, immediately after the fall of Donelson, N. Orleans, Memphis, Island No. 10, &c. It is true my principle of "<u>Sanguinity</u>" places me on the weak side of a discussion sometimes, & occasionally betrays me into what some people might call untenable assertions, but I make up in confidence for what I lack in argument. I am done with despondency, it is worse than yellow fever & more disfiguring than the smallpox to the countenance. I took a walk into town a morning or two ago and came across two fellows most piteously afflicted with it. They were the two remaining representatives of the "Jackson Mississippian," the paper which disseminated such encouraging views of Vicksburg, its impregnability, unlimited supply of provisions &c &c. The town was all deserted, stores shut, & silence & desolation reigned supreme. News hunting being one of my objects & I paused at the Mississippian office where the two victims of despondency were seated at the steps, exhibiting in their countenances painful evidences of the ravages of the disease. "Where is the Mississippian now?" "Scattered all about." "Ever get news now?" "None that's good." "What of Charleston?" "Enemy on Morris Island &c." No. 1 having remarked that Charleston was now the key of the Confederacy, No. 2 said "No, the key has been taken" meaning Vicksburg of course. "What of Lee?" "Retreating, [barren] victory &c &c." I laughed & left, & have been ever since waging war against despondency.

Apropos of the above, I have just learned as a profound secret, which I would not divulge to anyone but yourself, that we <u>are</u> to fall back at 10 o.c. tonight to Brandon, 20 odd miles from here. Of course it will cease to be a secret by the time it reaches you. What the object is I don't know, but have no doubt it is all right.

And now I will conclude for the night and leave my remaining page for some point on our anticipated march. Brandon is on the R.R. & I hope the luxury of a mail is not to be lost to us.

Yesterday I received two & today one letter from you, one enclosing the Bp's. They were more than welcome & have been a sweet treat to me after the few days dearth that preceded. I got one also from Sister Anne.

19th. I have had no opportunity of resuming until this morning & now have only a few minutes. We left Jackson on Thursday night and last night reached this place (17 miles from Brandon and 29 from Jackson). I wish I had time to detail the incidents of the march, which has been a hard one, but I have not. We marched the last three or four miles through a deluge of rain, but fortunately it cleared up after dark & we dried ourselves & slept comfortably. Today up to 10 o.c. we have no orders to march, probably because the roads are impassable. As to our destination & Grant's movements I know nothing & have no time now to speculate. I am well & do not mind the personal discomforts to which we are subjected. They are too small in comparison with the weightier interests of the day.

And now, my darling wife, I must say Goodbye, with much love. You had better direct to Jackson as usual, or to Meridian Miss. The letters will come straight. We are in <u>French's</u> division. Much love to all.

Your loving Husband
W. P. DuBose

Tuesday, July 21st 1863

I sent you on Sunday, my dearest wife, a note which brought me up to the end of the second day's march from Jackson. We rested there until midday on Monday where we took the road again & stopped yesterday evening. We are likely to rest again today. I don't know exactly where we are going. We started East & have been traveling in that direction until yesterday afternoon, since when we have been looking South. I hear we are to be in Pemberton's Corps. Evans, French, Pemberton! I cannot say I admire our generals much. Johnston does not seem to have lost confidence among the officers or men, and I do not believe he will disappoint the country when he is fairly tried. He could not have relieved Vicksburg.

We received yesterday intelligence of a general repulse of the enemy at Charleston on the 18th.[1] It does much to cheer us, to hear such good news from the Old City. I do believe that the prayers of its people will be heard and that Charleston is to be spared. I have not seen a newspaper for a very long time. Those that you sent have not been received. I do not know why they should be so much more uncertain than letters, but they certainly are. I cannot get anything definite about the battle of Gettysburg.

I have not regretted assuming the Chaplaincy. I have not had an opportunity of preaching a regular sermon as, so far, the only Sunday day service we have had was performed by Mr. Girardeau. But we have a short service every night, except in extreme cases & I generally make a brief address, in a very informal way. The attendance is very good & I have no doubt that the fact of my being an officer in many respects is an advantage to me. Anything that I tell you as a secret, you are at liberty to communicate to Sue or not, at your own discretion. Mr. Girardeau & I have ridden a great deal together during the last few days march, and I find him a very delightful companion. Fortunately our regts are next to each other, and I hope to be thrown still more intimately with him. He is a man of very clear mind, independent character & strong personal piety.

With regard to the Bp's letter, I don't see that he could expedite matters more than he is doing. The fact is, in this crisis of affairs I would not care to hurry out of the military service, particularly now that I am in a measure engaged in the work of the Gospel. Still as I allowed him to decide for me, I will of course be ready whenever the matter is arranged. I confess the prospect of getting home, for a while, increases somewhat my desire for the change, but I would dislike to desert this army in its present position, nor would I do it at all if I had had the initiation of the matter, or if it had been first proposed to me in the present aspect of affairs. I am perfectly willing to leave the matter to its own development, trusting that Providence will decide for me according to the will of God.

I see Creighton frequently. He often asks about you & regards me as having "married into the family." He is polite & gentlemanly, but in other respects has not struck me very forcibly. One of the best things about him is his evident devotion to his wife, who I have no doubt is too good for him; not that there is anything very wrong about him, but he certainly must be inferior to her if she is what I have heard her represented from various sources. I don't admire volunteer aids anywhere, but a volunteer aid to Genl. Evans, & one of a half a dozen, must be one of the last positions in the service. If he had occupied one more to my taste, it is probable I would have spoken more favorably of our cousin.

The weather is very warm & redbugs & ticks are eating me bodily, but I contrive to keep comfortable. I have become quite accustomed to the petty annoyances of bivouacking at this season & do not lose my equanimity as easily as I did at first. Thank Sue for her little note, & tell Margie that I do not like to promise, when writing is so precarious & inconvenient a thing, but she need not be surprised to see a letter from me when times improve a little. In the meantime she can write to me & give me as much pleasure as my letter could possibly give her. Give Lise & herself a kiss for me.

I have not rec'd a letter from you later than that enclosing the Bp's, or since you heard of the Fall of Vicksburg. I hope you did not relax your writing, and that the next mail, of which we are in daily hopes will bring me several from you. I am glad the Barnwells did get to you after all on so pleasant a visit, & only wish I could have met them & heard Miss Mary's music.

Goodbye, now, my darling wife. May God soon bring us safely & honorably through all our troubles & unite all those whom His Providence now separates! Much love to all. Remember me to the Whitners, Winthrops, Miss Hetty Breese & all enquiring friends. Give my love to my cousins of the spiders web & to your Brother & Sister Martha when you write.

Your affectionate Husband

W. P. DuBose

1. On July 18, 1863, Union forces, led by the Fifty-fourth Massachusetts (Colored) Infantry, launched their second assault on Battery Wagner. The attack failed, and Union forces suffered over fifteen hundred casualties, including Col. Robert Gould Shaw, the Fifty-fourth's commanding officer. See Long, *Civil War Almanac,* 387.

In the woods. I don't know exactly where. July 28th 1863
I was much disappointed today, my Darling, at not hearing from you by the first mail we have received for a week. I am afraid the news of the fall of Vicksburg and the uncertainty of our movements in consequence may have discouraged you from writing for a while. However arrangements have been made, I believe, to have the mail regularly forwarded from Meridian to Morton, the nearest village to us on the R.R., and I will not have to wait long I trust for the delinquent letter or letters, which, after all, I have no doubt were written. We have settled down into a camp of Instruction to revive our drill & discipline, "preparatory to offensive operations against the Enemy in Mississippi." This will give us a breathing spell for some time to come. You may direct to Jackson, Meridian or simply to Mississippi, if the brigade & division are designated the letters will come straight. We are within a mile or two from the place from which I last wrote; I don't know where Grant is or what he is doing. Probably he is satisfied with Jackson for the present. I wish you only knew that I was at leisure now to enjoy your letters to my fill, so that you might give me enough to occupy my leisure.

Your letter of the 10th has just reached me and is old enough for me to indulge the hope that the next mail will bring me another. I have fortunately been enabled to write regularly through the retreat, siege & on the march, and I am sorry my letters have been delayed longer than usual on the way just when they were most needed to relieve your anxiety. You must not pay much attention to rumours or anything short of ascertained fact in the papers. For instance there was never any prospect of a battle at Clinton. We hear today that Jackson has been evacuated by the Enemy. I would not be surprised if it is so, as I thought it probable that Grant w'd wish to send the bulk of his force to some other contested point, leaving enough only to defend Vicksburg. If this is so, we are as far off from a fight as ever, & may be sent to defend Mobile or reinforce Bragg or something of the sort. You would be amused to hear how easily & how often the rumour gains ground that we are to be sent to Charleston. The men w'd be delighted to go and listen greedily to the wildest reports on the subject. I hear now that we are in Hardee's and not Pemberton's Corps. I hope so.

Suppose that after all we should be in Charleston for a portion of the summer, and, the danger all blown over, should be enabled to realize the project which we planned before I was suddenly ordered out here! I have long since ceased to look forward to the time of our permanent reunion. I am as confident as ever of final success, and I bear up cheerfully under temporary disaster, but the end is far off & I feel that all I have to do is to make the most of my present mode of life and turn it to the best account. My separation from you is the most painful feature of it, and yet the longer the war seems to lengthen out the more I rejoice that we did not postpone our marriage to the indefinite future. Far as we are apart it is very much better to be married. I am glad you find the climate of Anderson so pleasant. It seems to me a week with you would be Elysium & I sigh for it sometimes when I permit my mind to dwell upon it. We have very warm weather here and the red bugs surpass anything in the way of petty annoyances. Just think of living in the woods where the supply is inexhaustible & unceasing. However I bear them with much more equanimity than I ever thought I could command. I hope their time will soon be over.

I received a letter from Sister Betsey together with yours. As she had written to you, you may have heard how much Col. Bratton is opposed to my accepting the Chaplaincy. His main objection is based, I think, upon an error. He thinks that a Brigade Chaplain would be a supernumerary, the Regulations only providing for Regimental Chaplains, and so it would be if the Regts were supplied. But this is only an effort to supply as far as practicable the deficiency of regimental chaplains. The mail boy is upon me & I must stop abruptly. Love to all.

Your loving Husband
W. P. DuBose

My Darling Wife,

I write from the same point from which my last letter was sent, the movement towards Enterprise having been indefinitely postponed. Our location has one great advantage, that of abundant good water. Independently of this there is nothing in it very attractive, but I have settled down into a sort of dogged independence of circumstances, which . . . [has] been that so many have formed, that I am afraid many have done so without due consideration, and that it may prove imperative from its very size and the want of genuine interest in many of its members. It working however remains yet to be tried; it is not fully organized yet. I read a portion of John's Gospel every evening and give a short address upon the leading thought in it. I have finished three chapters in this way. When the Association is completed, I will propose a "Prayer Meeting" one or two evenings in the week.

Your note of the 20th reached me this morning. I am very grateful to you, my darling, for writing so regularly <u>in faith</u>. My letters have been more regular than those of any other member of the mess, & it has been a great comfort to me to hear so constantly. I am sorry that my letters have been so irregular in reaching you; besides those of the 3rd & 12th which you acknowledge, I am sure there are as many as four. It is strange that when there is most need for promptness, the mail should be the most uncertain. . . .

. . . glad I had an opportunity at last of learning more of his disposition & character. I wish we could be together but I believe he was right in the course he took. Besides, he was of great assistance to me. He has considerable energy & capacity for work, & as he never liked to be idle, was always glad when I called upon him. The departure of his serv't & himself has made Wm. quite homesick, although he says he would not leave me if he could. The other night I woke up in the night in the midst of a heavy rain and heard Wm. condoling with himself on the desolateness of his situation "so far from home." He was sitting out in the rain, and his spirit as well as his body were considerably dampened. Generally he is very cheerful & has very popular manners. I called him up [just] now and gave him a little lecture, telling him that no matter what the rest of the Regt was, he & I were always & under all circumstances to be cheerful. He repudiated the idea of being anything else. . . .

. . . consideration however convinces me that, as it was not mine, no circumstances can excuse my taking it. I found it very readable as it brought to my notice a class of personages whom I was glad to meet so familiarly.

Perhaps in the dearth of new books, you & Sue may find time to enjoy it. And I will try & make the Judge amends some of these days. Capt. Cain leaves on Friday. Rutledge is better & has not succeeded in getting his furlough. Furloughs are being granted again at the rate of one to every twenty five men, 14 days at home. Very few officers can go, and of course having been so recently at home, I have not the face to apply. But w'd it not be sweet to be fourteen days with you? Of course I feel very anxious about Charleston, but of course also I am very hopeful. Lee's army I believe is to be in better after the battle of Sharpsburg, & therefore I apprehend no fear from that quarter. Bragg's army has not been damaged, & we have a pretty good one here. The enemy are not the stronger for having . . .

. . . [now], my dearest wife, I . . . as the mail is about to be closed. [Give much love] to Sue & tell her I will write to her in a few days if we continue quiet. Love also to the household & to my cousins in the other house. Remember me to the Whitners, Miss Carrie W., Miss Kate &c. Kiss Margie & Lise, & tell the latter I am glad she is so good a little scholar to you. I can do so little for you myself that I am grateful to all who in their [several] ways & degrees are good to you.

Your loving Husband
W. P. DuBose

Holcombe Legion
Aug. 3rd 1863

I am afraid I have allowed more days than usual to pass, my dearest wife, without writing to you. At any rate I do not remember on what day my last letter was sent, and it is fair to infer that it was a very long time ago. The fact is I am afraid too much <u>sedentariness</u> has stagnated me somewhat & is making me slow. There is little temptation to walk; it is so hard to get out of soldiers, & my horse's back being sore prevents my riding, so I lie down, & having a plenty of time, do very little in it, as usual. However I do a "power of thinking" sometimes, like the Hindoos[1] who lie flat on their back & "contemplate" their lives away; and you may be assured, my darling, that my reflections, or dreams, or whatever they are, turn not infrequently to you.

But sedentariness is no longer to be the order of the day. We have this moment been startled into life by an order to prepare immediately to move for Savannah Ga. Such shouts as the announcement elicited through the

Brigade, I have not heard for months. No man realizes, or reflects, that we are possibly going to meet the Enemy in deadly conflict; a soldier seldom does now, until whistling bullets rudely thrust the fact upon his consciousness. All they think of is that their faces are turned <u>homeward</u> and the very idea is happiness. Oh for the time when our faces shall be turned finally homeward, never to be turned away except for peaceful purposes! Just now it is hard at this distance to discriminate between going <u>homeward</u> & going <u>home</u>; we will realize soon enough, I expect, the difference between these when we get to Savannah or some point on the coast & find ourselves as much separated as ever from those who make home dear. I am tempted sometimes to hope that I may be situated that you can come to see me, but in the uncertain state of affairs I will build no castles, even to entertain so desirable a guest as yourself in.

Forrest. Aug. 4th. I was obliged to stop last night, this morning we marched 10 miles to this place and are now waiting to take the cars. I would not be very much surprised if we are after all sent on to Charleston. I hear that troops are much needed there. However Savannah is still our destination & I will not look further yet. I met this morning a man who was taken prisoner at Boonesboro, and confined in the same building with me in Frederick City. He has just returned from the North, having been there ten months, detailed as nurse in F'k city & Baltimore. He told me a good many interesting things concerning persons & places known to us in common, and being somewhat hungry, after an early & scant breakfast, I took considerable pleasure in recalling with him the multitudinous repast or series of repasts furnished us by the ladies of Frederick City, how after fasting from Sunday until Wednesday (almost), we were feasted continuously for six or eight consecutive on the last named memorable day, on liquids and solids & solids & liquids, on deserts [sic], meats & soups, soups meats & deserts [sic], until it was a wonder that any of us lived to tell the tale. One man did die, he told me, after I left, of that day's excess. <u>We</u> survived however to repeat it the next day, & the next, after which he was rescued by being sent to the Hospital, and I by being plunged into a second fast which lasted until I reached Ft. Delaware. He told me of one [of] our party, a captain, who was with me in Ft. Del. & who is so unfortunate as to be a prisoner there now, having been captured at Chancellorsville for the 2nd or 3rd time. He seems to think that Maryland, & certainly Baltimore, is more Southern in sentiment than it was a year ago, that Lee was certainly expected in Baltimore, by both parties, that the officers whom he met called Gettysburg a drawn battle, Meade having retreated to

Frederick & Lee to Hagarstown &c &c. On the whole the conversation with one just from the North did not discourage me.

Mobile. 6th. We arrived here about 8 O.C. last night and are waiting this morning for orders to march to the Montgomery depot. Before going out to take a peep at the city, I will finish my letter so as to mail it here. The morning paper contains no news, and I have heard nothing to fix our destination at any other p't than Savannah. Rutledge, whose family are just in our route, has permission to go ahead & stop a few days at Oxford. Why do you not live on the route too, instead of on that obscure little R.R. by which no one ever travels? I am afraid the letters I am leaving behind will take a long time to find me. My last from you was begun on the 22nd & finished on the 24th, so there must be several on the search for me.

Give much love to Sue and the family generally as well as to those of the other house. Tell your Sister Martha I am sorry her visit to Charleston was so rudely interrupted, & that when energy & 15 inch guns have failed to take Charleston, & she returns, I hope you will have an excuse to accompany her. And now my Darling, I must close. Remember me to all enquiring friends and
Believe me

Your loving Husband
W. P. DuBose

1. DuBose means people of the Hindu faith.

∞

Isle of Hope. 9 ms fr. Savan.
Aug. 11th 1863

The fortunes of war find us once more in a peaceful haven, my Darling, where for a brief space we may forget the horrors of war and luxuriate in the rare pleasures of security & repose. I have not a map & cannot determine our precise location, with reference to the Sav. River. It is a place similar in many respects to Young's Island[1] [*sic*], on which the Marions were encamped, connected like that to the mainland by a causeway over a marsh. I have not seen much of the island, but it seems to be used principally as a summer resort. Bathing houses abound, and the dwellings look as if they were built for summer. We are situated at "Grimball's place" on a creek, & with a fine shade of Live Oak trees. Our Hd. Qrs. are in the piazza of the house, with a fine place for bathing immediately in our front. Altogether the attractions of the spot and the feeling of rest after all our toils make it very delightful. There are some families on the Island, in our immediate vicinity, and the thought frequently suggests itself to me how sweet it would be to have you pleasantly domesticated with one of them, during my stay here. I could be with you almost constantly & I am sure we w'd have a delightful time. If I could only be assured that we would be allowed to remain here a reasonable length of time in our present security, I would not hesitate to propose the plan, but in the present uncertainty it would be folly. Still it is a pleasure even to dwell upon the fancy, & to imagine how sweet it would be to enjoy the reality. I could have a horse always at your disposal too & we could take charming rides together. Oh that it were practicable to see something of you, my dear wife! But before this reaches you we may be on our way to some scene of strife.

I have just received your letter of the 29th forwarded from Meridian. I am truly sorry to hear of the death of Prioleau Ravenel.[2] I have heard Sue & yourself speak of him with so much affection, and his poor mother has always felt so deeply the anxieties & trials of the war, that I know it must be a peculiarly sad case. I hope your Mother will prove as successful a comforter to her as she has always been. I suppose Sue has returned by this time, if so give her my sympathy for the loss of so dear a Cousin, & tell her I will take advantage of my present situation to write to her.

I did not know that John Elliott was to take a tour, but am exceedingly glad to hear that it is so. I know it will do him good, and he certainly needs it. I suppose he has left by this time. I wish you would tell me where he has gone & if possible his direction. I must try to write to him during my leisure. I was about to say I would like to take his trip with him, but if I were set at liberty for a time, I do not think I could be enticed away from you & home. I wish Miss Catherine had said something about John. I am anxious to hear where he is & what he is doing. When I last heard from home Sister Betsey was about starting on a second visit to Col. Bratton at Richmond; she has continued to see a good deal of him lately.

I must close my letter now, my Darling. I am in such a crowd that I can only go through the form of writing a letter, without entering much into the spirit of it. I am anxious for a fresh letter from you, only one or two days on the road. Give much love to Sue & the family & to your Mother when you write. I appreciate Cousin Clelia Gibbe's[3] kindness, which was all the same as though the work had really been done for me. Give my love to all my cousins, & remember me to the Whitners & other enquiring friends.

Yr loving Husband
W. P. DuBose

1. Yonges Island, South Carolina.

2. Elias Prioleau Ravenel (1837–63) was the son of Henry Ravenel (1795–1859) and Elizabeth Peronneau Coffin (1807–69). See *South Carolina Genealogies*, 2:73.

3. Clelia Finley Gibbes (1837–1906) was the daughter of John Reeve Gibbes and Sarah Peronneau Gibbes. See *South Carolina Genealogies*, 2:227.

Isle of Hope Aug. 15th 1863

I can only write a note this afternoon, My Darling, to enclose in Sue's letter, which I will direct to you in case she may not have returned home. Two of your letters reached me yesterday afternoon, an old one of June 26th (but not less acceptable for being old) and one of the 11th. I am glad you have faith enough to write so often, and trust that experience will always continue to prove to you that with me there is at least one "good thing" of which there cannot be "too much." I am afraid you will be disappointed in one thing & that is that my being at Savannah is not quite being at home. I realize that fact most deeply just now, and feel very much tantalized at being so near the object of my desires without being able to reach it. I do wish there were some shadow of certainty about our movements so that we might contrive some place of meeting. The war seems to be so indefinitely prolonged that no opportunity ought to be lost. I have not received Jim Davis' letter but suppose it will find me out after a while. I wonder what progress the B'p has made. After the recent disasters I was on the point of writing to him to request him to drop the matter for a time at least, if not finally. But I dislike to change, & concluded to let matters take their course. I am still doubtful however about the propriety of leaving the service at such a critical time and therefore cannot feel anxious to see him succeed too soon. I trust that Providence will decide for me in the best way.

Our Christian Association is organized & in operation. The only thing we have done yet is to hold meetings for prayer, which we are to do twice a week; our first was last night. I have a short service every night, which is very well attended. Of Sunday preaching I have had little experience so far. The Regts have been encamped so near together that it would have been not only useless to have separate services, but very often they would have interfered with each other, if held at the same hour. The 18th Regt and ourselves are now within 50 yards of each other and as they have a good chaplain, Rev. Mr. James, and I am very anxious to get to church once more, I will invite him to preach for both Regts tomorrow and ride into Savannah. I may hear Bp. Elliott if he is there. Have you any relatives or friends in Savannah? I may take it into my head to do some visiting.

I have heard nothing of Robert since he left me, and do not even know whether he went home. I am anxious to hear something too of Tom Stoney[1] who was formerly my dearest friend, and a favorite cousin with us all. We are faring very well here in the way of provisions, and are all in good health & spirits. There are a great many fish but we have caught very few yet.

I must close now, my dearest wife, as I have a report to make out before dark for tomorrow. I trust that some way will be opened for us to see each other, before we are again separated further. May our Saviour be very near to you to strengthen, comfort & guide!

Yr loving Husband
W. P. DuBose

Give much love to "Auntie" & all the family, & remember me to all our friends.

1. Thomas Porcher Stoney (1835–91) was the son of Peter Gaillard Stoney. See MacDowell, *Gaillard Genealogy,* 305.

Isle of Hope
August 18th 1863

A cool, rainy day, as it always does, has turned my thoughts with peculiar force today to home & you, my dearest wife. I am sometimes quite susceptible to the influence of meteorological changes, and next to a fine thunderstorm there is no state of the weather that affects me so pleasantly as a set wintry rain, which this resembles. It suggests more strongly than anything else the comfort of a cozy room with books & good society. When the sweet atmosphere of love is added, the picture is complete. Alas that it is only a picture today. Such a day spent with you in such a room, and ended with a brisk little walk through the driving misty rain, to nerve & brace our bodies & spirits, would be delightful.

On Sunday I went to Savannah to church and enjoyed two services at Christ Church. In the morning Bp. Elliott preached a fine sermon on the nature of a national fast to prepare the people for the observance of the fast appointed by the Pres't for next Friday. He read the Prests proclamation appointing it which is a perfect [model] I think. In the afternoon the sermon was preached by a young man who seems to be the Ass't Minister, & who at the distance at which I sat startled me by his likeness to Jno. Elliott. The only drawback to my enjoyment of the day was the long interval between the services, 12 ½ to 6, which I did not know what to do with. The Hotel furnished little attraction except at dinner, & that was very indifferent. The next time I go I will carry my haversack and devote part of the time to you, unless I find or make some friends in the meantime. It is fully nine miles from our camp to the city, and after service I had a long dark ride by myself. On my arrival at 10 o.c. I found your letter of the 4th Augt, and today, two have come to hand, one of the 7th from Miss. and one the 14th direct. I have no doubt all the Miss. letters have reached me now. The last contained Jim Davis' letter, which is very kind. The Bp. in his letter mentioned the fact that he had been for some time under religious conviction, which I was very glad to hear, on his father's as well as on his own acc't. John & Jim are the only two now left out of the church, & I trust he will live to see them brought to the knowledge & love of the truth. These last letters from you, my darling, have been particularly precious. I am glad to hear that our good friends have been exercising their ingenuity to devise some scheme for our meeting. I wish you would select the least visionary of them & proceed to put it into execution. You need not waste time to consult me, but simply apprise me of it in time for me to take my part. Gen. Evans went some days ago to Charleston & is now at Cokesbury. We do not know yet what our final destination is to be, but it seems to me more likely than it appeared at first that we will remain quietly here until we are called upon to take part in the great struggle for Charleston, unless some sudden emergency calls us to Tennessee or Va. One presumption against our remaining here we have drawn from the fact that although Gen. Evans ranks Gen. Mercer,[1] he has been ordered not to take command at Savannah, but to hold his brigade "as a reserve." Although matters are in this uncertain state I would be delighted if you would think it not too imprudent to risk a trip to Savannah. A very short visit would be worth a great deal under such circumstances, and there would be little or no danger of your missing me altogether. Even if we were ordered away after you left home for Savannah, it would take several days for the brigade to leave & I could remain for the last, or even after that. If we went to Charleston I could go with you via Augusta & Columbia. Under any circumstances I could send William with you. I would like him to pay a visit home. You might be able to pay me a good long visit, and under any circumstances would allow me an opportunity of seeing you. You could stay in Savannah or on this island as circumstances directed and I could contrive to be with you most of my time. I do not urge this prospect or even request it. I am so anxious to see you that I am afraid to trust my judgment, but if it should seem feasible to you or any of your counselors who are more impartial, I hope you will not allow any other considerations to deter you from acceding to it. There are several families, among them a Mrs. Habersham, living on the Island and I have no doubt some of them could make you tolerably comfortable for a while. Otherwise I could spend a good deal of my time in Savannah where I could find you pleasant lodgings at a private boarding house. Any plan though by which we may meet will be agreeable to me and I give you full authority to choose & decide. I was very much surprised to hear that Col. Bratton was at home. I have not heard directly from the girls since I left Mississippi. I am sorry to hear of [his] having been unwell, but glad that he has got home on the girls' acc't as well as his own. It always sets them going to have him with them for a time.

Our evening services continue to be very pleasant. It is very little exertion to me, or at least I feel it very little. I deliver a sort of little sermon every night in an easy familiar style & find it improving to myself, if not to my hearers. I do not care for you to keep . . . secret, but do not care for it to be generally spoken of. You may use your own discretion.

I am afraid we are very much alike in our want of system in the management of time. It has a very unaccountable way of slipping away from me. Give much love to our cousins of the other house. Of course I approve you lending Tanhauser[2] [sic] to Cousin Clelia & hope she will enjoy it. Tell her I am sorry her Captain is not here too. I have not heard of Gen. White yet and did not know the island belonged to him. I have not explored it yet but will do so and describe it to you. And now my darling I must close. With much love to the household & to your Mother when you write.

Your loving Husband
W. P. DuBose

1. Brig. Gen. Hugh Weedon Mercer (1808–77) of Virginia commanded Confederate troops in Savannah at the time of this correspondence. See Warner, *Generals in Gray*, 216–17.

2. Tannhauser was a German lyric poet. William Porcher DuBose may be speaking of his writings or a ballad or opera based on his legend.

Isle of Hope
Aug. 25th 1863

Your letter of the 21st, my Darling wife, had just reached me. I think I will deliver the note of introduction to Mrs. Elliott, as I feel quite in the humour for seeing ladies, and I would like to become acquainted with the Bp. I did not know you were so intimately acquainted with Mrs. E. I thought of going in to church again on Sunday but I find that the Reg't do not attend service as well in another camp as they do in their own & so determined to remain & have a service of our own. As the place where Mr. James preaches is not over fifty or a hundred yards from our camp, and he is quite a good preacher, I feel no hesitation in sending the Reg't to him when I feel like attending church, particularly as I have service every night. I never accept invitations to any other regt as they have chaplains of their own and my ministrations are limited strictly to our own Regt. The evening services I enjoy very much and the men also seem interested. I think they are calculated to do more good than the Sunday services even.

The Bp. seems to be really making progress towards effecting my transfer, and it does not look by any means so far off as it did. The nearer it comes, the more distrust in my ability to do good rises before me as an insuperable obstacle. Sometimes I am encouraged by the reflection that industry & prayer can effect wonders, but then it seems as if I make no progress in the use of those instrumentalities. I see that you & I have the same trouble. "Redeem the time," "redeem the time,"[1] is constantly ringing in my ears, and yet the time continues to glide away and leaves me standing still. Sometimes I ask myself in despair, "Is this to be always?" and a feeling of mental dread comes over me that I am to spend my life in a sort of inefficient mediocrity, when I feel within me the power, with industry & the grace of God, to do something more. I don't think I seek for applause or praise. At least when I disappoint myself in my efforts I don't trouble myself about not making a good appearance before my friends. I almost enjoy that humiliation as the just penalty of a want of diligence & prayer. My only comfort is to forget the failures that are past and to hope always for better success in the future.

Your sympathy seems to be excited for the brigade. It is true that we were rather a soiled & ragged set when we arrived from Miss. But when the men recovered their baggage which had been sent back from Jackson & had renewed their long interrupted acquaintance with water they began to improve decidedly in appearance. The Qr. Mr. deprtmt [quartermaster's department] too is rapidly supplying their wants and we will soon be about as well clad as we have been accustomed to be. With regard to myself, I have as much with me as I can carry and am very well supplied for the approaching winter.

We have just got orders to march to Savannah tomorrow morning at 5 o.c. preparatory to leaving for Charleston. This of course nips all my hopes of seeing you in Sav. in the buds. I am not surprised at this sudden summons. I have all along expected that when the emergency came we would be called to Charleston and sweet as the rest here is I am ready to take part in defence of the dear old city. I hope that if the place is to fall its defence will exhibit a heroism and devotion which will make the name of Charleston sacred in the history of this great struggle. We probably have hard service before us but we have the advantage of being more accustomed to exposure & heat than any of the troops now there. As for the danger let us trust in that power which has hitherto shielded me from harm & which can carry me safely thro' all the risks of the future. I must begin to prepare for the move & will therefore close. Give much love to all the family. Remember me to my cousins and all friends and believe me my darling wife

Your devoted Husband

W. P. DuBose

1. Ephesians 5:15–16: "See then that ye walk circumspectly, not as fools, but as wise, redeeming the time, because the days are evil."

Mt. Pleasant

Sept. 5th 1863

It will be some days, my darling, before our correspondence will find its equilibrium again. I am still in uncertainty as to yr direction as you spoke of spending only some days in Aiken. I wish I could have written to you to come & spend a few days in Charleston but I heard so [much] of the difficulty of ladies getting into the City that I quite despaired of you doing so. I do long to see you, my precious darling, & find it very tantalizing to come so near to it without succeeding. I went into Town on Thursday to see Jno. Johnson, whose wound has at last compelled him to leave Ft. Sumter and take a short rest.[1] It was acting sluggishly and looking badly and had become more painful than at first, & the Dr. insisted on his taking [fifteen to] twenty days' rest. He is going to his Sisters on Monday and in the meantime wrote to me to go & see him. I spent Thursday night with him & returned yesterday evening after dark. Besides other business which I transacted yesterday morning I had my likeness taken—at last. I am afraid you have thought me very unmanageable on that point. The truth is I have a peculiar aversion to having my picture taken; besides the trouble of shutting my mouth for so many seconds, I always sit down with conviction that it is not going to give satisfaction when it is done. I know you will be disappointed, but have come to the conclusion that it is better to disappoint you by sending a bad picture than by sending none. I thought I would try a photograph this time. I have not seen it yet but Mr. Cook[2] said it was good. I told him to prepare me three cards,[3] two or all of which I will send to you next week. I don't care to multiply impressions of myself. I met your brother, who seemed to think it not altogether impracticable that you might come to see me & said he would make inquiries for me. I told him I would [be] very much obliged to him if he could effect it for me. Mr. Sass says if you come you must stay at his home. He has a great deal of influence with Genls Beauregard & Jordan,[4] and has exerted it to get permission for several ladies to return to the city to remove valuables &c. From his experience I should judge it to be no easy matter to effect, & therefore I have very little hope of seeing you here, sweet as it w'd be, my darling.

I received the box from Dr. DeSaussure, but have not opened it yet. I am waiting for midday when I can test the Cherry Shrub[5] [better] & when our Hd. Qrs. will be less assailed by business applications. I will tell you the result of my experiment, before the close of my letter. The two Mrs. Snowdens[6] are still in town, hard at work for the soldiers. I made arrangements with them to send vegetables for our reg't occasionally. They are very useful & have certainly devoted themselves to the good work. All my friends sent love to you, or begged to be remembered, or rather all our friends.

I suppose you have been waiting to hear from me & have wondered at my delay. I hope my last letter explained my silence satisfactorily. I have opened the box & find the bottle sound. The Shrub has been favourably tested & will furnish a refreshing drink for some time to come. I have never tasted it before and like it very much. I would like anything from you of course but this has intrinsic merit to commend it to my taste. The other articles were all equally welcome, but what is sweetest to me, my darling wife, are the indications of thoughtfulness which this box, as everything that comes from you exhibits & which is the best proof of that love which I prize so highly. The tapers are one evidence of it, although I can see how you read that want, a want which I have been trying for some time to supply. But I cannot conceive what put it into your mind to send me Pascal,[7] unless it is that you have learned to read my thoughts at a distance. You have several times anticipated my wishes in the same mysterious way, which is always most gratifying to me. I wanted that very book.

I will send this letter to Aiken although I feel very uncertain whether you are there. Give my love to your Mother & remember me to the family. I must stop now my darling.

Your affectionate Husband

W. P. DuBose

1. Lt. John Johnson was engineer in charge at Fort Sumter beginning April 4, 1863. He was wounded on July 17, 1863, but he remained in the fort until September 2, 1863, when he left due to the lingering effects of his wound. See Johnson, *Defense of Charleston Harbor,* 121, 147.

2. George Smith Cook (1819–1902) of Charleston was described as "the premier southern photographer" during the war. See Teal, *South Carolina Photographers,* 22–23.

3. William Porcher DuBose refers here to a *carte-de-visite,* a photograph the size of a visiting card. See Teal, *South Carolina Photographers,* 38.

4. Brig. Gen. Thomas Jordan (1819–95) of Virginia was assistant adjutant general, which made him second in command under General Beauregard during the siege of Charleston. See Warner, *Generals in Gray,* 167–68.

5. This is a beverage made with cherries and sugar. See Leslie, *Directions for Cookery,* 358.

6. Reference here is to Mary Amarinthia Yates Snowden (1819–98) and Isabel S. Snowden (d. 1881). During the war these sisters became well known for their war work, which included organizing groups of women to feed and clothe Confederate soldiers. In 1886 Mary A. Y. Snowden organized the Ladies' Memorial Association; she was also one of the principal founders of the Confederate Home and College in Charleston. See *Memorials: To the Memory of Mrs. Mary Amarinthia Snowden;* WPA Cemetery Index.

7. William Porcher DuBose writes here about the *Pensees* (Thoughts) of Blaise Pascal (1623–62), a French mathematician and religious philosopher.

Mt. Pleasant

Sept. 10th 1863

Your Sunday letter reached me yesterday, my darling wife, on my return from the City, where I had spent the day. If I had met the mail boy in the morning as I had hoped to do, I could very easily have gone to see your Uncle Amory which I would have liked very much to do. As it is I am afraid he will be gone by the time I get there again. One of my objects in going to town was to get the photographs to send to you; there was still something to be done to them, & I left them for a day or two longer. You will be no better satisfied with them than with the other likenesses of me you have seen. There is the same fault, which cannot be remedied. I will send them all three to you as I do not think anyone else would care to have them. We have had a warm time in the harbour for several days past. On Tuesday evening, I started over to see Dick Dwight & got on the island just as a heavy bombardment was opened with the Monitor. The fire was so hot that I stopped at Battery Bee, where I stayed until after dark & had a good view of the fight. Although all the batteries participated, the enemy's fire was directed mainly against Ft. Moultrie, so that I was in no danger. I could see the Monitor struck repeatedly without any apparent injury, & the fire from the Ironclads was terrific. On Wednesday fire was opened on a Monitor which was aground; when the others came up to her relief & a terrible fight ensued. After the Enemy had withdrawn I went over to see the result of our work. The principal damage to life was from the explosion of an ammunition chest, of which you have of course seen an acc't. It occurred in Press Smith's Co., of which thirteen men were buried that afternoon. The casualties from the enemy's fire were remarkably few, considering the no. & character of the missiles thrown. Dick's splendid Brooke gun bursted during the engagement. Two of the bands broke, but he still thought it could be used. In the afternoon to test the question he took a shot at the grounded Monitor. The bolt struck her fairly, but it split the gun. Several guns were broken by the enemy's fire & some ugly holes were made in the walls of Ft. M. It is <u>hoped</u> that one or two of the Monitors were injured.[1] That night an assault was made on Ft. S.[2] of which you have seen an acc't. Stephen Elliott,[3] you know is in command there now, Col. Rhett having gone to James Island, so your friend has had another opportunity of distinguishing himself. Everyone says that he is about the best man we c'd have there. The Ft. is now garrisoned by the Charleston Battalion.

11th. We were at work on the fortifications yesterday, several miles from here. I began my letter there under so many difficulties that I could not finish it & so lost today's mail. My letter had now probably better be directed to Anderson as you expected to leave Aiken yesterday afternoon. I feel as if you had got out of my reach again, & the prospect of seeing you seems as far off as ever. It is a great disappointment to me, my darling, but God knows what is best for us, & we have both felt His love often & strongly enough to have faith in it. Col. Stevens came over the other evening & spent the night with

214

us. You may imagine how much I enjoyed his visit. It was the night for the prayer meeting of our Christian Association, in which he w'd have partici- pated, but unfortunately the meeting was interrupted at its very beginning by an order for the Regt to go on picket. The next morning I went to town with him, and had a good long talk with him. He says that if the enemy had not taken me prisoner at Boonesboro, he thinks he would have been in ser- vice still.

I have an opportunity of sending my letter and think I had better do so, so I will have to close prematurely. Accts represent Sister Anne as looking badly & she has been thinking of going to Greenville for a change. If she does so I hope she will see you. The Mrs. Snowdens are as indefatigable as ever & have been very kind to me, sending us some very acceptable articles from their provision fund, as well as supplying the Regt with vegetables &c. My boy cannot wait any longer on me so I must close. Much love to all.

Your loving Husband
W. P. DuBose

1. The action described occurred on September 8–9, 1863. The monitor that ran aground was the USS *Weehawken*. See *Official Records Army,* 28(1):716–18.

2. During the night of September 8, 1863, Union sailors and marines launched a boat assault against Fort Sumter. The fort's defenders easily repulsed the attack and captured around 125 Union sailors and marines, five boats, and five stands of colors. See *Official Records Army,* 28(1):724–28.

3. Maj. Stephen Elliott (1830–66) of Beaufort, South Carolina, took over the command of Fort Sumter on September 4, 1863. He later was given command of the Holcombe Legion, and in May 1864 he was promoted to brigadier general. See Barnwell, *Story of an American Family,* 152, 204.

Mt. Pleasant
Sept. 19th 1863

Your letter reached me yesterday, my darling wife, not long after mine had been dispatched. Slow as the mail is, letters by private hand always take still longer to come; the difficulty & delay is in getting from the City to this point & that exists in either case. I knew you had written, & the delay of the let- ter will only make the interval shorter between this & the next, which will be delayed by your traveling. I am very much obliged to Mrs. Finley[1] for the box. I sent up an application to town for it today, but a stringent order against going to the city came in the meantime & I did not succeed. I have sent for it however by an officer who had got a pass before the order, & hope it will come safely. It was very kind in her, & I promise to show my appreciation of her goodness by enjoying its contents fully. I will write to you on the subject again after the box has been received. Will it be enough to thank her through you, or should I write to her myself? I have been faring unusually well here & am in no danger of starving, but that will not prevent a thorough appreciation of the box. As far as you ever sending me one like it, you need not trouble yourself about that. You have already given me so much that nothing you c'd add to it in the way of boxes would make any appreciable addition. If you had a plantation to draw upon, I would not object to occasional favours, but as it is I will be more than grateful so long as you are comfortable yourself & continue to give me such sweet assurances in your letters of what is my chief wealth in this world—your love.

I have sent William home on a short furlough. He has served me faithfully & cheerfully & so far from applying for permission to go, seemed to dislike going without me. I know he is enjoying himself. He will bring me a box when he comes back. I am sorry that I have lost so good an opportunity of becoming acquainted with your Uncle Amory, and particularly of seeing him with Amo. I am prepared to find him a very loveable man from all that I have heard from you & others. I do not know when I will get to the city again, as only "urgent necessity" will entitle me to the privilege. The talk there now is all about the "Anglo Rebel fleet"[2] which both the Yankees and ourselves are expecting. That there is such a fleet, there can be no longer any doubt. And the question with me now is, how much are we to expect from it; whether they expect, or are likely, to be able to cope with these terrible Monitors. I only hope that our fleet will not, like our English gun, prove a failure.[3] I am afraid that Rosencrans has already attained his object in the possession of E. Tennessee & will confine himself to the task of securing himself there in which case our reinforcements may effect nothing.[4] I have not heard the rumour of Gen. Lee's transfer to that deptm't confirmed.[5]

I suppose that you have once more fallen into your old routine. I hope you find your scholars good, and glad to see you again. Give Margie & Lise each a kiss for me. I will write to Sue in a few days. In the meantime give her much love & ask her to send me word what effect your travels have had upon you. I hope she shows no evidence of overwork during your absence.

We are having real Fall weather, which somehow or other always recalls you most strongly & constantly to my mind, and makes me long for some of the glorious walks we have taken together in just such weather. The very recollection of some of those walks braces and invigorates me. But it is not only the Fall weather that recalls you to me, my own Darling. The other night on picket I stood on the beach with the wind blowing in my face from the sea, the clouds flying over my head and a scarcely perceptible drizzle falling upon me & thought how I would enjoy a walk with you. I sometimes look forward to the time when all seasons of the year and all states of the weather will have a new charm for me from being spent with you. God grant that that time may soon come, but there are certainly no signs of its approach yet. And yet I have no cause for dissatisfaction as I am, and have no doubt that my life even in the war has far more than an average of earthly happiness. Generally I can gratify my taste for reading, I am engaged & interested in the work which duty & inclination have both always conspired to indicate to me as my "calling," I have health & the power of enjoyment, and then the fountain of spiritual joy is as much open to me here as anywhere else in the world. It is true that there is the constant trial of separation from you, my love, but then even at this distance the sweet assurance of your affection & prayers, and the regular arrival of your letters are my chief source of earthly happiness. As long as you are comfortably fixed and surrounded by loving friends, our marriage even in our separation will be the happiest fact of my life.

Sunday Morning. I sent a note to Amo yesterday, begging him to deliver the box to the bearer & he writes in answer that it has never been sent to him, but that Parker Ravenel[6] had told him he had sent it with your letter to me. One of our men handed me the letter, and I was so glad to get it, that I did not stop to see who it was or to ask him how he got it. He said nothing about the box, & I have heard nothing of it. Amo says he will find by whom it was sent & let me know. I hope it is not lost, and have no doubt I will get it in a day or two.

Evening. I was interrupted this morning and after our service, went to dine with Dick at his request. I am finishing my letter tonight by one of your tapers which I have just used for our little night service. All of my services are pretty well attended and I think the interest is on the increase. I trust that by God's blessing they may be the means of doing some good. One of the Capts is an unusually pious man and assists me very much.

Dick is as full of marrying as ever. I give him my advice decidedly in favour of doing so as soon as possible and confirm him in the opinion that the married state is under any circumstances more satisfactory than the engagement. If he can get off he will be married early in Nov'r. He always sends his love to you. Robert has been for some time at Pocotaligo in the R.M.R.[7] We have several cousins in it.

One reason that I would have liked you to go to Winnsboro is that you might have got acquainted with our dear old Grandmother, one of the sweetest old ladies in the world. She is very anxious to know you. I hope you got my letter before leaving Aiken. Those people will think that I do not treat you well in the way of letters.

Goodnight, my own precious wife. May you be filled with the Grace of Christ! Love to the household.

Your affectionate Husband
W. P. DuBose

1. This could refer to Clelia Lightwood Peronneau Finley, the wife of William Finley. See Patey, *Whaley Family*, 199.

2. On September 11 and September 18, 1863, the *Charleston Mercury* printed stories regarding rumors that French shipbuilders in Le Havre and Bordeaux were building Confederate vessels. The *Mercury* also noted a *Times* article about the British construction of Confederate vessels.

3. Charleston's defenders received two 600-pound (12.75-inch) imported Blakely rifled guns without instructions for loading and firing them. The first gun was damaged during test firing in early September 1863. See *Official Records Army*, 28(2):387–88.

4. On September 16–17, 1863, Union major general William S. Rosecrans concentrated his Army of the Cumberland near Chickamauga Creek in Georgia. Simultaneously, Confederate lieutenant general James Longstreet and two divisions of his corps were arriving from Virginia to reinforce Gen. Braxton Bragg's Army of Tennessee. See Long, *Civil War Almanac*, 410.

5. Gen. Robert E. Lee did not transfer to the Army of Tennessee, but he did send Lt. Gen. James Longstreet, who was Lee's most experienced corps commander. See Long, *Civil War Almanac*, 410.

6. This was probably William Parker Ravenel (1832–87), the son of Henry Ravenel (1795–1859) and Elizabeth Perroneau Coffin Ravenel (1807–69). See *South Carolina Genealogies*, 2:73, 88.

7. Robert DuBose served as a private in the Rutledge Mounted Riflemen, Company B, Seventh South Carolina Cavalry. See Compiled Service Records, Seventh South Carolina Cavalry, M267, roll 45.

∞

1863

I received your letter of the 21st this morning my darling and feel very sorry that you should have been so long without hearing from me. There must certainly have been several of my letters lost as I feel very certain that I wrote regularly at least twice a week. I sent over some of my letters by irregular opportunities, which may not have been mailed. I rec'd today by accident from the Mt. Pleasant P.O., an institution of whose existence I was not aware, an old letter of Sept. 1st, which will explain my failure to hear from you about that time. I am very sorry I did not receive it as you must have thought it strange that I did not notice its contents. For example, you appeal to me in it to assist you in deciding whether to remain in Aiken or to return to Anderson. However I do not think that would have made much difference as the practicability of a furlough has never been sufficient to justify me in advising you to remain there on that acc't.

I was to have gone to the City today but was detained by some unexpected work until it was too late for the boat. So I have had my pass changed for tomorrow. I will call on Amo and learn what I can of my missing box. The book & the soap & the little jar of preserves at least will not be spoiled if I can still recover it. The glorious news from Bragg continues to improve and puts us all in good spirits. I feel very grateful for this light in our darkness, just where we most need it too. If Bragg can only follow up his success it may prove the turning point in our affairs. Several good results must ensue from what has already taken place. The moral effect upon that army will be very great, the cloud of defeat and failure will be lifted up from "the West," when we have learned to expect nothing else. And foreign nations will see that though we have been "cast down," we are not yet "destroyed."[1]

25th. I began my letter yesterday because I knew I would have little time to write today. I have spent the day in the city; without however effecting the objects for which I went. One was to get some testaments for the men, & Hughes[2] has been shut down all day. Another was to see Amo & learn something about my box. He was out this morning and I did not have time to call again this evening as I wished to do. Still another was, to hear something good from Bragg, and I have failed in this as badly as in the others. Rosencrans appears to be strengthening himself at Chattanooga and Bragg to be giving him time for that purpose. However I ought to be grateful for what has been already vouchsafed us, and not too impatient for the results.

The position is as anxious a one as ever, but the advantage is now vastly more on our side than it was before. Our army is elated with victory & theirs depressed by defeat, and I trust that the next encounter will be more signally in our favour than the last. Chattanooga is said to be not particularly defensible from an attack on this side, and we are thought to have very nearly as many fresh troops on hand as Burnside[3] could bring to the aid of Rosencrans. I got these items from Col. Lay[4] & Dr. Brodie[5] of Gen. Beauregard's staff, with whom I dined today at Mr. Sass'. Among our fresh troops is Jenkins' Brigade which c'd not have been in time for the battle. I did not know positively until yesterday, by a letter from Col. Bratton, that they had gone west. Col. B. formed the brigade on the passage. I called on Mr. Gadsden this morning & spent a pleasant hour with him. Just as I was leaving Mr. Pinckney called. I was very glad to hear from him that Miss Carrie continues to improve. He seems to think that she is recovering her health, & says that her improvement dates from her visit to Anderson. I hope he is not too sanguine.

The people of Charleston seem to feel more hopeful about their City than they have been for a long time. I don't know whether it is an indication that the prospect is actually brightening or only that they have recovered from the trepidation produced by the vigorous operations of the Enemy at first and are now deluded by his apparent comparative inactivity. Whatever be the case it is cheering to see men hopeful & in good spirits. I think that it is very evident that the fall of Charleston cannot be effected in less time than several months at least and independently of my "habit of hopefulness," do think that in time, with proper energy we can prevent it altogether. It is reported that Farragut is about to relieve Dahlgren in the command of the fleet & the former is said to be a far more daring and energetic man.

I am glad to hear, my Darling, that you do not submit patiently and amicably to not hearing regularly from me, particularly if it should prove my fault. I hope you will never be satisfied with, or submit to, one particle less than you are entitled to from me. Your love cannot be too exacting for me. So I will expect you to assert your rights & scold me whenever I neglect my duty to you in the slightest degree. Do not put Mt. Pleasant on your letters anymore or others of them might fall into this dead letter P.O. Give much love to all the family, particularly to Sue. Do you object to my crossing?[6]

Good night my own precious wife. May you be strengthened and guided by the grace & power of God!

Your affectionate Husband
W. P. DuBose

1. This is from 2 Corinthians 4:9: "Persecuted, but not forsaken; cast down, but not destroyed."

2. The 1860 *Charleston City Directory* lists the store of William N. Hughes, a bookseller and stationer, at 67 Meeting Street. His establishment also was a depository of the American Sunday School Union.

3. Union major general Ambrose E. Burnside (1824–81) of Indiana was a corps commander in the Army of the Potomac when he brought his corps to Chattanooga to help defend it against the Confederate Army of Tennessee. See Warner, *Generals in Blue*, 57–58.

4. This was Capt. John F. Lay. See Index to Compiled Service Records Raised Directly by the Confederate Government and of Confederate Officers and Non-regimental Enlisted Men, M818, roll 14; Crute, *Confederate Staff Officers*, 73–74.

5. Dr. Robert Little Brodie (1829–1913) was medical director of the Department of South Carolina, Georgia, and Florida. See Roman, *The Military Operations of General Beauregard*, 208.

6. This refers to cross-writing, or writing vertically across lines already written on the page of a letter.

Mt. Pleasant
Sept. 28th 1863

Your letter of the 24th & 25th was rec'd two days ago, my Darling. I was just looking at the date and disappointed to find it so recent, because it removed my hope of getting another today, when the mail arrived and brought your Saturday's letter. I am very much obliged to you for writing so often, but you must not think that the impatience to hear from me of which you accuse yourself somewhat reproachfully needs to be atoned for to me. I am ready enough to excuse anything which springs out of love to me. Thank Sue for the little piece of music which she sent me. The one which you thought you had lost was enclosed to me in the letter which was dug out of the Mt. Pleasant P.O. the other day. Thank the giver for it when you write there again; as she is your adopted Aunt, I suppose she is mine too. I have not learned to sing either of them yet, but will try to do so.

I must really try to answer some of your questions. I am afraid I do not always do it. We got a tent the other day, in which I sleep at night, before that, I always slept in the open air, & preferred it while the weather was mild. I seldom go into it in the day, but live at my desk, reading writing &c the greater part of the time. Every fourth night the whole Reg't, & of course I with it, go to guard the bridge between Mt. Pleasant & Sullivans Island. It is quite an exposed position but with that exception our picketing involves no hardship to veterans like us. I generally go over the bridge & spend the evening with Dick & he & I take glorious moonlight walks on the beach. We were encamped at first near this end of the bridge, but during the fight with the Monitors several shells came in our direction, and we removed to a safer location at the other end of the village where there is no danger of being disturbed. Some time ago a no. of shots were fired at the ferry boat some of which came tolerably near. It has not been repeated lately. When the batteries are completed on Morris Island it will be unsafe at any point in the harbour in daylight. The boats will have run then at night. From Northern acc'ts I have no doubt that a heavy fire is to be opened on the City from Morris Island as soon as they are ready. Our brigade is intended to meet a land attack by Sullivans Island if it sh'd be attempted. I think it more probable that the approach will be by James Island. One of the Micklers I hear went to Port Royal the other day on a scout; he reports that an Army Corps recently landed there and that the purpose was to take the City by James Island. I should think that that plan w'd suit us exactly. A good deal of confidence is felt now in our ability to hold the City, among officers & citizens. Ft. Moultrie has some pretty ugly holes in her walls; the wall was protected by what is called a "glacis" i.e. a bank of sand about 10 or 15 ft. in front of the wall and sloping out very gradually to the beach. This glacis was built by Anderson who anticipated an assault upon the Fort & therefore left this interval, which acts as a deep ditch between the glacis & Fort. It was thought it would protect the wall but the Enemy contrived to throw balls just over the glacis so as to strike the brick wall. The holes have been stopped & all the old bricks & debris from the [houses] in the Ft. which have been pulled down are being heaped against the wall to be covered with sand. Sometimes the Enemy, by small [changes], would roll their shells up the beach & the glacis & pitch them over into the Ft. Press Smith, in whose Co. that fearful explosion took place, from which he has buried eighteen men, saved his own life by promptly jumping down from the parapet into the ditch between the wall & glacis.[1]

I hear that twelve negro men whom we have down here on the fortifications were in Ft. Sumter during some of the bombardment. What heroes they will be at home! One was even scratched by a piece of shell.

I have heard nothing of Johnston (I w'd not have him to see that "t" for anything). I hope that Cousin Clelia has heard from the Capt. by this time and that he is uninjured. I see that Genl. Wofford[2] is not killed; he married a

Miss Dwight, Dick's 1st cousin. Dick wanted me to go with him to town today to see his father but I could not do so. I hope to go there on Sunday as it is Communion day, if I can get Mr. Girardeau to preach here. The last place I communed was I believe Jackson Miss. before the march to the Big Black. Did I commune there?

You may depend upon my remembering the 1st of October, my darling. I do not fear that the day will ever come when I will cease to look back upon it with joy. It would be a sad day for me if it should come. I don't know that I ever went into battle as slowly & with so much trepidation as I did to that house in Tradd St. two years ago. That was the only campaign that I ever conducted & the only battle in which I ever commanded in chief. I thought the campaign proved me a bungler & the battle, a coward, but the true criterion, success, has convinced me that I must have been a great General in both respects. I promise, my dearest wife, that the return of the day shall be celebrated with grateful prayer. This time last year I was in Ft. Delaware. I hope that this time next year I will be at home. I feel quite hopeful just now, not simply from principle or habit. I believe that the aspect of affairs is about to change once more in our favour & I cannot think that the North can arouse itself to another great effort. The draft is said to be a failure by their own papers. I think the accts from Chattanooga are quite cheering. I hope the starving process will operate upon Rosencrans & force him to an attack before he can be reinforced too heavily. The possession of Lookout Mt. is said to give us a great advantage. You see that Jenkins holds it.[3]

Give much love to Sue. I have not written to her yet as I sh'd have done, but hope to do so soon. Give my love also to "Auntie" and to both households and remember me to all friends. I will write to Mrs. Finley but am sorry to have to tell her that the box has never reached me. I have not heard yet how it got lost or anything about it. Sister A. has not given up her visit to Greenville and I hope very much she will go as she does not seem to be well.

And now I must close my darling, with much love & many prayers.

Your affectionate Husband
W. P. DuBose

1. *Official Records Army,* 28(1):717–19.

2. Brig. Gen. William Tatum Wofford (1824–84) of Georgia commanded a brigade in Kershaw's Division from the battle of Chancellorsville until January 23, 1865. See Warner, *Generals in Gray,* 343–44.

3. Following his defeat at the battle of Chickamauga, Union major general William Rosecrans withdrew his forces to Chattanooga, where they were besieged

by Confederate general Braxton Bragg's Army of Tennessee. Lookout Mountain was an important feature of Bragg's siege lines. See McPherson, *Battle Cry of Freedom*, 674–75.

Mt. Pleasant
Oct. 9th 1863

I should have written yesterday, my Darling, but allowed the day to pass without doing so, and in the evening we went on picket. The fact is I was completely overwhelmed by a letter which reached me from the B'p, enclosing my appointment as Chaplain, & ordering me, if I accepted it, to report to Gen. Kershaw. There is still something to be done in connection with it, but I have not decided yet exactly what it is. I think it is necessary to send on my resignation of my present position and have it received & published here. Under any circumstances I think it best to remain here until the end of the present month at least. The Bp thinks it probable that I would prefer to be ordained about December. All this I will have to think about & determine at my leisure. I am afraid I have not sufficient enterprise & go-ahead-itiveness in my disposition. I do shrink dreadfully from responsibility such as that which I am about to assume. Horror of an unprofitable ministry and distrust in my capacity to meet the varied demands upon me which such a position involves, are the predominant feelings which disturb me. On the other hand I feel that God has been preparing my mind for this thing by increasing my faith in His power & readiness to help those whom He calls by His Providence & Grace to the performance of His own work. I know my Darling, that your prayers will be offered up in my behalf. So after all there is a pretty strong probability of our meeting. My mind has been so taken up with other considerations that I have not begun yet to realize the happiness before me. May God prepare us both for a true & spiritual enjoyment of the blessing of being once more together! I have made no plans yet & do not know how long I may be able to be at home. I am glad that this time is to be in the Fall or Winter and trust that I will be stronger in all respects than I was in the Spring.

The B'p is to be in Anderson on the 25th. He told me to write to him there if not before. Your letter also reached me yesterday and was by no means so eclipsed by the Bp's communication as to lose any of its interest. On the contrary, the prospect of an early meeting with you added very much

A native of Camden, South Carolina, Gen. Joseph Brevard Kershaw (1822–1894) served throughout the war with distinction. His cousin William Porcher DuBose became chaplain of the brigade bearing Kershaw's name. *The Photographic History of the Civil War* (New York: Review of Reviews Co., 1911), 10: 115

to its enjoyment. After reading them I rode over & took dinner with Dick, and enjoyed some cake and other luxuries from Pooshee, the home of his intended & the present goal of his most ardent desires. The 10th Nov. draws near and he still indulges the hope of being on that day made the happiest of men. He sends his love to you and begs to be remembered to all his friends in Anderson.

I think you misunderstood me about my campaign of 61. I <u>thought</u> myself during my operations a bungler &c, but <u>know</u> myself now, by the issue, to have been one of the most expert strategists & successful generals of the age. I am afraid I would not have valued an easy victory and would spurn the idea of my foe having been otherwise than a most formidable one. I can say what I am sorry that no general of this war can of any of their battles— that my victory when it was won was complete & decisive & put an end to all hostilities.

Give my love to the household, particularly to Sue and kiss the girls for me. I hope to see them all very soon. I have not the courage yet to inform a single member of the Legion that I am so soon to leave them. Several of them knew the circumstances several months ago but have forgotten all about it by this time. My first taper has just reached its end and I conclude this letter by its last rays. You must try & have me one or two more ready to take West with me. I may find them as useful there as I have here. For some little while past I have not used them for the Prayer meetings. The Christian Association has supplied itself with candles as we are forced to use a lantern.

Good bye my own Darling.

Yr loving Husband

W. P. DuBose

Mt. Pleasant Oct. 17th 1863

We had a review this afternoon, my own Darling, and I feel quite tired tonight but I may not be able to write tomorrow and I am afraid you will not be satisfied with a share in Sue's letter. I received your letter of the 14th today and also a long one from Sister Jane with a note from Sister Anne. The latter is at last a little better & has made up her mind to go with Grandmother to Abbeville & thence to Greenville. But I do not know when Gr.Mother will leave & I am afraid that my visit home will interfere with this prospect. Of course I w'd insist on her going under any circumstances but she will not consent to be away during any portion of my stay at home. I have made no plans yet as to the disposition of the time which I shall take, but I must employ it as much as possible in preparing for my examination and ordination, and must be wherever I will be able to use it to the best advantage. This will hardly be in Anderson, & therefore I can scarcely expect to spend more than a few days there when I go for you which will of course be the first thing I do. If I have any time after my ordination I will try & do better. I wrote to the Bp some days ago & directed to Greenville. I told him that he could talk with you on the subject & you would answer it for him. In case the letter may miss him I will repeat that portion of it which needs answering & you can get the necessary information for me. Find out what sermons I will have to prepare for the examination. The Bp said that if I preferred I could be ordained on a simple examination on the Bible and Prayer Book & defer the three regular examinations for my ordination to the Priesthood. Get some idea of the nature and subjects of these examinations and also of the character of the examination on the Bible & Prayer Book.

Learn something of his movements during the next month or two and when he thinks my ordination can take place most conveniently to himself. It will be better on his acc't that it should be in Camden & I don't know but that I w'd prefer it myself to Winnsboro. As for preaching I hope I will have as little as possible of that to do as I don't know when I am to prepare any sermons. It is very certain that I have none on hand that I would be willing to preach.

I am going to town on Monday with Dick to meet his father and we will all probably dine with Mr. Sass. I am sorry to hear that your brother is having trouble with his eye. I know from experience that nothing can have a more depressing effect and no doubt that that has much to do with his low spirits.

We have moved our Camp a small distance and I now enjoy the privilege of a room for my reading & writing, a portion of it only as I have not the exclusive use of it, but still it is a considerable help. I still sleep in the tent. We are faring sumptuously this month. DuBose Porcher sent me a 2nd basket just as my box gave out, or rather just as the butter &c was exhausted. The solid portion of its contents will last some time yet. And today another box has come to the mess.

Good night now, my dearest wife. May the precious Grace of Christ be multiplied upon you!

Your loving Husband
W. P. DuBose

Mt. Pleasant

Oct. 21st 1863

I returned from town on Monday, my Darling, to find your letter awaiting me. Altogether it was an unusually pleasant day. Dick & I went to meet his father and we all three dined at Mr. Sass', where a delightful dinner was quite a secondary feature of the day. One hour in the morning was spent with Johnson whom I found like a hermit at home, busily engaged on a journal of his time in Ft. Sumter. In the streets I met Henry Peronneau, and was glad to see him so fresh from Anderson. He is looking remarkably well I think. He gave me your love, which I hope to carry back to you in a few weeks. I also saw Harry DeSaussure driving out Mrs. Wm. Sinkler, but did not speak to him. The Ct. martial which I attended some time ago was at the Citadel. If Amo Coffin & Henry had been there, my five hours waiting would have been more endurable. On my return as I said, I found your letter awaiting me to give a happy termination to a pleasant day. I have been so much a creature of circumstances all my life, that I have acquired the habit of adapting myself to my situation & living almost too exclusively in it. Dick Dwight on the contrary is always living in some time & place other than the present. His spirit & his body live very little together, and the former seems to find the union decidedly uncongenial, to judge by the time it spends away from home. He points to me as an evidence of the demoralizing effects of the war—a man with a wife so well contented away from her, and I quote Pascal on him: "We never <u>live</u>, we always <u>hope to live</u>." I tell him that while I would be happier to be with my wife, I am quite happy to have a wife even without the additional happiness of being with her. We are two extremes which are mutually benefited by meeting sometimes. He has more domesticity, more home feeling about him than any man I know. He refuses to live anywhere else. His body may be imprisoned elsewhere as it is now on Sullivans Island, but his spirit will only live where his heart is.

My "Theologia Germanica" is a treasure, and I am grateful for having found it. I would not be surprised if I end by ranking it with Luther & [Bunsen],[1] next to the Bible. No doubt some people could call it Pantheistic and Mystical, but it suits me, and if it does me no more harm than it did to Luther I will not complain. The great want of the Christian life of this stirring age is contemplation, reflection; and anything that savours of this we call mystical. Again I think one cause of the want of faith which exists on the subject of Providence arises from the fact that we separate God too much from His creation. Old Dr. Hume,[2] my former professor at the Citadel, whom people call an infidel (justly I am afraid) said to me the other day, "They call me an infidel. The difference between us is that you Christians worship God in churches & I worship him in Nature." I don't think he worships Him much anywhere, but I think we could worship Him much more in Nature without being Pantheists.

My books now are just what I need, & they are inexhaustible. If Sue reads "Les Miserables" tell her I don't endorse the book beyond Fantine. I have not read anymore although it is within my reach & I was very much struck with what I did read. Cosette opens it is said with the most graphic acc't of the battle of Waterloo ever written. Marius I have looked at but have not read for want of time. The book is more extravagant & rhapsodical in style in

English than it would be in French where it is more common. If Sue wants any of the series so far as they are out, I can get them.[3]

Your mother must have fallen in love with Aiken. She is enjoying the luxury of being useful and necessary. Give her much love when you write. Give my love also to Sue & the family. Excuse this scratchy epistle & believe me

Yr loving Husband

W. P. DuBose

1. Christian Charles Josias, Baron von Bunsen (1791–1860), a German diplomat and scholar, was the author of *God in History*.

2. This was probably William Hume (1801–70), a physician, planter, and educator. See Waring, *History of Medicine in South Carolina*, 248–49.

3. William Porcher DuBose writes here of Victor Hugo's *Les Misérables* and the characters in that work.

Mt. Pleasant Oct. 25th / 63

Your letter today, my own darling, was an agreeable surprise, coming so soon after that of the 20th which I don't believe I have yet acknowledged. I have therefore two to answer, & two such letters as I know I cannot make one of mine worthy of.

Today I know has been a sweet day to you. How I wish I could have been with you this morning! There is nothing which interests & affects me so much as a confirmation. To see young people, & particularly those in whom I am interested, coming out from the world to enlist under the banner of Jesus Christ & to consecrate their hearts & lives to him & his service, almost always awakens in me a sort of spiritual enthusiasm. I do not believe I ever witnessed it, and can scarcely think of it even now, without tears. I feel very grateful that Jno. Elliott has been so strengthened and encouraged by the work in his parish. In Miss Carrie Winthrop I feel the deepest interest. Oh, what it must be to find Jesus after so many perplexities & trials as she has passed through! I trust that this day has been blessed not only to those confirmed but to all who have been permitted to witness the touching ceremony. I hope you will give me an account of it & tell me how many & who that I know have been confirmed. If it is such a day with you as it is with us, I am afraid the weather has interfered somewhat with its enjoyment. Although it has not rained the clouds have been dull & heavy & the air cold

& raw. I did not succeed in drawing very many men away from their camp-fires this morning, but we had a pleasant service in spite of the cold & wind & clouds. I have not quite the <u>resistance</u> today though that I usually have. I have been for a day or so a very little unwell, just enough to demoralize me & give the weather an advantage over me. It was produced by sitting up until two o.c. with a sick man. I am by nature physically incapacitated for dissipation by the fact that in my best health the slightest irregularity revenges itself upon me. This is a piece of dissipation however that I wish I could afford often to repeat. In the room next to ours a young man of our reg't has been most painfully sick for several weeks, and now I am very much afraid he will scarcely recover. He is a man of high character & good mind & education and we feel very much interested in him. I read & pray with him every evening but have not had an opportunity of talking with him as I would like, as there are several of his friends who live in the room with him & are always there.

I received a sweet affectionate letter from Sister Anne yesterday. Grand-mother has given up the idea of going to Abbeville and Sister Anne has given up the trip to Greenville. She insists that she is better & that our visit will do her more good than anything else. After I leave she will come down to St. Johns. She says that Greenville would probably be too cold for her if she were to go.

It is impossible for me to say yet when I will probably leave. I do not even know whether I can leave before my resignation is accepted and they take very long to attend to these things in Richmond. There are several other things which keep me in suspense but I still hope to be able to get off about the end of the month. I think it very probable that I will be able to accommodate Anna Parker's friend.

I am going to the city tomorrow if nothing prevents to exercise a little diplomacy in reference to Dick Dwight's furlough. I hope I will spend the day as pleasantly as I did last Monday.

Our men have availed themselves largely of our situation here to buy salt at the neighboring salt works and ship it to their homes. They get it at about eighteen dollars a bushel. Would you not like to make a present of several bushels to your housekeepers? I have no doubt it is more convenient than money in buying supplies in the neighborhood. The idea is suggested to me by the fact that I have a nice large box in which I can carry it with me, and in this way it can be got more cheaply. If you desire it and if I can draw some pay before leaving, which I have no doubt I will, I will get it.

It is too dark to write more.

God bless you my Darling
W. P. DuBose

Mt. Pleasant
November 1st 1863

My resignation has arrived, my Darling, and I am now free to leave when I please. I will wind up my affairs in a few days & probably be with you at the end of the week. I have written to Miss Belle Glover that unless she hears from me again we will take Friday night's train. The time draws very near, my love, when we are to be allowed the happiness of being together once more. May the Spirit of God sanctify this meeting to our spiritual good & growth in Grace! With me much depends upon how this interval is spent. Much depends upon how a good work is <u>begun</u>, & the beginning will depend upon the immediate preparation. So pray for me now, as I hope you will pray <u>with</u> me very soon that God's will may be accomplished in me & by me.

Since the steamboat has ceased to run regularly, our mail has grown very irregular. In consequence of which I have not heard from you since my last. In answer to this direct to me in care of Mr. J. K. Sass, as I will probably be there during the last few days of my stay here. Yesterday, the last day of my official connection with the brigade, I was sent eight miles off to muster & inspect the 28th Regt, a pretty tiresome job. On Tuesday or Wednesday I have to ride there again to sign the Muster Rolls which are to be made out from yesterday's muster. We have had to exercise a good deal of perseverance & diplomacy to get Dick off, on acc't of certain complications which I will explain when I see you, but I think we have paved the way so that he can scarcely fail now.

The terrific fire upon Ft. Sumter still continues, as you see by the papers.[1] On Friday night or Saturday morning twelve or fifteen men were killed by the falling of a portion of wall, as you have no doubt also seen. I have been several times to Sullivans Island to see the damages. All the sea face has been knocked away so that on that side it looks like a [sand] fort. The other faces are also terribly battered. Of course I know very little of the strengths of the bombproofs of sand bags which they have been building within, but I hope when the whole structure has been pounded into a mass of sand & debris upon those bombproofs that the Enemy will have reached the limit beyond which they can inflict no further injury. The resistance of the old fort is becoming heroic. I believe Major Elliott is still in command. I am beginning to think the Greek Fire is a humbug and that they can do the city very little damage from their present position.[2]

Yesterday's mail has just reached us bringing me your letter of the 29th. You need not have minded Jno. Elliott's not writing as I have all the information I need. His Hand Book will be of great service to me. Remember me to him & tell him I hope to hear him preach on Sunday.

My sick friend is still very ill although we hope him a trace better. I have spoken to him several times but the crowd in his room still prevents my doing so as I would like. He is so weak & suffers so much that I am afraid he cannot think much on my subject. Poor fellow he is so reduced that if he recovers he will have a tedious time before him.

I called a meeting of the Christian Association today to take my formal leave of it as I was prevented meeting with them last night, but something induced me to postpone it until tomorrow night, when I will dissolve my connection with them. It makes me feel sad, and I believe that my departure will be felt by many friends here. I have no doubt it will be better for the Regt to have a regular chaplain if they can get a good one, who can devote his undivided attention to his work. We have already written to a man who is said to be admirably adapted to the post & who may accept.

I am inclined to think I will not be ordained until December. I am afraid that we'll be staying rather longer at home than would be quite right, but I would like to have about a month to prepare to begin preaching regularly, and if I were ordained on the 22nd I would have to preach during the remainder of my stay at home which would interfere with my preparation. I don't know that it will be necessary to go to Camden for books &c though. There are several there that I would like to have. I will write to the Bp before leaving Charleston.

Uncle Dwight represents Sister Anne as better decidedly. I am glad there is a likelihood of the girls seeing something of you at last, and you may see Grandmother too. I only wish Sue could go too. Give much love to each member of the family and remember me affectionately to all the members of the spider's web. Remember me also to Miss Carrie Winthrop and all other remembering friends. May God be with you, my dearest, to sanctify & guard you!

Your affectionate Husband
W. P. DuBose

Dick is very anxious for us to come down to his wedding on the 12th & if I could spare the time I would like it very much as it would give you a view of St. Johns as it is. And you may never see it again, if the Enemy should get there.

1. This refers to the second major bombardment of Fort Sumter, which began on October 26, 1863, and ended on December 6, 1863. See Burton, *Siege of Charleston,* 200.

2. The "Swamp Angel," a Union battery located in the marsh adjacent to Morris Island, fired incendiary shells at Charleston in an attempt to burn the city. The shells were defective and did little damage. See Burton, *Siege of Charleston,* 255.

4

WITNESS TO WAR

February–July 1864

"...there is still strength & even joy in the knowledge that the Rock of my salvation & of my hope changes not."

July 7, 1864

As a new chaplain, DuBose traveled to eastern Tennessee to assume his duties with Kershaw's Brigade. He traveled with Kershaw's Brigade to Gordonsville, Virginia, during spring 1864 to participate in the Overland campaign. The brigade played an important and costly role in the battles of the Wilderness, Spotsylvania Courthouse, and Cold Harbor. By July the brigade was in Petersburg, Virginia.

Kershaw's Brigade
Feb. 8th 1863 [1864]

We have at last reached the end of our journey, my darling wife, safe & sound in spite of the bushwhackers. I sent a letter back from Asheville by Henry Gaillard[1] whom I met there on his way home. I begged him to mail it at the first P.O., and hope it has reached you punctually. Our subsequent journey was not so pleasant in all respects as it had been up to that time. We left Mr. McDowel's on Saturday morning in a rain, and traveled to Marshall, a little town on the French Broad twenty one or two miles this side of Asheville, with rain & snow beating in our faces every step of the way. To retard our progress & add to the discomfort of the ride we were obliged to bring in front of our saddles twenty five pounds apiece of corn for our horses, as there is none to be had between Asheville & this place. My overcoat protected my body, but my feet soon became wet & suffered a good deal. On acc't of the condition of my horse's back I was obliged to come down from the jogtrot which had been our traveling gate [*sic*] to a walk, & so Frank arrived at Marshall an hour ahead of me, & when I rode up after dark wet & cold, I found him by a roaring fire which with a good supper at the public house soon made me forget the hardships of the day. The next day was cloudy but we had no rain only an occasional flake of snow. As this was the bushwhacking stage we did not part company, besides that the road was too bad to go over a walk. Near the Warm Springs we passed by several horses which had been killed by the bushwhackers in an attack on a party of Morgan's men a week or two ago. These men had been engaged in hunting deserters & had become obnoxious to them & so they laid an ambuscade for them & killed two men & several horses. At Paint Rock we left the Valley & climbed up the m't. The road is very tortuous & we were told that there was a more direct route through the mts to Caney Branch where we were to spend the night. We were told of this short cut at Marshall, and advised not to take it as it was blind and there was some danger of being fired at by bushwhackers. However we could not resist the temptation of making five miles, particularly as we were told by a man on the mts. that it was a good road for horses as the other, & we had come to the conclusion that the stories about bushwhackers were very much exaggerated, so we struck into the short cut and traveled on very comfortably for a while when we met a lone woman in the wild mts, whom Providence had probably sent there to save us from a terrible fate. To our inquiries she replied that we were out of our way & directed us how to proceed & so we got across the mts & found our way to Caney Branch where we spent the night. We found there a Capt. Nelson with a company of Cavalry.[2] He lives in the neighborhood & is perfectly familiar with the mts. He told us that there was some danger in the route we had taken, that there was a gang of forty or fifty bushwhackers who had a den in that mt. When we described the road we had taken by mistake, he said that if we had gone a mile or so further we would have walked into their den & that the woman we had met was the wife of a man in the Yankee army. When Confederate soldiers & bushwhackers come into contact there is no mercy shown on either side, & we might have been disposed of in those mts without a trace of us ever being discovered. Our conclusion was that there was little or no danger in the right way, but if we had strayed among them I doubt if we would have come out again. In spite of all drawbacks I would have <u>enjoyed</u> both days journeys but for the soreness of my horse's back. The river was beautiful, the mts covered with snow were magnificent, and when we got up into the mt the scenery was indescribably wild & grand. On Sunday the sun came out occasionally & lit up the snow clad m't summits which lay piled one upon another on every side.

At Marshall we met an old man named Mr. Davis who told us that he lived at Caney Branch & insisted upon our spending the night with him. He expected to come along with us but was prevented; he told us however that his wife was a S. Carolinian & a staunch Southern woman & w'd be glad to see us. So when we got to Caney Branch we enquired for Mrs. Davis' & found it one of the most wretched & unpromising looking hovels you ever saw. We w'd have been glad to back out of it, but it was after dark, & our horses were tired so we determined to make the best of a bad bargain & went [in]. The interior was not very neat but we found Mrs. D. what the old gentleman had described her & spent a very pleasant night. While we were there Capt. Nelson came in, a fine looking & very gentlemanly man. During the course of the evening after learning our names where we were from &c, he informed me that he & I were cousins, which I found to be the case. His Grandmother was Miss Esther Marion from St. Johns. His father was a wealthy man & a good stock raiser from the neighborhood. This man used to go to S.C. with horses & mules and a number of years ago met Father at Winnsboro who had discovered the relationship. I remember perfectly Father informing us that he had met a horse drover who was a cousin of ours, but I never expected to meet him in this way. He was very kind to us & we were very much pleased with him.

We arrived here today at three or four o'clock, & my friends all seem glad to see me. We have just finished an egg-nog to which I contributed the white sugar. I have no doubt I will be pleasantly situated. These fellows have a dozen hens which keep them in eggs. My horse is better off than I expected her to be at the end of the journey. She is a fine little animal & did not mind the journey except her back. I will not undertake to say anything about my situation or friends so soon. My tea lasted me to the end of the journey and kept well. We w'd have had no use for the lunch if we had had it.

I hope you got your box safe. Remember me affectionately to Sue & all the family & all my friends.

It is late & I am sleepy, as you may see by my writing. May God bless you my darling & make us duly grateful for all the blessings both of His Providence & of His Grace! I meant to write a note to Mr. Miles. I hope you gave him a good message for me with the books. I may yet write to him. Moultrie sends his love. William is not here with my baggage. I presume he is with Col. Bratton, whose brigade is at New Market about 22 miles from here. I hope to get him very soon. I will write home tomorrow if possible.

Goodbye my Darling. Moultrie has got a letter from Lizzie written last Monday.

Your affectionate Husband
W. P. DuBose

1. This likely refers to Henry Augustus Gaillard (1837–1921) of Winnsboro. See MacDowell, *Gaillard Genealogy,* 22.

2. This was probably Capt. W. R. Nelson, Company F, Twelfth Battalion Tennessee Cavalry. See Compiled Service Records, Twelfth Battalion (Day's) Tennessee Cavalry, M231, roll 32.

Near New Market
Feb. 14 1864

My darling wife

I feel ashamed of myself for having allowed almost a week to elapse without writing to you. Never mind, I do not think it will happen again. On Wednesday we began to move to this place, 20 miles nearer Knoxville than Russelville is, and I have been so unsettled that I have scarcely been able to write. When the troops began to move on Wednesday I determined to ride ahead & see Col. Bratton who was at New Market, or rather whose Hd. Qrs. were. He happened to go up on that very day to attend a Ct. Martial at Russelville, & we passed each other at Morristown five miles this side of R. When he discovered it, he rode back after me & did not overtake me for nine miles. I then rode back with him, spent the night at M. with him, and after he had finished with the court on Thursday we rode down to his place. On Friday we moved camp again to get nearer to water. So you see we have been very unsettled. Col. Bratton starts here tomorrow morning. I am very sorry he did not get home while we were there. Besides our moves I have met so many friends, & not having a tent of my own, have found it so utterly impossible to be private that it has worried me.

I have made arrangements at a farmhouse a few hundred yards off for the use of a room during the day, where I can be undisturbed, & I have no doubt it will be a great convenience. I commenced my services today but not very satisfactorily. The day began with rain which [bid] fair to continue all day. About 11 o.c. it had held up & as one or two men assembled I determined to have a little prayer meeting. As it progressed, quite a large congregation collected, for which I was not as ready as I could have wished. This afternoon I had a good congregation again at one of the regts. but I am sorry to say that I did not enter into the services as I sh'd have done. I was not prepared in mind or spirit for the days [*sic*] work. May God help me to do better next time! Still I am encouraged if not by myself, by the field which is open to me. There is but one Chaplain present with the brigade, and the men all seem disposed to attend service. This was a very unfavourable day to begin, because besides the threat of rain, I have to confess that the men were hard at work. They came here yesterday with orders to build temporary winter quarters. They set to work on their huts but of course did not finish them last night. Today looked like the beginning of a bad spell & very few have resisted the temptation of pushing on their work. A great many of these fellows do not know when Sunday comes.

I have a great many friends in the brigade, and they all seem glad to see me. What do you think, the very first night in camp I broke the crystal of our little watch, and there is not another to be had in our reach. I have sent it home by Col. Bratton & will not bring it out again as the same thing is constantly liable to happen. But you do not know how much I miss it. I did not anticipate how dear that little thing was to be to me. When I got clear out here I felt as if I had a part of yourself with me, & when it got broken I felt as if I had injured you. Besides the sentiment of the thing, there is not a watch in the reach of these Hd. Qrs. & it is great inconvenience to be without a timepiece. I never know when to come to meals, or when service hour comes. I hope you will have an early opportunity of getting it from Winnsboro.

Your letter reached me yesterday, my Darling, having been a longer time on the road than I hope the next one will be. I am anxious to hear from you in Anderson. And so you got into the Bee store; I am glad you succeeded, & got what you most needed. I wish very much I c'd have been with you in Columbia, and am glad you were pronounced so much improved. You must keep it up now & let me hear good accts of you. And I hope to hear good accts of Sue & your Mother too.

You must have been mistaken about Bosey Eggleston's[1] [*sic*] having got home. He is still here, applying for a furlough. We are living well & have a pleasant mess of which I will write more when the absent members return. We have a number of hens to lay eggs, and have occasional rooster fights to while away the monotony of camp for those who have time to kill. We are creeping down the R.R. nearer & nearer to Knoxville & may have active operations before we expect it. As furloughs are granted freely I do not suppose anything very serious is apprehended immediately.

I hope you got the box safely & without trouble.

And now, my dearest wife, I must say goodbye. God bless you, my darling, in soul & body, & enable us both by His grace to do His will & live to His Glory! He has been very good to us & will continue to be so if we are faithful. Give much love to all in both families & remember me to all friends.

Write me about Sue's school, about Thos. Gadsden, about Mr. Miles' school, & the Rev. Mr. M. and everything about yourself. I miss you very much & your letters are very sweet to me.

Your affectionate Husband
W. P. DuBose

1. DuBose Egleston (1843–94) of Winnsboro, a cousin of William Porcher DuBose, was a second lieutenant in Company A, Second South Carolina Infantry. See MacDowell, *DuBose Genealogy,* 205, 270; Compiled Service Records, Second South Carolina Infantry Regiment, M267, roll 155.

Near New Market
Feb. 16th 1864

My dearest wife

Our mails have grown quite irregular since we left Russelville, and for fear that a letter which I sent off yesterday may not reach you punctually, I will send another by a friend who is going across the country to Greenville. As I did not have time to write by Col. Bratton, I begged him to make some of the girls write to you & tell you he had seen me, in case my first letter did not reach you. The weather looks like clearing off and it is turning cold, so we have our boys busy today building us a chimney to our tent. In the meantime I am seated down in my farmhouse reading and writing. I want to do some studying & hope I will soon be able to order & systematize my time as to be able to effect something in that way. I have a good long morning. We break-fast at 8 o.c. dine at 4 & have no supper, an arrangement which suits us all admirably well. Very few of our regular mess are present in camp. Gen. Ker-shaw will scarcely return to us again. It is reported that he has been made Maj. Genl. & ordered to Johnson's [*sic*] Army. He returned a few days ago & is now at Div. Hd. Qrs. I have not seen him yet. Moultrie Dwight is the only regular member of the mess present, & a young Dunlap from Camden, a clerk.

The command of the brigade devolves upon the Junior Col. present, who up to this time has been an old friend of mine, Rutherford.[1] He is now about to go home & will carry this letter for me. This is a mess of young married men. Those who are present, Dwight, Rutherford, Dunlap & myself have all been married since the war. The two latter are happy in the prospect of starting home very soon.

I did not see the little sentences you wrote in my Prayer Book until this morning. I happened to be in a mood when those very verses were the thing

I needed, & it was very sweet to have them suggested by you. You see you can speak a word in season, although you are so far absent. I think you know me remarkably well for so short an acquaintance as ours has been. I flatter myself with the thought that only love c'd have given you such an insight into my tastes, feelings and wants. You don't know, my darling, how I value these little indications of thoughtfulness & of sympathy in my deepest feelings. I hope you are beginning to see that we are sufficiently alike in many respects & congenial enough in all respects to explain of my falling in love with you. The other day riding through N.C. many of the incidents of that eventful summer came back to my mind. I saw the place on the French Broad where I got out of the stage with the young ladies to walk & pick ferns. Everything was very different on this day, with mud beneath me and snow all around. I looked at the walks I used to take from the warm springs, but nothing that I saw excited such associations as those which were connected with the French Broad at a point much nearer to its source. My mind would always run forward to that portion of my campaign of the summer of 1860, & I lived over a good deal of it again.

It is night & I am writing now in my tent by a comfortable fire in the chimney which William built today, of bricks, pine poles & mud. You have no idea how comfortable it makes the tent. The weather has turned very cold, & the wind renders outdoors fires insupportable. Our chimney draws admirably & we are perfectly free from smoke. The weather yesterday & today has been too bad for me even to visit my friends as I wished to do. I don't like to think of Sue trudging to school in such weather as this. By the by did you try to get a pair of india rubbers in the Bee store? She must have a muddy walk. Give her much love & give me an acc't of her school.

I have just commenced today our reading of the Old Testament. I will have to skip all the intervening chapters & begin afresh at the lesson for the day. You must read by the lessons, & also keep in mind during the week the Collect Epistle & Gospel. It will be sweet to know that we are reading & thinking together. My traveling &c threw me a little off my balance & I am just recovering it again. How is it that we will so often stray away from God when it is so sweet to be near Him & so full of discomfort & wretchedness to be far from Him? If our hope rested on our own faithfulness how miserable we w'd be! But blessed be God, it rests upon His faithfulness & not ours. Is not God's patience & forbearance a mystery! I am almost tempted sometimes to feel that it is useless to try Him again. I have been so often faithless to my most sacred vows. Then I feel that I cannot live without Him & I always find Him more than ready to receive me. Oh how I wish I could be more consistent & steadfast. The hymn beginning "Jesus my strength my hope" is a very sweet one to me.

Among other friends whom I have met out here, Frank Parker[2] is a surgeon in Jenkins brigade, now acting on his staff. Another classmate, Carlisle, whom I had lost sight of, is a surgeon in this brigade.[3] The people in this country are rough specimens of humanity. It is hard to tell whether they are Lincolnites or rebels, and they are very noncommittal. My friend of the farmhouse is eminently so. I think he values my presence as a sort of protection against the soldiers. He wanted me to sleep there but I prefer the tent.

Good night now, my dear. I am writing in my lap & my back is breaking. It is too cold to have the fire. Give much love to your Mother, Auntie and <u>all</u>. Kiss Lize & Margie for me. I am getting impatient for another letter.

Your affectionate Husband
W. P. DuBose

1. Col. William Drayton Rutherford, Third South Carolina Infantry, was a Newberry County lawyer. His law partner was James Drayton Nance, who organized the Quitman Rifles in 1860 and was later colonel of the Third South Carolina Regiment. Rutherford succeeded Nance as commander when the latter was killed. Rutherford married the daughter of Col. Simeon Fair in 1862. His daughter's name was Kate Stewart Rutherford. He is buried in Rosemont Cemetery in Newberry, South Carolina. See Kirkland, *Broken Fortunes,* 306; Pope, *History of Newberry County,* 198–99; Compiled Service Records, Third South Carolina Infantry, M276, roll 176.

2. This probably refers to Francis Lejau Parker (1836–1913), a physician. See Parker, *Genealogy of the Parker Family,* 27, 42; Index to Compiled Service Records Raised Directly by the Confederate Government and of Confederate Officers and Nonregimental Enlisted Men, M818, roll 18.

3. Richard Coleman Carlisle (1835–1906) was an assistant surgeon in the Seventh South Carolina Infantry Regiment. See Compiled Service Records, Seventh South Carolina Infantry, M276, roll 215; Abrams, *Newberry County Cemeteries,* 7.

Near New Market
Feb. 21st 1864

Sunday has come again, my darling, and with it a snow storm which excludes the possibility of any ministerial duties. The fact is the climate & the weather at this season are exceedingly unfavourable for outdoor operations of any sort, and I am afraid that this season of tranquility for the army is going to pass away without my being able to effect much. I have not even made a good start in the visiting line. It is God's weather, however, as well as God's work, and with His help I will try to adapt myself to the situation in which He has placed me & to do the best I can under the circumstances with which He has surrounded me. My spiritual health depends very much upon the regularity with which I am enabled to discharge my duties, and this irregularity & constant uncertainty is quite a severe test to me. I have had one or two other little trials. One is the failure to find that privacy which I needed & which I hoped to receive at the farmhouse of which I wrote. I soon found that I was not free from constant interruption from not only the family but soldiers & officers. The children would come & look over my book or my paper; men would come in to warm & to read, and as it was the most comfortable room in the house & one which was not only used for a bedroom but had evidently been used as a parlour also. Of course I said nothing although I had been promised the use of it. For the last few days I have not gone there at all but have done the best I could in our tent which is of course often invaded by visitors on all sorts of business. The last trial which I will enumerate is a toothache which attacked me last night, but for which I am happy to say the oil of cloves has proved a sovereign remedy. You will be glad to hear that I have such a specific against that old enemy. There now, you have all my trials. There is not another one which I can think of, except that greatest of all, from which none of us are free, my own sins & shortcomings. Thank God, His grace more than sufficed for them all, and I hope by patience & prayer to rise more & more above all my difficulties & to grow in grace & in obedience. There is not a chaplain present in the brigade except myself & there is only one who is certain of returning. The field is a large & an important one and the men seem pretty well disposed to attend service. I am going to begin this very evening to see what I can do in the way of visiting as I see little hope from public services.

It is curious how your little mementos have come to me one by one at pleasant intervals. I discovered your note during my ride, as I wrote you. The verses in the Prayer Book I found a week or two ago as I also told you. The verse in the Testament I never saw until a few days ago. Each was a fresh surprise & pleasure to me. I have so little thoughtfulness in that way myself that I am never prepared for it from others, but I do not enjoy it any the less on that account, particularly from you my Darling.

Your letter of the 11th reached me on the 20th, in better time than any of the others. I am glad to hear your Mother is so much better again, and hope as her improvement has been so gradual, it will prove permanent. I suppose you are in your own house again. It makes me almost homesick to imagine you anywhere where I have been in the habit of seeing you, and to recall the little incidents of my visits. I am glad to hear that you too are better my Darling and hope you will continue to improve. It does me good to hear that Sue & Cousin Nannie & the school agree so well. Thank the former for her note and give her a good deal of love. Tell Auntie that I haven't the face to describe the sensations of the first kiss in a letter to you. I may give her my experience at first hand one of these days when you are not near. Whether we began like the Dr. & his wife or not, we will hope that the sequel may be somewhat like theirs: "a happier couple never spent a longer & more useful life together."

We have orders this afternoon to march back to Greenville Tenn. It is a pity to have to leave so soon the comfortable winter quarters which we have just finished. We have been expecting the order all day and when it arrived this afternoon it gave occasion to a small annoyance which is liable to happen at any time to a preacher in the open air. It cleared off today after I began this letter & I determined to have a service this evening. The congregation was very respectable considering the circumstances & the fact that the men were expecting every minute to get orders to move. In the midst of the sermon I heard a horseman ride up to the office tent just behind me, and saw every face in my congregation turn away from me to him. I knew the expected orders had arrived & felt I had lost the attention of my audience. Of course it disconcerted me & I felt it all through the sermon. I hope it was not very perceptible to others. The sooner I get accustomed to all these little things the better & I am glad I was somewhat prepared for them before.

We move at 7 o.c. in the morning. I do not know the object of our movement & will not speculate on the subject as you would probably read the fact in the papers before you read my conjectures. Our papers tell us of important movements against Mobile.[1] God grant that this campaign my not open with disaster to us! I feel very anxious of course, but I am willing to leave it all in higher & wiser hands.

I am by myself in my tent (in our tent) writing by the taper you made. I wish you could drop in & see how comfortable it is. Our chimney performs admirably, & the fire is cheerful & beautiful & comfortable. And we must leave all this tomorrow. How sweet it is to know that we have better & more enduring possessions which never change or can be taken from us!

I was very sorry to hear of the afflictions of the Winthrops.[2] Please express to them my deepest sympathy.

I am trying to make this Lent profitable to me too, although like you I am not actually fasting. I find it a hard thing to [keep up under] my body & bring it into subjection. I am often troubled & perplexed about my spiritual state, but God keeps me from despair. I am learning to trust more in his goodness & faithfulness & am more independent of myself. The chaplains in this brigade have about all given up & resigned. God give me grace and patience to hold on to the end! I am disappointed to hear of Thos. Gadsden's failure to get an appointment. I wonder if he would be willing to take a Chaplaincy in this brigade. I don't know at all that he c'd get it but it may be possible. I believe I will write to him on the subject. It w'd be a comfort to me to have him here and Thos. would be patient & faithful enough to redeem the Chaplaincy here. I forgot to tell you that I attended on last Wednesday a meeting of the Chaplains of this Corps. There were about a dozen present, among them two old University contemporaries & friends, Craig a Presbyterian preacher now in [S.C.] Jenkins Brig.[3] and Toy[4] a Virginian in a Georgia regt., both unusually intelligent men. The meeting was very harmonious and pleasant and I got some good hints about Chaplains work. We are to have two meetings every month, 1st & 3rd Wednesday. It was not a particularly able body but the men seemed to be in earnest.

I must stop now, my love. Give much love to all the family and remember me to all friends. And now my Darling Good bye. May God bless you & fill you with His grace! I have written home only once since my arrival in Tennessee.

Your loving Husband
W. P. DuBose

1. Minor Union probes, including ship and shore operations and the bombardment of Fort Powell, took place from February 16 through late March 1864. See Long, *Civil War Almanac,* 464.

2. One of the "afflictions" mentioned may have been the death of Henry Winthrop (1859–64), son of Francis Winthrop (1832–1909) of Charleston. The child died in Anderson, South Carolina. See Mayo, *Winthrop Family,* 280, 389.

3. John N. Craig was a chaplain in the Fifth South Carolina Infantry. See Compiled Service Records, Fifth South Carolina Infantry, M267, roll 191.

4. C. H. Toy was chaplain in the Fifty-third Georgia Infantry Regiment. See Compiled Service Records, Fifty-third Georgia Infantry, M226, roll 61.

Blue Springs Tenn.
10 miles from Greenville
Feb. 25th 1864

As we have drawn up at this place, my Darling, & may remain here a day or two, I will try to get a letter off to you. We left our last camp on Monday morning at 7 o.c. with orders to march to Greenville, as I wrote you on Sunday. The weather has been admirable for our move & we have done remarkably well. We have spent every night in a house near to the brigade. Monday night we spent at a Mr. Gates' at Panthers Springs, a very respectable old fellow who treated us well & complimented my singing. He said he had not heard a preacher for several months and seemed anxious for an opportunity, so when we were ready to go to bed I told him, as we could not have regular preaching we might have family prayers. I gave out a hymn & he raised the tune, followed by his daughter & myself (when it was not too high). I thought we got through pretty well. The next morning before daylight while I was dressing, the old gentleman came to say that if the preacher had no objection we w'd have prayers again. When we were all ready, I suggested another hymn, but the old fellow said he thought we had better dispense with the singing. "He was not such a hand at it himself, & I did not seem to be much better." The next night we stayed at a very unpromising looking home belonging to a woman with nine children, whose husband had gone to the Yankees. She gave us the use of a room. Last night we came to this place & are again in a house & very comfortable. We have no orders to move today & are very willing to remain.

I have begun to have prayer every night with one regiment or another and find it very pleasant. The men attend very well & are very attentive. The main difficulty is that I cannot get round to each reg't more than once a week, and it is almost impossible to exert much personal influence in the regts. All the Chaplains have now resigned except one who is now on furlough, a Mr. McCallum, whom I used to see in Camden, a faithful & useful man. I thought for a while that I might succeed in getting an old friend of mine in one of the regts—Toy who is now in a Georgia brigade, but he has decided against coming. You need not be afraid of my working too hard or not taking enough recreation. The difficulty all lies the other way. Last night on my return from prayers, I found everybody reading letters & the two waiting for me from Sister & yourself. You may depend upon it that we were a happy crowd. I was distressed though to hear that some of Sister Anne's bad symptoms had returned & that she was depressed in spirits. Bosey also, they said, was looking badly. I trust that they will both be better very soon again.

I could not help feeling disappointed that you had not yet received my first Tenn. letter which was written on the 8th. Although you had scarcely had time to get it by the 15th. I am in hopes I will get another letter tonight acknowledging its receipt. I know you must have felt a little anxious until you got it. And so you are back in the old house again & have no school to occupy your time. I know it was hard to leave Auntie's, pleasant as it is to get back to your old haunts. I am glad your Sister Martha decided to send Lise to school. I am not afraid of your not finding enough to do and hope among other things that you will soon make your Mother quite well again. I am sorry to hear she improves so slowly. I am glad to hear, Darling, that you have such pleasant recollections of the three months we spent together. It is all sweet to me, and I thank God for the blessed privilege which we had so little right to expect in these war times. May He hasten the day when our intercourse may become permanent & uninterrupted! Several efforts have been made to get this brigade to S.C. to recruit but there is no hope of it now. If we ever become stationary in your reach, you must not let your past experience discourage you from making the attempt to come to me again. I doubt if I can expect a furlough before next winter and we are not accustomed to such long separations.

I have not learned yet to make the best use of my time. I haven't systematized yet & therefore lose a great deal of time. I hold two services every Sunday when the weather permits. The Episcopal service, modified, at Hd.Qrs. in the morning and an informal service in the brigade in the afternoon. I have prayers every night. I have not been in reach of any hospital yet and there are no sick men with the brigade. When I get my daily routine better defined I will tell you exactly how I spend each day. And you must do the same, my Darling, so that we may, as you say, live as much as possible together in imagination & in spirit. I am glad to hear that the Marions have had an opportunity of distinguishing themselves without experiencing any loss. James Davis got a letter from [Jim], describing the affair and sympathizing with the two dead Yankees whom he had been, in his measure, instrumental in killing, at which these hardened old veterans laugh very heartily. They say there is nothing prettier than a dead Yankee. I hope a little real service will make the Marions better satisfied with their Captain. And so Thos Gadsden has fairly broken ground. God grant him success in his undertaking! Has he not told his family his intentions? I must close now, my dearest. I may write some more tonight. Love to all.

Your loving Husband
W. P. DuBose

Greenville [sic] Tenn.
March 2nd 1864

My own darling wife,

I have been very nearly prevented from writing this week, and have time for only a short letter this morning which I wish to send by a friend about to start through the country. I have been writing a sermon under very adverse circumstances, and you may imagine how difficult it is for me when I find it so far from easy under the most favourable circumstances. Besides the necessity of writing always in a crowd, I have had several ministerial calls made upon my time. Yesterday I was sent for in Greenville by a family, a member of which had died the night before. I was engaged yesterday afternoon & will be so this morning making preparations for the funeral which is to take place this afternoon. I had to take some of the responsibility upon myself, such as furnishing an ambulance for a hearse, several additional pall bearers &c, there being a dearth of male citizens in Greenville as elsewhere. The deceased is an old lady of eighty two and must have been a remarkable woman. She was very much venerated by the whole community.

If I remain here long I will be virtual pastor of this church. The minister although a man of Southern sympathies, was from the North & returned there early in the war. The congregation seem glad to have the church opened again after so long an interval.

I received a day or two ago your letter of the 22nd inclosing Charlie's. It worries me very much, my Darling, that my letters had not reached you more regularly. My first was written on the 8th and I have written regularly twice a week, about Sunday & Wednesday. Thank you, my dearest wife, for writing so regularly with so little encouragement. Your letters have come to me regularly and are always a great comfort to me. I am glad that you do not give way to uneasiness on my account. I will tell you something of the contents of Charlie's letter in my next. It was strictly confidential, but he had sense enough to expect a man to share his secrets with his wife. I would let you read it if were present, but I am ordered to burn it up immediately.

I think after my experience here I will be trained to write under any difficulties and will be in no danger of ever being distracted by your presence. Not that I ever was so, my Darling, or if I was, it was by the happiness of having you near me. I must confess that you would be more of a distraction to me now than all the crowd which is walking around me & shaking my table.

I have heard some exquisite music since I wrote to you last, piano, violin &c. Last night we had a serenade. But I will have to reserve this too for my next letter.

I am glad to hear that your Auntie is so kind to you. It is a great comfort to have her, or them, with you. I cannot write another word. My letter carrier has already started & I have to overtake him in Greenville.

Excuse this scratch my Darling. Much love to Sue, your Mother & all.

Your loving Husband
W. P. DuBose

∞

Greenville March 4, 1864

Some damage to our R.R. & the raid about Richmond[1] have delayed our mails, my Darling, so that your letter of the 22nd is still the last which I have received. I have been so busy this week that I have scarcely had time to write a line. However I did write a note in a great hurry to send across the country, but the bearer gave me the slip & so I gave it to an officer going by R.R. I have written regularly twice a week, Dearest, except I believe the first week, and am very sorry you had failed to hear from me as late as the 22nd. Your letters have come to me regularly & you would be satisfied if c'd read the disappointment in my heart at even the short interruption of the last few days. I know, my love, how you must have felt during that long interval of almost a month without a word from me. I almost felt that it was selfish in me to be enjoying your letters so regularly, when you were so cut off from the same enjoyment. The fact is though, I am afraid my letters, when they did reach you, have disappointed you. I have felt all the time so behind [hand] in my duties here, & so incapable of doing anything properly, that I could not even write to you as I wished. Living in a crowd as I do, a great deal of my time is lost; and although I am often doing nothing, yet the sense of what I am failing to do takes away some of my interest in what I do do. However I am becoming rapidly accustomed to my circumstances & am learning to do better under the difficulties.

With the aid of a bed quilt & an oil cloth I have partitioned off a corner of our room & made a nice little closet for myself. In it I have a desk, & some shelves and a chair, & am very comfortable. The only difficulty is that my partition does not shut out any of the sound, but I am getting accustomed to that & I have the privilege of at least not seeing or being seen. I am getting a little more into harness too & shall do as well as I could expect. But my Darling, if I have not written as I could have wished, you have been more in my mind than ever and I have never felt a greater yearning to be with you than sometimes possesses me. Every night I go to sleep longing for the sweet consciousness of having you at my side and very often I wake up in the morning with the same thought on my heart. Homesickness is a thing I very seldom ever feel—it is simply a longing for you.

You speak in a letter which I will acknowledge directly, of my old dinner table glances at Mr. Eubanks'.[2] Although others may have seemed to share them with you, you were responsible for them all. It was never my nature or my habit to be guilty of such ill manners until you tempted me by sitting opposite to me. Then because I was obliged to look at you, I had to look at others too to keep up appearances. I used to feel very rude, but what could I do! It makes me feel desperately in love again to think of those old days. You did not think you had made so deep & wide a breach so early in the engagement. After all however, my Darling, I would not exchange the calm, tranquil, confident love of our sober married life for the feverish, anxious & uncertain excitement of those days, sweet as they were. Still I like to go over them all & recall the incidents & feelings of that eventful period, until I imagine myself dead in love again, trembling with doubt & uncertainty, trying in vain to interpret your looks & to fathom your thoughts. You used to think I had the same looks & manners for all. Do you not know that it is the nature of love to embrace all who are connected with its especial object? I was in love with everybody at Mr. Eubanks' for your sake. You <u>kindled</u> all my devotion even if you did not receive it all. You <u>would</u> not receive it all then, & so I was obliged to give some of it away. You are ready enough to take it all now, and my Darling, I am just as ready to give it. All I want in return is your own. We are well enough paid in each other's love. Let us learn together to become better & purer & more worthy of the love of Him whose love it is much harder to repay, but who overlooks more shortcomings than we can ever discover in each other.

I have just heard of the birth of another little nephew. I have no doubt a girl would have been preferred this time but we will be satisfied if he is as fine a boy as his predecessors. How fortunate that Col. Bratton was at home. I wonder if he begins as ugly as the others did. Col. B. has also been busy dividing the estate as far as it was practicable. That was one reason why I was anxious to be at home with him. I have heard very little of the result of the division. I heard that the books came to me. And Stephen & William have both fallen to me. I wonder who our cook, Beck, has gone to. It troubles me to think what I, & three girls, too are to do with these negroes. There is not a better nor more devoted set of negroes in the state than ours. I would be glad if Farmington could be kept up, but I disapprove of owning negroes if you cannot live with them. Nor do I believe in a joint stock affair. . . .

1. From February 28 to March 2, 1864, a Union cavalry raid under the command of Maj. Gen. H. Judson Kilpatrick (1836–81) struck toward Richmond in a failed attempt to penetrate the city and free Union prisoners held there. See Long, *Civil War Almanac,* 469–71.

2. DuBose is apparently referring to the keeper of an inn near Dunn's Rock in Transylvania County, North Carolina, where he first met Nannie during a summer vacation in 1860. In his reminiscences (which name the innkeeper as Ewing), DuBose briefly described his first encounter with his future wife, seated across from her at the inn's dinner table: "At that table, literally at the first sight of Nannie Peronneau my fate seemed to be determined." See DuBose, "Reminiscences," 66, SCL.

March 7th [1864]

I began my letter late on Friday night but did not progress very far with it. On Saturday I was invited to take tea & listen to music [at] Gen. Arnold's,[1] the old gentleman whose office we occupy. As we are indebted to the family for various little attentions & I am the only one of us who have [*sic*] not been very attentive in return, I made it a point to go and had a very pleasant evening. It is a large family, all Episcopalians, & thoroughly Confederate, except the old gentleman, who while he is a good Southerner & hates Abe Lincoln, Andy Johnson, Parson Brownlow[2] & the Yankees generally, was opposed to disunion & "is afraid he was right." The women are as sound as they can be, as the best families about here are, although it is a Union place. We have a magnificent band of stringed instruments in the brigade, & several of them were present & gave us delightful music. Mrs. Marshall—Miss Arnold that was—also played & sang for us. She plays sweetly on the organ in the church; the choir had been practicing that day. She took the liberty of suggesting two metres to me for Sunday. I told her I would be glad if she w'd take your place & give me the Psalm & hymn, but she declined. She is a sweet lady. I meant to finish my letter on Sunday night but our room was full.

Sunday was again a beautiful & delightful day. In the morning I had an overflowing congregation & preached a sermon which I wrote last week on Phil. II &c, an expansion of what I said in that text in the sermon in your possession. We had full chanting. Even the Te Deum & the service was a very pleasant one. In the afternoon I preached to the brigade with much less effort

& strain upon my voice than on the Sunday before. My voice seems to be getting stronger already. Altogether I trust I am in some measure overcoming the little difficulties & obstacles of my situation & entering more & more into the work. Comparatively speaking, I have very few difficulties to contend with. Being at Brig. Hd. Qrs. gives me a great advantage over the chaplains who are connected with regts. The main obstacle I had to contend with was myself. You need not, in your answers to my letters, allude to the little trials I write about. It is sweet, Dearest, to have your sympathy in all matters, even the least; and that is the reason I tell them all to you. But very often by the time your answer comes they are over & forgotten & I am ashamed that I even ever thought or spoke about them. However when I come to think about it I w'd not change your letters in any respect & so you may write as you please. Your letter of the 26th ult. came to me yesterday, & that of the 1st, today, a few minutes ago. I had been a long time without any & was delighted to have them. You are skeptical about the desirableness of only two meals a day. I am in earnest about much preferring it, & want you to prepare yourself for the arrangement when we go to housekeeping. It saves a great deal of time, & a lunch is not impracticable although I feel no necessity for it. We have plenty to eat & only adopt these [hours] because we find them best.

I repeat that there is no danger of my [confining] myself too closely, but I will keep your directions in mind. The elocution I must confess I have neglected. In a big army it is hard to get a private place. But I will try to do this too. I know I need practice. I will be very glad to get the money from Jno. Elliott. I [am] just about to raise some in the brigade for that purpose. I spoke about it yesterday afternoon. I am delighted to hear that Jno. Elliott & his congregation have been doing so well for each other, he in spiritual things & they in temporal things. Do remember me affectionately to him.

Would you believe that I never remembered your birthday. Never mind, I remember you, and you can rely upon my prayers, Dearest, for all that you need. I am delighted to hear that Sue is getting on so well with the school. Give her much love. You must direct to Longstreet's <u>Corps</u> & we are in McLaws' Division, but you need not put that. A Major General commands a Division & L't General a corps. It makes no difference practically but I like my wife to do all things right as she generally does.

Much love to all the family including those at "the web" & kiss the girls for me. Remember me to all friends including Mrs. Glover & Miss Carrie Winthrop &c &c. And now my Darling good bye. God bless, guide & help you with His Holy Spirit. I am disappointed to hear bad accts still from Sister

A. I feel very uneasy about her. I am sorry your box has not turned up & hope it may still do so.

Your aff. Husband
W. P. DuBose

1. Gen. Thomas Dickens Arnold (1798–1870) was a resident of Greeneville, Tennessee, and a United States representative from the twenty-second and twenty-seventh United States Congresses. See *Biographical Directory of the American Congress,* 650.

2. William Gannaway Brownlow (1805–77) of Tennessee was a Methodist minister and radical supporter of the Union. After the war he became the governor of Tennessee and wanted to disenfranchise all those who had supported the Confederacy. In 1866 he made speeches warning that another, final war against the South might be necessary: "As for the rebel population, let them be exterminated." See Cazauran, *Democratic Speaker's Hand-Book,* 370.

Bristol April 4th 1864

Three of your letters have reached me, my Darling, since I last wrote. One by Col. Stiles[1] on Friday, one of the 28th on Saturday, & today a laggard dated the 20th. Thank you for the tea & envelopes. You need not fear that I will not use & enjoy the former. Col. Nance[2] & myself have been drinking some of my old stock, we being the only two who like it without milk & sugar. I have learned to make it myself & never entrust it to anyone else. I have several packages so that I have not begun yet upon the one you put in my saddle bags. Now however that I have learned to make & to like it I will soon be able to give a good acct of it all. Col. Stiles is on an examining board with Col. N. which has brought him over here several times. I hope I will continue to see something of him. Some of his brigade got into a terrible difficulty on Saturday night. The troops have been on rather short rations for some time & the Georgia troops have made several raids on the Commissary deptmt. Finally on Saturday night several hundred of Woffords brigade attacked the Com. store house in Bristol & took a large amt of flour & bacon. They were resisted by the Guard who fired into them, killing several & wounding a good many. Some were also captured and are to be tried immediately. There were officers among them, one of whom was killed. The Post Commissary, whose store house was attacked, is an Episcopalian & a devoted Christian apparently. He is the man who sent to invite me here on Good

Friday. He is from this place & has a large [Pork] press (gov't establishment I believe) which employs a no. of poor people. The children of these & others he has collected into a Sunday School near here and yesterday afternoon he called by to be introduced to me & invite me to it. He is anxious for me to have services in town & is going to try to make arrangements for that purpose if we remain. You need not think it a double tax on me. I w'd generally have the same no. of services anyhow & I find it much easier in a house than in the open air. There is no Ep. Church in Bristol, but there are other vacant churches that are willingly lent. I could not attend the S. School yesterday afternoon because of another call upon me. Capt. Marshall,[3] Gen. Arnold's son in law, who left Greenville the day we did, was taken sick on the way & stopped at a farm house 4 miles from here. Yesterday he was very ill & sent to beg us to send him a physician. We did so, & in the afternoon Moultrie & I rode to see him. We found him better but still very sick. Of course we owe him every attention, on acct of the kindness of his family & himself to us, if for nothing else. I want to go see him again today. I sympathize deeply with himself & his wife on acct of their indefinite separation, & pity him in his sickness away from her.

We have had wretched weather for one week. Yesterday was a pleasant day, as all Sundays have been, but today the weather has had a relapse. The mts are covered with snow & the whole country with mud. Under these circumstances it is pleasant to be in a good house as we are. Up to today we have been boarding with the family & living delightfully, but as all the provisions in the country have been impressed & only a small allowance left to each family we thought it an imposition to do so any longer, and so have fallen back upon our old mode of life, still occupying their rooms however. Mr. King in two nights after we got here had 17 pieces of meat & three horses stolen from him. Joe Haskell too had a fine horse stolen from him some days ago, so I am not alone in my misfortune in that line. It is quite a common thing, in fact, I am sorry to say. As I got my other horse before we had to move, I have never had to walk, but besides this several of my friends could have kept me mounted, & offered to do so.

I had service only once yesterday, in the brigade. I am sorry to say I have done little in the way of personal intercourse with the men & see little hopes of doing better. Eighteen hundred men is enough to discourage one from beginning such a thing & so far I have found it so hard to do what I have undertaken that I hesitate to undertake more. I am still the only chaplain present. I certainly have not overworked myself yet, nor have I kept late hours, 11 o.c. generally finding me in bed. Of reading I have done little or none & see no hopes of doing more; my music books I have not opened. Sue does not wish me to be "exhausted, body & soul & brains" before she becomes one of my parishioners. Tell her that my body will thrive, I hope, under its present treatment. I would be sorry to think that the draft I make upon my brains could exhaust it, but I am fearful that it is deteriorating for want of discipline & management. As for my soul, that is too serious a matter to talk lightly about, but I am afraid it requires great vigilance, perseverance & effort than I have hitherto made to preserve it too from retrogression. May God wake me up more fully to the necessity of striving more earnestly & constantly after conformity to the character & obedience of Jesus Cr't! Everyday teaches me more of my helplessness & of God's wonderful goodness & patience. I seem to myself weaker than ever, but I hope that it [is] only because, by comparing myself with my work, what I do with what I ought to do, I have learned to know myself better & to have higher ideas of what <u>obedience</u> should be.

I am distressed to hear that your Mother is worse again & trust it has proved only a temporary backset. I am glad, Dearest, that you have had it in your power to be useful to her. I would be glad to think that she would never lose the services which I know gives you so much happiness to render. I want her to be able always to feel that I have not deprived her of her daughter. It is not every daughter who has enjoyed to such an extent the privilege of being so necessary to both Father & Mother.

Thank Sue very much for her note. Beg her to take what you please to read her of my letters for those which I would write to her under more favorable circumstances. Not that I don't intend to answer them directly, which I certainly do. Tell her she would be gratified if she knew how much a note from her enhances the value of even a letter from you. You must always be sure to tell me everything about the school. Col. Stiles seemed to have enjoyed his visit to Anderson but it must have been hard to be there without his wife.

Thank you Darling for the bookmark which I am using. It will remind me of you every time I go to read, if indeed I need to be reminded of you at any time.

The idea of mounting the Corps seems to have been abandoned. The men were crazy about it for a while but we hear nothing of it now. You have heard no doubt that the Hampton Legion[4] has gone home to convert itself into cavalry, to be used for the defence of Richmond. Logan Hampton is no longer in our Corps. I think my letters can scarcely reach you regularly. The loss of my mare & several other things you have been obliged to learn first from other sources. My intention is my Darling never to keep anything from you which concerns or interests me. If my letters do not come twice a week you may be sure that there is a failure in the mails, unless I explain it in some other way myself.

The Mrs. Williams in Anderson is a daughter in law of the old lady I saw in Greenville & who was very kind to me. Col. Nance has been superseded in command of the brigade by Col. Kennedy[5] from Camden. He is the fifth officer who has been in command since I have been here & every one except one was an old personal friend of mine. I am glad Capt. Parker thinks well of Tom Stoney,[6] and am very sorry that so many have been [excluded] from his company whom I w'd like to see in it. A good deal of the cavalry from S.C. is ordered to Va. and I hear the R. M. Rifles among them. If so Robert of course will go with them.

My ink flows miserably, & I fear has made my crossing illegible. Give much love to all & kiss the girls for me. How is Judge Whitner?[7] Good bye my Love.

Your affectionate Husband

W. P. DuBose

1. This was Lt. Col. Benjamin Edward Stiles (1835–64) of the Sixteenth Georgia Volunteers. His wife was Clelia Finley Peronneau (1840–87) of Charleston, Nannie's first cousin. See Stiles, *Stiles Family,* 680; Patey, *Whaley Family,* 199.

2. James Drayton Nance (1837–64), a Newberry attorney, was elected colonel of the Third South Carolina Infantry Regiment in May 1862. He was killed on May 6, 1864, at the battle of the Wilderness, and his body was brought home and buried in Newberry. See Wallace, *History of South Carolina,* 4:605; Compiled Service Records, Third South Carolina Infantry, M267, roll 176.

3. This perhaps was Capt. Richard S. Marshall, Thirty-seventh Regiment Tennessee Infantry (Seventh Infantry, First East Tennessee Rifles). See Compiled Service Records, Thirty-seventh Regiment Tennessee Infantry (Seventh Infantry, First East Tennessee Rifles), M231, roll 37.

4. On March 17, 1864, the Hampton Legion was ordered from Tennessee to Greenville, South Carolina, to receive further orders. By May 19, 1864, the unit was classified as mounted infantry and ordered to Richmond, Virginia. See *Official Records Army,* 32(3):646; 36(2):1023.

5. Col. John Doby Kennedy (1840–96) of Camden, South Carolina, commanded the Second South Carolina Infantry. He was promoted to the rank of brigadier general in December 1864. See Compiled Service Records, Second South Carolina Infantry (Second Palmetto Regiment), M267, roll 156.

6. Pvt. Tom Stoney was in Captain Parker's Company. See Compiled Service Records, Captain Parker's Company, South Carolina Light Artillery (Marion Artillery), M267, roll 104.

7. Joseph Newton Whitner (1799–1864) was a judge and a South Carolina state legislator. He died in Anderson on March 31, 1864. See Bailey, *Biographical Directory of the South Carolina Senate,* 3:1717–18.

Bristol April 8th 1864

Your letter of the 31st reached me today my darling wife, together with one from Sister Anne. I feel now about the expressing the pleasure which your letters always give me, as I have always felt about praising a piece of music after hearing it played or sung. It gets so common that it sounds formal & then I can't say it. Still I can feel it, which is better, & I know you do not doubt that I do that. Today is our national fast day.[1] It rained all the morning, as it has been doing for over a week past, & I despaired of being able to observe it in camp. However this evening was better & we had service, a large congregation attending. I find it very hard to prepare extempore addresses with as much care as I should, & consequently I am always dissatisfied with them, even more than with [more written] ones. I should think it a great temptation to extempore preachers. I hope the day was faithfully observed throughout the Confederacy, & may God bless it to the immediate good of our cause. How much depends upon the character of this Spring's campaign. If it is successful I believe it will be decisive.

I am invited to officiate in the Presbyterian Church on Sunday morning, & as one of the two invitations I rec'd was in the form of a pleasant note from a lady, Mrs. Blackford. I have not of course refused. I will miss the chant very much, both as a delightful portion of the service & as a great help to me. There are a good many Episcopalians in Bristol, mainly refugees I believe. I was unfavourably impressed with the appearance of the place on first sight. It has somewhat risen in my estimation since I have seen it in rather better weather. The Blackfords find the society better than that of Greenville. The main street of the town is the line between Va. & Tenn.; the Va. Half of the town is called Goodson, the Tenn. Bristol. Our destination is as much a matter of speculation as ever, & we may be here for some time. I have one great advantage here that I may seldom expect to enjoy & that is some degree of privacy. We have two rooms, a sitting room & a bedroom, the latter without a fireplace which gives me the command of it during a considerable portion of the day. I have much though to censure myself for in the poor use of which I make even the opportunities which I have. Sometimes, I am paralyzed & feel perfectly helpless & destitute of resources at the prospect of what I have to do. One most distressing thing is that when I have to speak extempore, for some time beforehand, I can do nothing at all, not even think of what I am going to say, & the consequence is that I go to the service not only unprepared [in matter], but in an undesirable condition of mind & speech. All these however are trials incident I suppose to my calling, & it is a consolation to feel that neither I nor my hearers are the judge to whom I am responsible, but only J C't [Jesus Christ], who can sympathize with my infirmities. I find it hard to believe sometimes that he can accept & recognize such an obedience & service as I render; the faith that He does own me & my work as His own, fills me with gratitude & heightens my conception of the mystery of grace. That little piece of poetry "One by one the sands are flowing"[2] often recurs to me & helps me. I think I try to "grasp" too many "moments." By the by I have lost one verse of it & have been racking my brains in vain to find it. It['s] the 6th or 7th (not the one beginning "Every hour that fleets so slowly"). I wish you w'd furnish it to me from your book.

I am glad to hear that your Mother is improving again & hope that the mild weather when it does come will hasten her reversal. It must be a trial to her to be so much confined. Give her much love & tell her that as she was good enough to give me her daughter, I feel very grateful for the privilege of being able to furnish her a nurse; & that I hope to find her, when I return as strong & as active as I have been accustomed to see her. I am very much gratified at her kind offer of the watch. It w'd be a great accommodation certainly, but you can judge better than I whether it would be proper for me to accept it. If you know its value & the service it does her. If you think I sh'd do so, I will do it gratefully. The difficulty then w'd be to get it here. I do not see any prospect of an opportunity. When I sent your watch home I neglected to send the key & yesterday Frank Parker was so much in want of one that I gave it to him.

Frank dined with me yesterday and sent his love to you. He always was impudent. I am very fond of Frank but his affectation & vanity amuse me as much as ever. He is Division Surgeon in Genl. Field's[3] staff, Hood's[4] successor. I believe he stands well.

I am distressed to hear that Mr. Hutcheson[5] has resigned the parish & is to go to Nassau. I had become attached to him & will miss him very much. I think he expects to return eventually but will be absent probably during the war. His father wrote him such an urgent & imploring letter that he could not resist it any longer. Another motive too is his health which he told me he thought w'd compel him to resign that parish. He suffered almost incessantly in winter from neuralgia, which he thought interfered seriously with his usefulness.

I am very glad that the lost box has turned up, as it has got [Jeffrey] out of his box & you into yours. It is nearly 11 o.c. & the rain is pouring down with as much energy & intensity as though it had had a month to replenish its supplies. Sister A. writes cheerfully of herself, pronounces herself cured by milk punch, Dr. Bratton's prescription. She approves of the plan which I suggested of taking William's wife for our cook. He has a son and a daughter who we both think would do well for house servants. The latter, Sally, was in the house for a little while. Remember now that she belongs to you, & not to the estate, & that if you need a maid at any time, you need not hesitate to take her. Sister A. suggests that you might take her now if you need her.

I would much rather you have kept the [SH][6] Mr. Sass sent you & hope you have not sent it. Give much love to Sue & all the family. I think every now & then I see indications that you don't get my letters punctually & regularly. I can see in your mention of Randolph Fairfax's[7] life that you had not rec'd a letter which was mailed I think several days before those papers were.

Your speaking of missing me sets me to speculating as to the probable time of our next meeting. The casualties of war are no longer to be looked to as a source of furloughs & my visits will I am afraid become more like angels' visits, in the only respect in which I object to the resemblance. I am peculiarly hopeful just now, however, about the issue of the war, & look forward to a permanent reunion before very long. I have seen the Richmond papers regularly & have read some fine articles on the times. I expect much from the presidential election & its attendant agitations.

Tell Sue while you are taking care of your Mother I will look to her to make you take care of yourself. Good bye now, my Love. May all blessings attend you & those who are dear to us both!

Your loving Husband
W. P. DuBose

1. Confederate president Jefferson Davis declared Friday, April 8, 1864, a day of humiliation, fasting, and prayer for the Confederacy. See *Official Records Army*, 32(3):748–49.
2. This is from a poem by the English poet Adelaide A. Procter (1825–64) published in 1858: "One by one the sands are flowing, / One by one the moments fall; /

Some are coming, some are going, / Do not strive to grasp them all." See Stevenson, *Home Book of Verse,* 3761–62, 3894.

3. Maj. Gen. Charles William Field (1828–92) of Kentucky commanded Gen. John Bell Hood's old division in the First Corps of the Army of Northern Virginia from February 12, 1864, until it surrendered at Appomattox. See Warner, *Generals in Gray,* 87–88.

4. Maj. Gen. John Bell Hood (1831–79) of Kentucky was in command of Longstreet's First Corps when he was wounded at the battle of Chickamauga on September 20, 1863. He was promoted to lieutenant general and command of a corps in the Army of Tennessee on February 2, 1864. See Warner, *Generals in Gray,* 87–88.

5. This was Rev. James Theodore Hutcheson. See Thomas, *Protestant Episcopal Church,* 625.

6. DuBose is possibly referring here to a soldier's hymnal or sacred hymns.

7. *A Sketch of the Life of Randolph Fairfax* by Rev. Philip Slaughter was first published in 1862. Fairfax (1842–62), a young private in the Rockbridge Artillery of the Stonewall Brigade, was killed in action at the battle of Fredericksburg. Ten thousand copies of Slaughter's memoir, based on the letters of Randolph Fairfax, were distributed to the Confederate army at the expense of Gen. Robert E. Lee and other officers as a "stimulating tract upon the Christian soldier." See *Appleton's Cyclopaedia,* 17:207–8; Harrison, *Virginia Carys,* 114.

Bristol April 11th 1864

Your letter of the 5th came in an unusually short time, my Darling, in order to reach me, I presume, on my birthday. It was even smart enough to foresee that there would be a failure of the mail today, & so came to hand yesterday (just as I was about to start to church, so that I had to carry it in my pocket some hours before reading it). I am grieved to hear that your Mother is not improving & sympathize with you deeply in your anxiety on her account. I hope your next letter will bring more favourable accts, & I shall therefore expect it with unusual interest. She must miss very much Jno. Elliott's services and sermons which she has always enjoyed so much. And I am glad that he is so willing to do all that he can to supply the deficiency by private readings. I received his little note to you and will accept the advice, although I am afraid I am in no danger of overtaxing my nerves. I feel grateful that his very useful labours are spared to the church and that you, dearest, & those who are near & dear to you are all well provided for in spiritual things.

Yesterday morning opened with rain & I was uncertain until the hour was upon me whether I would be able to fulfill my engagement in town. As it was not actually raining at the time I went in & found to my surprise quite a large congregation, and a good many ladies. If you c'd conceive, which I am sure you cannot, what a place Bristol is, after two weeks' steady raining, you would give them considerable credit for enterprise for turning out on such a day. They say however that anyone who undertakes to live in the place must accept mud as an established fact & get reconciled to it as early & as well as possible. I think it w'd appall even as staunch a walker as you. I preached the sermon you sent me, with some changes. The Presbyterian choir officiated & sang very well indeed. Of course we had no chants sung. During the service I recognized among the congregation an old U.V. friend, an ordnance officer, whom I had never seen since I left the University, James Boyd.

In the afternoon I wanted to brave the weather & have service in the brigade, but the rain came on & prevented. It is very unpleasant to be in suspense about having service, & must very often be the case in open air preaching. It does look today as though the weather is about to break up, although it has rained this morning. Our friend Capt. Marshall is up again & called by to see us yesterday on his way to his reg't. He has heard not one word from his wife since he left, & supposes that by this time she is within the enemies' lines. Are you not sorry for them!

I have caught up to you today, my Darling. May God bless us both during the coming year in body & soul & grant us the privilege & happiness of spending at least a portion of it together! I do not think it wrong or ungrateful in you to find my letters no compensation for my presence. At any rate if it is a fault it is one which I find very easy to make allowance for. It is one of my happinesses to be missed, and another of them, to be assured of it, even though I never doubt it. I hope your Mother is not too sick to enjoy being read to; it would alleviate the irksomeness of the sick room for both of you. Not that I object to your having time for reflection, when it turns your mind to me.

We are faring pretty well in every respect. The King's [sic] are very kind to us sending butter &c & inviting us occasionally to a nice breakfast or dinner. Moultrie & I dined with them yesterday. Mr. K's father, an old gentleman of seventy five, is the pastor of the Presb. Church here. Rumours are very current in the brigade that we are about to move to Va., but I do not see any indications of an early move in any direction. The fact is the continuous rains of the last two or three weeks must delay operations for some time. Then will begin the decisive campaign of the war.

I have several grounds for hoping that it will be the last of the war, all of them based upon the contingency of Grant's defeat which I will not allow myself to doubt. The first is that if Grant is defeated they lose their main, & so far as I can see, their last dependence as a general. The second is that failure in his campaign will defeat Lincoln in the approaching election, & perfect the formation of antagonistic parties at the North. The last is the old hope of financial difficulties at the North. The late Richmond papers are filled with Northern extracts & editorials upon them which have raised my hopes considerably. I hope you will have more faith in my foresight than Moultrie has been able to instill into his wife. She wrote some days ago that they had all grown very hopeful at home since he had stopped prophesying peace.

Well, we have just had orders to be ready to take the cars tomorrow with four days' cooked rations. Virginia of course must be our destination; what particular point remains to be seen. It is a strange thing how prophetic these rumours among the soldiers almost always are.

I must close now my Love. Love to all.

Your devoted husband
W. P. DuBose

Gordonsville Apr. 30th / 64

I cannot allow this memorable day to pass, my own darling wife, without writing to you, although Saturday is a day on which my thoughts are all required [for] other duties. I have to preach tonight, besides preparing for tomorrow's work. Is it not strange that after our wedding day was undesignedly fixed the same as Brother's, Robert should have come so nearly being married on the same day. Nothing prevented it but the fact of its being Saturday. You have, no doubt, heard of Robert's sudden determination to get married before leaving for Virginia. The day was fixed for the 27th & I [presume] it came off on that day. I wish very [much] I could have been present on the occasion. Robert was in a state of insupportable excitement . . . accounts. I hope he continued to endure it until the momentous evening arrived. In spite of all that was said, I think I was creditably cool & self possessed this time one year ago. Still I am perfectly satisfied never to repent the ordeal. I hope that Rt. after one year's experience of married life, will have no more cause to regret his step than your husband has, my Darling. They have in the army a very homely & pertinent (or <u>im</u>pertinent?) query which nevertheless involves a generally admitted truth. "Are you a married man, or a dog?" We laugh very much at Capt. Holmes[1] who lately returned from a sixty days furlough still in the latter category. He claims one great advantage however over his brother "dogs," that he is one against his will. Holmes is a very fine fellow; I have been delighted with him. He is an admirable officer too, Asst. Adjt. [Gen.] of the Brigade. He says he used to be a classmate of yours at Miss Lovell's. I hope [he] is going to get a good wife. He is certainly very happy in his engagement. You see on this day marrying is the theme which naturally & appropriately suggests itself. The fact is, it is a very popular subject in camp. While I write there is a discussion going on outside of the tent on the subject between a newly married man, an engaged man, & an old batchelor. Our mess is an exceedingly pleasant one & we have . . . times occasionally. I have been remarkably fortunate in that respect during this war. I received a good box from home several days ago, which came in good time & has helped out our mess considerably. We <u>have</u> suffered a little from the ration act of the last Congress (for which I believe Col. Orr[2] is responsible). As long as we were Greeneville & were a separate army Gen. Longstreet took the responsibility of allowing us to purchase a few rations. [That] was revoked as soon as we reached Bristol [and] became a part of the army of Va. For a few [days] we were quite short of provisions in consequence . . . mine so I expect than many refugees have often. . . . Since then we have been pretty well supplied [and] are now doing well. You need never fear that I will suffer. I wish I were always sure of your living as well as I do, & keeping in as good health as I am enjoying at present.

We had a grand review of our Corps on Friday. I wish you could have witnessed it. There were two parallel lines of battle over a mile in length, about eleven thousand men in all. The President & Genl. Bragg were expected, but did not come. Genl. Lee reviewed the Corps & as he rode on the ground was received with tremendous cheers. A great many ladies were present, the day was pleasant, the troops looked well & did well & everything conspired to make it quite a day with us. Genl. Lee, whom I have not seen since the first Maryland campaigns, looks greyer & older & rather stouter than he did then. His health they say is fine & his spirits good. What must his feelings have been as those 11,000 men marched by him in review, who have fought so many battles under him, & not one of whom does not venerate & love him. I think of that man's burdens & responsibilities & what a help & comfort it must be to him to be supported by the confidence of the Army & the nation. He is a grand old man. May God bless him & the country in him, in the future as in the past.

Our . . . very regularly, & there has been a great deal to encourage us. We have service every day, or rather every night & they are largely attended. Besides this there are little prayer meetings kept up by Xtians in the brigade. There is a great deal of religious feeling among the men & I have had conversations with a good many of them.

I promised to write you something about the prayer meeting. It was begun by several very zealous Xtians from the different regiments, the most prominent of whom is a lieutenant whom I first met in Ft. Delaware, Lt. Jennings from Fairfield District.[3] I take a great deal of interest in this meeting which has been growing steadily until now it is regularly & largely attended. In this meeting we have [appointed] a committee of two from each reg't, from whose cooperation I expect a great deal. The fact is we are getting things into working order & I trust with God's blessings that some good may be accomplished. In the morning I have fixed an hour for conversing with whoever desires it, & several always come. I send you a little note which I received last night from a man with whom I had a very interesting conversation this morning. I am getting more accustomed to public speaking in the open air so far as its physical effects are concerned. I feel little or no effects now at all. As I practice it, it is certainly much less laborious than writing. But I am afraid I do not devote sufficient labour to the preparation of my sermons. You must not attach too much importance to my confessions of my weaknesses & of the temptations which I encounter in my work. I very often find it impossible to control my mind & the excitement of having to preach extempore often paralyzes & distracts . . . when I most need my collected [powers I have] them least at command. I have trials & temptations enough but I trust they will be overruled to my good.

I wrote the greater part of my letter on Saturday & have not been able to finish it until today (Monday). So that I have allowed a week to elapse between my two letters. I will try to make it up, my Darling, & in spite of your permission will try & not let it occur again. I do not feel right unless I write at least twice a week. Your letters of the 19th & 22nd reached me yesterday & the day before, the former last. I was shocked to hear of the shipwreck[4] by [which] Odenheimer & Phil Porcher were probably drowned. Your visit must have been a sad one.

From your acc't of the matter I think Jno. Elliott was right in his course in the run away affair, although it was a trying situation. As to the discipline case I am not so clear. He must have secured a high standard of piety in his flock if the offence in the case c'd be treated in so extreme a way.

You ask me about a calico shirt. Which one do you mean? I have never got one from you. Some time ago Sister A. sent me a homespun shirt which had been made w't my knowledge. She implied also that she had made several others. As she had my measure & a seamstress for whom she was glad to find work, & moreover the shirts were already made or making, I determined to write & tell you to keep the calico for a future occasion, but neglected to do so. I infer that you have sent me a shirt which I have never received.

My paper has given out my Darling & I must close. Love to all & as much as you wish for yourself.

Your loving Husband W. P. DuBose

1. Alfred Holmes was a captain and adjutant of the Twenty-fourth South Carolina Infantry Regiment. See Compiled Service Records, Twenty-fourth Infantry Regiment, M267, roll 339; Kirkland, *South Carolina C.S.A. Research Aids.*

2. Jehu Amaziah Orr (1822–1921) was a Confederate congressman. A native of Anderson, South Carolina, he was the younger brother of James L. Orr.

3. This was First Lt. Robert H. Jennings, Company G, Third Battalion South Carolina Infantry. See Compiled Service Records, Third Battalion South Carolina Infantry (Lauren's, James'), M267, roll 180.

4. The Confederate side-wheeler *Helen* (formerly the *Juno*), carrying 220 bales of navy cotton, foundered while running the blockade from Charleston to Nassau. Lt. Philip Johnstone Porcher (1835–64) of the Confederate States Navy (C.S.N.) was in command. He was DuBose's cousin and probably also related to Nannie. He is buried at Magnolia Cemetery and named on the Confederate memorial at St. Michael's Church in Charleston. Lt. William Henry Odenheimer Jr. of the C.S.N. was the husband of Sophia Malbone Ball (1837–91) of South Carolina; he was the son of Bishop William Henry Odenheimer of Philadelphia and New Jersey. See Porcher, "Porcher, a Huguenot Family," 177; Wise, *Lifeline of the Confederacy,* 152–53; WPA Cemetery Index; Deas, *Recollections of the Ball Family,* 148–49, 188–89; Jervey, *Inscriptions in St. Michael's,* 16.

Near Spottsylvania C.H. [sic]
May 9th 1864

The telegrams have no doubt explained, My Darling, the cause of my long silence. Since last Wednesday we have been almost continuously on the move, marching & fighting & maneuvering. Our brigade has been particularly active & deserves the credit I think of having saved the army. Thursday night we encamped eight or ten miles from the field of battle. Friday morning at daylight the enemy attacked desperately, hoping no doubt to decide the day before Longstreet got up. We started at one o.c. and marched rapidly arriving on the field at sunrise. Just as our brigade which was in the advance came up, some N.C. troops on the right gave away & Genl. Lee thought the day was gone. Our troops filed rapidly into the woods & faced the enemy, but the N. Carolinians broke thro' their ranks & threw them into some confusion, which would have been fatal with inferior troops. The Yankees followed close but found themselves in contact with more solid stuff & were soon hurled back. This saved the day & in all their subsequent attacks the enemy made no impression upon any point of our lines. But the brigade suffered severely.[1] Two of my best friends & the two best officers in the brigade, by general concession, were among the first killed. You have no doubt seen their death announced in the papers. Cols. Gaillard & Nance. Nance was killed outright. Frank breathed several hours but was never conscious. I had him buried in a graveyard several miles from the field of battle. I read a portion of the burial service over him. The only ones present besides myself being Dick Gaillard[2] & Frank's servant, a faithful & intelligent old negro. The battle was going on while we buried him. He will be very much missed in the Brigade; there was no more popular man in it. Frank Gaillard has been for several months very perceptibly serious on the subject of religion. I noticed him closely without appearing to do so, but I was not the only one who observed it. He rather avoided direct conversation on the subject, & while his mind was evidently turned towards it I did not press it upon him, contenting myself with trying to help him indirectly & watching his progress. I told Bosey Eggleston several days before the battle that I meant to delay no longer questioning him on the subject but I did not see him again until I shook hands with him as he marched into battle. I have reproached myself bitterly for delaying until it was too late. I believe if I could have induced him to open his mind to me, that there would be much to comfort his friends. He used to read regularly as many other men do who have no serious thoughts, but besides this I have seen him spend almost the whole of Sunday reading & evidently reflecting & meditating over the Bible.

On Saturday night we marched round to this place a distance of about twelve miles & confronted Grant moving down towards Fredericksburg. Our brigade which was again in advance formed lines of battle & moved in to relieve the cavalry who were retarding their progress. They had hardly got into position when they were violently assailed by the enemy, who charged in overwhelming numbers three times & were every time repulsed with terrible loss. At points on the line the fighting was hand to hand. We have a good many men wounded with the bayonet, two of them struck through the body & doing well. Our men had no bayonets but not one gave way & the enemy were finally driven away with great slaughter. The brigade never did better & never killed more Yankees. Our loss from first to last is about four hundred & fifty.[3]

I regret to say that Moultrie was taken prisoner & is now in the hands of the enemy. After the fighting was over he rode unexpectedly into a party of Yankees & was captured. No gun was fired & therefore he could not have been injured. No one else has been wounded of our particular friends. After Gen. Jenkins was killed,[4] Col. Bratton assumed the command of the brigade. He is well. The enemy are moving down our right towards Fredericksburg & we are conforming ourselves to their movements. We may move at any moment, are ready to do so at a moment's notice, & I had better close my letter. God has blessed us signally so far. May He continue to do so & give us deliverance from our enemies! I rec'd a dateless letter from you one or two days ago which refreshed me much. My time has been spent principally in the hospital. Of my experience there I will write you hereafter.

Much love to all.

Yr loving Husband
W. P. DuBose

I don't know how I will send my letter.

1. This action occurred on May 6, 1864, at the battle of the Wilderness. See Rhea, *Battle of the Wilderness,* 297–99, 302, 304, 308–13.

2. Richard Walter Gaillard (1830–1905) was a captain and quartermaster in the Twelfth South Carolina Infantry. See MacDowell, *Gaillard Genealogy,* 22.

3. These events occurred on March 8, 1864, during the battle of Spotsylvania. See Rhea, *Battle for Spotsylvania Courthouse and Yellow Tavern,* 52, 65–66.

4. After the second day of the battle of the Wilderness, Generals Longstreet and Jenkins were making a night-time reconnaissance of the battlefield when their own troops fired on them. Both men were wounded; Longstreet survived, but Jenkins died on May 6, 1864. See Warner, *Generals in Gray,* 155.

Spottsylvania C.H.
May 14th 1864

I wrote you some days ago, my Darling, & sent a short note this morning, but am doubtful whether they will reach you. What with raids & other causes we have had little or no communication with Richmond. This has prevented my writing regularly as I w'd otherwise have done. Besides this I had my haversack stolen from the Hospital on Sunday with all my little conveniences &c.

I trust that this protracted & bloody battle is over at last, but we do not know it to be so. Grant was always obstinate & now he is desperate. He is determined not to give up until he is obliged to do it, & may be preparing for another attack. If we have gained a great victory the nation has much to be thankful for. Grant's army was a powerful one & it has never made more vigorous & obstinate efforts to gain its object. Both sides have lost heavily in General Officers, otherwise our losses have been proportionately smaller I suppose, than in any other battle of the war. You have no doubt heard, if not from me, of Frank Gaillard's death. His loss both as an officer & a man will be severely felt in the Brigade.

Moultrie Dwight will also be very much missed. I wrote you that he was captured, unhurt. The greatest loss to the brigade is undoubtedly Col. Nance who would have been put in command of the brigade when Gen. K. is promoted, which he certainly will be.

You will learn more from the papers than I can tell you, so I will say no more about the battle until it is certainly over. Today we hear good news from Richmond, the Trans. Miss. deptmnt &c.[1] If our success continues we will certainly have a great national thanksgiving.

I have been much at the Hospitals & I trust have been of use there. Many of the wounded have been sincerely anxious about their spiritual condition, & some who were not Xtians before have died praying & apparently believing. On the contrary there have been some end cases of men who could not, & others who would not, think of those things. Those who are not dangerously wounded I talk with & cheer up, & only introduce religious topics incidentally as occasion offers. They generally seem glad to see me & I like to talk to them, tell them the news, &c.

Monday. 16th. I have had no opportunity of sending off my letter & consequently have not finished it. I have a little ink but it is so bad that I cannot write with it. Our suspense still continues with regard to Grant's [intentions].

Nothing has occurred worthy of note for two or three days. I think he is trying to provoke Lee to attack him. Lee however seems to know what he is about, & I am willing to leave it all to him. We have had very large rains & the roads are almost impassable. I am still near the hospital & spend part of every day there. It is very interesting work & there has been much to encourage me. I talked yesterday with a man who will probably die, but may get well. Four or five days ago I spoke to him but got so little encouragement that I put him down among those who could not or would not think seriously. I saw him several times in the interval but did not sound him again until yesterday & I have never seen such a change in a man. He talked intelligently, feelingly & with assurance of the spiritual change that had come over him after my first conversation. That is one of several interesting cases.

We are cut off from news here. I have seen no paper later than the 9th. My latest from you was postmarked April 30, & I don't know when we will get another mail. You have no doubt heard all about Robert's wedding. I suppose he is in Va. by this time.

Gen. Seymour[2] is among our prisoners. Miss Sarah's friend, I suppose. He is very defiant. As a crowd was looking at him the other day at Gordonsville, he told them he "hoped we w'd whip Grant & take Washington, we would [then] find out how strong & how much in earnest the North was." I saw Gen. Wadsworth[3] dying. He was Seymour's opponent for Governor of N.Y. & one of the richest men at the North.

I must close now my darling. Love to all. May God bless you & unite us soon in peace!

Your aff. Husband

W. P. DuBose

1. DuBose is referring to the efforts of General Lee's Army of Northern Virginia in the Overland campaign and Confederate major general Richard Taylor's victory over Union major general Nathaniel P. Banks during the Red River campaign in Louisiana, March 10–May 22, 1864. See Long, *Civil War Almanac,* 473–510.

2. Brig. Gen. Truman Seymour (1824–91), of the Army of the Potomac, was taken prisoner at the battle of the Wilderness and exchanged in August 1864. See Warner, *Generals in Blue,* 432.

3. Brig. Gen. James Samuel Wadsworth (1807–64) ran for governor of New York on the Republican ticket in 1862 but lost the election to Horatio Seymour (1810–86). He was shot in the head at the battle of the Wilderness and died two days later in a Confederate field hospital without regaining consciousness. See Warner, *Generals in Blue,* 532; *Appleton's Cyclopaedia,* 6:312–13.

∞

Spottsylvania C.H.
May 21st 1864

After a long dearth of letters, my darling wife, your sweet one of the 30th reached me yesterday & has refreshed me more than I can express. It almost repaid me for my long privation. I am glad you were able to enjoy so much our first anniversary. May we never spend another apart from each other, of which I believe there is now a reasonable hope. How much I would have enjoyed the little "festival" at the web. I long to see flowers & ladies and especially yourself, my Darling. Our situation is in striking contrast to all these things. We have been now for over two weeks confronting the enemy, in line of battle all the time except when on the march & during the last day or two, when we have been in reserve, just behind Col. Bratton's brigade. Most of the wounded have been sent off by R.R. only four or five being left. Since the Brigade has been in reserve I have resumed my duties in it.

There seems to be much serious feeling in the brigade & I believe there is an opportunity of doing much good. We have service every evening & a large prayer meeting besides, and a good many seem interested. The enemy are reported moving against our right, evidently trying to get to the York River & try the Chickahominy approach again. We may move at any moment & are expecting orders. This uncertainty interferes considerably with my systematic religious efforts but we do the best we can. I was deeply interested in the Hospital work & more encouraged than I could have hoped. There were more interesting cases there than I can tell you of. One of the most so was that of a man named Robuck,[1] formerly a captain in the Holcombe Legion, a fine officer, turned out in the reorganization. He received a wound which he knew to be mortal but which gave him little pain & did not impair his strength at all for some days. It was hard to face death almost in sound health but he did it right bravely. He had been a Xtian for several years & his faith scarcely deserted him for a moment & he died happy on the 4th or fifth day. Not more than half a dozen died in this hospital & several of them I believe were prepared for their change on their deathbed. Many of those who will I believe get well seemed before they were sent off to have made up their minds to become Xtians. God only knows how genuine all these conversions & purposes of amendment are, but there has been much to interest & encourage me in the work.

The men are sanguine & in good spirits but are getting tired of the anxiety & suspense. Grant is evidently determined to leave nothing untried. His hope was to run over Lee by force of numbers & hard knocks. He has discovered that he cannot do this & I think the general impression is that he will creep down the Mattaponi to the York River & try the Peninsula & regular approaches. May God continue to bless us as He has begun and give us a decisive victory & peace!

I hope your letters will reach me more regularly hereafter. They are a great comfort to me, particularly at such a time. Thank Sue very much for her letter; it was a very sweet one & came very opportunely. I would not have enjoyed it so much if it had come in time. She is good to return so much good for evil. Thank Auntie & "Cousin" Nannie for remembering me on our wedding day. Thank the latter for the flowers too. The doves came in good preservation & were duly appreciated. Give much love to your Mother & all the family & remember me to all friends. May God bless & strengthen you my Darling.

Yours with much love W. P. DuBose

Have you seen that Wm. Edmund Stoney[2] was badly wounded near Richmond. He is at Petersburg under Dr. Porcher[3] who writes favorably of him. Frank Gaillard's & Moultrie's servants are about to go home & I may send this by them. We miss those men very much. My health is perfectly good, but I do not like Spring much.

1. Capt. William P. Roebuck of Spartanburg County, South Carolina, was mortally wounded at the battle of Spotsylvania. See Compiled Service Records, Holcombe Legion, M267, roll 378; Landrum, *History of Spartanburg County,* 671.
2. Capt. William Edmund Stoney, William Porcher DuBose's cousin, was the brother of Tom Stoney. He was adjutant inspector general of Hagood's Brigade. See MacDowell, *Gaillard Genealogy,* 305; Index to Compiled Service Records Raised Directly by the Confederate Government and of Confederate Officers and Non-regimental Enlisted Men, M818, roll 23.
3. This was Francis Peyre Porcher.

Hanover Junction
May 25, 1864

The newspapers have no doubt apprized [*sic*] you by this time my Darling, of our movements during the last few days. Grant, having grown tired of butting against our lines at Spotsylvania attempted on Saturday & Sunday to slip around our right flank, as he had previously done at the Wilderness, & get ahead of us in the race to Richmond via this junction. We had hard marching to get here before him. We left Spotsylvania at sunset on Saturday, marched until 2 or 3 A.M., started again at 5 & got here by midday on Sunday. We established our lines on the S. bank of the North Anna which gave the enemy a great advantage as the heights on the N. bank were much higher & commanded us entirely. After dark we adopted a new line quarter of a mile in the rear & fortified it strongly. The enemy after spending Sunday night in posting batteries & preparing to assail our first lines was no doubt surprised & disappointed on Monday morning to discover that his labour was all in vain. Our rear line is an admirable one, the enemy being able to use very little artillery against it, & in fact hardly able to discover it until right up on it. Grant if he attempts to force it will suffer more I think than he did in the Wilderness or at Spotsylvania C.H. As the battle has to be fought out somewhere, I hope it will be at this place. Before this letter reaches you, if it travels at the usual rate, you will no doubt see in the papers the issue of the last battle of this long & tiresome campaign I trust, of the war. Yesterday & today Grant seems to be feeling our lines & preparing for the big attack, which may come at any time now. One disadvantage of our move to a point nearer Richmond will no doubt be that the enemy have forgotten their recent sufferings & imagine, as their generals have tried to persuade them, that they have been victories & have pursued us to this place. This on the other hand may be an advantage to us if it encourages them to charge more boldly & consequently suffer more terribly. After their heavy losses on the other battle fields, they could not be brought within damaging distance.

Our friends have not suffered since Sunday the 8th when Moultrie was captured. My telegrams & letters had not reached Winnsboro up to the 18th or 19th. It is distressing that our friends sh'd have been kept in sad suspense. Lizzie's letters to M. arrive regularly, postmarked as late as the 19th. I wish he had them to soften the rigour of his captivity. I know he finds it hard to reconcile himself to his situation.

Your letters have not behaved as well as usual. While my friends have got letters of as late date as the 18th & 19th & I have rec'd as fresh date from Winnsboro, up to last night. My last letter from you was that of the 30th. Last night I got one of the 5th. And yet while it has been hard to be so long without letters, in one respect it has been a comfort to me. Your letters written before the fighting began are more refreshing to me amid the trying scenes through which we are passing than probably the later ones would be, filled as they are with the anxiety & seriousness which such times impart. It is like getting out of this turmoil & trouble to read one of these letters written under such different circumstances. I breathe a fresher & purer atmosphere of peace & tranquility. To read of flowers & weddings & sweet little collations & books and such things is to leave this world of strife & carnage & enter another & a very widely different one. Not that your life or your letters are made up of such things exclusively. You too have your strife, & your trials, but there is enough of these little entertainments by the way to refresh me even in your accts of them. I have scarcely seen a flower; in fact I hardly know that it is Spring, although the trees which had hardly begun to put out on the 1st May are now in full Spring dress. I have not experienced my usual Spring feeling except for two or three days. My health is as good as possible, but I have today an eruption on my face which is disagreeable. Although I have never in the Army worn anything but a cap in the Summer & have never objected to the tanning, my cap now has suffered my face to become almost blistered. There is something of eruption coming too which makes me fear that besides the burning I may have touched poisonous oak, which may very well have happened in lying down on the ground. I hope it will not prove so however. I received Robert's card, which helps me to realize that he is really married. I wish we could have been present on the occasion; I w'd like to have witnessed the ceremony & the subsequent happiness. I propose however that if you & I ever get married again, instead of Spring, we have the wedding the winter before. Robert & M. spent some of their time at Roseland which must have been delightful, particularly as they look forward to it as their house. Roseland must have been looking very sweet too, & I can answer for it that love invested it with a beauty & glory which it alone can impart. May love ever be strong in their hearts to clothe the plainest house with beauty and joy! Robert's short furlough was cut two days by the stirring events near Richmond, where he now is, I presume, as he mailed a letter from home for me there on the 23rd. Those last companies from the coast contain a large number of young men whose loss would be irreparable to the state. I was very glad to hear that Nat Barnwell[1] had followed Stuart's example. I know how much it must lighten the weight of their father's anxiety.

May 26th. I carelessly lost this morning's mail, by which this letter should have been sent. I am afraid it has been a long time since my last; I cannot measure time here. This morning I received your letter of the 9th. I hope to be getting them every day now for some time until all come up. I am sorry to hear of the sickness in your house. What a pity your Sister M. sh'd have been taken sick during the Capt's furlough. As your acct's however are nearly three weeks old, I hope she is quite well again by this time. Give my love to her & also to your brother. However I have no doubt you are in Abbeville by this time, to which place I suppose I had better direct my letter.

Everything is quiet today except occasional firing from the skirmishers in our front. Grant is slow to begin the battle; & he may well hesitate to attack us in our present position. I will keep my other page for tomorrow. Good bye for today my own Darling.

May 27th. The enemy are moving & we are about to do likewise. Love to all.

Yours W. P. DuBose

1. Nathaniel Berners Barnwell (1845–83) was the twin brother of James Stuart Barnwell (1845–64). They were the sons of Robert Woodward Barnwell (1801–82) of Beaufort, South Carolina. At age sixteen Nathaniel enlisted in the Rutledge Mounted Rifles, which in March 1864 became Company B of the Seventh South Carolina Cavalry Regiment. His brother also served in the Rutledge Mounted Rifles and died of typhoid fever in Richmond in July 1864. See Barnwell, *Story of an American Family*, 112, 214; Compiled Service Records, Seventh South Carolina Cavalry, M267, roll 45.

Hanover County
8 miles N. E. Richmond
May 30th 1864

We have moved again, my Darling, since my last letter, and are as you see nearer to Richmond. Grant would not attack at Hanover Junction as we were all anxious for him to do, but moved down the North Anna & crossed a portion of his army over the Pamunkey. Lee as usual was ready to confront him & here we have been since day before yesterday waiting for him to develop his plans. The only troops who have been engaged since the last move, so far as I have learned, are the 4th & 5th Regts of cavalry just from S.C., Rutledge's and Dunovants.[1] The 4th I hear lost severely, the Charleston Lt. Dragoons seventeen out of thirty nine who went into action.[2] I have heard no names & feel quite anxious as I have several relatives & a good many friends in that company. We are quiet here & had the privilege of a sweet day of rest yesterday. We had three interesting services. In the afternoon Dr. Pryor[3] of the Presbyterian Church, from Petersburg, preached for us, one of the finest sermons I have heard for a long time. There continues to be a good deal of religious interest manifested in the Brigade. There is no doubt that battles & the prospect of battles do much to startle men into seriousness.

273

The night before the battle of the Wilderness, we stopped at dark after a fatiguing march. I knew that a battle would come off the next day & although the men were very much worn out I determined to hold a short service, in the course of which I invited any who desired to converse with me to do so after we separated. So many came that we had a little meeting, in which a serg't, a very nice & intelligent fellow, stated publicly that up to that evening, no serious thoughts had crossed his mind, but that when the drum beat that called us to that service it had startled him into anxiety & that he had made up his mind not to rest until he had found peace. That was nearly a month ago & he shows no signs of wavering yet. What is to be the effect upon their good resolutions when the battle is over & security returns, God only knows. Many of them certainly seem to be in earnest now.

I am anxious to go to Richmond for a day for several reasons & may try to do so tomorrow if the battle does not seem more imminent than it does today. I suppose Robert is there as he mailed a letter for me there some days ago. He was to have left a bundle for me at the Dudleys [sic], but I sent for it & it was not there. The Dudleys have sent me several pressing messages to come if only for a few hours.

We hear this morning that the big fighting has begun in Georgia & are very anxious for further news from Johnson. I believe I feel more anxiety about Atlanta than I do about Richmond.[4]

My last letter is still that of the 9th. Everybody's letters are behaving better than yours now, a state of things I have not been accustomed to. Maybe I have boasted too much of my superiority hitherto to others in the regularity of my letters from you. Capt. Holmes & myself sympathize very fully in our enjoyment of letters from Anderson Dist. but he is so far ahead of me now that I am growing envious. However remiss your letters may be, though, Dearest, I do not need them to assure me that you are not so; and fortunately the last two or three letters which I have are enough to keep me in a good humour under my privations.

We are all doing well—the poison in my face got no worse & is nearly well, but I have a little of it on my hands. My skin is too tough to be much affected by it. I got a little on me in Mississippi. We are living quite well & are in good spirits.

I hear that Miss Julia McCord is engaged to Capt. Feilden[5] on Beauregard's staff. I know him very well & like him very much. If it is so I suppose it means that he intends to settle permanently in this country. He has good friends in Charleston.

I hope the sick are all better. Give much love to your Mother, Sue & all the family.

Your aff. Husband

W. P. DuBose

1. Col. Benjamin Huger Rutledge (1829–89), a Charleston attorney, commanded the Fourth South Carolina Cavalry, and Col. (later Brig. Gen.) John Dunovant (1825–64) commanded the Fifth South Carolina Cavalry. Both regiments were engaged heavily at the battle of Haw's Shop on May 28. See *Cyclopedia of Eminent Men of the Carolinas,* 148–50; Warner, *Generals in Gray,* 78–79; Compiled Service Records, Fourth South Carolina Cavalry, M267, rolls 24, 29, and Fifth South Carolina Cavalry, M267, rolls 32, 33.

2. At the battle of Haw's Shop on May 28, 1864, the Charleston Light Dragoons and other companies of the Fourth South Carolina Cavalry suffered heavy casualties when they failed to receive word that Confederate forces were withdrawing from the battlefield. See Emerson, *Sons of Privilege,* 69–77.

3. Theodorick Bland Pryor (1805–90) was pastor of the Second Presbyterian Church of Petersburg, Virginia. See Claiborne, *Seventy-five Years in Old Virginia,* 84.

4. The battle of Resaca was fought on May 15, 1864, with the result that Confederate general Joseph E. Johnston (not Johnson) withdrew his forces closer to Atlanta. See Long, *Civil War Almanac,* 502.

5. Henry Wemyss Feilden (1838–1921) was a British army officer who resigned his commission to serve in the Confederate States Army. In October 1864 he married Julia McCord (1837–1920), daughter of David J. McCord of Columbia. After the war he returned to England with his wife. Reinstated in the British army, he served as a naturalist on the British Polar Expedition in 1875–76. His friend Rudyard Kipling called him "the gentlest, gallantest English gentleman who ever walked." See *South Carolina Genealogies,* 3:83–84; *Confederate Veteran* 29 (1921): 440.

Hanover Co. June 2nd 1864

I write, my Darling, from a point four or five miles east of the place from which I sent my last letter, & near the Gaines' Mill which was the scene of one of the hardest of the battles around Richmond.[1] Grant seems to be trying to get as near the City as possible by a system of flank movements &, since the Spotsylvania affair, with as little fighting as possible. I do not see, however, how he can keep up this system any longer & in fact yesterday afternoon he made quite a vigorous assault upon our lines, an acc't of which you will of course see in the papers.[2] Our brigade properly behaved as usual, but have lately rec'd a large accession to our ranks without apparently adding to our efficiency. Col. Keitt's[3] reg't came in a few days ago and was assigned to this brigade of which Col. K. assumed command. The reg't was larger than our entire brigade & was a splendid looking body of men. Its actions however have not been in keeping with its appearance. It acted badly yesterday morning & caused an attack on our part to miscarry, which I think w'd have been successful without the assistance of these reinforcements. Col. Keitt was badly, probably mortally, wounded, though he is still alive. The enemy were very obstinate in their attack yesterday evening, gaining possession of a portion of our lines for a while. Several of our reg'ts, particularly the 2nd, acted handsomely recovering the works lost by another brigade & capturing the enemies' colours.[4] Fighting is going on as I write, half a mile in my front but I can learn nothing definite. The papers must inform you.

I rec'd the day before yesterday your letters of the 15th, 20th & 25th which bring me up once more with the rest of the world. If they did come together it was not too much for me to enjoy. I hope hereafter they will be more punctual & regular. I am glad that you went to Abbeville, but very much disappointed that your Mother has improved so slowly. Very often the benefit of these changes is felt more afterwards than at the time & I trust it will be the case with her. Give her much love for me, & if you are still in Abbeville remember me particularly to old Mrs. Parker. And to any others who know me.

Our S.C. Cavalry has suffered very severely since they arrived here. The C.L. Dragoons lost 18 out of 39 on Saturday the 28th and 12 out of 33 on Monday the 30th.[5] A good many of my friends are among the casualties, & one cousin Percival Porcher,[6] shot through the thigh. Shingler's reg't, in which Robert is, also lost heavily on the 30th. You have no doubt seen that Trenholm,[7] Alick Haskell[8] & others were wounded. David DuBose,[9] Mattie's brother, & Capt. of Boykins Co. from Camden, was painfully wounded through the thigh, & Alick Porcher,[10] Cousin Louisa's brother, is one of the missing. Robt is safe. I just missed seeing him yesterday morning. He is now 14 miles from me.

Capt. Holmes is the only one of our staff left. Gen. Kershaw & himself have been most remarkably spared in this war. They have been as much exposed as any other two men & have never been wounded. Holmes' orderly was killed at his side yesterday. We had several killed but there are none dangerously wounded at the Hospital & we are so near Richmond that all who can bear removal are sent there immediately, so that I have not the field for hospital duty, which I had at the other hospitals.

I have seen no strawberries, but I eat [*sic*] yesterday some very nice cherries, the first I have seen. I hear that Col. Ste. Elliott has been made a brigadier general. If it is so it is not impossible that he might be put over our brigade as we have no men now likely to be promoted.

I must go now to the Hospital, which is several miles off. I have not been there this morning. I hope my letters have begun to reach you regularly by this time. Good bye now my Darling. May God bless, guide & keep you!

Your aff. Husband W. P. DuBose

I am very sorry to hear of Thos. Gadsden's rebuff. He c'd not have said that I advised him to act promptly. Did you not read my letter to him? I did advise him however if he did adopt a rapid policy not to be discouraged by failure at first. If she wavered at first, I think if he is judicious he will succeed in the end. So I am still hopeful about him. He <u>ought</u> to succeed.

1. The battle of Cold Harbor, June 1–3, 1864, was fought near the site of the June 27, 1862, battle of Gaines Mill. See McPherson, *Battle Cry of Freedom*, 733.

2. Late in the afternoon of June 1, 1864, Grant's forces attacked Lee's army near Cold Harbor in the first phase of the battle of Cold Harbor. See Long, *Civil War Almanac*, 512–13.

3. Lawrence Massillon Keitt (1824–64) of Orangeburg, South Carolina, was a Confederate congressman. Early in 1862 he raised the Twentieth Regiment of South Carolina Volunteers and was elected its colonel. In May 1864 his regiment was ordered to Virginia, and he was mortally wounded at the battle of Cold Harbor.

4. At a critical point in the battle of Cold Harbor on June 1, 1864, the Second South Carolina Infantry Regiment and the Third South Carolina Battalion filled a breach in the Confederate line and recaptured a portion of the Confederate earthworks from the Forty-eighth and 112th New York Regiments. Pvt. John Pickett of the Second South Carolina captured the Forty-eighth New York's colors. See Rhea, *Cold Harbor*, 255.

5. The Charleston Light Dragoons, which had been in Virginia only since May 24, suffered heavy casualties at the battles of Haw's Shop (May 28) and Matadequin Creek (May 30). See Emerson, *Sons of Privilege*, 69–83.

6. Percival Ravenel Porcher (1829–64) was a member of the Charleston Light Dragoons. He was shot in the thigh at the battle of Haw's Shop and died of gangrene on June 3, 1864. See Emerson, *Sons of Privilege*, 75; Owings, "Cousin Isaac," 43–44.

7. William Lee Trenholm (1836–1901) was the son of George Alfred Trenholm (1807–76) of Charleston, the second Confederate states secretary of the treasury. William was major of the Rutledge Mounted Riflemen, which was incorporated into the Seventh South Carolina Cavalry. He was severely wounded at the battle of Matadequin Creek. He returned to active service and was made a lieutenant colonel of a new South Carolina regiment. See Compiled Service Records, Seventh South

Carolina Cavalry, M267, roll 48; *South Carolina Genealogies,* 4:313–14; Wakelyn, *Biographical Dictionary of the Confederacy,* 414.

8. Col. Alexander Cheves Haskell (1839–1910) was the son of Charles T. Haskell and Sophia Cheves Haskell. He was given command of the Seventh South Carolina Cavalry Regiment in March 1864 and was badly wounded at the battle of Cold Harbor. See Daly, *Alexander Cheves Haskell,* 222; WPA Cemetery Index; Brooks, *South Carolina Bench and Bar,* 70.

9. Capt. David St. Pierre DuBose commanded Company K of the Seventh South Carolina Cavalry. His sister was Margaret "Mattie" Ann Boyd DuBose, William Porcher DuBose's sister-in-law (Mrs. Cowan McNeely DuBose). See Compiled Service Records, Seventh South Carolina Cavalry, M267, roll 45; MacDowell, *DuBose Genealogy,* 12.

10. Alexander Mazyck Porcher (1831–93) was a private in Company B, Seventh South Carolina Cavalry. His sister was Louisa Ashby Porcher (1830–91). See Compiled Service Records, Seventh South Carolina Cavalry, M267, roll 47; Porcher, "Porcher, a Huguenot Family," 135–36.

Hanover Co.

June 4th 1864

I enclose, my Darling, a note to Jno. Elliott informing him of the condition of his brother Ralph.[1] You may read it if you wish to see how he is. I have often intended to write to you about Capt. Elliott, but do not know that I have ever mentioned him. I did not become acquainted with him for a month or two after I reached the brigade but have since seen a great deal of him. He was very much thought of in the Reg't & in the brigade both as an officer & a man & his loss will be much felt. He was in the 2nd Reg't, Col. Gaillard's, who had great confidence in him. As he has never been sufficiently sensible to talk since his wound, & I knew nothing of his religious status before, I can say nothing whatever on that point.

About the time that he was shot, Wednesday the 1st, we heard of the promotion of his brother Stephen. The latter is probably now in command of Evans' brigade. If he has been promoted, he has risen very rapidly, and certainly without any effort on his part. I received yesterday a long letter from Jno. Johnson in which he says that Col. E's promotion to Colonelcy was altogether unexpected to him & this last must be equally as much or more so. Johnson is one of a board of three or four officers appointed to prepare a history of the siege of Charleston. He is still in Ft. Sumter & very busy. He says they are still engaged in the work of building [in] & upon the ruins of the old Ft. a new fort with protection for 500 men, & mounting 6 very heavy & 6 light guns.

We had pretty heavy firing along our lines yesterday. The enemy made repeated assaults at several points & were bloodily repulsed with a marvelously small loss on our part. We are still fighting behind works, which gives us an immense advantage, although I am afraid our men are learning to rely too much upon them, & will be more cautious about charging them when the time comes than they have been hitherto. Capt. Elliott was shot in the very gallant charge by the 2nd Reg't for the recovery of our lines on Wednesday, about which I wrote you.

We have not had many wounded & most of them have been sent to Richmond. The condition of the rest has been much improved by the very efficient & timely labours of the Relief Committee of this State who have found out all our hospitals near the various battle fields & do much for the wounded in the way of soups, coffee & attentions of every kind. I recognise one or two acquaintances among them. The weather for a day or two has been remarkably favourable for the wounded, cool with occasional rain.

I have just seen Dick Gaillard, who has lately seen Robert. He says he looks remarkably well & happy. I discussed with Dick some of the wedding cake which Miss Fanny sent him.

I have not been to Richmond yet but still hope to go there in a day or so if nothing prevents.

I hope your Mother begins by this time, my Darling, to show evidences of improvement. It makes me sad to be forced to the conclusion that her health may be permanently breaking. She was so active, & valued her activity & endurance so much. I shall still hope to see her her old self again. My dear old Grandmother seemed a few years ago to be failing but after a year or two of ill health, became again as well as ever.

I was interested in the little you told me of the proceedings of the Church Council. About the Episcopal College, I am doubtful whether it would be practicable in so small a state. The first difficulty w'd be to get sufficient patronage & the second to get competent professors. Unless these two things are secured it will be, to use a slang phrase, a "one horse" concern of which we w'd have no cause to be proud. That is if it is designed to be a College & not a school. [Tavey] makes an admirable teacher & manager of boys; to make him a professor of young men might raise him above the sphere of his efficiency. As they constantly make in the army very poor generals out of first rate colonels. He is not a sufficiently profound scholar for such a College as I w'd like to see & his forte is with boys. Jno. Johnson, while he is not much of a scholar, in the limited sense in which the word is used, w'd make a good professor of Literature. Mr. Holmes could not help expressing to me the other day at the U.V. his regret that Johnson had not been willing to accept such a position. He says he could have got him a good place the year after he left the U.V.

I wonder if it may be possible for [Jno] to supply my place here for a little while, when things get quiet & spend a few weeks at home. If you can make a bargain for me, you are at liberty to do so & I will try to get the furlough. Would it not be sweet to have a month at home, especially after this long & anxious stretch. How sweet the rest would be. And yet my labours are not fatiguing or wearing. The universal experience is that after much dealing with pain & suffering the effect upon the sensibilities is very much diminished, while the disposition & the aptness to help & relieve are proportionately increased. Bp. [Butler] expresses this in much more philosophical terms, & but for his explanation of the fact, I should have feared that I was becoming too callous. Another thing is that men do not as a general rule suffer very much from bad wounds & when the suffering is not great, the relief from the fatigue & dangers of battle is so great that they are generally cheerful & contented. They are almost without exception glad to receive religious conversation.

As you are probably still in Abbeville I had probably better direct my note to Jno. Elliott himself. His brother was shot in the head, exposing the brain. His pulse is still good but he must die in a day or so.

Good bye my darling.

Your loving Husband W. P. DuBose

[Enclosed note:]

Sunday Morning. 5th

Capt. Elliott has revived somewhat this morning, has taken nourishment & was for a while conscious. He knew Maj. Barnwell his cousin who is now here, recognized me by my voice & talked a little. There seems yet to be a possibility of his recovery, but I am afraid a very slight one. He is asleep now & it is very hard to rouse him. I have written to Jno. directly and also to his brother Stephen.

1. Capt. Ralph Emms Elliott (1834–64) was the commander of the Palmetto Guards, Company I, Second South Carolina Infantry (Second Palmetto Regiment). He was mortally wounded in the battle of Cold Harbor and died on June 5, 1864. He was the brother of the Reverend John Elliott and Gen. Stephen Elliott. See

Compiled Service Records, Second Infantry (Second Palmetto Regiment), M267, roll 155; Barnwell, *Story of an American Family,* 153, 204.

A. N. Va.
June 9th 1864

I received today, my Darling, your letter of the 28th; my last before that was the one of the 25th. The R.Rs are running again but the clerks are doing military not P.O. duty, & the state of things is not materially improved. I hope your experience is a more favourable one & that my letters have continued to reach you. I am distressed to hear no better accts of your Mother. I hoped from your letter of the 25th that the long delayed improvement was becoming apparent at last. I have been directing my letters to Anderson up to this time, and I am afraid that I will end by making the change just about the time that you are returning home. If no change takes place in her, however, I am afraid it will be long before she will be able to be moved. Under such circumstances I am glad that you are among such genuinely kind & hospitable people. Please remember me particularly to Mrs. W. H. Parker & tell her that I would be glad enough to be her guest if it were practicable.

We have been very quiet for several days. All the wounded have been sent to Richmond & as the men are all the time in the trenches & exposed to a fire from sharpshooters which keeps them very close, I have had nothing to do. Under the circumstances I have been reading Hugh Miller's[1] "Testimony of the Rocks" & having a very tranquil time. I have had a good many letters to write too, & have spent some of my time in that way. I wrote to Sue yesterday & enclosed a letter to Jno. Elliott giving him the circumstances of Capt. Elliott's death. If she is in Abbeville the letter will be longer in reaching him than I expected. But he was not dependent upon me for notification of the fact, as the body was sent immediately to Richmond & received there by at least one of his brothers & other relatives & friends. His death was a disappointment to us as his case seemed decidedly more hopeful for a day or two before his death.

I have been trying for several days to go to Richmond, but it is necessary to get a pass from Genl. Lee through the regular channels, & it is a slow business. I have had one up for two days & have heard nothing from it. The cavalry moves about so much that I despair of finding Robert. I hear of him occasionally however & he seems to be well & in good spirits. I was very sorry to hear from Mr. Jno. G. Barnwell[2] that his brother Nat is among the missing. He was captured I believe on a scout with three others.[3] When is all this to end, & who are to emerge in safety from this period of insecurity & distress? These are questions which will suggest themselves to me. We are likely to be in the stretch for some time longer as Grant is determined not to withdraw until he has exhausted the men & resources of the North. The more I think of it the more I am struck with the magnitude of the combination against Richmond. As a <u>combination</u> it has failed signally. <u>One</u> great army now threatens the City, and that is an army every corps of which has been whipped already. How much "fight" remains in it, after their past failures, we have yet to see. May God continue to bless us as He has done hitherto.

I begged Sister Anne some time ago to send you some money, but my letter to her was delayed several weeks on the road. You must not let it distress you, my Darling, to apply to me for help in any form. Am I not the one to whom you should apply? I am only sorry that you should have an opportunity of doing so. It would be much pleasanter to anticipate your want & I could very easily have done so under ordinary circumstances. I have seven months pay due me, & no prospect of drawing. I am in no need of any myself as the Gov't is my principal creditor as well as debtor. As far as the plantation, with no one to attend to it, it finds it as much as it can do to support itself. Taxes however on that species of property are much more moderate than on other forms and I think they are not paid before the end of the year. You must always be candid with me and let me know all your difficulties. It is a mystery to me how refugees live.

Much love to your Mother & all.

Your aff Husband
W. P. DuBose

1. Hugh Miller (1802–56) was a Scottish geologist and a creationist. His *Testimony of the Rocks* was first published in 1857.

2. This was Capt. John Gibbes Barnwell (1831–88), Company H, First South Carolina Infantry (McCreary's). See Compiled Service Records, First (McCreary's) South Carolina Infantry (First South Carolina Infantry Provisional Army), M267, roll 126; Barnwell, *Story of an American Family,* 112–13.

3. Nathaniel Berners Barnwell was captured at Dabney's Ferry, Virginia, on May 27, 1864. See Compiled Service Records, Seventh South Carolina Cavalry, M267, roll 45.

Frazier's Farm (near Malvern Hill)
June 14th 1864

I have suffered a longer time than usual to pass without writing to you my Darling, in consequence of movements both private and public. On Saturday I went to Richmond & returned to camp on Sunday evening. My visit was an exceedingly pleasant one in every respect. My friends seemed glad to see me, & I was as usual fortunate in meeting them. I stayed at the Dudleys of course where I am as much at home as I am anywhere else. Tom Dudley has a sweet little cottage just out of Richmond—Gothic architecture, stained windows, grassy shady yard &c &c. Here we spent the night & had a pleasant time. Tom's family is in Charlottesville just now & he I were alone. On Sunday morning I attended service in a private capacity & in the afternoon rode home. Alick Haskell is staying at the Dudleys. His wound is doing well but it is a long one & it will be some time before it is sufficiently healed for him to resume the saddle. He is a very attractive man & I expect an admirable officer. He is Col. of Robert's Regiment, you know, 7th Cavalry. On Monday we left our lines near Cold Harbour [sic] & marched to this place to conform to Grant's movements. We found Hill skirmishing with the enemy when we got here, but they disappeared very mysteriously [last] & today we are all completely mystified. Except (I hope) Gen. Lee, whom they have never yet deceived, & I trust never will. We move tomorrow morning at 7 o.c. Today we have had a day of rest which was very grateful to the men after their long confinement in the trenches followed by yesterday's hard march. I have spent it pleasantly. This morning I had a visit of half an hour from Robert, which I enjoyed very much. He is well & likes this service, which is very hard, much better than their activity in S.C. It suits his active restless disposition. He says that Minnie writes to him everyday; also that he received "a very sweet letter" from you for which I must thank you until he can do so for himself. Robert is a very improving man & very attractive to me. I am sorry to learn that Col. Logan[1] was severely, though I hope not dangerously, wounded yesterday. He is said to be a first rate officer.

After Robert left me today I rode with Genl. Kershaw & others over the old battle field at Malvern Hill. It is a powerful position & a beautiful place, & I enjoyed my ride very much. From its summit we could see the Yankee transports in the river, and innumerable wagons at Bermuda Hundreds. All this to [classic] ground. We are encamped on the battle field of Frazier's Farm, where Jenkins' brigade distinguished itself. On every side of us lie the bleaching bones of those who fell in that battle & I have studied phrenology on at least one skull, which I hope was a Yankee's. A dentist might make a valuable collection of teeth; I have seen one beautiful set.

This afternoon Col. Bratton paid me a nice long visit; he is looking remarkably well. Tonight I had service in the brigade. In fact this has been quite like Sunday for us. Our Sundays having been converted into weekdays, we have to convert weekdays when we get a chance into Sundays. I think I told you of our accessions in the way of Chaplains in the brigade; a Mr. Duncan came with the 20th,[2] & one of the resigned Chaplains has returned. We have now a Presbyterian, a Methodist, a Baptist, & an Episcopalian. The religious feeling of the brigade continues strong & services are always well attended.

May God give us grace to be faithful & efficient laborers in so rich a harvest! That he should own me at all for his servant & accept my service, is an incomprehensible display of His grace & forbearance which strikes me more every day of my life.

My last letter from you was the 5th. There is still one before it which I have not received. They pass very slowly thro' the Richmond P.O. I am afraid it is still more the case with those going your way.

It is 12 o.c. p.m. & I must stop for [trumpet]. I hope I will be able to add something tomorrow.

15th. 9 o.c. An order came this morning that the enemy were reported advancing & that instead of marching we must hold ourselves in readiness to meet him. I have heard nothing since & we are very quiet. The papers this morning report the death of Gen. Polk in Ga.[3] This settles the question of his returning to his bishopric after the war. Speaking of bishops, James Davis tells me that his father has lost his little remaining sight and cannot now distinguish between day & night. It will make him more helpless & dependent but will not deprive him of very much more than he had lost before.

I wonder whether you are still in Abbeville or are once more in your house in Anderson. In either case, I hope your Mother continues to improve. William insists that he & I are to take a furlough after "this fracas" is over & seems to be worried that I seem so indifferent on the subject. He says he has to do all the talking about it. He is very much opposed to the principle of marrying in such times & says that if he had no family he would not care about going home. I have no doubt I am as anxious as he is, but the prospect seems so distant that I do not indulge the thought very often. And yet how sweet & peaceful would it be to take a walk with you this morning. The weather last night was cold and today it is delightful although the sun is shining brightly. I feel just in the humour for taking an easy indolent walk in company which would impart a charm to even the natural attractions of so sweet a day. We have had remarkably pleasant weather so far this summer; the dust is the main inconvenience now.

What do you think of this specimen of soldier life? One of our soldiers this morning beat up his coffee (in the absence of a mill) in a skull for a mortar with a leg bone for a pestle. It is wonderful how matter of fact they become. Though I do not think I could quite do that, I find much of my "sentiment" on such matters wearing off. The mind becomes easily accustomed to almost anything.

Gen. Kershaw is at last, as you have seen a Major General. Who is to be our brigade commander is a question which is now interesting us all. I do not think any man in the brigade will be promoted. Col. Nance would have been the man if [he] had lived; next to him Col. Gaillard. After these we have no Colonels who would do.

I must close now, Dearest. Give much love to your Mother and all the family if you are at home. Johnson in my last letter from him inquired particularly about you & begged to be remembered.

Your loving Husband
W. P. DuBose

1. Thomas Muldrup Logan (1840–1914), a native of Charleston, South Carolina, was the son of Judge William Logan and Anna D'Oyley Glover Logan. He was colonel of the Hampton Legion when he was wounded on June 13, 1864, at the battle of Riddle's Shop. In February 1865 he was appointed brigadier general, the youngest at the time in the Confederate army. See Compiled Service Records, Hampton Legion, M267, roll 367.

2. William Wallace Duncan (1839–1908) was listed as chaplain of the Second (not Twentieth) South Carolina Infantry. He was later a minister and bishop in the Methodist Episcopal Church. See Compiled Service Records, Second South Carolina Infantry (Second Palmetto Regiment), M267, roll 155; Landrum, *History of Spartanburg County,* 470–72.

3. Lt. Gen. Leonidas Polk (1806–64) of North Carolina was a bishop of the Protestant Episcopal Church and a Confederate corps commander in the Army of Tennessee. He was killed by Union artillery fire at Pine Mountain, Georgia, on June 14, 1864. See Long, *Civil War Almanac,* 522; Warner, *Generals in Gray,* 242–43.

Petersburg June 20 1864

I have but little time to write this afternoon, my Darling, but I must write at least a note to send by Capt. Holmes tonight. After passing thus far through the war without a scratch he has at last been put hors de combat for two or three weeks at least. He was shot by a sharpshooter through the thigh, inflicting no injury upon the bone or artery. He is staying in a private house in the city, but I hope to get him off tonight. He has a servant & I am going to send William with him as far as Columbia. They will have to carry him in a litter, & it will no doubt be painful but this city may be shelled at any time & I do not know what that might subject him to. I have all along promised Wm. a furlough, about this time, so it comes in very well. He seems to hate to go without me, but there appears to be so little prospect of my getting off that there is not use for him to wait. There are other servants here who can take care of me in his absence though not so good.

I have actually forgotten where my last letter was written from. We came from Malvern Hill to Drury's Bluff,[1] staid [sic] there a day & then crossed by the pontoon bridge & came here on Saturday. As we marched by Drury's Bluff by the bright moonlight, we passed the little huts erected by the artillery officers in charge of the guns. They have been stationed there so long that they have accumulated around them a good many evidences of civilization & comfort. Their little well cultivated gardens, their fowl houses & neat grounds looked strange to men whose experience of war has been so difficult. To cap the climax, as I rode by one of the nicest of the cottages a nice looking lady came to the door with a child in her arms. This glimpse of the inner life was better than all the exteriors. As we used to say at the U.V. "it produced me a curious effect," this vision of peace in the midst of war. And this Drury's Bluff is the point that they say Grant is fighting for. "An indispensable necessity to the capture of Richmond," the Northern papers say. The enemy were not very far from the possession of this place when we got here. We have things all straight now & I think Grant has been as completely foiled as he has been elsewhere. When we gave up our outer lines, along with them "went up" as the soldiers say the farm & property of the gentleman who now entertains Capt. Holmes & with whom I spoke last night. On that farm moreover, is located the battery which has shelled the city & from which one shell has struck the fence of his town lot. His negroes & stock are all gone, and yet here three days after he is as generous & hospitable as possible. He is a cousin of Mr. Dudley in Richmond, Mr. Friend.

Yesterday our brigade being under fire, I attended a delightful service at St. Paul's Church, where they have chimes like St. Michaels [sic], sweet music, & a minister, Mr. Platt, who reads beautifully & preached an admirable sermon. There were about a dozen generals present, Lee, Hill, Anderson, Pendleton, &c. It was a sweet day.

We have had some men killed & wounded by sharpshooting, but no engagement since we got here.

I am writing against time & must now close. Love to your Mother & all.

Your aff Husband
W. P. DuBose

Gen. Elliott was struck five or six times the other day without being wounded. I have seen a good deal of Dr. Porcher who inquires particularly about you. I received Tavey's letter. I am amused at the simplicity with which he gives advice in points on which I hope you did not need it. However it [came] to me with . . . him than anyone else.

1. This was Drewry's Bluff, Virginia. See Long, *Civil War Almanac,* 920.

Petersburg June 24 1864

We have real hot weather today, Dearest, which [recalls] my old philosophy on the subject without enabling me very successfully to practice it. The weather sometimes seems to have a physical effect upon my mind, attenuating it like a gas or volatilizing it like a liquid; so on such occasions you must not be surprised to find my letters correspondingly thin & empty.

When we look at all its consequences, it is no unimportant part of the economy of Heaven that there is to be no heat of the sun there. The sun affects the mind & the mind affects the spirit. But the contemplation of "the Lamb who is the light thereof" will perfect mind as well as spirit, and raise us above all such variations & inequalities of intellectual condition. I long for a time when I will be liberated from the bondage of mental indolence, & be able to <u>think</u>.

I have not been writing on regular days lately & the consequence is I can never remember when I wrote last. I believe since my last I have rec'd two letters from you, a laggard of about the early part of June and a late one. The enemy have been cutting heavily at the R.R. lately & I am afraid our mail communications may be interrupted.

I think a general attack was contemplated by Genl. Lee this morning but there was some hitch in it which I have not heard explained & it did not come off. I am convinced that Grant's whole army is composed of either old whipped troops or of new & inefficient ones & that they are ready to be defeated whenever we can get fairly at them. Our men still suffer a good deal from sharpshooting but are gradually protecting themselves better. They (the wounded) are sent off pretty rapidly so that I have little to do at the hospitals, nor can I go to the lines & therefore I have but little occupation. I have been reading with much interest the Testimony of the Rocks, which I should have read long ago & which every educated person ought to read. The light which Geology throws upon the age of the earth, upon the true nature of the Flood &c is becoming pretty generally known, but the changes produced in the popular views on these subjects are so great that every intelligent man ought to be more familiar with them than most of us are. I got today & am going to read as a sequel Guyot's[1] "Earth & Man," a book which I have been long intending to read.

Did I tell you what a pleasant service I attended on last Sunday. I am going to try to repeat it on Sunday if we are still here, although I want to have one service at the Hospital for the Drs & nurses & what patients are there.

I was very much surprised to hear of Bosey's engagement[2] & then of his hasty marriage. I have seen only as much of Marion as you have & was not particularly struck. There is one thing in her favour & that is that she is the niece of Aunt Carrie & her sister Miss Rebecca Couturier, & was reared by the latter, which ought to have developed all the good in her. I have heard that she is a fine girl & I hope she will continue to make him happy. The saddest thing about it is his uncertain health. You have never said anything about Miss Julia McCord's engagement. I was very glad to hear of it; I like Capt. Feilden very much, but I am afraid they will have a slow start in a pecuniary sense. Mr. Sass however will no doubt help him into business. This settles that senseless report about him.

I am glad you can see something of Sue. I think you are mutually dependent upon each other, she as much upon you as you are upon her. I sympathize very heartily with her in her labours, the more so because I know it has its peculiar trials. Even if there were not a material necessity for it, I would admire her for undertaking it. I think every life should have its work, its ministry, & I think she is suited to this. Oh how I long to work with, & sympathize more directly with you all. But we lead a separate life & our paths ever cross but seldom.

I had a funny conversation with two old gray haired men in a book store today. One of them remarked incidentally that he had communicated to the French Emperor through the consul his views of the English policy with regard to us. They agreed that "the old Cockade City"—Petersburg—was by the defeat of Grant to become the Yorktown of this Revolution & witness the winding up of the struggle.

A day or two after William started home a letter came to him announcing the birth of a fine daughter. All are doing well. I am very glad under the circumstances that he went, although I miss him very much. Robert had a boy who ran away from the coast several months ago & was thought to have gone to the Yankees. I heard of him several days ago in Elliott's brigade, waiting on someone. He says he was "pressed into service."

I am very sorry to hear that Mr. Johnson gives so little satisfaction. I was never particularly pleased with him but the Church has grown so rapidly with him & the people used to seem to like him so much that I was in hopes that there was more in him than I could see. I know nothing that grieves me so much as to see men as capable of doing good as Mr. Arthur & himself really doing so little. God spare me from a similar spirit, or cure me of it if I have it! If these men had the <u>spirit</u> of Jno. Elliott they could rival or at least approximate his usefulness. They are not "<u>separated</u> unto the Gospel of God." I wish that I could feel that I was. Indolence and self-indulgence are powerful hindrances.

I hope your Mother continues to improve. Give her much love and remember me to the good friends who have been so kind.

I have just heard that our division has come back in reserve, & I will therefore go to them & hope to be able to have some services.

Goodbye now, my Darling. I hope communication will not be too long interrupted between us. Much love to Sue & all.

Your loving Husband
W. P. DuBose

1. Arnold Henry Guyot (1807–84) was a Swiss American geologist and geographer. His *The Earth and Man: Lectures on Comparative Physical Geography, in Its Relation to the History of Mankind* was published in 1849.

2. DuBose Egleston married Mary Louise Aiken (b. 1848). See MacDowell, *DuBose Genealogy*, 205.

Petersburg July 7th 1864

After writing my last letter, Dearest, I found an opp'y of sending it by private conveyance to a point on the Weldon R.R. from which I hope it was safely transmitted to you. I was sorry afterwards that I had not known while writing it that there was a probability of its being thus favoured. I might have written it with more interest, & then made it more interesting. We are encouraged now to hope that regular R.R. communication will be resumed in a few days. In anticipation of this I have experienced one disappointment this morning. Two letters were handed me with an air which justified me in hoping that one at least was from you, but they were both from Richmond, one from Robert & the other from Tom Dudley. Robert is suffering from the combined effects of no letters from "his wife" and cornbread & fat bacon. Otherwise he is doing well having passed safely through several fights since I saw him last.

I have moved my residence since I wrote last to a point nearer the brigade. We are in a pretty grove of beeches and poplars called "Poplar Lawn." I am writing perched up on one of the lower limbs of a huge beech which makes a tolerably fair seat. There is everything in my situation to inspire the thoughts & feelings which would make an interesting letter, but alas so much more depends upon what is within than what is without! I have tried in vain to reflect the beauty & light of the things around me, but somehow the poetic & religious faculty is not strong in me today. Under such circumstances there is still strength & even joy in the knowledge that the Rock of my salvation & of my hope changes not & that however variable my condition or my mood my life & my peace rest upon a foundation which cannot be removed. I think if you were seated by my side I could be much more readily amused & awakened to the inspiration of my surroundings. It would not be the first limb upon which we have sat together & your presence has never yet failed of its influence. I wish you were with me, my Darling. I begin to feel this long separation & to long for its termination. Robert seems fully satisfied with his choice of a wife & boasts of the fact that Mr. Wm. Robertson accuses Minnie of "writing every day & sometimes twice a day." The girls also speak affectionately of her & I am in hopes she will prove all he thinks her. I pity the poor man who is condemned to live his life with a wife who disappoints him, and I thank God that, if my wife is as little what I sought as she represents herself, he has so mercifully left me in my self-deception.

There has been but little change in the situation of things here. Our brigade is still in reserve & we have a service every evening and a prayer meeting after it. I preach about three times a week. Our sick & wounded have been removed from our own hospital to the S.C. Hospital now about two miles out of town under the charge of Dr. Porcher. I ride out there about every morning & spend several hours with our men & sometimes those of other brigades, who are always glad to see a chaplain. They lie in tents, five or six in a large tent, and I have prayers with them as I go round. I generally see Dr. Porcher & am going to dine with him again in a day or two. The hospital is on the grounds of an old gentleman, Mr. Coxe, the father of a friend of mine who took his degree at the U.V. a year before I did, & died after the breaking out of the war. He was very proud of that son, the only promising child he had, & seems still to grieve very much for his loss. In his yard there are a number of refugees living in tents, apparently very comfortably. In fact the citizens of Petersburg are almost all abiding in these tabernacles now, scattered all over the country west of the city. I always considered that it was the healthiest & in many respects the most sensible mode of life, & I have no doubt these people could enjoy it if they could only get enough to eat. Would you not like to try it for a while? With a large tent & several plain articles of furniture, a table & a few chairs, a bed, in a nice shady grassy yard with a few pleasant neighbors. I think it would be very pleasant indeed. And then if you were at Mr. Coxe's you could walk a hundred yards & revive the sick & wounded with the sight of a lady. There is a pretty young lady there whose acquaintance I am going to make. She is a little fast the Dr. says but quite pleasant, & I heard her playing the piano the other day. Some music would do me good, I think.

I hope you are not all suffering for want of rain as we are. One unfortunate consequence of the drought is that vegetables are cut short and therefore hard to get. And they are very important to an army fed as ours is on bacon. I never knew until lately the value of onions. I am afraid I am contracting an incurable fondness for them. I never eat [*sic*] them before the war, but now we cannot have a better treat. These very occasionally & cowpeas a little oftener constitute our variety. We have for two months had coffee & sugar regularly and generally abundantly. The staple of our fare now is ham or bacon, rice, & cornbread, about a third of the time wheat bread. This with the coffee & vegetables ought to satisfy any reasonable man in such times. We have two regular meals a day & coffee at night.

I must close now, my love. I hope your Mother is much better. Love to her & Sue & all the family.

Your affectionate Husband
W. P. DuBose

Petersburg July 13th 1864

I received yesterday, my Darling, the little packages of socks, tapers &c which you sent me some time ago. It is so long since anything has reached me from you that it was peculiarly welcome. Thank you very much for all the articles.

I am now well supplied with clothing for the summer, having several pairs of summer socks before these came. The tapers I will be sure to put to good use and you must not be offended if I return you the envelopes, one by one, at intervals of about three or four days. We are still without letters, and still hopeful of receiving them daily. Trains have come in by the Weldon R.R. but have brought no mails yet. It is about a month since I have heard from you, Dearest, and I cannot help feeling anxious for news of you all. So many things can happen in a short time. I was distressed to see a day or two ago in the Richmond papers, the announcement of the death of your friend Stuart Barnwell. Nat missing and Stuart dead, and only a few months after the death of their sister![1] I am sincerely sorry for Mr. Barnwell and the other surviving members of this afflicted family. I hear that he was very much affected when he heard about Nat, and then Stuart's death coming so soon after must have made it peculiarly hard to bear. I feel a deep interest in those young men, not only on acc't of your affection for them, but also on acc't of the high terms in which I have heard them spoken of by others, Robert &c. What an unspeakable comfort it is that they were not taken away before they had made their peace with God, young as they were. If their sister's death was the occasion in God's Providence of turning their hearts to God, she did not die in vain. One of them at least is with her; I trust the other is safe. I hear also that Lilly Trapier[2] is dead—a sad invasion into that happy family. She always seemed to be very delicate.

My life is as it has been, my professional duties divided between the Hospital & the Brigade and my leisure time devoted to reading &c in this pleasant grove of beeches and poplars. I have made the acquaintance of Mr. Gibson,[3] rector of Grace Church in this place, and one of the best men I have ever known. He began here as a missionary and endeared himself to the whole city by his piety and usefulness. His little church was several times enlarged until now he has a fine large & handsome one holding seven hundred persons. I preached for him on Sunday morning & dined with him. I was delighted with both himself and his wife and am going to see him again. It was in his former church that Tom Dudley was confirmed in May 1857 and [I] came very near being introduced to him then. He is a friend of Mrs. Dudley. We still have service everyday in the brigade but there are four of us now and we have occasional help from without, so that I do not have to preach more than two or three times a week. The prayer meetings are still kept up too.

I dined on Monday with Gen. Bratton. He is well & we had a very pleasant time. The last time we heard, Willie & The [Theodore][4] were both unwell, particularly The. I hope they are all right again. On Tuesday I spent the day with Dr. Porcher at the S.C. hospital now 2 ½ miles out of town. Most of our sick & wounded are there, and I found there Henry Gaillard who has been sick but is better. I learned from the Dr. for the first time of the death of his brother, Cousin William Porcher,[5] who was killed near Charleston. I don't think you ever saw him.

I have been reading a novel lately, a thing I don't often do. I am reading Waverly,[6] will you believe it for the first time. Although I was once a great novel reader & very fond of Scott there are a good many of his novels which I never read.

We are hearing all sorts of exciting rumours of Early's movements in Maryland. All our acc'ts are from Northern sources but there is no doubt that he has the Yankees in a great state of trepidation.

I have just found an opt'y of sending my letter by private hand & so must close in order to avail myself of it. I am exceedingly anxious to hear of your Mother but in the absence of news will hope that the improvement which had began [sic] when I last heard, has continued. Much love to her & Sue &c. Goodbye my Darling.

Your loving Husband
W. P. DuBose

1. Mary Gibbes Elliott Barnwell was born in 1838 and died on January 3, 1864. See Barnwell, *Story of an American Family*, 112.

2. Elizabeth Shubrick Trapier (1850–64), the daughter of the Reverend Paul Trapier, died in Camden, South Carolina. See Trapier, *Incidents in My Life,* 57; Trapier, *Private Register,* 111.

3. The Reverend Churchill J. Gibson (1819–95) founded Grace Protestant Episcopal Church in Petersburg and was its rector for fifty years. See Tyler, *Encyclopedia of Virginia Biography,* 4:153.

4. William Porcher DuBose's nephews William DuBose Bratton (1860–97) and Theodore DuBose Bratton (1862–1942) were the sons of Gen. John Bratton. See Bratton, "Letters," [ii, v], SHC.

5. Pvt. William Edward Porcher (1823–64), Company B, Second South Carolina Cavalry, was the brother of Dr. Francis Peyre Porcher. He was killed in action on Johns Island, South Carolina, on July 7, 1864. See *South Carolina Genealogies,* 2:71; Compiled Service Records, Second South Carolina Cavalry, M267, roll 13.

6. Sir Walter Scott (1771–1832), a Victorian novelist, wrote *Waverly, or 'Tis Sixty Years Since.*

∞

Petersburg July 18th

My darling Wife,

After one month of non-intercomm. your letters begin to drop in one by one. Day before yesterday brought me one of the 19th, yesterday one of the 22nd & today one of the 7th of this month. The latter brings the sad intelligence that your Mother had on that day passed beyond the reach of human means and was calmly awaiting the summons to a better and a happier world. I was not altogether unprepared for this. Your letters for several months, although they have not always expressed immediate apprehension & have even sometimes been hopeful, have convinced me that her health was slowly and surely failing. A letter from Sister Anne [too] rec'd several days ago, but of a later date than any of yours, prepared me still more for the intelligence which today I get from yourself. All during this long & painful month of silence I have felt apprehensive that when the curtain was once more raised and revealed the events transpiring at home, there would be changes, of which none was more probable than this.

Ere this reaches you, my Darling, you will probably have taken leave of her whom God appointed your first & nearest friend. Yours has been the sad but precious privilege of comforting and assisting the last days and moments of both of those who were the loving guardians of your infancy & youth. It was natural & therefore right that this should be so; & I am glad that my claims upon you have in no respect interfered with the efficient exercise of this pious duty & privilege. I thank God sincerely & heartily that he has mingled the anxiety & sadness of your office with so much of comfort & hope. In such a death as hers there is more of joy & peace than of sadness. God's providence has collected around her all who were dearest to her, and His grace fills & satisfies her heart. She has lived beyond the term of years allotted to most, & has finished her appointed work in the world. God calls her away before her powers of mind & body have become impaired by the infirmities of age; & cheers her last moments by the presence & loving offices of friends whom she loves. And then she has the precious assurance that a better friend awaits to welcome her to more blessed abodes, where soul will be freed from the weariness & sickness of this earth.

Especially in such times as these, such a death has for me far more blessedness than pain. One more whom we loved, released from the trials of this life & safe & at rest with God!

I have written as though there were no probability of your mother being still alive. Your note of the 7th evidently thought her incapable of lasting more than a few days. Tomorrow will no doubt bring me later intelligence.

I rec'd also yesterday the gloves and cravat you sent through Sue. Thank you, Dearest, for knowing & supplying so well my wants. They were both articles which I particularly desired. I believe all my wants are now supplied.

I have seen more of Mr. Gibson & preached for him yesterday afternoon. He is the hardest working man I know & I am glad I find it so easy to assist him by preaching my old sermons. Is not Mr. H. Peronneau Brown of this place named after your father? It is a fine family; one of them, Col. Thompson Brown, was killed lately.

I want to finish this in time to send it by a private opp'y, as I still distrust the mails. God bless & comfort you my Darling! Love to all.

Your loving Husband
W. P. DuBose

Near Drury's Bluff
July 25th 1864

My letter has been delayed, my Darling, several days by a rather unexpected move from Petersburg to this place. The enemy were reported crossing to the north side of the James River and our division was suddenly dispatched to meet them on Saturday morning. We now occupy the line of works north of the James, but the enemy, if they have crossed in any force, have made but little demonstration towards Richmond.[1]

My last letter from you contained the sad intelligence which I had been for some days expecting. You need not regret having filled your letters with the details of her last hours. There was nothing which did not interest me. And you may always be assured that your letters are most interesting to me when they are filled with what interests and concerns you. I anticipated in my last letter most of what my feelings now suggest, but I need not fear repeating too often, my Darling, the assurances of my deepest sympathy. How I would like to have the privilege of being with you in these days of your sad bereavement!

I was distressed to hear of her terrible suffering during the last two days, but that brief anguish only sweetened the bliss in which it has been swallowed up & forgotten. You have no doubt ere this returned to a house which will be very different without her presence, but these changes are appointed and natural, & you have to mourn nothing but the loss which you yourself have sustained.

The girls write that they hope to have you move with them now that home has fewer claims upon you. Nothing in fact would give them more pleasure than that their home should be henceforth your home, until we get one of our own, & that you should feel this to be not only their pleasure but your right. I should urge this upon you, my Darling, but for Sue, who I suppose considers herself fixed in Anderson for the present. As it is, I leave it entirely up to you, to act as you think best. Your home is in Winnsboro, ready to receive you whenever you please to go to it for all or any part of your time. Do not let Sue forget for a minute that she belongs to us, not in part but entirely. As long as we have not a home of our own she may dispose of herself as she pleases, but she must prepare to surrender herself when that time comes. In the meantime I know that the girls will be more than glad to have her whenever she can spare herself to them. I feel very helpless at not being able to do anything more than make suggestions for you, but in these days ladies have to think, act, & shift for themselves. Make your arrangements with the assurance that a house in Winnsboro is not only urged upon you but that it belongs to you by right & that it would give all concerned the sincerest pleasure if you should accept it; also that Sue would be always secure of a hearty welcome there whenever she could go & for however long a time.

I had hoped, Dearest, that we would all be spared to see your Mother in our own house, but it has been ordered otherwise. Give much love to Sue, your Sister Martha, Auntie, Cousin Nannie and all of both families. I hope your brother's eyes have improved & that he is in better spirits about them. I am very sorry to hear of Miss Carrie Pinckney's sickness and hope she is better than when you last wrote.

Soon after you wrote to me about Robert & enclosed Sister A's letter about him, I received one from her on the same subject, giving some extract from Robert's letter. I agree with you perfectly & wrote to him to that effect. That was my second letter to him on the subject. I thought when I saw him that I detected in his manner a good deal of seriousness. I had no opp'y of talking with him but he asked me for one or two little books which I gave him. God grant that he may be led to the knowledge and love of the truth! It is what he needs to make him a fine man. I was very much struck with an extract from his letter which I cannot now recall. Robt attracts & interests me very much & I think I feel more concern about his spiritual condition than on any other subject I know. I am deeply interested in Gen. Bratton too, but I find it particularly hard to approach him. He is far from indifferent on the subject I believe, & I do not see enough of him to [know] what his difficulties are. [Boggs] is not with him now since his promotion. I believe

Frank Parker to be a changed man, although he does not seem ready yet to make a public profession of religion. It has improved him wonderfully. We continue to keep up regular daily services & the prayer meeting continues to increase in interest. Nearly twenty in the brigade joined the diff't churches while we were in Petersburg & there is considerable interest among the men. I am becoming very well acquainted with the brigade & I believe making friends. I am now engaged in organizing a Christian Association which will assist me very much, and from which I anticipate much good.

I received a very confidential and candid letter from Thos. Gadsden[2] a few days ago in answer to mine. It is an admirable letter & I would like to show it to you. From what he tells me I fear that Miss Mary's rejection of him was a decided & final one. She certainly did her best to make him regard it as such & to impress it upon him. You know better than I how much hope remains after such a refusal. He himself feels but little, & thinks that success if it ever comes must be very far in the future. He feels it deeply but of course bears it admirably & extracts a blessing from it. He is an "Israelite indeed in whom there is no guile." I have never known a more simple-minded, single-eyed Christian, and Miss Mary would help him so much by her practical turn & sound judgment that I could not help hoping that the match had been all arranged. But God is wiser than man.

I came very near having quite a misfortune befall me a few days ago. My old horse John got a kick on his knee & the joint became so inflamed that it was pronounced by all the judges a permanent injury or at least one that would disable him for several months. At this juncture came the order to march 20 miles, which left me the alternative of leaving him to [starve] or to drag him along on three legs. I was obliged to choose the latter never imagining that he could accomplish it. But to my amazement he did, & what is more it has cured him. He started off literally on three legs & in evident agony, my servant leading him. He is now nearly well.

I send you a few of your envelopes which you may use again. Goodbye my Darling wife.

Yours, W. P. DuBose

1. On July 25, 1864, Grant sent the Army of the Potomac's Second Corps and two cavalry divisions to the north bank of the James River to move toward Richmond and destroy railroads. See Long, *Civil War Almanac,* 545.

2. Thomas F. Gadsden married Mary Trapier (daughter of the Reverend Paul Trapier) in September 1866. See Trapier, *Incidents in My Life,* 36.

5

FAITH TESTED

August 1864–April 1865

"Nothing remains for us but to prepare & brace ourselves for the patient endurance of trials & sufferings of which God only knows the extent or the issue."

February 8, 1865

From the summer of 1864 until the end of the war, DuBose and the men of Kershaw's Brigade were on the move. The brigade, as part of Anderson's division, was transferred to the Shenandoah Valley, where it participated in a number of actions. From there the brigade returned to Petersburg and then moved to Charleston. It abandoned the latter city with the withdrawing Confederate forces and then faced Sherman's troops at Cheraw before retreating into North Carolina. The brigade participated in the battles of Averasboro and Bentonville before surrendering at Greensboro on April 26, 1865.

Orange C.H. Aug. 10 1864

My darling wife

I completed and mailed a letter to you in Richmond on Sunday morning informing you of our move in this direction. I was subsequently persuaded by Tom Dudley to remain in the city until the evening, assisted in the service & communion service at the Monumental Church, dined with Tom, & started on my lonely ride at sunset. Do you know that the little daughter of his who is also my God daughter, has been waiting on me to baptize her several months. My friends in Richmond are fully bent on having you come and see them, and I have promised them that if I have an opp'y even during the war you will do so, [so] get ready, if I should happen to be stationed for any length of time near Richmond. They are all very affectionate to me. I was very glad on Sunday morning to have at last an opportunity of communing. It is long since I had done so.

On Sunday evening at sunset I started after the wagons which had started early in the morning. My horse being a little lame still, I walked him leisurely until midnight by myself all the way & without any moon, rather a lonesome and dismal ride. I stopped then for the night & slept on my overcoat by the side of the road. At daylight I resumed the chase and over-took the wagons in the course of the day. We reached this place, about eighty miles from Richmond, at 10 o.c. this morning and are resting until afternoon when we expect to reach the troops about 12 miles from here near Cedar Mt. My horse has stood the trip unexpectedly well, for which I am sincerely thankful. He cannot go over a walk but does very well at that. A day or two ago I had a valuable halter stolen from me, & today my bridle has suffered the same fate, so that in these respects I am dependent on charity.

My ride was free from incidents of interest until today when its monot-ony was relieved by a very pleasant visit to some ladies near where we now are. When we rode up they sent down & invited the gentlemen to come up and drink some cider. A Qr. Mr. & I accepted the invitation, and when we walked up to the house found three or four ladies seated in the piazza. We introduced ourselves & sat for an hour or two talking with the ladies and drinking iced cider. It is a beautiful place and the ladies were very pleasant so that I enjoyed the visit very much. I found that we had a good many mutual acquaintances and friends. I am also acquainted with the minister of their parish, Mr. Richard Davis of Charlottesville, who is absent just now. One of our mutual friends is Mrs. Sam. Preston, formerly Miss Texie Saunders of Charlottesville.[1] Her husband, one of my dearest friends, I was distressed to hear in Richmond, was mortally wounded in the explosion the other day at Petersburg.[2] These ladies tell me however that there is yet hope of his recovery. I trust so.

I heard in Richmond too for the first time of Johnson's injury in Ft. Sumter.[3] I heard that the wound, tho' severe, was not dangerous & that he was doing well. I am anxious to hear more definitely, & hope he is with his sisters. We launch out now, my Darling, I suppose, into the region of no mails. We have no grounds for conjecture as to where we are going or what we are to do. But we have at least to expect that we are in great measure to lose for a time the blessed privilege of regular communication with those we love. However, God can & will take the same care of our families & coun-try, whether or not we get letters regularly or read the daily papers. Do not write less than twice a week, however uncertain the mails may get. Next best to getting letters regularly is to get a handful after long abstinence or deprivation. My letters will no doubt get to you more regularly than yours to me. I will avail myself of every opp'y of mailing them.

I have not been able to say anything in reply to what you wrote about your former S. School scholar, nor can I now, writing under such disadvantages. You must tell me more about her case, in which I feel much interest. I do not infrequently have such cases and experience the same inability to give the needed comfort, of which you complain. All we can do is to do the best we can with prayer and leave the rest to God. To one so much in earnest as she seems to be, I have no doubt God will in the end send the necessary light and strength.

This month two years ago we started from Gordonsville on the first Maryland campaign. I trust that the sequel in this case will prove less sad and eventful than that, unless it is more happily eventful.

I must close now, my dearest. May God be ever with you to make you strong in His service. Love to all.

Yours lovingly

W. P. DuBose

1. Samuel Davis Preston married Texie G. Saunders in 1861. See Preston, *Preston Genealogy,* 50.

2. Capt. Samuel Davis Preston, Company C, Thirty-fourth Virginia Infantry, was killed on July 30, 1864, at the battle of the Crater. Union soldiers tunneled under a portion of the Confederate lines held by Brig. Gen. Stephen Elliott's South Carolina brigade. The Union troops filled the tunnel with explosives, which they detonated to begin a Union assault on the Confederate lines. Even though the explosion blew a massive hole in the Confederate lines and buried many Confederate soldiers, the Union assault was a costly failure due to poor leadership and execution. See McPherson, *Battle Cry of Freedom,* 758–60; Compiled Service Records, Thirty-fourth Virginia Infantry, M382, roll 44.

3. On July 28, 1864, Capt. John Johnson was severely wounded when he was struck in the head by a fragment of a mortar shell after eight months and twenty-eight days of duty in the fort. See Johnson, *Defense of Charleston Harbor,* 231.

Near Brucetown

Aug 29th 1864

My darling wife,

Since my last letter, of the 25th, three of your letters have reached me—14th, 17th and 21st. I am sorry I have abandoned the mail so much. We have fared tolerably well both in the way of letters and newspapers, and in our present situation we get a daily mail. Why do you object so much to my getting several letters at a time? Why not judge me by yourself, and infer that, as only a number of letters can satisfy you after a long privation, a single one would not satisfy me under similar circumstances. The best rule is to go regularly on as though there were no obstacle to communication. You cannot write too often, my Darling, and I would rather get ten letters any day than one. I do not say this because you have not written regularly, but because you seem so "disgusted" at the idea of my getting more than one letter at a time.

On Thursday we passed through Charlestown and our brigade occupied the advanced lines about a mile beyond the town. On Friday the enemy attacked our pickets who were off their guard and captured about eighty and killed and wounded about twenty. Bosey Eggleston had his neck scraped by a minnie ball, a narrow escape. On Saturday we retired to this place, fourteen miles south of Charlestown and encamped on the spot occupied by the brigade two years ago, after the first Maryland campaign. Our tent is on the spot occupied then by Col. Gaillard's. I was at that time in Ft. Delaware. Yesterday we had a quiet tranquil Sunday, the first for a long time, and everybody seemed to enjoy it. Our situation is a pleasant one and the weather perfectly delightful. The services are as well attended as they have ever been and the interest seems to be as great. The Christian Association works admirably and I expect much good from it. The prayer meetings, which are its main instrumentality, begin to rival the regular services in size and I think surpass them in interest and usefulness.

The second member of the Association was killed on Friday. The first was Sergt. [Brearly] killed at Deep Bottom, about whom I wrote at the time. This was Bacon of Greenville,[1] color-bearer of the 2nd Regt. His father is Mr. Arthur's organist, and <u>he</u> performed the same office for me in the church in Greenville Tenn. I think this young man played for his father the day I attended service in Greenville. He was a nice fellow and a pious man, & behaved very gallantly on the occasion of his death. He was shot through his body and died almost instantly, exclaiming with his last gasp to a comrade to whom he handed the colours, "Hold up the flag." These instances of individual heroism are more frequent than one would suppose, but in a big war like this not many of them are recorded. There is a young fellow with whom I used to converse at Gordonsville & who has since become a member of the Baptist Church. He has no parents nor home and always excited my interest by his manliness and modesty. In this campaign he has carried the flag of the 7th Regt. and has attracted the admiration of everyone by his conspicuous gallantry in battle.

I am anxious to learn the cause of Sue's non-appearance. I suppose it was owing to some detention on the road. I wonder how long you have had to keep school and whether you got back to Miss Carrie Pinckney. You began your reading with a very interesting subject and I should like to have formed one of the reading party. I think the plan adopted an admirable one; it awakens interest and curiosity and prepares you to read with relish and profit. I have seen the "Yahweh Christ" but never read it and am therefore not prepared to pass judgment on it.

Please remember me particularly to Miss Mary and Miss Carrie Pinckney. I hope the latter has begun to improve more rapidly.

I must close now my Darling and reserve the portions of your letters which are still unanswered for the next time. It is quite late and my letter must go early in the morning. William and John are both well and beg to be remembered. I am sorry to see that my letters do not reach you as regularly as yours do me. I thought it would be the contrary. Much love to Sue and all. Good night my love.

Your aff. Husband
W. P. DuBose

My ink is bad and my light worse.

1. Randolph Bacon (b. 1841) was the color sergeant for the Second South Carolina Infantry Regiment. See Compiled Service Records, Second South Carolina Infantry (Second Palmetto Regiment), M267, roll 153; Wyckoff, *History of the Second South Carolina Infantry,* 135, 156.

Winchester
Sept. 2nd 1864

My own darling wife,

Your sweet letter of the 21st reached me yesterday and whether it was that the letter itself was more touching than usual, or that I was more impressible, or that the lovely Fall day had something to do with it, it had a perfectly delightful effect upon me. This month here is what October will be with you, cold nights bright and glorious days and a bracing atmosphere that makes one enjoy life and—wish [himself] at home. These are the days for long walks with you, when the sun is not hot enough to [drive us] to the shade, nor the weather cold enough to [drive us] to the fire. And so you think that you . . . make me so unhappy after all. . . . when [the time] comes for us to lean upon each other . . . I long for the time to come for you to try the experiment and have no fears for the result. So you see we are at Winchester again. Our movements are inexplicable to our [selves] and therefore I will not attempt to explain them to you. One thing is certain, that the newspapers know nothing of our doings. You need never read them to see what we are about. We do more maneuvers than fighting and the main object of both sides seems to be to mystify each other as much as possible. I am surprised that my letters take so long to reach you. The cause of it no doubt is a petty little quarrel which the papers are talking about between the P.M. [Postmaster] General and the President of the [Central] R.R. in consequence of which no mails [pass] over that [road]. There seems to be a special [arrangement] for the Army mail coming here. You will [be rewarded] for writing so regularly by learning that your letters have all reached me without much delay, and always one at a time. I [have written] regularly also and hope they are reaching [you] now. On the 24th you had not yet heard . . . [Stiles' death] which occurred on the 16th. . . . Genl. of this corps[1] told me that he had telegraphed the fact to Savannah, or signaled it to some point from which it could be telegraphed, so that I supposed you would hear it before that time. It made me sad to hear that . . . day you were hearing of me from . . . when I had, a week before communicated such [sad] news of him.

I was sorry to leave our last camp. We were so pleasantly situated, and I had a nice little grassy and shady retreat to which I retired for several hours every morning and enjoyed in perfect privacy my reading, meditation and prayers. There [also] I would read over my letters and enjoy sweet thoughts of you and all the other dear ones at home. Here I cannot get such a nice, nor such a private place but I have one which answers my [purpose] pretty well. A place of retirement has become a matter of necessity with me and I wonder . . . I ever in the army imagined I could live [without] it as I did too long. I have been trying [under] them [even] of late to live in constant [communion] with God and He has I believe blessed [my] efforts. May He strengthen both of us my Darling, more and more for. . . . The . . . solution of all perplexities, and the only . . . for all the trials and weaknesses of life [is] to be found in a living union with Him. I [find] too, my Darling, that the more I love Him the more I love you and the greater [interest] I take in all the gifts He has so lovingly lavished upon me.

We have a sudden order to move, [where] I do not know, so I must hasten to close what I intended to be a long letter. I hope Sue arrived safely on the 20th [not] too much reduced by her earache. Give her much love and tell her I hope she [feels] strong to begin her duties afresh. I got a note from

Thos. Gadsden [today] and am rejoiced to learn that he [may] probably be the Chaplain of Robt's [regiment].[2] He will be pleasantly situated [with] Col. Haskell and will find some [friends in the] R.M. Rifles at least. . . . a large number of . . . I hoped to be able to accomplish have. . . . Goodbye now, my Love.

Yours with much love
W. P. DuBose

I have lost my pocket book, with . . . , but all my stamps which I cannot . . . here.

1. This was Maj. Gen. John Cabell Breckenridge (1821–75). See Warner, *Generals in Gray,* 34–35.
2. This was the Seventh South Carolina Cavalry, but Gadsden's name does not appear in the Compiled Service Records for this regiment (M267, roll 46).

Winchester
Sept. 8th 1864

My darling wife

My last letter was written, I believe, from Berryville on Sunday evening. You see we are once more at our old stand. The enemy fell back on Sunday to a strong position beyond Berryville where it was not deemed advisable to attack them, and so on Monday we retired to this place. The little affair of Saturday evening was considered, I hear, by Early[1] & Anderson[2] quite a handsome thing as we were much inferior to the enemy in force.[3] I am glad it happened as our division has been somewhat unfortunate lately, and Gen. Early had begun to laugh at us for letting the Yankee cavalry pick us up at Front Royal and Charlestown. On Monday the 5th I received your letter mailed on the 29th. It is provoking that when your letters reach me so speedily and regularly, mine should be so long getting to you. It is all caused by a trifling quarrel between the P.M. General and the Prest. of the Va. Central R.R.[4] I was distressed to see that you had not heard of Col. Stiles' death.

We have been having for several days a cold wintry rain, such as you never enjoy before November—very supportable in a house by a cheerful fire and in good company, but harder to bear in a little tent filled very often with the smoke of camp fires of which you can only enjoy the heat by taking the rain. The only solace, humanly speaking, is derived from the consideration of how we <u>could</u> enjoy such a day under certain imaginary circumstances, which I hope will one of these days be realized. I ought never to complain however. I enjoy peculiar advantages for keeping comfortable. I have always a tent & much more transportation for clothes &c than is usually allotted to soldiers. On Saturday night while the belligerents were taking the rain in the trenches at Berryville, I was sleeping dry and comfortable in a tent. The soldiers, however, contrive to be much more comfortable themselves ordinarily than would be supposed possible. They are most of them provided with little Yankee flies[5] which they carry on their backs. Two or four of these buttoned together as they are made to do, make quite an efficient shelter for two three or four men sitting or lying. Our main difficulty is the want of shoes. There are several hundred of our men barefooted. This want will soon be supplied I hope. Gen. Connor[6] is at last, we hear, on his way to take command of this brigade. Do you know him? I am glad that we are at last to have a permanent commander.

We get the daily papers pretty regularly, two days after they come out. Yesterday we received final confirmation of the fall of Atlanta.[7] Of course the news has depressed us all more or less, but I am still rallying rapidly from the temporary defeat into which it threw me, and have thrown Atlanta into the category of Nashville, New Orleans, Memphis, Vicksburg &c—spilt milk, over which it is needless to cry. "Forgetting those things which are behind &c"[8] is a maxim that holds good in war and courtship as well as in higher things. I practiced it successfully in courtship and I am trying it now in war. We in camp find it easier to rise above despondency than you at home.

Oh for a living faith to lift us above the reach of despondency and distrust! It is hard to practice what we profess. Did you see the other day a description from a Northern paper of the Rebel prisoners at the North? It is in striking contrast with the acc't you gave sometime ago of the Yankee prisoners in Ga.[9] The acc't spoke of much of their orderly conduct, and particularly of their frequent religious services, prayer meetings &c and of the strong religious feeling apparent among them. I heard a rumour the other day that Gen. Winder[10] who has been in charge of the Yankee prisoners has been removed for incompetency and brutality.

On acc't of frequent moves &c we had not had a service for a week until yesterday. I spent the morning looking up our wounded in Winchester, all of whom I found doing well, and in the evening we had a service and prayer meeting which I enjoyed very much after the long interval. Today it is raining steadily.

I received a letter from Charlie Dwight a few days ago which was over three weeks coming. He [is] somewhere in Western Virginia in Pierpont's dominions, and surrounded by deserters & tories who however do not molest him.[11] He is getting tired of the [sameness] and <u>safety</u> of his life. I believe I told you all about courtship which has been for some time past in suspense. He says he is going to renew and terminate it very soon. He [is] not hopeful of the result. It is sad to see [that] a man of his character, intelligence and solid attractions should be doomed to mortification failure and single unblessedness for a little physical defect. This I am convinced is the secret of it all. He does not speak much of his matrimonial prospects in his letter. It is not a pleasant subject. He says he has become used to disappointment and will be prepared for it. I have heard nothing of Dick since his transfer to the Medical Department.

I suppose you are still in Pendleton. I hope you will mention what you learn of Holmes' wedding. I have written to congratulate him on his happy transformation from a "dog" to a married man. I have written to Thos. Gadsden also on the subject of the chaplaincy of the 7th Cavalry. I am going to write to Col. Haskell and recommend him. Thos. wants some important qualifications of a chaplain but he will make up for these in the essentials of piety, faithfulness & courage. In these he is unsurpassed and they will effect much.

I must close now, Dearest. Much love to Sue and others. Remember me [to] Miss Mary and Carrie Pinckney.

Your aff. Husband
W. P. DuBose

1. Lt. Gen. Jubal Anderson Early (1816–94) of Virginia was made commander of the Second Corps of the Army of Northern Virginia after the departure of Lieutenant General Ewell. Early commanded Confederate forces during the Shenandoah Valley campaign of 1864. See Warner, *Generals in Gray,* 79–80.

2. Maj. Gen. Richard Heron Anderson (1821–79) of South Carolina was a division commander in the Army of Northern Virginia until he was temporarily promoted to lieutenant general on May 31, 1864, to command the First Corps after Lieutenant General Longstreet was wounded. His corps was part of Jubal Early's Confederate forces in the Shenandoah Valley campaign of 1864. See Warner, *Generals in Gray,* 8–9.

3. On September 4, 1864, Early's and Union major general Philip Sheridan's forces skirmished near Berryville, Virginia. See Long, *Civil War Almanac,* 566–67.

4. John Henninger Reagan (1818–1905), Confederate postmaster general, and Edmund Fontaine, president of the Virginia Central Railroad, clashed over the railroad and its delivery of Confederate mail. See *Correspondence.*

5. DuBose refers here to tents.

6. This was Brig. Gen. James Conner (1829–83) of Charleston, South Carolina. In a letter to his mother dated September 20, 1864, he writes of William Porcher DuBose, "I have a Chaplain, a Brigade Chaplain, Episcopalian at that, the Rev. Mr. DuBose . . . good parson they say. We do things up brown, have grace said regularly." See Moffett, *Letters of General James Conner*, 154.

7. Confederate forces evacuated Atlanta, Georgia, on September 1, 1864. See Long, *Civil War Almanac*, 564.

8. Philippians 3:13–14 (King James Version): "Forgetting those things which are behind, and reaching forth unto those things which are before, I press toward the mark for the prize of the high calling of God in Christ Jesus."

9. The prisoner-of-war camp at Andersonville, Georgia, was the most notorious camp of the Civil War. See McPherson, *Battle Cry of Freedom*, 796.

10. This was John Henry Winder (1800–1865) of Maryland. At this time he was in charge of prisons in Alabama and Georgia. In November 1864 he became the commissary general of all prisoners east of the Mississippi. William Porcher DuBose may be referring to accusations made against Winder by Col. Daniel T. Chandler, who submitted a report on the Andersonville prison. In his biography of General Winder, Arch Fredric Blakey states that Chandler accurately described the conditions at that place but that they were not created deliberately, as Chandler alleged. See Warner, *Generals in Gray*, 340–41; Blakey, *General John H. Winder*, 191.

11. Francis H. Pierpont (1814–99) was a unionist and the first governor of West Virginia, which was formed of the northwestern counties of Virginia that opposed secession. See Sifakis, *Who Was Who in the Civil War*, 164; McPherson, *Battle Cry of Freedom*, 298–99.

Winchester
Sept. 12 1864

My darling wife

For once I believe I have no change to report since my last letter. The weather has been cold & rainy and we are fortunate in having been allowed to remain quiet in camp with tolerable facilities for protecting ourselves— although I did hear a <u>Captain</u> exclaim this morning that it was "a hard thing to be a thousand miles from home with one blanket and no tent"; some of the men might have added "and no shoes." Yesterday (Sunday) opened with quite a storm but it closed off into a lovely morning, in time for me to go into Town and attend service, some of my brother chaplains remaining to preach for the brigade. I have hardly ever enjoyed more the privilege of <u>going to church</u>. The Winchester congregation is an old one and they have a fine church. Then the music is about the best I have heard for a long time and I did enjoy it very much. And finally I heard a very fine sermon from a man I have long been anxious to know. I don't know whether you have ever heard me speak of Randolph McKim.[1] He came to the U.V. just after I left and inherited many of my friends there, from whom I heard so much of him that I have long been anxious to know him. He is a very striking young man, physically, intellectually & religiously. He was at that time a Presbyterian, but preferring the Ep. Church, he left the army some time ago, studied for some months at Staunton & was then ordained & entered as a Chaplain. The minister of the church is also a U.V. man, Mr. Maury, and I waited after service to introduce myself to them, but they gave me the slip. I will make another opp'y, if I can.

I was on the point on Saturday evening to call on some young ladies whom I formerly met at the U.V. but was prevented by some little cause. And on Sunday morning an invitation was given to the funeral of their brother that afternoon. It is strange how hard it is for me to make up my mind to visit ladies, and yet it always does me good to see them even at a distance. The fact is, bashfulness (or modesty, or something) is increasing on me painfully. I have been trying hard to pay several visits in this town and have not succeeded yet; the people here are worth going to see.

We are still doing well in this country—get beef and flour enough, plenty of apples, & occasionally tomatoes, &c. The main difficulty is with our horses. They have nothing but hay & a little grazing which cannot last much longer. It will be impossible for them to live after winter sets in, and they are getting poor already. My old horse's disposition and temper are getting [ruined] by starvation. He was chiefly valuable for his amiability & docility, and now even William, his dearest friend, admits that he is getting to be a "mighty mean horse." If I let him go to graze, I cannot catch him when I wish to; if I take the bit out of his mouth for the same purpose, he shuts his teeth obstinately & refuses to take it again. The very expression of his face is becoming soured. However, to quote William again, "you cannot blame the old fellow, he is always hungry." This is a serious feature of our situation. We cannot stay here without horses, and horses cannot stay here without forage.

I believe I told you that Gen. Conner had joined us at last and assumed command of the brigade. His first evening was celebrated by quite a demonstration on the part of his new command. The men gave him a serenade, in the course of which Gen. Kershaw introduced the new brigadier to his brigade in a very appropriate little speech. Gen. Conner then followed in a telling & effective speech which rec'd with considerable enthusiasm. He has made a good impression & will no doubt give universal satisfaction. His aide is young Magrath,[2] just from the Citadel.

I have seen in the papers that Jno. Morgan[3] was betrayed into the hands of the Yankees by Mrs. Joseph Williams, the young lady whose only child I buried at Greenville last winter. She rode fifteen miles at night to give them notice that he was at her mother-in-law's house. The effect of his death has been swallowed up by the fall of Atlanta, but it will be a loss to us and a triumph to the Yankees. Half of old Mrs. Williams' family are true Southerners and half are traitors.

I received yesterday, my Darling, your last letter written just one week before Sunday 4th. My sympathy was much revived by it for poor Mrs. Stiles. I would have written to her long ago but I knew that she would expect me to say something of his religious character & hopes, of which I knew not one thing. I never met him except in company with others and had no opportunity of forming any judgment of him in this respect. I remember being struck several times by one thing to which you allude—his evident respect for men of consistent religious character. He several times spoke openly of pious men in terms which w'd have convinced me that he was a religious man himself. As you think I may do her some good by writing I will of course do so without delay. I will consult Col. Stiles' friends in the brigade & see if I can gather any further particulars. I am almost inclining to the opinion that it is a sad thing in these uncertain times for a young lady to marry one who is constantly exposed to death. And yet after all I believe that "it is better to have loved & lost than never to have loved at all." Thank you, my own precious wife, for the sweet assurances of your increasing love. May I prove worthy of it all and may we both show in our lives our gratitude for [the] loving manner in which God has dealt with us!

Love to Sue & all.

Your loving Husband
W. P. DuBose

1. Randolph Harrison McKim (1842–1920) of Baltimore, Maryland, served in the Army of Northern Virginia but left the service after the battle of Gettysburg. He returned to the Confederate army as a chaplain in 1864. In 1910 he published his diaries as *A Soldier's Recollections*.

2. This was probably First Lt. Andrew Gordon Magrath Jr. (1845–94), the son of South Carolina governor Andrew Magrath. See Index to Compiled Service Records Raised Directly by the Confederate Government and of Confederate Officers and Nonregimental Enlisted Men, M818, roll 15; Hewett, *South Carolina Confederate Soldiers*, 300; WPA Cemetery Index.

3. Brig. Gen. John Hunt Morgan (1825–64) was famous for his raids behind Union lines. He was killed in Greeneville, Tennessee, on September 4, 1864, as he attempted to evade capture. See Warner, *Generals in Gray,* 220–21.

Near Mt. Sidney
Oct. 3rd 1864

I hope, my Love, that you spent our engagement day under brighter skies than I did. It was hopelessly dismal with us—such a day as the Ettrick Shepherd[1] himself would have been forced to pronounce a <u>bad day</u>, if he had regarded it from my standpoint and not from the interior of a cheerful "snuggery." It was such a day that my mind refused to connect it with the sweet association which belonged to it, and the eventful moment had almost arrived (about 11 ¼ A.M., was it not?) before I remembered what an important anniversary it was. Even then my sluggish mind had to be prompted. And I am indebted to Gen. Kershaw for the suggestion which awakened the slumbering association. He rode up to me as I was splashing thro' the mud & rain, and asked me very innocently what the day suggested to me. I started into recollection & told him that it was much fuller of suggestion than he probably dreamed of—& then explained. He meant that the arrival of October suggested the approach of furloughs, which by the way was not a bad suggestion itself. But to describe the day; it was a cold rainy day, spent on the road, bad enough for us on horseback but desperate for those on foot. After a heavy march northwards, in the direction of Winchester, we halted in the afternoon and consoled the outer man by a rousing fire & the inner man with a fine dinner, worthy of better times. Yesterday we rejoiced in being allowed to rest, and it cleared off a beautiful Sunday. We had two services & a prayer meeting, the pleasantest we have had for a long time. I preached in the afternoon on the Vine & the branches, the necessity, nature, and marks of a living union with Jesus Xt.

Today we had orders to be ready to move at sunrise but we have not done so yet and it is now 10 or 11. The enemy are a few miles ahead of us, but only cavalry I believe. I suppose we will push as far North as we can to prevent Sheridan's sending off any portion of his force. William is better again; he had quite a severe little attack.

My last letter from you, my Darling, was that of the 19th Sept. two weeks ago, the longest interval that I have been without them for a long time. If I only had one this morning I could spend a delightful morning. The bands are playing all around us, and everything, except a letter, conspire to make it enjoyable. I see that the enemy have renewed operations on the North side of the James,[2] and I feel anxious again about Robert. I have heard nothing of him except from home since we left Richmond. Minnie the girls say spent the whole time with them very pleasant & agreeable. I would like very much to see Robert and herself together.

I had a long conversation yesterday with an old friend on peace subjects. He is the only young man I know who is going to make literature—writing—his profession; and I think he has the abilities & qualities to succeed at it. There is little prospect of his soon entering upon his chosen occupation, but it was refreshing amid all these "wars & rumours of wars"[3] to become interested with him on subjects so much more congenial to us both. You no doubt have heard me speak of V. Dabney[4]—he is on Gen. Gordon's staff.[5] We pictured to ourselves the pleasure of a general reunion in Richmond at the end of the war—Dudley, Strother, Blackford, V. Dabney, Leigh Robertson, Hutcheson, Minor, Chamberlayne, Johnson & myself and others. I would like to introduce you to some or all of them. A few of the best of them are gone, Haskell for instance. It gives me a great deal of pleasure to meet old friends and renew old times.

We have been living very well lately, but have several days breakfasted at sunrise and dined at 9 or 10 P.M. Once we dined after the interval on a cracker apiece. But we enjoyed pumpkins hugely next morning.

Much love to Sue, Miss Sarah and all of both families, and as much for yourself as you can accommodate.

Yrs with much love,

W. P. DuBose

1. Hogg, a Scottish poet of the romantic movement, was known as the "Ettrick Shepherd."

2. On September 29, 1864, the Union Tenth and Eighteenth Corps captured Fort Harrison, which was north of the James River, with the expectation of driving toward Richmond. See Long, *Civil War Almanac,* 575–76.

3. Matthew 24:6.

4. Capt. Virginius Dabney (1835–94) was an attorney and an author. In 1886 he published a popular novel, *The Story of Don Miff.* He was the son of Thomas Smith Gregory Dabney (1798–1885), a Virginia planter whose life was recorded by his daughter Susan Dabney Smedes in *A Southern Planter.* See Index to Compiled Service Records Raised Directly by the Confederate Government and of Confederate Officers and Nonregimental Enlisted Men, M818, roll 7.

5. Maj. Gen. John Brown Gordon (1832–1904) of Georgia was a division and, later, corps commander in the Army of Northern Virginia. See Warner, *Generals in Gray*, 111.

New Market Va.
Oct. 8th 1864

As I expected, my Darling, we resumed the march yesterday morning and made twenty miles to this place, where we have the promise of a few days rest. Yesterday was a lovely day, such a day as the 1st of October ought to have been, if anything in nature <u>ought to be</u>, which is not. We got up for a sunrise start but did not get off until an hour or two later, an interval which I spent in the enjoyment of the most exquisite scenery, and in reading, to which the situation lent an inexpressible charm. How much our physical condition and external circumstances do sometimes influence the mind and the spirit when we open ourselves to them! Some of these late days have been indescribably sweet to me. I have seemed to myself to <u>live</u> more than at other times. The weather has been so delightful, the scenery so lovely & spiritual things so sweet to me. The mts up here are clothed in their Autumn hues, the brightest & most variegated colours. As the sun rises over the Blue Ridge it illuminates the Alleghanies [*sic*], and as it sets over the Alleghenies it lightens up the Blue Ridge. And then all day long the shadows sailing over the mt sides is a sight that never loses its beauty. The Valley itself is a picture of desolation. The enemy as they retired destroyed everything, sometimes even dwelling houses. We can trace their course in the distance by the huge smokes. I do not know how the inhabitants themselves can live, much less subsist an army. Therefore I do not think we can remain here very long and besides this there has been a rumour that the enemy themselves are about to cross the mts and move towards Lynchburg by another route, by Orange & Gordonsville, which would necessitate a corresponding movement on our part. This is probably only a rumour.

My hopes & spirits have recovered their normal state, and things to me look cheerful & promising. The effects of the Valley disaster are disappearing rapidly—things are looking up decidedly in Ga, and Price[1] seems to be getting on swimmingly in Missouri. I cannot help feeling anxious about Richmond on acc't of the fearful disparity of numbers, but I have a strong faith in the safety of that much tried city. Gen. Lee will do all that can be done with the means in his possession and if he can only hold out until active work ceases elsewhere, we can reinforce him sufficiently to secure the safety of the place during the winter. With regard to the condition of things at the North, after McClellan's[2] letter of acceptance I began to think his election would probably be less desirable than that of Lincoln. There is no doubt that he is sincerely & honestly for the Union at all hazards, by war if by no other means. We have nothing therefore to hope from him; he is no more our friend than Lincoln is. But if there is nothing to hope from him, there is something to hope from his party which may control him when it gets into power. And the change <u>cannot</u> hurt us; it may benefit us, therefore I am for McClellan. I think Lincoln will be elected, but it is by no means certain. In the meantime, it is pleasant to see that the English papers regard our success as a foregone conclusion, ever since they have learned the fall of Atlanta. They say that if the Yankees attempt to secure reunion by negotiation and pacific means, no doubt "negotiation will fail as force <u>has</u> failed." The impressions of a third, & disinterested, party deserve attention. We who are so near and so interested cannot judge correctly. Therefore I think on the whole, things look brighter, & I, who try to be bright under all circumstances, am brighter in consequence. So my immediate circumstances, natural & spiritual, and political circumstances conspire to make me feel bright. And there is another circumstance which plays an important part in the conspiracy, which is the continually approaching prospect of seeing you once more my love. Christmas is rapidly approaching and we will certainly meet, if it be God's will before it comes. November or December will carry me to you without fail, I trust. Does Sue have any holiday about that time? I wish she could be at leisure while I am at home.

I am now reading "Heroes & Hero Worship" by Thos. Carlyle & am deeply interested in it. It is an awakening & stimulating book & has roused me considerably. You ask about my daily life. I have no such thing under existing circumstances. Everyday has its own routine. We breakfast at daylight when we are going to march, otherwise at 7½ or 8 o.c. on beef, biscuits & pumpkin—all nice & nicely cooked—occasionally extras in the shape of butter, apple butter, cabbage &c. After breakfast I walk & spend where practicable several hours in such solitude as I can secure. This is my most precious time, & I thank God that it becomes daily more precious to me. Then I return to camp & read or write until dinner, which is the same as breakfast. All the afternoon, sometimes till long after dark, I devote to service, prayer meetings &c. When we march, I read as well as I can in the rests. In all the odd moments & very many of the serious ones I think of you, my darling wife.

The [soap] cakes will be very welcome when they come which will no doubt be after a while. I am sorry to hear that Miss Sarah thinks there is no chance for Thos. Gadsden. I have no doubt that he loves her earnestly, but I cannot blame her for refusing him if his attentions have impressed her & others as they seem to have done. I believe in a blind, transfiguring sort of love, after you have <u>selected</u> with judgment, just short of Marius & Cosette's.[3]

I am very glad to hear of Miss Margaret Blake's change of life. If you should write to her be sure to give her my congratulations. I had seen the refutation of the story of Jno. Morgan's death in the papers before you wrote, substantially as you gave it.

I am very sorry to hear that the Y. Fever is so bad in Charleston & am truly sorry for the Gadsdens.[4]

Goodbye now my Love. Love to Miss Sue, Miss Sarah & all. Tell Margie I would like to be one of the listeners at her Shakespearian readings.

Yr loving Husband

W. P. DuBose

1. In September 1864 Confederate major general Sterling Price (1809–67) led a twelve-thousand-man force in an invasion of Missouri. Price suffered a series of defeats in October, which forced him to retreat from the state. See McPherson, *Battle Cry of Freedom*, 787–88; Warner, *Generals in Gray*, 246–47.

2. Union major general George B. McClellan (1826–85) was the Democratic candidate in the 1864 presidential election. See Warner, *Generals in Blue*, 290–92.

3. These young lovers were two principal characters in Victor Hugo's *Les Misérables*.

4. On October 8, 1864, an obituary appeared in the *Charleston Mercury* for Mary, the wife of the Reverend Christopher P. Gadsden of St. Paul's Episcopal Church, who died on October 5, 1864.

Woodstock, Va

Oct. 12th 1864

My darling wife,

Yesterday when I should have been writing to you, I was spending the day with some friends in one of Early's divisions. Today we unexpectedly resumed our march and tonight just before going to bed I am lying flat on my face making up for past delinquencies. I think my last letter was written on last Saturday. On Sunday we had quite an exciting time. Our Cavalry elated with the success which they had gained a day or two before pressed on about twenty miles ahead of us & on Sunday afternoon we were hurried out to save them from demolition. The whole Yankee force had turned on them, taken most of their artillery & wagons & sent them flying back.[1] The Yankees did not follow far & we did not become engaged.

I had service on Sunday morning but we are beginning in this as in other respects to feel the effects of the cold weather. Men as thinly clad as ours will not leave their fires. I expect now to rely mainly upon little services around the camp fires at night. We had ice on Monday morning.

I spent yesterday with Randolph Hutchinson[2] and Lewis Randolph,[3] of Gen. Rode's,[4] now Gen. Ramseur's[5] staff. These have both been confirmed within a year. They were not at all religious when I knew them & I am delighted to find them truly changed men. Hutcheson [sic] was to have been married about the time the war broke out to a young lady in St. Louis where he was living. He has never seen her since and only occasionally hears from her—nearly four years!

You have no doubt heard of Gen. Bratton's wound.[6] It is reported "serious" in the papers, but I am relieved to hear from an officer just from Richmond that Mr. McMaster had told him it was not dangerous. My friend Col. Haskell is reported "severely" wounded, which makes me anxious to hear from Robert, who is in his regt.[7] May God spare Gen. B. & himself to the girls!

We are now thirty miles from Winchester and are to resume our march at daylight. Our men are in good condition & fine spirits, but our force is very far inferior to that of the enemy.

I must close now my Darling. I hate to send you such a scrawl but I am writing under many difficulties & I ought to be looking for daylight. Love to all.

Yr loving Husband

W. P. DuBose

1. On October 9, 1864, Union cavalry in the Shenandoah Valley routed Confederate cavalry at the battle of Tom's Brook. See Long, *Civil War Almanac,* 581.

2. This was Col. Robert Randolph Hutchinson (1837–1910) of Virginia. See Index to Compiled Service Records Raised Directly by the Confederate Government and of Confederate Officers and Nonregimental Enlisted Men, M818, roll 20; *Confederate Military History,* 12:325–26; Bratton, *Apostle of Reality,* 33; Crute, *Confederate Staff Officers,* 167–68.

3. Capt. Meriwether Lewis Randolph of Virginia was a descendant of Thomas Jefferson. See Index to Compiled Service Records Raised Directly by the Confederate Government and of Confederate Officers and Nonregimental Enlisted Men,

M818, roll 12; Page, *Genealogy of the Page Family,* 243; Crute, *Confederate Staff Officers,* 167–68.

4. Maj. Gen. Robert Emmett Rodes (1829–64) of Virginia was a Confederate division commander. He was mortally wounded on September 19, 1864, while leading a counterattack at the third battle of Winchester. See Warner, *Generals in Gray,* 263.

5. Maj. Gen. Stephen Dodson Ramseur (1837–64) of North Carolina was a Confederate division commander. He was mortally wounded at the battle of Cedar Creek on October 19, 1864, and died the following day. See Warner, *Generals in Gray,* 251–52.

6. Brig. Gen. John Bratton (1831–98) commanded Jenkins' brigade after Jenkins's death. He was wounded in the shoulder on October 7, 1864, at the battle of Darby-town Road. See Warner, *Generals in Gray,* 33–34.

7. On October 7, 1864, at the battle of Darbytown Road, Colonel Haskell was shot through the eye, with the bullet exiting behind his ear. He survived the wound. See Daly, *Alexander Cheves Haskell,* 151–54.

Near Strasburg
Oct. 15th 1864

I wrote you a pencil note on Tuesday night, my Darling, from near Mt. Jackson. My time since this has been spent rather sadly. On Wednesday we reached the place and found the entire Yankee force in position a few miles beyond the town. Gen. Early immediately put a few pieces of artillery into position and opened fire upon them. An attempt on the part of the Yankees to capture these pieces brought on a partial engagement in which our brigade alone was actually engaged. Gen. Conner made a very handsome little fight, killing and wounding a large number of the enemy, and taking one hundred prisoners.[1] Our loss was about one hundred & thirty. Gen. Conner had his knee shattered by a piece of shell necessitating amputation. The shock was terrible to his system, as is always the case with shell wounds, and he was so prostrated after the operation that the Dr. was afraid he would not rally. He did so, however, and is now getting on admirably. The leg which he has lost had never recovered from a wound received at the Battle of Seven Pines, so it was no very great loss to him. The loss of Gen. Conner to the brigade is an irreparable one. I consider him the best officer I have ever known & he was getting the brigade into splendid condition. I think he expects to return on a wooden leg.

My friend Col. Rutherford was mortally wounded in the centre of the body. We got the Genl. and himself into adjoining rooms in a house where he died yesterday at 1 o.c. P.M. after about twenty hours of torture. I was with him all the time and have never had my heart more wrung by the sight of suffering. He had been trying for some weeks or months to prepare for death, but could not feel that he was accepted & his sins forgiven. As his end drew nearer & nearer he seemed to trust more & more in God's mercy and at the last he told me he was willing to go. But his efforts to be patient under his great suffering were most touching. He felt that it was God's hand laid upon him and never once rebelled. He kept praying "if it be possible let this cup pass away from me," and when I asked him if he could finish the prayer he said "Yes, but not my will but thine be done."

The whole scene was the most heartrending and affecting that I have ever witnessed. There is another poor young widow added to the number made by this terrible war. He married a very sweet girl after the war commenced and has one little daughter. She is a cousin of the Bryces. I had to be so constantly with Col. Rutherford that I saw very little of the other wounded, most of whom were sent off yesterday morning early. Our friends are all safe.

After the battle our forces occupied the line of "Fisher's Hill"—the point from which Early was so summarily ejected after the battle of Winchester.[2] There has been skirmishing but no fighting of any consequence since Tuesday. The two armies confront each other and fighting may begin at any time.

Major Goggin,[3] Asst. Adjt. Genl. of the division has been assigned to the temporary command of the brigade & is now with us. He is a first rate man and a good officer.

I have heard nothing further of Gen. Bratton & nothing at all of Robert, about whom I cannot help feeling uneasy. I look every day for "Lists of Casualties" in the papers but have seen none yet.

I received yesterday a long letter from Sister Anne written on the 7th more than a week later than my last from you. The time is not very long before I hope you will be with the girls. I know you do Sister Anne good, and she looks forward with great pleasure to your visit, as indeed they all do. You will probably see Gen. Bratton, as I suppose he will be carried home as soon as he can be moved. And, my Darling, I hope you will not have to wait very long there for me. As the time approaches I long more and more to be with you. It is an ever increasing trial, my Love, to be so much away from you. Letters are an inexpressible comfort to me, but after all there can be very little real interchange of sympathy when letters take so long to pass between us, that is, except in the great unchanging subjects of sympathy such as our mutual love and our common faith and hopes & trials and joys. All smaller things pass away before we can receive the sympathy which is so sweet to us. However I ought to make no complaints against the letters which do more to supply yr [*sic*] place than anything else can. I feel today the effects of my watching night before last. This morning my hour in the woods was inexpressibly sweet and comforting to me. I wonder how I ever tried to live without these moments of solitude, which I now find so necessary to my spiritual life.

I must close now my own Darling. Much love to Sue and all the family. May God bless & keep you!

Yr loving Husband
W. P. DuBose

1. On October 13 and 14, 1864, skirmishing took place along Cedar Creek and near Hupp's Hill. See Long, *Civil War Almanac,* 583.

2. On September 19, 1864, Union major general Philip Sheridan's superior forces defeated Confederate lieutenant general Jubal Early's Army of the Valley at the third battle of Winchester. On September 22, 1864, Sheridan's troops routed Early's men from their defenses along Fisher's Hill. See Long, *Civil War Almanac,* 571, 573.

3. Maj. James Monroe Goggin (1820–89), a native of Virginia, commanded Conner's, formerly Kershaw's, Brigade at the battle of Cedar Creek. See Sifakis, *Who Was Who in the Civil War,* 252.

Fisher's Hill
Oct 18th 1864

Just after my last letter had been sealed and dispatched, my Darling, on last Friday or Saturday, two of yours were handed me, of the 1st & 6th, the first written on our engagement day. According to the ancient custom that day ought to have been written with chalk but in our separation I believe I prefer ink. May the day never come, my own precious wife, when its annual return will fail to fill me with gratitude and happiness. Your love is one blessing for which I think I have never neglected to be thankful, and the trials to which we have been subjected have only made me value & prize it all the more. It does seem strange to me that our love is only three years old, even dating it from Oct 1861. In <u>fact</u>, I think <u>mine</u> is nearly, if not quite, a year older than that. I cannot speak for yours, nor do I think you can either, exactly. One of these days I will make you tell me approximately when it did begin. I do not mean to submit to having loved a whole year without any return. If you insist upon it, you will have to love harder to make us even. Your "passing thoughts," Dearest, are never "foolish" or idle to me, particularly when they relate to me, and I like your letters best when they sometimes seem emptiest to you. The assurances & expressions of love when they are the most playfully uttered, & seem lightest, are the evidences of what is to me, next to God's love, the highest & most precious reality. I do not know but that this separation so painful and trying has had the effect upon me of elevating & spiritualizing my love, not only for you, but for my sisters & others. Human affection seems to me a more sacred and holy thing than it used to, and while I believe I have acquired a larger capacity for loving myself, I learn to look with more interest upon the love of others. One thing is true, that the love of God strengthens & sanctifies every other kind of love.

Gen. Conner became a good deal worse on Saturday and I spent that night with him, fearing that he might at any moment begin to sink; but he was better on Sunday and this morning was well enough to start off in an ambulance for Staunton. We made a daylight start yesterday morning and thought we were off towards Winchester, but after going a mile or two, we returned to our old position where we are still at rest. It was only a reconnaissance in force, I suppose. It is impossible for us to remain here much longer. We have to draw our supplies from Staunton and the supply of forage is about out. Luckily I got old John right fat while it was more abundant. I discovered the other day that John is a remarkable trotter. He could make a buggy spin and I am very anxious for an oppt'y of getting him in one with you in it. If I could get him home while I am there, which I may do, I hope we will have a trial of his accomplishments in that line. William is quite well; he sends his love to Sally & says he hopes she will continue to behave well. I suppose she will enjoy your visit to Winnsboro. Tell her howdy for me too. I think William is pleased with the idea of your having her. We are enjoying beautiful weather and the mts look glorious in their Fall dress.

Our services are pretty regularly kept up. Instead of regular services in the afternoon in the week we have begun to have less formal meetings around the camp fires in the separate regiments at night. The prayer meetings keep up pretty well in numbers and interest and even a few days rest and regularity produce an evident improvement. The hardest thing to secure is a regular attendance of the higher officers at these regimental and brigade services. I have been long intending to commence, in addition to the regular brigade services, holding on Sunday mornings at Brigade Hd. Qrs. a regular Episcopal service. This would secure the attendance of many who seldom attend now. It would give to many in & out of the brigade the privilege of a full service, and it would be a pleasure to me, but I have not succeeded in carrying it out yet for several reasons, one of which is that we are seldom quiet on Sundays. In the brigade services, all I can do in the way of using the liturgy is to use some of the prayers from memory. And most Episcopalians will not attend non-Episcopal services. I at least cannot blame them for this because I have only lately myself been able to do so with profit, and I long for an opp'y of using the regular service.

I am sorry to hear that you find the [German] so tough. You must encourage me by your success to undertake it when I have an opp'y. I am afraid though that I can no longer hope to learn either that or Hebrew, two objects of my ambition.

Give much love to Sue, Miss Sarah and all the family. Also to Clelia & all at Auntie's. And remember me to all friends. I was much disappointed to hear the decision in Thos' case. I had not written to Col. Haskell. I thought the thing was secure. Good bye now my Love.

Yr loving Husband
W. P. DuBose

New Market
Oct 31st 1864

Our life is becoming so uneventful, my Darling, that I begin to be thrown back more than usual upon my internal resources for materials for my letters. There certainly ought to be no lack of these there, when I have inexhaustible stores of love, material sympathies & common interests, joys & hopes to draw on. But one who usually has battles or at least marches to begin his letters with, feels somewhat empty when he takes up his pen to write. There is something wanting to <u>open</u> the fountain & start the flow of thought & sentiment. I write from the same spot from which my last letter was sent. We have subsided into an unbroken calm, with only drums, drills and dinner to interrupt the monotony of the day. When military operations cease, religious operations have an opp'y to revive, and it is so with us. The religious interest which at times seemed to have died out, has revived very perceptibly. Our daily prayer meetings and services are well attended under the most unfavorable circumstances & there are increasing numbers of individual instances of deep interest. We have built a "rail" church, composed of seats, [fire] stand & book stand, with William for sexton. We have brigade services again at dark, and they are the most interesting we have ever had. The weather is quite cold at times, but the men turn out with blankets around them.

Col. Kennedy of Camden has returned & assumes the command of the brigade today. He is a very intelligent & pleasant gentleman but I wish it were possible to retain a commander permanently without such frequent changes.

Two of your letters have reached me, my darling, since I last wrote, 21st & 24th. I always find them awaiting me on my return from service at night and they furnish a sweet termination to the by no means arduous labours of the day. I begin to regard each of them as a sweet foretaste of the joys in store for me at our approaching meeting, a prospect which ever brightens as it approaches. I strive, my Love, as that time draws near, to purify and elevate my affections & to become more worthy of the enjoyment which God provides us in his providence. I have a constant feeling that a low view of God's blessings will bring disappointment. Blessings as well as trials need preparation of spirit. The fact is that since that unfortunate reverse of the 19th[1] I have been laboring harder to make my life & ministry what they ought to be. I hope, Dearest, that God will enable us to help each other in our spiritual life and approaches unto Him, make us helpmeets to each other. When we are together I need more strengthening than you do, and you can give it to me.

I am glad that Sue has promised to spend her short holiday with us. It is sufficient inducement for me to delay my furlough until that time. I will probably apply for it from about the 5th Dec. I wrote to her a day or two ago & expressed the hope that she w'd do just what she has promised to do. I am sorry to hear of the troubles in Charleston & that the Yellow Fever has invaded your sister's family. I hope it will not prove serious. The direction which you admire so much is Capt. Holmes'. He does write a very pretty hand.

I suppose that this letter will almost certainly find you at Winnsboro. I think you were right to wait for the Bp's visit. I would not like to have missed such a pleasure if it had been in my power to enjoy it. I am very glad to hear of Anna Parker's coming forward, & giving such evidence of a serious change of heart.

I am reading now M'Cosh's "Divine Government,"[2] a book which I have long been wishing to read. It is quite long and will occupy me until I get home, I suppose, even if my opp'y for reading continues as good as it is. I read with a good deal of relish but have not Sue's happy faculty of turning to acc't the odds & ends of time.

The late fight enriched me to the extent of a pr [*sic*] of shoes. At least it gave me an opp'y of buying a nice captured pair, just when I was getting to be in serious need. [It] also supplied the army with portable tent flies for the winter, although it w'd certainly have been better for us if they had not stopped to take them.

I must close now my Love. Much love to all the household & tell Sister A. if she has not sent my things by the [Association] she need not do so.

Your loving Husband
W. P. DuBose

[An undated, damaged letter was folded with a letter of October 31, 1864; the legible portion follows.]

I do feel deeply for that family in their many trials. I must draw to a close now, my Love. I find and said in my last letter that I cannot even write to you in this period of suspense . . . as I have never done before, how precious you are to me, my own dear wife. Much love to the girls. Your devoted Husband, W. P. D.

1. The battle of Cedar Creek took place on October 19, 1864. Confederate lieutenant general Jubal Early's Army of the Valley surprised Union forces with a dawn attack that routed them and sent them into a four-mile retreat. Instead of pursuing their foes, the Confederates stopped to pillage the Union camp. That afternoon Union major general Philip H. Sheridan led a determined counterattack, which forced the Confederates to retreat. See McPherson, *Battle Cry of Freedom*, 779–80.

2. DuBose refers here to *Method of the Divine Government: Physical and Moral* by the Scottish philosopher James McCosh (1811–94). See Borchert, *Encyclopedia of Philosophy*, 6:70–71.

Blue House
Feb. 5th 1865

We were so unfavorably situated for writing, my Darling, at Salkehatchie that I had determined to make up in frequency for the character of my letters;

but my good resolutions were frustrated by very unexpected circumstances. On Friday night just as we were on the point of retiring at 11 o.c. we were startled by a dispatch from Genl. McLaws[1] stating that the enemy had crossed Broxton's Bridge, & that we must fall back from the line of the Salkehatchie. We did not get off however before daylight, but we did not sleep a wink the whole night. We marched yesterday to this point & are to take the cars tomorrow for the Edisto River which I suppose to be our new line. Today (Sunday) we have been visiting & I have held my first services. It has been a charming day, after the incessant rains which had prevailed for several days. I wish I had been able to write during the day. Tonight you may imagine me writing in a perfect hubbub of business &c, in a single room used for all purposes. Possibly communication with you may be interrupted at Branchville even before this letter reaches you. Sherman must be very near Branchville by this time & I am afraid there can be but little doubt of his taking the place. Your letter of the 31st was such a sweet comfort to me that it is hard to think of being deprived again even temporarily of such a source of strength & happiness, particularly in these times when we need all that we can get of both commodities. I am afraid my Darling that my letters will fail very far of expressing half how much I miss you or how sweet your letters are to me; & I long for a quiet opp'y of pouring out my heart to you. In the meantime, I know you can well supply all that I fail to say. You would appreciate the difficulties under which I write if you could only look in upon me at this time.

I was getting settled at Salkehatchie before we left & had finished the 3rd vol. of Joseph II & was beginning Ansted's view of the Creation.[2] I am afraid we are destined not to remain stationary for any length of time & that I will do very little at reading. I can imagine you all, reading together at night & would give very much to spend at least that portion of the day with you. Capt. Holmes has gone off for a few days to Charleston & Florence, where his wife is. William & John arrived safely & in good condition on Thursday, or Friday I believe, just in time for our march on Saturday which was a terribly hard one on the men, most of it being through mud & water. If Wm. had not arrived until Saturday, which I thought very probable, he w'd have found us gone & might have been captured.

We are ordered, I just learn, to Raysor's Ferry on the Edisto, not very far below Branchville. So we will take the S.C.R.R. in Charleston.

You may tell the girls that it is not thought down here at all probable that Sherman will take their route for Va, even if he sh'd be perfectly successful down here. Gen. Johnson [*sic*] says that Sh. w'd not have the temerity to make such an attempt.[3] It is generally thought he will try the Wilmington route. So they may not quit, no matter how things go here, at least until Columbia falls or is seriously threatened.

I wonder my Darling when you are to go to Anderson. I know how different your home there must be since your Mother's death & I love to think that I can in some measure supply her place to you. There are still two at least who are dependent upon your love & care. The little watch is a great comfort to me & I am very precious of it. I regard it as a representation of you, & it is quite a companion to me.

I must close now, my Love. Give much love to the girls, & kiss all the children for me. I have had the mumps & was consequently not a subject for it. I hope the children will get well through with it. Much love to Sue & others in Anderson.

Your ever loving Husband
W. P. DuBose

1. Maj. Gen. Lafayette McLaws (1821–97) of Georgia commanded a division in the Army of Northern Virginia's First Corps until Lieutenant General Longstreet relieved him of command. He later served under Johnston in the Carolinas campaign. See Warner, *Generals in Gray,* 204–5.

2. The British geologist David Thomas Ansted (1814–80) was the author of *The Ancient World: or, Picturesque Sketches of Creation,* published in 1848. See University of Cambridge, *Alumni Cantabrigienses,* 1(2):61.

3. Confederate general Joseph Eggleston Johnston (1807–91) attempted to check Maj. Gen. William T. Sherman's march north in 1865. See Wakelyn, *Biographical Dictionary of the Confederacy,* 259–60.

George's Station
Febr. 8th 1865

Today finds me still, my Darling, on the spot from which I wrote yesterday, & in the same state of uncertainty. Half of the brigade is in Charleston & half at Raysor's Bridge & our wagon train with William & my bags & baggage somewhere on the road between Salkehatchie & this place. The road between here & Raysor's Bridge is in places waist deep in water & so I am reduced to the necessity of waiting here for transportation of some sort. Meanwhile I am quite comfortable, except that I am much in need of a change of clothing.

I am also enjoying more quiet and privacy than are usually vouchsafed to me, to which you are indebted for this second letter in two days. I am seated now by myself in a large pleasant room by a good fire & with little prospect of interruption before dinner time. If I had only received a letter from you this morning, which however I had no right to & did not, expect, my satisfaction would be complete. This would be a nice place for us to keep house if we were only permanently established in the neighborhood. I could easily ride out to the brigade & back everyday but the situation does not admit of any such dreams of happiness. It is remarkable how completely we are in ignorance of what is going on even at Branchville only twelve miles off, but I fear we are offering very inadequate resistance to Sherman's progress.

And so the Peace Commission has ended in nothing.[1] Nothing remains for us but to prepare & brace ourselves for the patient endurance of trials & sufferings of which God only knows the extent or the issue. May His grace be found sufficient for us in every time of need! It is a hard struggle for me to submit my will to His in this matter, but I trust that He will give me strength to stand even this bitter test. I feel now how far I have unconsciously been borne away from God, & how much I love my own will.

The weather has cleared off beautifully once more & it would be a sweet day but for the wind which makes it chilly. Unfortunately I have none of my books with me & I feel I am losing precious time. I have been thinking since I left home how pleasant it would be to extend our reading on all the subjects in which Joseph II has interested us. Contemporary histories of the courts of France, Prussia & Russia read just now would impress upon us quite vividly the history of that interesting period.

It is sad to feel my mind becoming deteriorated and wasted by the want of cultivation & discipline. The only consolation is that if these times are unfavorable to the training of the mind, they are as certainly favorable to the strengthening & discipline of the character & the soul. He who is not overwhelmed & destroyed by such circumstances as these must certainly be strengthened & purified. May we who do lean only upon the hope of His Heavenly Grace, be ever more defended by His mighty power!

My companions here are [Dunlap] & Radcliffe. The former is about to be transferred to the cavalry & the latter is to take his place as clerk at Hd.Qrs. During these moves my basket has come in remarkably well. All that remains of it now is one ball of butter & a little syrup. I tasted the other day some home-made syrup made of the regular sugar cane which I admit was better than sorghum can be made, far better than the old molasses.

I have seen or heard nothing of John Johnson nor of any of my friends on the coast. The former is I believe somewhere about Branchville & of course very busy. I must close now my Love, with much love to the girls & a kiss for the children. Give my love also to Cousin Ellen & tell her I hope to hear of her being established in Winnsboro. Remember me also to Miss Kate. May God bless & strengthen you all.

Yr. affectionate Husband

W. P. DuBose

1. The Hampton Roads Conference occurred on February 3, 1865, aboard the *River Queen* off Fort Monroe, Virginia. Abraham Lincoln and his secretary of state, William H. Seward, met with Confederate vice president Alexander H. Stephens, John A. Campbell, and R. M. T. Hunter to discuss the possibility of peace. Lincoln and Seward demanded the unconditional restoration of the Union, which Stephens and the Confederate delegation could not accept. See Long, *Civil War Almanac,* 633.

Cheraw Mar. 2nd

My darling wife

We have just heard a report which we can scarcely doubt that our house in Wbo [Winnsboro] has been burned. Nevertheless I do doubt it; I cannot conceive of their turning out so many women & children to burn the house. I write this [note] by Bosey not knowing whether he will succeed in reaching W'bo, or whether if he does so, he will find you there. You may imagine my anxiety to get home & I have been sorely tempted to make an effort to accompany him, but I would do no more than <u>he</u> will do, & it w'd cut me off indefinitely from my command. I long to know something from or of you. I leave Bosey to tell you all about me as it is impossible to write.

I hope you are not disheartened by . . . events. The spirit of the army is more hopeful than it has been for a long time. And as for you & all who are so dear to me at home, I am willing still to trust you to God, assured that as your day so will your strength be.

. Send me little notes by every possible opp'y, & some of them may reach me. This is my third note to you since I arrived here. The other two were sent to Camden.

Your devoted Husband

W. P. DuBose

N. Carolina Richmond Co.
11 P.M. March 6th 1864 [1865]

My darling wife

Bosie after giving up his original design of going to W'bo, went off afterwards suddenly & without my knowledge with Major Barker, who was wounded at Cheraw. Capt. Parker had a narrow escape at the same time, but escaped with the loss of his horse. We evacuated Cheraw Friday morning intending to burn the bridge behind us, but the enemy pressed so closely that the latter would probably not have been accomplished but for Capt. Parker who having been detained to the last moment in town gathered a few men & defended the bridge until it had time to ignite. He had his horse killed but escaped unhurt. He had however most of his horses & 35 men cut off on the way to Cheraw, & probably captured, among them Tom Stoney[1] & Bruce & Jim Davis.[2]

I saw today for the first time your brother. He is in the Engineer Corps, under Johnson & pleasantly situated, but, he says, rather unprepared for a campaign in the way of clothes, blankets &c. I hope to see a good deal of him. I see all my & your relatives quite frequently. They are all well. We expect soon to form a [junction] with Johnson from Charlotte & do something. I fear there can be no doubt of our house being burned, but I hope that you were not there. I will say nothing of it however until I have heard definitely.

I have just stopped to eat dinner & it is now nearly 12—time to be getting ready for tomorrow's march. We marched last night until 10 O.C. took dinner near midnight, got to bed at 2 A.M., got up at 10 A.M., breakfasted at 11 & marched at 12. And with all this irregularity my health was never better.

Your brother left a note & book from Sue to me at Dr. DeSaussure's, which I am sorry I did not get. Much love to her. I hope you are both comfortably at Auntie's.

I must close now my Darling. How much I w'd give for a letter from you tonight. May God be ever with you!

Yr aff. Husband
W. P. DuBose

1. This was Pvt. Thomas P. Stoney, Captain Parker's Company. See Compiled Service Records, Captain Parker's Company, South Carolina Light Artillery (Marion Artillery), M267, roll 104.

2. These were Pvts. F. Bruce Davis and Jim T. Davis. See Compiled Service Records, Captain Parker's Company, South Carolina Light Artillery (Marion Artillery), M267, roll 103.

10 miles from Smithfield
March 17th 1865

I cannot describe, my Darling, the joy with which I [hailed] this morning your letter of the 22nd & 25th Feb. It was the first word that I have heard from W'bo since your letter of the 12th Feb, rec'd before we left Ch'ston, & the first contradiction to the report, which reached me from so many sources that I could not doubt it—that our house had been burned. I had persuaded myself too that you must have gone to Anderson. Your acc't of things was a great relief to us, Robert & myself, quite as much to William. I feel grateful for your remarkable exemption from injury & insult & shall, I trust, feel hereafter more than ever willing to leave those who are dear to me to the keeping of God. I never allowed it to trouble me much, feeling that you were all capable of enduring bravely anything which was likely to occur.

We had yesterday quite a serious engagement with the enemy, of which you will have seen an account before my letter reaches you.[1] Rhett's brigade rec'd the brunt of it. It fought well & suffered heavily, particularly in officers.[2] Press & Porcher Smith[3] are both severely but I hope not dangerously wounded. Willie Martin[4] was shot in the side, not dangerously. The enemy failed in all direct attacks but succeeded in flanking us out of two advanced lines. The third line they made no impression on & that night we resumed our march. Robert was not in the fight. His leg incapacitated him from walking & he was at our wagons unconscious of what was going on until it was almost over. His Capt. & the Lt. of the Co. were respectively wounded & killed, Julius Rhett & [Henry] Stuart.[5] [Capt.] Bacot[6] was wounded, I have not heard how.

21st. I have to tell of more severe fighting, my Darling & am sorry to have to mention Robt. among the wounded and Allie Gaillard wounded & a prisoner.[7] Robt. was struck in the chest by a piece of shell & terribly shocked. He was carried to the wrong hospital & I did not find him until the next morning, when he was so much prostrated that I was for a long time fearful that he could not rally from the shock. He was wounded on Sunday & all day Monday (yesterday) he had scarcely any perceptible pulse. Then he was brought ten or twelve miles in a wagon over the worst road I ever saw. But for the stimulant which I procured him & Wm's attention & care on the way, I do not believe he w'd have survived the journey. I stopped here at this pt. four miles short of Smithfield; got a tent & bed from our Qr. Mr. and have made him tolerably comfortable. This morning he has at last reacted; his pulse is very good & I hope there is no more cause for anxiety. Wm. will stick to him & if possible get him home & I will keep his boy. He is fortunate in having Wm. I have not succeeded in learning anything about [Allie] except the bare fact which I have stated. I will write all the circumstances as soon as I can investigate them. John Minott[8] is severely but I believe not dangerously wounded in the thigh or hip. Bosey Eggleston was slightly wounded in the chest on Sunday evening & returned to his post the next morning. I did not see him but was told so. I neglected to mention [M.] Horlbeck,[9] shot in the eye in the first fight. His brother did not consider the wound mortal.

All of Johnson's [sic] forces have concentrated here. Sunday's battle resulted in our favour, but was not decisive. Yesterday nothing much was done up to the time I left & today I am too far off to know what is going on. Our brigade has lost but five so far. May God grant us the victory in this crisis of our affairs! The troops are doing well & are cheerful & hopeful. They are much encouraged by their success thus far. As I write the cannonading has become quite brisk & I expect that fighting has been resumed. Since I began my letter, I have received the long one you sent by Gen. Boggs.[10] He gave it to one of our surgeons who brought it safe & directed it to me. You have no idea how you have relieved me by writing so promptly & fully.

So far I know I am the only member of the brigade who has heard directly from S.C. since the passage of the enemy. I was too distressed to learn of the loss of Sister Jane's rings. May the grace of God console her in all her trials. The heartlessness & vandalism of those wretches surpasses all my expectations. I hear that in Camden Mr. Trapier's house fared worse than any other—completely stripped and plundered.[11] Fairfield seems however to have fared worse than any other portion of the State. I bought a mule and gave it to Harrigan (Mrs. Geo. McMaster's brother) to take home for me. He is here looking for some horses taken from his mother by Wheeler's[12] men. I expect to start home in a day or two. A day or two ago I was quite affected at the sight of one of our carriage horses in the possession of one of Wheeler's men. He said his Colonel had the other. The one I saw looked pretty well but heartily sick of the service.

I am rejoiced to hear of the fidelity of the faithful negroes at home. I wish you w'd tell them how grateful we are to them for their sympathy & help. As for my losses I do not regard them for a moment if the girls & you can make out. I am sorry for Daughter's & Sister's losses. Tell Sister I see Jno. Henry quite often. He sends his love. Your brother is well. I saw him yesterday & gave him your message. Capt. Parker went with his battery to Raleigh to replace his horses & caissons & has not returned. Tell the girls to send the bridle that goes on the mule to old Mr. Bayley. It was lent me by his son, who is ill.

I do not care to disturb Robt. to make him send a message, but will send his love for him. Tell Minnie I am taking good care of him & will try to send him to her. I hope my letter will get as speedily to its destination as yours have done.

Very much love to all. May God bless & comfort you!

Yr. aff. Husband
W. P. DuBose

I am much distressed about John & hope soon to hear of his return. I have not told William.

I enclose a letter from Fra. Porcher to his mother for some possible opp'y of forwarding.

1. The passage refers to the March 16, 1865, battle of Averasboro, North Carolina. See Bradley, *Last Stand in the Carolinas,* 121–33.

2. Rhett's Brigade blocked the Union advance for most of the battle's first day while receiving little support. See Bradley, *Last Stand in the Carolinas,* 121–33.

3. These were Capts. Robert Press Smith and S. Porcher Smith, Company B, Manigault's Battalion, South Carolina Artillery. See Compiled Service Records, Twenty-seventh South Carolina Infantry Regiment, M267, roll 360, and Manigault's Battalion, South Carolina Artillery, M267, roll 88.

4. This was Pvt. William D. Martin. See Compiled Service Records, Captain Parker's Company (Marion Artillery), South Carolina Light Artillery, M267, roll 104.

5. This refers to Capt. Julius Moore Rhett (1840–95), the son of Benjamin Smith Rhett of Beaufort, South Carolina, and First Lt. Henry M. Stuart. See *South Carolina Genealogies,* 4:25; Barnwell, *Story of an American Family,* 168; Compiled Service Records, First South Carolina Artillery Regiment, M267, rolls 64–65.

6. This was probably Capt. Peter Brockington Bacot (b. 1838), acting assistant surgeon. See Index to Compiled Service Records Raised Directly by the Confederate Government and of Confederate Officers and Nonregimental Enlisted Men, M818, roll 2; *Transactions of the Huguenot Society* 77 (1972): 112.

7. Capt. Alfred Septimus Gaillard (1839–70), Company K, First South Carolina Artillery, was wounded and captured at the battle of Bentonville, North Carolina, March 19–21. In 1863 he married Margaret A. DuBose (1842–1919), sister to Susan DuBose, who married his brother Samuel Isaac. See Compiled Service Records, First South Carolina Artillery, M267, roll 59; MacDowell, *Gaillard Genealogy,* 23, 40.

8. This was Second Lt. John C. Minott, Company G, First (Butler's) South Carolina Infantry (First South Carolina Regulars). See Compiled Service Records, First (Butler's) South Carolina Infantry (First South Carolina Regulars), M267, roll 115.

9. This probably refers to First Lt. J. Moultrie Horlbeck (1841–67), Company H, First (Butler's) South Carolina Infantry. See Compiled Service Records, First South Carolina Infantry, M267, roll 114; WPA Cemetery Index.

10. This was possibly Brig. Gen. William Robertson Boggs (1829–1911) of Georgia, who was Gen. Edmund Kirby Smith's (1824–93) chief of staff until late in the war. See Warner, *Generals in Gray*, 29.

11. The Reverend Paul Trapier lived at an estate in Camden, South Carolina, known as Kamchatka (or Kamschatka), which was formerly owned by Gen. James Chesnut, the husband of Mary Boykin Chesnut. See Trapier, *Incidents in My Life*, 65.

12. Maj. Gen. Joseph Wheeler (1836–1906) commanded Confederate cavalry units during Sherman's campaign through Georgia and the Carolinas. He and his men were much criticized, especially by Confederate civilians, for their lack of discipline in Georgia and South Carolina. See Warner, *Generals in Gray*, 332–33.

Near Smithfield
April 3rd 1865

Moultrie Dwight expects to leave tomorrow morning, my Darling, for W'bo & I have not acquired sufficient confidence in the mail not to prefer such a direct private opp'y. In fact we get so few letters by mail that I doubt whether those which we trust to its conveyance ever reach their destination. I have only trusted one or two to it, but have sent letters quite regularly by private opp'ies, most of which I hope have reached you at last. Your letter by [Kumma] to W'bo found Moultrie on the point of starting for the army & he brought it on to me. He came to see what he could gather about Allie Gaillard reported mortally wounded on the 19th March. He arrived on Friday & found Moultrie Brailsford & myself just concreting an expedition to Bentonville for that purpose.[1] On Saturday morning we set off for the battlefield, 25 miles distant, & spent the afternoon there visiting hospitals (established by the enemy) & the scenes of the conflict. The results of all our investigations & inquiries were that he had been carried to Goldsboro, that since all the seriously wounded were left in the neighborhood there was a strong hope that he was <u>not</u> dangerously wounded. I trust that there is good ground for these conjectures & that, as has so often & happily happened before, the mourning for his death may be changed into joy for his restoration. As the result of our trip was favourable we quite enjoyed it. The weather was lovely, the birds & blossoms gave the first decided evidence which we have had of approaching spring & Moultrie's being just from home & having seen you also added decided interest to the ride. Then we had some adventure in the way of swimming creeks (the bridges having been burned) bivouacking for the night &c &c. We reached camp at 12 o.c. yesterday,

Sunday, tired & hungry, having ridden fifty miles & done a good deal more in a little over 24 hours.

Yesterday we had a lovely day as everyday is now. I had supplied my place during the day & so had no regular preaching to do. I have however prayers with a little address every night in the dif't regts & this evening we are to begin again the Xtian Association prayer meetings. I hope we may be able to turn to some acct this little season of rest & quiet which no doubt precedes a storm of unparalleled fury & violence.

Today everybody is out on a big review & I am left in quiet & solitary possession. The solitude is sweet, but it is just such a day as we have spent so charmingly together at Dungannon & elsewhere, that I long for you to share its enjoyment with me. Spring is very sweet when one can enjoy it, & I am in hopes that the little twinge of disability which visited me at its first approach will leave me free during the remainder of its stay to do so. We are encamped in a grove & as I write the song of birds are mingled with the distant music of bands at the review. If you could just step into my tent at this moment there would be no one for probably an hour to disturb our quiet possession, and unless you w'd prefer to mount John to go & look at the review, we could have a nice long talk, which would be an infinite improvement on this slow & ineloquent pen. And do not think I c'd not accommodate us both with easy chairs. I could produce a couple of camp chairs which for comfort would put to shame many of those which ornament drawing rooms. But I will not tempt you too much.

It was fortunate that you did not accept my invitation. The review is over much sooner than I expected, & our interview w'd have been rather rudely interrupted by the returning stream of warriors.

I am relieved to hear from Moultrie that Robert arrived safely at home & is doing well. All my wounded friends are doing well I hear. I see Johnson quite frequently. He is now chief Engineer of our Corps & as energetic & useful as usual. I wonder whether you [will] be able to see anything of your brother since he has been ordered to S.C.

I am anxious to learn how Sue is getting on with her school. Give her much love & tell her she owes me another note as the other did not reach me. Give much love also to Auntie & all the family & to Sister Martha, Aunt Eliza &c. Remember me also to all friends. I have met Dr. Winthrop several times; he introduced himself to me & I was glad to make his acquaintance.

9 P.M. Dr. Darby's spending the day with us interrupted my writing and as the evening belongs to my ministerial duties I have been unable to resume

until this hour which I had devoted to a letter to the girls. M. leaves tomorrow morning. I therefore my Darling must conclude for the present. With my heart's best love & most earnest prayers.

Yr devoted Husband
W. P. DuBose

1. This probably refers to Alexander Moultrie Brailsford (1839–1927), a cousin. See MacDowell, *DuBose Genealogy,* 228.

EPILOGUE

DuBose began the long journey home with $1.50 in silver, a horse, two mules, and his servant William. He arrived in Winnsboro and then traveled to Anderson to escort Nannie back to Farmington. He became minister of St. Johns Episcopal church in Winnsboro, which DuBose's father had helped to found and whose earliest communicants were families from St. John's and St. Stephen's parishes in the lowcountry. Sherman's men had destroyed the church, so DuBose's congregation worshiped at the courthouse in Winnsboro. On October 15, 1866, DuBose and Nannie's first child, Susan Peronneau, was born in Winnsboro. Another daughter, May Peronneau, was born in 1868, and a son, WIlliam Haskell, was added to the faimly in 1870. Their last child, Samuel, was born in 1872 but died as an infant. DuBose was ordained by Bishop Davis and remained in charge of the church in Winnsboro through 1867.[1]

In 1868 DuBose was placed in charge of Trinity Episcopal Church in Abbeville and took his growing family with him. He later commented on the upheavals that occurred in the town during Reconstruction, including the destruction of homes, presumably by freedmen.[2] DuBose remained in Abbeville until 1871, when in the spring of that year he was nearly elected bishop of the Diocese of South Carolina. He later commented, "It would have been the great misfortune of my life, if I had been elected—that I feel very forcibly." Later during the summer he was elected chaplain of the University of the South (Sewanee) and professor of moral science.[3]

DuBose was to have a dramatic impact on Sewanee. When he learned of his appointment there, he recruited a number of South Carolinians to attend the university and took them with him upon assuming his new position. DuBose later helped to found the School of Theology, of which he served as the second dean until his retirement in 1908.[4]

In his early years at Sewanee, DuBose experienced profound grief. His beloved Nannie died in April 1873, and their son Samuel followed his mother

In this photograph William Porcher DuBose appears to be in his late thirties or early forties. Courtesy of the Jessie Ball duPont Library, Sewanee, the University of the South

to the grave in 1874.[5] DuBose found solace in the family of faculty and students at Sewanee, and he contributed greatly to the vigor and growth of the university. He was beloved by his students, who urged him to publish his lessons and sermons, and once he began, he was a prolific writer. His publications included *The Soteriology of the New Testament* (1892), *The Ecumenical Councils* (1896), *The Gospel of the Gospels* (1906), *The Gospel According to St. Paul* (1907), *High Priesthood and Sacrifice* (1908), *The Reason of Life* (1911), *Turning Points in My Life* (1912), and eleven articles in the *Constructive Quarterly* from 1920 to 1930, which were later republished in 1957 as *Unity in the Faith.*[6]

DuBose's works were reviewed in journals published in Europe and the United States. During the early twentieth century he was referred to as "the wisest Anglican writer ... on both sides of the Atlantic" and "one of the foremost philosophical theologians of our time."[7] He later was called "the only important creative theologian that the Episcopal Church in the United States has produced" and "the most original and creative theologian to appear in the more than 200-year history of the Episcopal Church."[8] Today his life is commemorated on August 18 as a "lesser feast" of *The Episcopal Calendar of the Church Year.*[9]

Notes

1. DuBose, "Reminiscences," 136, 138–39, SCL.
2. Ibid., 143–46. In his reminiscences DuBose writes at length about the lawlessness in Abbeville during his time there.

3. Ibid., 150–51.

4. Ibid., 152; Armentrout, *Quest for the Informed Priest,* 121.

5. DuBose, "Reminiscences," 153–54, SCL.

6. DuBose, *Soteriology of the New Testament;* DuBose, *Ecumenical Councils;* DuBose, *Gospel in the Gospels;* DuBose, *Gospel According to Saint Paul;* DuBose, *High Priesthood and Sacrifice;* DuBose, *Reason of Life;* DuBose, *Turning Points;* DuBose, *Unity in the Faith.*

7. Chitty, *Reconstruction at Sewanee,* 149n; Moberly, "Theology of Dr. DuBose," 161.

8. W. Norman Pittenger, "The Significance of DuBose's Theology," in DuBose, *Unity in the Faith,* 21; Sanday, *Life of Christ,* 281; Slocum, *Theology of William Porcher DuBose,* vii. Slocum's volume is the most comprehensive regarding the theology of DuBose.

9. Slocum, *Theology of William Porcher DuBose,* vii.

BIBLIOGRAPHY

Primary Sources

Manuscripts

Bratton, John. "Letters of General John Bratton Written to His Wife during the Civil War." ("Made from typewritten copy lent to the Southern Historical Collection, UNC, Chapel Hill, by the Rt. Rev. Theodore D. Bratton, D.D., Jackson, Miss.").

DuBose, William Porcher. "Reminiscences." South Caroliniana Library, University of South Carolina, [#636]. ("Copied from typed copy lent by Mrs. Joseph M. Bell, 1017 Bull Street, Columbia, S.C., 1946").

Printed Sources, Public Documents, Reference, and Reminiscences

Adams, William Davenport. *Dictionary of English Literature.* Detroit: Gale Research Co., 1966.

Appleton's Cyclopaedia of American Biography. 7 vols. Detroit: Gale Research Co., 1968.

Augustine of Hippo and Henry Bettenson. *The City of God.* New York: Penguin Classics, 2003.

Badders, Hurley E. *Remembering South Carolina's Old Pendleton District.* Charleston, S.C.: History Press, 2006.

Bailey, N. Louise, ed. *Biographical Directory of the South Carolina Senate, 1776–1985.* 3 vols. Columbia: University of South Carolina Press, 1986.

Barnwell, Stephen B. *The Story of an American Family.* Marquette, Mich.: Privately printed, 1969.

Borchert, Donald M., ed. *Encyclopedia of Philosophy.* 10 vols. Detroit: Thomson Gale, 2006.

Bratton, Theodore DuBose. *An Apostle of Reality: The Life and Thought of Reverend William Porcher DuBose.* New York: Longmans, Green and Co., 1936.

Brooks, U. R. *South Carolina Bench and Bar.* Columbia, S.C.: The State Co., 1908.

Bruce, Philip Alexander. *History of the University of Virginia, 1819–1919.* Vol. 3. New York: Macmillan, 1921.

Carey, Rosa N. *Esther.* New York: Hurst & Co., 1895.

Cazauran, Augustus R. *The Democratic Speaker's Hand-Book.* Cincinnati: Miami Print. & Pub. Company, 1868.

Charleston (S.C.) City Council. *Census of the City of Charleston, South Carolina for the Year 1861.* Charleston, S.C.: Evans & Cogswell, 1861.

Claiborne, John Herbert. *Seventy-Five Years in Old Virginia*. New York and Washington, D.C.: Neale, 1904.

Confederate Military History Extended Edition. 19 vols. Wilmington, N.C.: Broadfoot, 1987.

Confederate Veteran. Nashville, Tenn.: S. A. Cunningham, 1893–1932.

Correspondence between the President of the Virginia Central Railroad and the Postmaster General in Relation to Postal Service. Richmond, Va.: Ritchie and Dunnovant, 1864.

Crute, Joseph, Jr. *Confederate Staff Officers, 1861–65*. Powhatan, Va.: Derwent Books, 1982.

Cyclopedia of Eminent and Representative Men of the Carolinas, Vol 1. Spartanburg, S.C.: Reprint Co., 1972.

Daly, Louise Porter Haskell. *Alexander Cheves Haskell: The Portrait of a Man*. Wilmington, N.C.: Broadfoot, 1989.

Davidson, Chalmers G. *The Last Foray: The South Carolina Planters of 1860*. Columbia: University of South Carolina Press, 1971.

Deas, Anne Simons. *Recollections of the Ball Family of South Carolina and Comingtee Plantation*. Alwyn Ball, Jr., 1909.

DeFontaine, F. G. *Army Letters of 1861–1865; Issued Monthly [by] "Personne" F. G. DeFontaine, War Correspondent . . .* Columbia, S.C.: War Records Publishing Company, 1896–97.

deSaussure, Charlton. *Lowcountry Carolina Genealogies*. Greenville, S.C.: Southern Historical Press, 1997.

Dickert, D. Augustus. *History of Kershaw's Brigade with Complete Roll of Companies, Biographical Sketches, Incidents, Anecdotes, etc.* 1899; reprint, Dayton, Ohio: Press of Morningside Bookshop, 1973.

Dictionary of American Biography. New York: C. Scribner's Sons, 1928–36.

Directory of the City of Charleston, to Which Is Added a Business Directory, 1860, Volume 1. Charleston, S.C.: W. Eugene Ferslew, 1860.

DuBose, William Porcher. *The Ecumenical Councils*. Vol. 3 of *Ten Epochs of Church History*, edited by John Fullerton. New York: Christian Literature Company, 1896.

———. *The Gospel According to Saint Paul*. New York: Longmans, Green & Co., 1907.

———. *The Gospel in the Gospels*. New York: Longmans, Green & Co., 1908.

———. *High Priesthood and Sacrifice: An Exposition of the Epistle to the Hebrews*. New York: Longmans, Green & Co., 1908.

———. *The Reason of Life*. New York: Longmans, Green & Co., 1911.

———. *The Soteriology of the New Testament*. New York: Macmillan, 1892.

———. *Turning Points in My Life*. New York: Longmans, Green & Co., 1912.

———. *Unity in the Faith*. Edited by W. Norman Pittenger. Greenwich, Conn.: Seabury Press, 1957.

Faust, Patricia L., ed. *Historical Times Illustrated Encyclopedia of the Civil War*. New York: Harper & Row, 1986.

BIBLIOGRAPHY

Ferguson, Lester W. *Abbeville County: Southern Life-Styles Lost in Time.* Spartanburg, S.C.: Reprint Co., 1993.

Gadsden, Charles C. *Gadsden Family Portraits.* New York: IKON, 2000.

Gardner, Helen. *New Oxford Book of English Verse, 1250–1950.* New York: Oxford University Press, 1972.

Gist, Margaret A., ed. *Presbyterian Women of South Carolina.* Greenville: Women's Auxiliary of the Synod of South Carolina, 1929.

Glover, James Bolan. *Colonel Joseph Glover (1719–1783) and His Descendants.* Marietta, Ga.: Glover Family Association, 1996.

Goodlet, Mildred W. *Links in the Goodlet Chain.* Easley, S.C.: Southern Historical Press, 1965.

Harrison, Fairfax. *The Virginia Carys: An Essay in Genealogy.* New York: De Vinne Press, 1919.

Haskell, John Cheves. *The Haskell Memoirs.* New York: G. P. Putnam's Sons, 1960.

Hedge, Frederic H., ed. *Hymns for the Church of Christ.* Boston: Crosby, Nichols & Company, 1858.

Heitman, Francis B. *Historical Register and Dictionary of the United States Army.* Vol. 1. Washington, D.C.: Government Printing Office, 1903.

Hewett, Janet B. *South Carolina Confederate Soldiers, 1861–1865, Name Roster.* Vol. 1 Wilmington, N.C.: Broadfoot, 1998.

Historical Catalogue of Brown University, 1764–1904. Providence, R.I.: Brown University, 1905.

Jervey, Clare. *Inscriptions on the Tablets and Gravestones in St. Michael's Church and Churchyard, Charleston, S.C.* Columbia, S.C.: The State Co., 1906.

Johnson, John. *The Defense of Charleston Harbor including Fort Sumter and the Adjacent Islands, 1863–1865.* Charleston, S.C.: Walker, Evans, and Cogswell, 1890.

Johnson, John Lipscomb. *The University Memorial: Biographical Sketches of Alumni of the University of Virginia Who Fell in the Confederate War.* Baltimore: Turnbull Brothers, 1871.

Jones, Hugh Percy. *Dictionary of Foreign Phrase and Classical Quotations.* Edinburgh: John Grant Booksellers, 1963.

Kirkland, Randolph W. *Broken Fortunes: South Carolina Soldiers, Sailors, and Citizens Who Died in the Service of Their Country and State in the War for Southern Independence.* Charleston: South Carolina Historical Society, 1995.

———. *South Carolina C.S.A. Research Aids.* Pawleys Island, S.C.: Randolph Kirkland, 1992.

Landrum, J. B. O. *History of Spartanburg County.* Spartanburg, S.C.: Reprint Co., 1977.

Leslie, Eliza. *Directions for Cookery in Its Various Branches.* Charleston, S.C.: Bibliobazaar, 2007.

Long, E. B. *The Civil War Day by Day: An Almanac, 1861–1865.* Garden City, N.Y.: Doubleday, 1971.

MacDowell, Dorothy Kelly. *DuBose Genealogy.* Columbia, S.C.: R. L. Bryan Co., 1972.

BIBLIOGRAPHY

————. *Gaillard Genealogy.* Columbia, S.C.: R. L. Bryan Co., 1974.

Map of the Seat of War in South Carolina and Georgia. Charleston, S.C.: Evans & Cogswell, [1861].

Matthews, James M, ed., *The Statutes at Large of the Confederate States of America Commencing with the First Session of the First Congress 1862.* Richmond, Va.: R. M. Smith, 1862.

May, John Amasa. *South Carolina Secedes.* Columbia: University of South Carolina Press, 1960.

Mayo, Lawrence Shaw. *The Winthrop Family in America.* Boston: Massachusetts Historical Society, 1948.

McCrady, Louis deBerniere. *Mrs. Edward McCrady, 2nd, and Her DeBerniere Family Papers.* Charleston, S.C.: [The Author], 1960.

Memorials: To the Memory of Mrs. Amarinthia Snowden, Offered by Societies, Associations and Confederate Camps. Charleston, S.C.: Walker, Evans & Cogswell, 1898.

Moffett, Mary Conner, ed. *Letters of General James Conner.* Columbia, S.C.: R. L. Bryan Co., 1950.

Moore, Samuel J. T. *Moore's Complete Civil War Guide to Richmond.* [The Author], 1973.

New Encyclopedia Britannica. 15th ed. Chicago: Encyclopedia Britannica, 1998.

Old, Hughes Oliphant. *The Reading and Preaching of the Scriptures in the Worship of the Christian Church.* Vol. 6: *The Modern Age.* Grand Rapids, Mich.: William B. Eerdmanns, 1998.

Page, Richard Channing Moore. *Genealogy of the Page Family in Virginia.* New York: Jenkins & Thomas, 1883.

Parker, William Henry. *Genealogy of the Parker Family of South Carolina, 1670–1935.* Privately printed, 1935.

Patey, James Garner. *The Whaley Family and Its Charleston Connections.* Spartanburg, S.C.: Reprint Co., 1992.

Pope, Thomas H. *The History of Newberry County, South Carolina.* Columbia: University of South Carolina Press, 1973.

Preston, William Bowker. *The Preston Genealogy.* Salt Lake City: Deseret News, 1900.

Quinn, Alice Hawkins. *Descendants of Robert Gibbes (1644–1715): Colonial Governor of South Carolina.* Privately printed, 1991.

Ravenel, Henry E. *Ravenel Records.* Dunwoody, Ga.: N. S. Berg, 1971.

Sanday, William. *The Life of Christ in Recent Research.* New York: Oxford University Press, 1908.

Sifakis, Stewart. *Who Was Who in the Civil War.* New York: Facts on File, 1988.

————. *Who Was Who in the Confederacy.* New York: Facts on File, 1988.

South Carolina Genealogies: Articles from the South Carolina Historical (and Genealogical) Magazine. Spartanburg: Published in association with the South Carolina Historical Society by Reprint Co., 1983.

Stanley, Arthur P. *Life and Correspondence of Thomas Arnold.* London: B. Fellowes, 1845.

Stevenson, Burton Egbert. *The Home Book of Verse, American and English.* New York: Houghton Mifflin Co., 1927.

Stiles, Henry Reed. *The Stiles Family in America.* Jersey City, N.J.: Doan & Wilson, printers, 1895.

Sutherland, John. *The Stanford Companion to Victorian Fiction.* Stanford, Calif.: Stanford University Press, 1989.

Thomas, Albert Sidney. *A Historical Account of the Protestant Episcopal Church in South Carolina, 1820–1957.* Columbia, S.C.: R. L. Bryan Co., 1957.

Towles, Louis P., ed. *A World Turned Upside Down: The Palmers of South Santee, 1818–1881.* Columbia: University of South Carolina Press, 1996.

Trapier, Paul. *Incidents in My Life: The Autobiography of the Rev. Paul Trapier, S.T.D. with Some of His Letters.* Edited by George W. Williams. Charleston, S.C.: Dalcho Historical Society, 1954.

———. *The Private Register of the Rev. Paul Trapier.* Charleston, S.C.: Dalcho Historical Society, 1958.

Tyler, Lyon Gardiner, ed. *Encyclopedia of Virginia Biography.* 5 vols. New York: Lewis Historical Publishing Co., 1915.

University of Cambridge. *Alumni Cantabrigienses: A Biographical List of All Known Students, Graduates and Office Holders at the University of Cambridge, from the Earliest Times to 1900.* 10 vols. Cambridge: Cambridge University Press, 1922.

Wakelyn, John L. *Biographical Dictionary of the Confederacy.* Westport, Conn.: Greenwood Press, 1977.

Waring, Joseph Ioor. *A History of Medicine in South Carolina.* Vol. 2, *1825–1900.* Charleston: South Carolina Medical Association, 1967.

Warner, Ezra J. *Generals in Blue: Lives of the Union Commanders.* Baton Rouge: Louisiana State University Press, 1992.

———. *Generals in Gray: Lives of the Confederate Commanders.* Baton Rouge: Louisiana State University Press, 1987.

Webster's Ninth New Collegiate Dictionary. Springfield, Mass.: Merriam-Webster, Inc., 1984.

Who's Who in America: A Biographical Dictionary of Notable Living Men and Women. Chicago: A. N. Marquis, 1899.

Articles

Dominick, Ethel Wannamaker. "Poinsett Genealogy: Additions and Corrections, also Descendants of Christopher Samuel Lovell." *Transactions of the Huguenot Society* 86 (1981): 68–74.

Ferrara, Marie. "Moses Henry Nathan and the Great Charleston Fire of 1861." *South Carolina Historical Magazine* 101 (October 2003): 258–80.

Luker, Ralph E. "The Crucible of Civil War and Reconstruction in the Experience of William Porcher DuBose." *South Carolina Historical Magazine* 83 (January 1982): 50–71.

"Memorial Tablets in the French Protestant (Huguenot) Church in Charleston, South Carolina." *Transactions of the Huguenot Society* 75 (1970): 49–90.

Moberly, W. H. "The Theology of Dr. DuBose." *Journal of Theological Studies* 9 (January 1908): 161.

Owings, Marvin Alpheus. "Cousin Isaac, a Vignette." *Transactions of the Huguenot Society* 88 (1983): 39–52.

Porcher, Catherine Cordes, comp. "Porcher, a Huguenot Family of Ancient Lineage." *Transactions of the Huguenot Society* 81 (1976): 90–186.

Porcher, Frederick A. "Upper Beat of St. John's, Berkeley: A Memoir." *Transactions of the Huguenot Society* 13 (1906): 31–78.

Smith, Henry A. M. "Willtown or New London." *South Carolina Historical and Genealogical Magazine* 10 (January 1909): 20.

Tison, John Laurens, Jr., and Samuel G. Stoney, eds. "Recollections of John Safford Stoney, Confederate Surgeon." *South Carolina Historical Magazine* 60 (1961): 209.

Government Records

Biographical Directory of the American Congress, 1774–1927. Washington, D.C.: U.S. Government Printing Office, 1928.

National Archives. United States Bureau of the Census. *Eighth Census of the United States (South Carolina), 1860.* Washington, D.C.: Government Printing Office, 1865.

———. War Department Collection of Confederate Records. RG 109. Compiled Service Records of Confederate Soldiers Who Served in Organizations from the State of South Carolina. Microcopy 267, Holcombe Legion, roll 372.

Works Progress Administration Cemetery Index. Unpublished card files at South Carolina Historical Association.

War of the Rebellion: The Official Records of the Union and Confederate Armies. 70 vols. Washington, D.C.: Government Printing Office, 1880–1901.

War of the Rebellion: The Official Records of the Union and Confederate Navies. 30 vols. Washington, D.C.: Government Printing Office, 1894–1922.

Secondary Sources

Abrams, George Carter, ed. *Newberry County, South Carolina Cemeteries.* Newberry, S.C.: Newberry County Historical Society, 1982.

Armentrout, Donald Smith. *The Quest for the Informed Priest.* Sewanee, Tenn.: School of Theology, University of the South, 1979.

Baker, Gary R. *Cadets in Gray: The Story of the Cadets of the South Carolina Military Academy and the Cadet Rangers in the Civil War.* New York: Palmetto Bookworks, 1989.

Barker, Frederick T. "Holiness, Righteousness, and Life: The Theology of William Porcher DuBose." Doctoral diss., Drew University, 1985.

Barrett, John G. *The Civil War in North Carolina.* Chapel Hill: University of North Carolina Press, 1995.

Batterson, Hermon Griswold. *A Sketch-Book of the American Episcopate.* Philadelphia: J. B. Lippincott & Co., 1878.

Blakey, Arch Fredric. *Gen. John H. Winder, C.S.A.* Gainesville: University of Florida Press, 1990.

BIBLIOGRAPHY

Boyd, John Wright. *A Family History: Boyd and Connected Families.* Tignall, Ga.: J. W. Boyd, 1980.

Bradley, Mark L. *Last Stand in the Carolinas: The Battle of Bentonville.* Campbell, Calif.: Savas Woodbury, 1996.

Burton, E. Milby. *The Siege of Charleston, 1861–1865.* Columbia: University of South Carolina Press, 1970.

Chitty, Arthur Benjamin, Jr. *Reconstruction at Sewanee: The Founding of the University of the South and Its First Administration, 1857–1872.* Sewanee, Tenn.: University Press, 1954.

Emerson, W. Eric. *Sons of Privilege: The Charleston Light Dragoons in the Civil War.* Columbia: University of South Carolina Press, 2005.

Ferris, Norman B. *The Trent Affair: A Diplomatic Crisis.* Knoxville: University of Tennessee Press, 1977.

Fetzer, Dale. *Unlikely Allies: Fort Delaware's Prison Community in the Civil War.* Mechanicsburg, Pa.: Stackpole Books, 2000.

Foote, Shelby. *The Civil War: A Narrative.* Vol. 1, *Fort Sumter to Perryville.* New York: Vintage Books, 1986.

Hugo, Victor. *Les Miserables.* Translated by Lee Fahnestock and Norman McAfee. New York: Signet Classics, 1987.

Lewis, Elizabeth Wittenmyer. *Queen of the Confederacy: The Innocent Deceits of Lucy Holcombe Pickens.* Denton: University of North Texas Press, 2002.

McPherson, James A. *Battle Cry of Freedom: The Civil War Era.* New York: Oxford University Press, 1988.

Miller, Hugh. *The Testimony of the Rocks, or Geology in Its Bearings on the Two Theologies, Natural and Revealed.* Boston: Gould and Lincoln, 1857.

Poston, Jonathan H. *The Buildings of Charleston: A Guide to the City's Architecture.* Columbia: Published for the Historic Charleston Foundation by the University of South Carolina Press, 1997.

Reuther, Galen. *Flat Rock: The Little Charleston of the Mountains.* Charleston, S.C.: Arcadia, 2005.

Rhea, Gordon C. *The Battle for Spotsylvania Courthouse and Yellow Tavern, May 7–12, 1864.* Baton Rouge: Louisiana State University Press, 1997.

———. *The Battle of the Wilderness, May 5–6, 1864.* Baton Rouge: Louisiana State University Press, 1994.

———. *Cold Harbor: Grant and Lee, May 26–June 3, 1864.* Baton Rouge: Louisiana State University Press, 2002.

Robertson, F. W. *Lectures on the Influence of Poetry and Wordsworth.* London: H. R. Allenson, 1906.

Roman, Alfred. *The Military Operations of General Beauregard in the War between the States 1861 to 1865.* New York: Harper Brothers, 1884.

Roos, Rosalie. *Travels in America, 1851–1855.* Carbondale: Southern Illinois University Press, 1981.

Sadleir, Michael. *Trollope: A Commentary.* Boston: Houghton Mifflin, 1927.

Sass, Herbert Ravenel. *The Story of the South Carolina Lowcountry.* 3 vols. West Columbia, S.C.: J. F. Hyer, 1956.

Scarborough, William Kaufman. *Masters of the Big House: Elite Slaveholders of the Mid-Nineteenth-Century South.* Baton Rouge: Louisiana State University Press, 2003.

Scott, Sir Walter. *Waverly, or 'Tis Sixty Years Since.* Edinburgh: James Ballantyne and Company, 1815.

Sears, Stephen W. *Landscape Turned Red: The Battle of Antietam.* New York: Ticknor & Fields, 1983.

Slocum, Robert Boak. *The Theology of William Porcher DuBose: Life, Movement, and Being.* Columbia: University of South Carolina Press, 2000.

Snowden, Yates, ed. *History of South Carolina.* Chicago and New York: Lewis, 1920.

The Soldier's Hymn Book. Charleston: South Carolina Tract Society, 1863.

Stone, DeWitt Boyd, ed. *Wandering to Glory: Confederate Veterans Remember Evans' Brigade.* Columbia: University of South Carolina Press, 2001.

Speer, Lonnie R. *Portals to Hell: Military Prisons in the Civil War.* Mechanicsburg, Pa.: Stackpole Books, 1977.

Stone, H. David, Jr. *Vital Rails: The Charleston and Savannah Railroad and the Civil War in Coastal South Carolina.* Columbia: University of South Carolina Press, 2008.

Teal, Harvey S. *Partners with the Sun: South Carolina Photographers, 1840–1940.* Columbia: University of South Carolina Press, 2000.

Tennyson, Alfred Lord. *The Poems and Plays of Alfred Lord Tennyson.* New York: Random House, the Modern Library, 1938.

Tinsley, Jim Bob. *The Land of Waterfalls.* Brevard, N.C.: J. B. and Dottie Tinsley, 1988.

Wallace, David D. *The History of South Carolina.* New York: American Historical Society, 1934.

Wilson, John M. *I Have Looked Death in the Face: Biography of William Porcher DuBose.* Kingston, Tenn.: Paint Rock Publishing, 1996.

Wise, Stephen R. *Lifeline of the Confederacy: Blockade Running during the Civil War.* Columbia: University of South Carolina Press, 1988.

Wyckoff, Mac. *A History of the Second South Carolina Infantry: 1861–1865.* San Diego, Calif.: Sergeant Kirkland's Press, 1994.

INDEX

Murden, Malvina, 9, 18, 131, 145
Murden, Victoria, 98, 100, 103, 106,
110–11

Nance, James Drayton, 241n1, 252, 255,
255n2, 265, 267, 285
Nannie. *See* DuBose, Anne Barnwell
Peronneau
Nelson, W. R., 235, 236, 237n2
Neuse River, N.C., xxi, 115, 121n1
New Bern, N.C., xxi, 73n3, 115, 129,
130, 166
New Jersey, 264
New Jerusalem, xviii, 48n2
New London, S.C., 28n1, 41n8
New Market, Va., 86, 236, 237, 239,
241, 312, 320
New Orleans, La., 305
New Testament, 133
New Year, 29, 30, 31
New York, 110n, 268; regiments, 48th,
277n4; 112th, 277n4
Newbern. *See* New Bern
Newberry, S.C, 134, 241, 241n1,
255n2
Noble, Mrs., 137
North, the, 126, 131, 144, 203, 204,
223, 247, 261, 268, 282, 305, 310,
313
North Anna River, Va., 271, 273
North Carolina, 5n1, 30n4, 73n3, 75n3,
96, 121n3, 129, 130n6, 144n3,
148n6, 151, 152, 166n3, 250n2,
285n3, 298, 316n5, 330n1, 330n7;
infantry regiments, 4th, 97n3

Old City. *See* Charleston, S.C.
Old Testament, 11, 240
Orange C.H. (Court House), Va., 91,
298, 312
Orangeburg, S.C., xxv, 3, 4n2, 7, 8, 12,
156n4, 277n3
Orangeburg Aid Society, 156n4
Ordinance of Secession, xvi, 80n1

Orphan House Chapel, Charleston,
S.C., 29, 30n2
Orr, Jehu Amaziah, 262, 264n2
Overland Campaign, xxiv, 234, 268n1
Ovid, 161, 177
Oxford, Ga., 204

Paint Rock, N.C., 235
Palmer, Francis Gendron, xvii, xxvii, 53,
55, 55n2, 98, 119, 125, 152
Palmetto Guards (Co. I, Second South
Carolina Infantry), 280n1
Palmetto State, CSS, 137
Pamunkey River, Va., 273
pantheists, 228
Panthers Springs, Tenn., 245
Paradise, 15
Paris, France, 30n5
Parker, Anna, 230, 321
Parker, Charles, ix
Parker, Charles Rutledge, 147, 148n2
Parker, Edward Frost (Ned), 2n1, 255,
327, 329
Parker, Edward Lightwood, 13n1, 30n4,
56n3
Parker, Francis Lejau, 240, 241n2, 257,
297
Parker, Mrs. W.H., 281
Parker, Serina Waring, 2
Parker, Thomas, 4n6
Parker, William McKenzie, 13n1, 56n3
Partridge Academy, Duxbury, Mass., xv
Pascal, Blaise, 212, 213n7, 228
patriotism, 109
Paul, Saint, 15, 45, 132
Pea Patch Island, Del., 97n1
Peace Commission, 325
Pearl River, Miss., xxiii, 168, 173, 176,
188
Pegasus, 10
Pemberton, John Clifford, 71, 188n1,
189, 190, 197
Pemberton's Corps, 197, 200
Pendleton, William N., 286